BASEBALL
FEVER

BASEBALL FEVER

EARLY BASEBALL IN MICHIGAN

PETER MORRIS

THE UNIVERSITY OF MICHIGAN PRESS
Ann Arbor

Copyright © by the University of Michigan 2003
All rights reserved
Published in the United States of America by
The University of Michigan Press
Manufactured in the United States of America
♾ Printed on acid-free paper

2006   2005   2004   2003   4   3   2   1

A CIP catalog record for this book is available from the British Library.

Library of Congress Cataloging-in-Publication Data

Morris, Peter, 1962–
    Baseball fever : early baseball in Michigan / Peter Morris.
        p.   cm.
    Includes bibliographical references (p.   ) and index.
        ISBN 0-472-09826-8 (Cloth : alk. paper) — ISBN 0-472-06826-1
    (pb : alk. paper)
        1. Baseball—Michigan—History—19th century.   I. Title.

    GV863.M52 M67   2003
    796.357'09779'09034—dc21   2002154229

To my mother, Dr. Ruth Rittenhouse Morris (1933–2001)

ACKNOWLEDGMENTS

This work would not have been possible without the kindness and generosity of many people. David Thomas had the original idea for this book. My editor, Kelly Sippell, believed in this project, championed it, and she and Kevin Rennells made it infinitely better with their perceptive suggestions and skillful editing. I also thank Ron Fraker for designing a beautiful book and Pete Sickman-Garner for his enthusiastic marketing approach. David MacGregor, Peter Levine, Howard Anderson, Delecia Seay Carey, Dick Clark, and Stephanie Berens read part or all of the manuscript and offered valuable suggestions. Any weaknesses and errors that remain are solely my responsibility.

The staff of many Michigan libraries and archives have patiently and professionally handled countless requests. I am particularly grateful to Bill Anderson, Randy Riley, and the entire staff of the Library of Michigan; Greg Kinney of the Bentley Historical Library, University of Michigan; Gordon Olson and M. Christine Byron of the Grand Rapids Public Library; Jim Zuleski of the Ella Sharp Museum; David Poremba of the Burton Collection, Detroit Public Library; Evelyn Leasher of the Clarke Historical Library, Central Michigan University; and Cathy Greer of the Michigan Technological University and Copper Country Historical Collections.

John Gelderloos and Mark Rucker were invaluable aids in helping me gather photos for this book.

Many members of SABR (Society for American Baseball Research) have contributed to my knowledge of baseball with the generosity that is the hallmark of SABR. These include Bob Richardson, Bill Deane, Joe Simenic, Bob McConnell, Tom Ruane, Scott Flatow, Carlos Bauer, Scott Harris, Jim Lannen, David Nemec, Jay Sanford, Marc Okkonen, Rich Newhouse, Cappy Gagnon, Debbi Dagavarian-Bonar, Reed Howard, David Vincent, David Arcidiacano, Bill Carle, David Ball, John Thom, Paul Hunkele, Steve Steinberg, Marty Payne, Bob Schaefer, and Tom Shieber. I especially want to thank Richard Malatzky, whose diligence constantly amazes me.

Many coworkers at both American Collegiate Marketing and the John Henry

Company offered encouragement and graciously rearranged their own schedules to enable me to research this book, especially Karen Henry, Mike Brighton, Lisa Bartlett, Alex Uschuk, Joel Schantz, Dave Spoelman, Sarah Wasson, Lee Schultheiss, Patti Tremblay, Missy Andrews, Amy Bergethon, Erin Muller, Elaine Rayburn, Debbie Wolf, Rachel Whitaker, and Jennifer Richmond.

Many friends offered support, advice and a shoulder to lean on, and I particularly want to thank Mary O'Malley, the Reslocks, Amanda DeWees, Katie Pickett, and the late Vic Steinman. My brother Douglas and my sisters Corinne and Joy are always there for me when I need them. My father Raymond is a constant source of strength and encouragement. My mother Ruth did not live to see this book's completion but she remains an essential part of everything any of her children accomplish. This book is dedicated to her memory.

CONTENTS

INTRODUCTION

Melville McGee, by then a prominent judge in Jackson, Michigan, reminisced in 1892 about the so-called raisin' games of his boyhood in rural Concord, Michigan. While no dates are specified, McGee was born in 1828, so it must have been in the late 1830s or early 1840s that these games of what was then called "base ball" took place.[1] McGee recalled that "the raising of a framed house or barn was an event that called together the entire neighborhood, and it was very seldom that any one invited to assist on such an occasion failed to be present. The event was looked forward to by the boys of the neighborhood with great satisfaction, as it gave them a half holiday from the labors of the farm and enabled them to enjoy a game of base ball after the building had been raised."

After the work was done, all joined in a hearty meal. Then, "the next thing in order was to select a good place and two of the young men chose sides and they played ball until it was time to go to their several houses. It seems to me now as I look back and recall those early days that the young people enjoyed their sports and games and entered into them with far more zest than young people do at the present day. There was no feeling of envy or superiority, or the feeling that you don't belong to my set. All were on a level, and everyone was just as good as any other."[2]

The nostalgia implicit in Judge McGee's reminiscences will sound familiar to modern readers, as every new generation of baseball fans feels the need to grumble that the game has become a business and is no longer played for the love of it as it was when they were children. In reality, baseball has been a business to the players since the 1860s.[3] In most instances, what such speakers are actually articulating is the unpleasant shock of recognizing that the same game they played for fun as children can provide a livelihood for a select few, but not for them.

Such sentiments also tap into the deeper reality that baseball is at heart a country boy's game that was fundamentally changed when it moved to the city. It is as though modern baseball fans who express their disillusionment possess a collective memory of the scene McGee describes. Or perhaps they are simply remembering the carefree days of their own childhoods. Either way, they are demonstrating an essential truth about the course of baseball history.

Judge McGee's belief that there had been a change in the way baseball was played and experienced was not merely rose-tinted nostalgia. His contention that the notion of superiority was a later addition to the game-playing ethos is a reality confirmed by modern sports historians. Historian Melvin L. Adelman concludes that "competition was often viewed as socially dysfunctional in premodern America" and that only with the rise of industrialism between 1820 and 1870 did "Americans firmly come to accept competition as a valued mechanism for achieving social progress."[4] As we shall see, no one witnessed this very real transformation in the way baseball was played more closely than did McGee.

McGee's account provides a particularly poignant description of the sense of belonging and community created by the pioneer lifestyle. This feeling of belonging extended naturally to ball-playing because all the players were equal participants—there were no spectators unless by choice. These half-holidays earned by honest toil were a celebration of a shared work ethic, and McGee understandably believed that a bond had been severed when changes in the way the game was played began to limit participation. Perhaps of all the changes necessitated by baseball's growth, the most fundamental one came when the game began to exclude many from participating—never again would "everyone [be] just as good as any other."

Nonetheless, modern baseball fans still feel a strong sense of belonging, in spite of being excluded from firsthand participation in the game. William Freedman's *More Than a Pastime: An Oral History of Baseball Fans* documents how fans have cultivated a new sense of belonging to replace the one that comes from playing. A fan identified as Sanford S., who grew up in the 1950s, recalls that "baseball was part of the beautiful romantic world I was excluded from, but only as a player. As a fan . . . it gave me a warm and wonderful sense of belonging and acceptance."[5] Sanford continues: "Lots of things seemed out of reach. But not baseball. Baseball was within reach, and it was part of a world I wanted to belong to. . . .

Judge Melville McGee (*seated*) began playing baseball as a boy in the 1830s and scored the tying run in the grand Detroit tournament of 1867. But controversy swirled around the club he represented, and McGee later wrote with sadness that the game was no longer played with the same spirit he remembered. *Courtesy of the Ella Sharp Museum*

Anybody could tune in, and when you did you joined all the others who were tuning in, all those neighbors sitting on their porches. . . . That was a world I could be a part of."[6]

Another fan named Bennett K. could have been responding directly to McGee. He describes attending a game at Fenway Park as "a return to an agrarian ideal where everyone has a chance to achieve the American Dream, where everyone gets a piece of land. At a ball game we all get to share this piece of land for two-and-a-half, three hours." He also comments on how complete strangers feel drawn to share memories: "I loved that kind of buzzy friendliness. It's a return to community, to small town agrarian life where everybody knew everybody or felt friendly even towards people they didn't know."[7] How is it that baseball managed to change so dramatically from the days of "raisin' games" without losing this sense of belonging?

This book will trace that quite astonishing development in the still primarily rural state of Michigan from the mid-1850s through the mid-1870s. Precisely because Michigan was never at the forefront of baseball's development, examining how its residents first became passionate about the game will help us understand a vital and forgotten part of baseball's history. While baseball first caught on as an adult activity in New York City, the country's big cities have produced countless fads that soon died because they had no appeal in the Midwest. Only when baseball became established in the country's heartland did it truly become the national pastime.

NOTES

1. Following current conventions, *baseball* will be spelled as one word in this book. During the period covered by this book, however, the term *base ball* was in common usage.
2. Melville McGee, "The Early Days of Concord, Jackson County, Michigan," 430.
3. Robert F. Burk's *Never Just A Game* offers an excellent account of the development of baseball as a business.
4. Melvin L. Adelman, *A Sporting Time*, 285.
5. William Freedman, *More Than a Pastime: An Oral History of Baseball Fans*, 161.
6. Freedman, *More Than a Pastime*, 162.
7. Freedman, *More Than a Pastime*, 164. "Bennett K." was born in 1950.

1

"The Good Old Days When the Result Was Merely a Question of Physical Endurance and Light"

Sporting activities understandably played a limited role in early America. A culture imbued with such a strong work ethic, and with plenty of "hacking and hewing" to keep it busy, had little need to devise new challenges.[1] Numerous accounts by British tourists in the 1830s and 1840s noted that Americans seemed obsessed with work, to the exclusion of recreation.[2]

Activities like hunting, fishing, and horseback riding were naturally viewed as means of survival, rather than as contests of skill. Early settlers in Michigan encountered a particularly harsh landscape, and creating diversions was hardly a priority. As one of Michigan's early pioneers later remembered, "In those days, amusements were scarce, and work was the steady employment of old and young."[3]

Nonetheless, by the 1830s the modern world was making rapid incursions into the traditional rhythms of American life. As early as 1839 the *Farmer's Almanack* wrote that "scarcely a tool . . . has not been altered for the better in some way or other."[4] These advances not only helped the farmer in the field and the farmer's wife in the kitchen; often they lured the couple's children to the cities to follow new careers. Around two-thirds of the population still farmed in 1840, but that percentage was slowly and steadily dropping.[5]

Travel was becoming a major part of Americans' lives. New roads were being built everywhere, while steamboats and trains would soon make the country seem much smaller. In the generation since Lewis and Clark's expedition, more and more of the continent had been "civilized"—wildernesses chopped down, wild beasts slain, and native people forcibly relocated by government policy. Suddenly, states like Michigan were no longer considered suitable only for pioneers, fur traders, and "that class who 'leave their country for their country's good.'"[6] A much wider cross-section of Americans began to catch the "western fever."

These changes meant that time for leisure activities gradually became available even to working men. Ironically, it was the setting aside of the Sabbath as a day of rest that made this most conspicuously evident. While other members of the family were content with a respite from their labors, the excess energy of boys needed some kind of outlet. One Michigan pioneer, Bela Hubbard, recalled: "On Sundays, parents and daughters rode to church in a sober, jog-trot style, on a cart drawn by a single pony, while boys raced on their nags, and returned in the grand style, racing, with whoop and hurrah! . . . In winter these races were exchanged for trotting matches on the ice, in their light home-made carry-alls. Long and eager were the contests for superior speed and skill."[7]

Ball sports were not uncommon, but they remained disorganized. The many settlers from the British Isles imported cricket, but that sport's already well-developed rules and customs were singularly ill-suited to channeling the energies of young boys. A proper match lasted most of a day and was limited to twenty-two participants, many of whom remained inactive for long periods. Cricket was thus best suited for those long on attention span and short on energy, hardly a description of young boys at any time.

More successful was the British game of rounders, a much less formal bat and ball game. Rounders and similar games that went by such names as *round ball, town ball, one old cat, two old cat, barn ball, field base, patch ball, stool ball, feeder,* and even *base ball* or *bass ball* were popular in America in the 1830s and 1840s. These games involved some of the essential elements of baseball—hitting, fielding, and base running—but lacked many of the modern game's complexities. They were far more flexible than cricket, being adaptable to any number of participants, not necessarily dividing the players into teams, and making every player at least potentially part of the action on every play.

The most detailed surviving account of a pre-1840 game resembling baseball describes one played on June 4, 1838, in Beachville, Upper Canada. This account was not written until nearly fifty years later, and since its author was seven or eight when the game was played, the precision with which he recalls details must be considered suspicious.[8] But even with some possibly spurious elements added, the Beachville game sounds as much like tag or dodge ball as baseball. The game featured five "byes" (bases), with the first bye placed a mere six yards from home in order to "get the runners on the base lines, so as to have the fun of putting them out or enjoying the mistakes of the fielders when some fleet footed fellow would dodge the ball and come in home."[9]

A Boston baseball journal gives a similar account of the loose structure of the predecessors of regulation baseball: "The game of ball . . . has been for years a favorite sport with the youth of the country, and long before the present style of playing was in vogue, round ball was indulged in to a great extent all over the land, whiling away many an hour of the school boy's holiday. Who of our readers does not recollect the ball games of their school days with the convenient trees, posts and pumps for bounds (no bases in those days), the distance not alike between any two, and instead of two sides of nine men each, half the time, five, would suffice for a game, with one at the bat, a catcher out, giver and a chaser or two, the fun would continue for hours."[10] In a society that placed great emphasis on the distinction between manliness and childishness, this loose structure created a damning perception of baseball as a juvenile diversion.

One of the earliest ball-playing clubs composed of men was the Olympic Ball Club of Philadelphia, which evoked a mixture of amusement and scorn when it began playing town ball in 1833:

> The first day that the Philadelphia men took the field . . . only four men were found to play, so they started in by playing a game called cat ball. All the players were over 25 years of age, and to see them playing a game like this caused much merriment among the friends of the players. It required "sand" in those days to go out on the field and play, as the prejudice against the game was very great. It took nearly a whole season to get men enough together to make a team, owing to the ridicule heaped upon the players for taking part in such childish sports.[11]

Another account of this club recalls that some players would go over to Camden, New Jersey, to play ball, "the prejudice against wasting time in that way being very prevalent in the Quaker city [Philadelphia] of that period."[12] Clearly, men in 1830s America were expected to have better things to do with their time than participate in the games of small boys, and their society discouraged such activities.

Who deserves the credit for reinventing this child's game as an adult activity? One claimant who can conclusively be dismissed is Abner Doubleday. The game in Cooperstown was played by small boys and was not an advance on earlier versions. As explained in appendix A, there are still many misconceptions about the Double-day story.

The much-ridiculed Philadelphians were not the only adults who tried to form a ball-playing club prior to 1840. A recently discovered 1823 article describes "witnessing a company of active young men playing the manly and athletic game of 'base ball'" in what is now Greenwich Village.[13] A club formed in Rochester, New York, around 1825 numbered nearly fifty members ranging in age from eighteen to forty.[14] But if these clubs introduced any innovations, the evidence is now lost in the murky past.

Accordingly, most of the credit for introducing the elements that helped transform baseball is given to the Knickerbocker Club, formed by a group of New York City residents in the early 1840s.[15] Significantly, the Knickerbockers held their practices on the Elysian Fields in Hoboken, New Jersey, a picturesque strip of land surrounded by woods and overlooking the Hudson River. One early participant described this location as "an opening in the 'forest primeval.' The open spot was a level, grass-covered plain, some two hundred yards across, and as deep, surrounded upon three sides by the typical eastern undergrowth and woods and on the east by the Hudson River. It was a perfect greensward almost the year around. Nature must have foreseen the needs of base ball, and designed the

THE AMERICAN NATIONAL GAME OF BASE BALL.

The Elysian Fields near Hoboken, New Jersey, were the Knickerbockers' home. One player later wrote of them, "Nature must have foreseen the needs of base ball, and designed the place especially for that purpose." *Courtesy of Transcendental Graphics*

place especially for that purpose."[16] The Knickerbockers thus embodied the duality of baseball's origins—residents of the nation's largest city returning to an (exaggeratedly?) idyllic countryside.

Although the Knickerbockers are sometimes inaccurately portrayed as snobbish blue bloods, the members of the club were a very homogeneous group of young men of the middle and upper-middle classes.[17] While there was considerable variation in their income levels, all members of the Knickerbockers whose occupations can be identified worked in nonmanual, white-collar jobs, which indicates that they were among the rapidly growing number of Americans who relied on the written word for communication. This was demonstrated by the correspondence of the Knickerbockers, which was "precise as to language, grammar, and spelling, reflect[ing] a high level of literacy."[18]

Membership in the Knickerbocker Club was restricted: "No person can obtain membership in the club merely for his reputation as a player; he must also have the reputation of a gentleman."[19] In addition, club members had to have an occupation that left them free after 3:00 P.M. on weekday afternoons in order to join in the practices. Throughout their history, the Knickerbockers engaged mostly in practice or intersquad matches and showed only limited interest in meeting outside competition.

The club's rules specified that nonmembers could participate only if there were not sufficient members present: "In all cases, members shall have the preference, when present, at the making of a match." In these seemingly innocuous ways, the exclusivity bemoaned by McGee and others entered baseball. With it, the feeling of belonging fostered by baseball began a long and complex shift from a communal sense based on shared values to an exclusive sense based on membership in a more selective group.

The Knickerbockers emphasized this more limited sense of community by introducing the first uniform, a dapper outfit that consisted of blue woolen pantaloons, white flannel shirts, and straw hats. They also changed the way the game was played, using a set number of players per side and specifying dimensions for the playing field and equipment. Of particular note, the Knickerbockers used four bases that were set a standard distance apart. The club measured this distance in paces, so it is debatable how closely this corresponded to today's ninety-foot distance, but the basic geometry of the baseball field was thus defined, with the primary action occurring in an enclosed space. It is quite possible that earlier clubs actually introduced some of these rules and customs. However, the Knickerbockers assured their place in history by writing their rules down, thereby helping baseball shift from an oral to a written tradition while the nation's workforce was making a similar transition.

The Knickerbockers' decision to put the rules in writing played a direct role in helping what became known as the "New York game" outstrip a more flexible rival known as the "Massachusetts game." Over a hundred copies of the Knickerbockers' rules had to

The Knickerbocker Club of New York was responsible for many innovations that helped transform baseball from a child's game to an adult activity. *Courtesy of Transcendental Graphics*

be printed to meet the requests from newly formed clubs. More converts were gained when the rules were published in *Porter's Spirit of the Times* on December 6, 1856, and in the *New York Clipper* a week later.[20] Historian Tom Melville concludes that "baseball was the first game Americans learned principally from print," noting that town ball was "handed down from generation to generation orally" but that baseball was learned by reading "printed regulations."[21] Baseball has retained an obsessively bookish element, and, as we shall see, its history has been intertwined with that of the newspapers.

Another important way in which the Knickerbockers injected literal elements into the game was the emphasis they placed on scorekeeping. Previously the score, if kept at all, was maintained by notches on sticks, a picturesque element of early games that is frequently cited in reminiscences. In contrast, the Knickerbockers kept elaborate scorebooks, and their rules even specified that an umpire be appointed at practices to record rules violations in "a book provided for that purpose."[22] These scorebooks, which still survive, allowed the performance of clubs and players to be judged by an outside audience and thus were another essential step to baseball developing a written history.

The Knickerbockers brought many of the rituals of fraternal organizations to baseball. The baseball matches played by this club and the many that followed its lead were formal events with specific rules of conduct. One club would issue a challenge and, once it was accepted, would act as hosts for the match. At the conclusion of the match, both clubs would give three cheers for each other and for the umpire, the losing club would present the winners with a new baseball, and then both clubs would join in a meal, often prepared by the hosts. Some clubs even had special songs that they sang on their way to the ballpark. These rituals helped to restrain competitiveness for awhile, although, as we shall see, it would become increasingly difficult for losing clubs to play along with the rituals.

Historian Robert Burk compares the functioning of the Knickerbockers to that of a religious congregation, as they used "dues, fines, and punishments to help maintain their exclusiveness, finance their activities, and define their purposes. Also as in congregations, violations of certain rules concerning decorum and behavior were more common than others, as club members tested the boundaries of group discipline while avoiding any challenge to the association's basic integrity."[23] The adherence to a shared belief system helped renew a sense of belonging and enabled the Knickerbockers to distance the game from its childish associations.

Some of the rule changes popularized by the Knickerbockers also appear to have been specifically designed to help distance the game from its juvenile associations. Previously, base runners could be put out by hitting ("soaking," "plugging," or "spotting") them with a thrown ball when they were between bases, an element recalled fondly in several reminiscences. This rule made it necessary to use a soft ball, usually one that featured an india-rubber center. When the Knickerbockers replaced soaking with tagging, the game began to be played with a much harder ball, an essential step in disassociating the game from its childish past.

Later on in the game's development, the Knickerbockers led the movement to do away with the bound rule, by which a player was out if a hit was caught on the first bounce. The crux of their argument was that this was a childish way to play and that men ought to have to catch the ball without it being cushioned by the ground. Henry Chadwick, the game's first great journalist, derisively described a bound catch as "a feat a boy ten years of age would scarcely be proud of."[24]

While the Knickerbockers commenced a dramatic transformation of the game from a boy's game to a competitive sport, their revolution took time to take hold. The Knickerbockers first wrote their rules down in 1845, and their activity for the next eight years was sporadic. But by 1854, urbanization and industrialization were touching the lives of more and more Americans, and they began to feel the same need for recreation that had inspired the Knickerbockers. The game spread at a near-epidemic rate, with the number of clubs in the New York City area soaring from 12 in 1855 to 125 in 1858.[25] By 1857, the rest of the country was learning the Knickerbockers' version, led by the Franklin Club of Detroit.

A New York-based organization, the National Association of

Base Ball Players (NABBP), assumed responsibility for the game's rules in 1858.[26] Clubs were not always well-versed on the latest updates, so the term "regulation base ball" was used loosely to denote the rules introduced by the Knickerbockers and modified by the NABBP. Since the specific rules used by a particular club cannot always be deduced, I have used this generic term.

However, the regulation game did not simply overwrite earlier versions in the way that the automobile rendered the horse and buggy obsolete. Instead, the surviving references to baseball in Michigan before 1850 are backward glances tinged with the same nostalgia expressed by McGee for the days when the game was enjoyed purely as a pastime. For example, an 1875 game in Hillsdale pitting fat players against lean ones was compared to the ones "which used to be in the days of 'town meetin's' and 'raisin's.'"[27]

Other contemporary accounts similarly seem to focus on what was lost in the game's transition to a formal activity. A Detroit newspaper observed in 1867 that "base ball, under various and rude shapes has of course been played in America for many years, but was never cultivated to any great extent or under regular rules and by numerous players of skill until twenty years ago."[28]

In 1877, a group of elderly men in Dundee, Michigan, played "a game of base ball . . . according to the rules in vogue fifty years ago." Most of the participants were described as having "made lively runs, notwithstanding their age," which is remarkable, as all the players were over sixty and many were in their eighties. The oldest player was David Van Pelt, described as being ninety-six years old and a veteran of the War of 1812, and he actually scored a run.[29] Many of these men had not grown up in Michigan, but their familiarity with the game from boyhood demonstrates the length of the game's prehistory and must have materially aided the acceptance of a game ostensibly coming from New York.

In 1875, a letter to the *Midland Times* described a loosely played game as being "not baseball, the way it is now played, but [as it was] was well known . . . in our grand father's time."[30]

The University of Michigan 1849 class president reminisced in

1921 that "athletics, back in the days of '49 were not regularly organized, nor had we any gymnasium. We played baseball, wicket ball,
two-old-cats, etc., but there was no football nor any trained teams.
There was mere extempore volunteering."[31]

In 1937, the *Jackson Citizen Patriot* noted: "In a field where the
Blackman park now stands, the first baseball game was played here
July 4, 1845, at which time two teams were selected to entertain the
crowd at an Independence Day celebration. But no record of this
contest was ever published for historical reference."[32]

A letter writer to a Cedar Springs newspaper in 1874 reminisced
about playing "'anti-i-over,' 'two-old-cat' and other species of the
game in our youth," including "old-fashioned base," in which "the
privilege to 'spot' a man whenever he observes him trying to run a
base, is a rare pleasure which is not incorporated within the rules
and regulations of the National Game."[33]

While these descriptions are short on details, such particulars
would be largely irrelevant in any case, since the quintessence of
these games was their flexibility. These games were also devoid of
the ritual elements that cricket possessed and that baseball would
later develop. There were no winners and losers, no score to keep,
and a game was readily abandoned at the behest of parents, a hint of
foul weather, or the whim of the players if a more interesting pursuit
beckoned. After competitiveness had changed the game forever, the
nostalgic fondly recalled "the good old days when the result of a
game was merely a question of physical endurance and light."[34]

A single tantalizing glimpse survives of a baseball club in Michigan before 1857. In 1897, the *Detroit Free Press* observed:

It may be of interest to lovers of the sport to know where the first club
was organized in the state of Michigan. Birmingham claims that distinction. Forty-three years ago, nine young men, ages ranging from
20 to 30 years, decided that it would be a good thing to have a baseball club and by practice become able to play that fascinating game,
not for gate receipts and grand stand money, but for fun, pure and
simple. Accordingly they practiced and, representing the town of

Bloomfield, challenged the adjoining township of Troy to a trial of skill. The two teams lined up in front of the National hotel (building still stands and is yet in use as a place of accommodation to the traveling public) one bright spring day at shortly after 12 o'clock, and the first game began. It was played for a supper of ham and eggs, the losing side to pay for the same. Bloomfield won by a score of 100 to 60. The game was not finished until after 5 o'clock in the evening. The ball played with was a soft one, weighing four ounces. Old time rules of course governed the game, one of them being that a base runner could be put out if hit by a thrown ball anywhere between the bases. Many men were put out in this way.

Elated by their victory, the young men of Bloomfield decided to organize a baseball team, the constitution and by-laws were drafted and adopted and every Saturday a certain number of hours were devoted to practice. That summer the team won many games.

The members, as far as can be learned, were as follows: Luther Stanley, Charles Gillett, Major Valentine, Eli Caswell, Ezra King, Clark Valentine, Ed. Valentine and George W. Mitchell. The latter, now a gentleman 67 years of age, is as far as known, the only surviving member of the team. He still lives [in Birmingham]. . . .

In those days the team that first secured a hundred tallies (generally marked on a stick with a jack-knife, opposite edges used for the two clubs) carried off the honors of the day.[35]

As this description suggests, the members of the Birmingham club were pioneers in organizing, even going to the extent of drafting bylaws. But since they were still playing the long-familiar childish game, their feats went unrecorded at the time, and this account is the only trace of their activities that seems to have survived. Undoubtedly, there were others like them whose exploits at early versions of the game were never documented.

It would only be a few years before clubs in Michigan would begin to compete at the "regulation game" popularized by the Knickerbockers, and their activities would soon take on a corresponding seriousness.

NOTES

1. Frances Trollope, *Domestic Manners of the Americans* [1832], quoted in Jack Larkin, *The Reshaping of Everyday Life, 1790–1840*, 1.

2. Benjamin G. Rader, *American Sports*, 28.

3. *Paw Paw True Northerner*, April 14, 1871.

4. Larkin, *The Reshaping of Everyday Life, 1790–1840*, 49.

5. Larkin, *The Reshaping of Everyday Life, 1790–1840*, 16.

6. Melville McGee, "The Early Days of Concord, Jackson County, Michigan," 430.

7. *Detroit Daily Post*, May 10, 1872. See Melvin L. Adelman, *A Sporting Time*, 280, for a description of how the strict proscriptions on any sort of Sunday recreation in New York City were gradually relaxed.

8. William Humber, *Diamonds of the North*, 18, calls the exact measurements in Dr. Adam Ford's account "preposterous," and the entire account must be viewed skeptically. It seems more plausible, however, that the general description of the extra base very close to home base is accurate.

9. Adam Ford, "A Game of Long-Ago Which Closely Resembled Our Present National Game."

10. *New England Base Ballist*, August 6, 1868.

11. John Thorn, *The Game for All America* (St. Louis: Sporting News, 1988), 13. This essay is also reprinted in various editions of John Thorn and Pete Palmer, eds., *Total Baseball*.

12. *Illustrated Sporting News;* reprinted in the *Kalamazoo Morning Gazette*, June 29, 1904. This article is about the first club in Philadelphia seventy years earlier. Newspapers in the period covered by this book frequently reprinted other papers' articles. Sometimes they credited the newspaper from which they borrowed the piece, but often they simply stole it. Exact dates were never given. My practice has been to cite the earliest appearance of an article that I could find along with any credit given. It is always possible that the piece originated elsewhere.

13. *National Advocate*, April 25, 1823. The discovery of this article and one the same day in the *New-York Gazette and General Advertiser*, by George A. Thompson Jr., received front-page coverage from the *New York Times* on July 8, 2001. See George A. Thompson Jr., "New York Baseball, 1823," 6–8.

14. *Autobiography of Thurlow Weed* (1883), quoted in Stephen Fox, *Big Leagues*, 168.

15. One of the leading figures in the Knickerbockers was Alexander Cartwright, and he is frequently credited with being personally responsible for most of the innovations I discuss herein. However, exactly how much credit Cartwright really deserves is disputed, so I have chosen to credit the club as a whole.

16. William Shepard, "Reminiscences of an Old-Time Ball Player," in Seymour Church, *Base Ball*.

17. Adelman, *A Sporting Time*, 123: "The occupational structure of the Knickerbockers indicates that the members were drawn from at least the middle class, but there is no evidence to support the contention that on the whole they were from the city's upper class or were wealthy urban gentlemen."

18. Fox, *Big Leagues*, 181.

19. Charles A. Peverelly, *The Book of American Pastimes*, 340–41.

20. James M. DiClerico and Barry J. Pavelec, *The Jersey Game*, 26.

21. Tom Melville, *Early Baseball and the Rise of the National League*, 18, citing the *Racine (Wisconsin) Journal*, August 4, 1867, and the *Whitewater (Wisconsin) Register*, July 27, 1866.

22. The scorebook of pioneer journalist Henry Chadwick has been described as "large enough and black enough to be the book of judgment" (Robert Smith, *Baseball*, 78), a metaphor reinforced by the custom of early players calling "judgment" when they wanted a ruling from the otherwise impassive umpire.

23. Robert F. Burk, *Never Just A Game*, 6.

24. Henry Chadwick, ed., *Beadle's Dime Base-Ball Player* (1860), quoted in Warren Goldstein, *Playing for Keeps*, 49, as part of a detailed discussion of the bound rule, 48–53. The change to the fly rule had many advocates in the late 1850s, having been proposed by the Knickerbockers at the first convention of ballplayers in 1857, but was not adopted until December 1864. Foul balls caught on the first bounce remained outs until the 1880s.

25. Adelman, *A Sporting Time*, 126–27.

26. The NABBP was officially formed in New York in March 1858, although there were two preliminary meetings in 1857 at which some rule changes were implemented.

27. *Howard Record*, August 12, 1875.

28. *Detroit Advertiser and Tribune*, May 2, 1867.

29. *Detroit Advertiser and Tribune*, August 1, 1877. Census records suggest that Van Pelt's age was exaggerated by a few years.

30. *Midland Times*, September 14, 1875. "Baseball" is actually one word here, but this is so singular that it is probably a typographical error.

31. *Michigan Daily*, March 24, 1921.

32. *Jackson Citizen Patriot*, September 19, 1937. Contemporary confirmation of the game, however, does not exist.

33. *Cedar Springs Wolverine Clipper*, September 9, 1874.

34. *Lapeer Democrat*, August 16, 1882.

35. *Detroit Free Press*, April 19, 1897. The paragraph omitted from the quotation claims that the Cass Club of Detroit secured a copy of the constitution and bylaws of this club and, with a few changes, adopted them as their own. Since the Cass Club was not formed until 1869, this is certainly a mistake. Possibly the writer was thinking of the Franklin Club or the Detroit Base Ball Club.

2

"THE NEW WAY MUST BE
AN IMPROVEMENT OVER THE OLD"

MICHIGAN'S FIRST REGULATION BASEBALL CLUB

In the generation after the Philadelphia club elicited amusement and mockery, the country's populace resettled in a way that contributed to Michigan's first regulation baseball club being taken more seriously. After the opening of the Erie Canal in 1825 and Michigan's entry into the union in 1837, a surge of "western fever" caused the population of Michigan to increase rapidly—from just over 30,000 in 1830 to 200,000 in 1840, then to nearly 400,000 in 1850 and to almost 750,000 in 1860 (see appendix B for additional population data).

Increasingly the new settlers were men and women accustomed to the amenities of life, and so they flocked to Detroit. A mere village two decades earlier, Detroit had swollen to a metropolis of 45,000 by 1860. Close proximity meant that almost anything could spread more quickly than before, whether it be fads, news, or fires. With sewage and waste management systems still primitive, fevers and other diseases spread especially rapidly and Detroit was ravaged by several deadly epidemics. Moreover, as Detroit developed into an industrial city, many workers shifted from hard physical labor to occupations that exercised few if any muscles. These unhealthy and unsanitary elements of city living thus led to growing concern about the physical well-being of urban Americans.

As leisure time increased, young men began to spend it in saloons and billiard halls, and concern broadened to include the health of the spiritual man. One Flint, Michigan, newspaper noted that cities seemed to spawn crime and remarked that this difference was puzzling since human nature is the same in either an urban or a rural setting.[1] This new concern with the relationship between physical and spiritual health is reflected in this sermon by a New York City minister:

> In country life there are no perilous excitements such as the city affords, and hence there is not such a wear and tear of either the physical or mental system. Hence a vigorous frame generally distinguishes those who come here from the rural districts, and if they pursue the right and virtuous path, they become mentally the superiors of such as are city bred, their mental organism being continually aided in its exercise by a healthful and robust physique. The country is constantly renovating the city, and pouring new life into its veins. Unfortunately, too, many of those who come here however, become by dissipation mere wrecks of humanity, ruin their prospects both for this life and the life hereafter, and sink into an early grave.[2]

With the effects of city living being viewed as a direct threat to men's salvation, the church began to promote the benefits of exercise for those whose work was sedentary in nature. The "Muscular Christianity" movement, which originated in Great Britain, contended that physical deterioration led to spiritual deterioration and consequently recommended sporting activities. The return to nature was emerging as a major theme of great American writers like Ralph Waldo Emerson, Henry David Thoreau, and Walt Whitman.[3] In 1858, a writer in the *Atlantic Monthly* even suggested that men return to childish pastimes: "To almost every man there is joy in the memory of these things; they are the happiest associations of his boyhood. It does not occur to him, that he also might be as happy as a boy, if he lived more like one."[4]

As a result, the leisure activities of boys and young men rapidly gained popularity and became more physically demanding. While baseball today is not perceived to be particularly strenuous compared to, say, basketball, it required much more energy than many of the sporting activities that were popular in the 1840s and 1850s. Pastimes such as horse racing, pigeon shooting, yachting, and billiards required little physical exertion, and young men began to seek out more physically energetic forms of recreation.

In a 1903 interview, a founding member of Detroit's second baseball club, David Peirce, described the arrival of competitive baseball as the logical culmination of a dramatic surge of physically demanding sports in Detroit in the late 1850s:

> The young men of the city were enthusiastic over athletics, and every noon and every night they met at Merritt's gymnasium, on Jefferson avenue, between Bates and Randolph streets. Mr. Peirce says the boys used to do about all the tricks that the athletes do in circuses today.
>
> Mr. Peirce did not have time during the days to take boxing lessons, so he got up early in the mornings and walked four miles to Canniff's farm on the Pontiac road, to take his lessons. He was very quick on his feet, and in those days he would rather box than eat.
>
> At night when the boys assembled at the gymnasium, the first event on the program usually was a foot race from Jefferson avenue to the foot of Woodward avenue and back. Then the boys adjourned to the gymnasium and boxed, wrestled and took part in other sports.[5]

In this environment, baseball became an acceptable compromise for channeling these excess energies. It allowed a young man tempted by the city's vices an outlet that offered reminders of the rural past and helped to renew his sense of identity. Baseball clubs were thus seen as upholding, rather than threatening, traditional values, and in baseball's early years there was little reason to view the function of these clubs as anything other than the culturally con-

servative one of keeping young men from the temptations associated with city living.

Although the advent of scorekeeping meant that the games now
featured winners and losers, baseball's adoption of the chivalric concept of tournaments helped to restrain competitiveness. The immediate inspiration for this mode of competition may have been the popularity of tournaments in the late 1850s in which the fire engines of
neighboring towns competed to see who could shoot water the far-
thest.[6] While these events evoked civic pride in the winners, the
competitive element was obviously less important than the protection all citizens received from the improved fire-fighting abilities
thereby inspired. Spectacle rather than competition was emphasized
by these tournaments, and the crowning of a champion was less
important than the message that the participants were ultimately all
on the same side, just as they had been in the "raisin' games."

While the essence of prehistoric baseball was the absence of
organization, there were hybrid clubs like the one in Birmingham
that assumed a formal structure while still playing by old-fashioned
rules. As the *Detroit Free Press* later summarized: "Detroit had long
possessed the felicity of base ball clubs, yet they were of the tran-
sient and evanescent order, playing on commons and by no well settled code of rules. . . . It was not until 1857 that one of the regulation
sort came to abide in the City of the Straits."[7]

By the summer of 1857, Michigan was ready for its first regulation baseball club, and not surprisingly it was in Detroit, the state's
only large city, that the club was born. The Franklin Club may even
have been the first club west of New York to adopt the Knickerbocker rules, but its members were modest in their claims. Henry
Starkey, a leading member of the Franklins, gave this account of the
club's early days in an 1884 interview:

> "I understand that you are the oldest base ball player in the
> world," said a reporter to Secretary Starkey of the Board of Water
> Commissioners yesterday.
>
> "Can't say as to that, but I organized the first base ball club in

Detroit, or assisted to do so. That was in 1857. Previous to that time, we had played the old-fashioned game of round ball. There were no 'balls' or 'strikes' to that. The batter waited until a ball came along that suited him, banged it and ran. If it was a fly and somebody caught it, he was out and couldn't play any more in the game. If the ball was not caught on the fly, the only way to put a batter out was to hit him with the ball as he ran. There were no basemen then; everybody stood around to catch flies and throw the ball at base runners.

"There was an old fiddler here in the city named Page. He is dead now, I guess, but has relatives here still—George Sparks for one. He used to take the New York *Clipper*, and one day he showed me a copy in which there was quite a lengthy description of the new game of base ball. By the way, Page was the man who shut up all the saloons—never would go home until they were all shut up.

"There was quite a number of us who felt an interest in the game, and we came to the conclusion that the new way must be an improvement over the old. Anyway, we decided to try it, so I wrote to the *Clipper* for a copy of the new rules, and paid $1 for it. After we got the rules we organized a club—the first in Detroit."

"What was the name of the club?"

"The Franklins."

"Who composed the team?"

"They were mostly printers from the *Free Press* office, though I was then clerk of the Recorder's Court."

"Are any of them living beside yourself?"

"Oh, yes. There's George Atkins for one. I think he is now employed on the Chicago *Times*. J. P. McMillan was another. He is working in some job room here in the city. I do not know whether there are any more of them living or not."

"Where were your grounds?"

"Out on the Beaubien farm where now is the corner of Beaubien and High streets. It was then a pasture."

"What became of the Franklins?"

"Oh, Bob Anderson and others soon formed the Detroit Club, got fine grounds out on Woodward avenue and so far eclipsed us that we died a natural death. Bob once knocked the ball four miles out into the country; took them three weeks to find it. I heard him telling about it the other day. It's a fact!"[8]

The *New York Clipper* did indeed publish the rules the Knickerbockers played by on December 13, 1856. But even without corroboration, the basic truthfulness of Starkey's folksy narrative would be evident. Although his anecdotes are exaggerated for comic effect, Starkey made no effort to claim any particular significance for the Franklins other than their having been Michigan's first regulation club. Starkey was only fifty-five when he made these remarks, and others were alive who could have corrected any inaccuracies.[9] Moreover, Starkey was one of Detroit's leading citizens, having served his city of Detroit in numerous capacities and his country in two different wars.

If a boy's game were going to be reinvented as a man's pastime, it needed the support of upstanding citizens. A more appropriate person than Henry Starkey can scarcely be imagined. Henry Mitchell Starkey was born in Binghamton, New York, on May 11, 1828, but his father, Lewis, a physician, moved the family to Michigan in 1833. Lewis Starkey eventually settled in Kalamazoo and served in the Senate in Michigan's second legislature. His son Henry initially apprenticed to a printer and then became one of the first students at Branch University in Kalamazoo. However, he ended his studies to fight in the Mexican-American War.

After the war, Henry Starkey moved to Detroit and succeeded his brother Richard as city editor of the *Free Press* in 1855. After two years in that position, he entered public service, serving as clerk of the recorder's court and as deputy county clerk. Although he was married and starting a family, he continued to participate in a wide range of civic activities, including being an active member of the volunteer fire department.[10]

When the Civil War came, the now thirty-four-year-old Henry Starkey reenlisted and was wounded at Gettysburg. After the war, his civic activities continued to expand. He was elected city clerk in

1865 and was twice reelected to two-year terms. In 1872, he became secretary of the Board of Water Commissioners. Though his war injuries prevented a return to competitive play, Starkey still found time for the sport he had helped introduce to Michigan. He served on the board of Detroit's Cass Base Ball Club and participated in many of the popular "muffin" games between sides representing various branches of local government.[11] After he had grown too old to play anymore, he continued to keep score or to umpire. In fact, just a month before his death in 1888, Henry Starkey dressed in a bell diver's costume to officiate in a game between fat and lean members of the Knight Templars.[12]

The club Starkey described was formed by frequenters of the Congress Hall Saloon, which was located at 3 Congress Street and run by Jeremiah Calnon. The Congress Hall's proximity to the three Detroit newspapers made it a popular watering spot for printers, and it was there that interest in the newly formalized game of baseball crystallized. In August 1857, a meeting was held at the saloon to form a club.

The exact date of this historic meeting is difficult to establish. George Catlin, a twentieth-century *Detroit News* reporter and an expert on local history, gave the date of the club's formal organization as August 1, 1857.[13] However, the *Detroit Free Press* reported on August 15, 1857, that "a Base Ball Club is about being organized in this city, by the admirers of the 'good old Yankee sport.' "[14] In addition, near the end of the month both the *Free Press* and the *Detroit Advertiser* reported the club's formation and its new officers.[15] So the date given by Catlin must have been either that of a preliminary meeting or an error.

When the club was formally constituted in late August, its first officers were Walter H. Foster, thirty-one, a *Free Press* printer, as president; Theodore P. Robinson, twenty-six, a bookkeeper, as vice president; and Clarence E. Eddie, an attorney, as secretary.[16] Twenty-four other men signed the bylaws. Their identities, as reconstructed from city directories, censuses, and other genealogical sources, were as follows:

Henry Starkey, twenty-nine, clerk of the recorder's court

George E. Atkins, twenty-five, foreman of the *Free Press* news-room

Franklin D. Ross, twenty-four, circulating agent for the *Free Press*

James H. Walker, Malachi J. O'Donnell, eighteen, Jordan P. McMillan, Henry R. Durney, and Ad Cowan, printers for the *Free Press*

Jonas H. Titus Jr., twenty-two, Michael Dempsey, twenty-four, Edward Atkins, and George Thurston, printers

John Atkins and John Hudson, forty-one, carpenters

John P. Phillips, a lumber dealer

Milo D. Hamilton, the commercial editor of the *Advertiser*

Jeremiah Calnon, the proprietor of the Congress Hall Saloon

Earl F. Plantz, twenty-six, collector

Eugene Robinson, twenty, surveyor

J. J. Maledon, circulating agent for the *Advertiser*

Charles C. Robinson, coppersmith

Frank Folsom, seventeen, bookstore clerk

Thomas S. Gillett, accountant

Marsh D. Robinson, twenty-five, printer for the *Advertiser*

As this list suggests, the members of the new club fit the profile of young men who had been left by urbanization with too much time on their hands. There were plenty of tempting ways to use that spare time. Historian Steven A. Riess notes that "in Detroit, a major billiard center that was the site of the first American championship in 1859, billiard halls were situated mainly in and around the downtown area in close proximity to the city's saloons and brothels."[17] With such unsavory alternatives, no one could object to young men like these redirecting some of their time to a healthy outdoor activity, even one that had traditionally been enjoyed by small children.

The Franklin Club was also representative of the rapidly growing Michigan population in another important regard. In 1845, the Michigan legislature had appointed an agent to live in New York and encourage immigration to Michigan. The 1860 census showed that 25 percent of Michigan residents had been born in New York State and that at least six of the Franklins' members were born in New York. So it is not surprising that the club chose to adopt the New York version of baseball rather than the rival Massachusetts version of the game.

The employment of so many of the Franklins by the Detroit newspapers was also appropriate. Newspapers had been part of Michigan's culture for decades, but their primary function was as advertising sheets for local businesses. However, in the 1850s the invention of the telegraph and enhanced printing technologies enabled newspapers to become the fastest medium of communication. They would lose this status to the telephone in the 1870s, but by then newspapers had established themselves as an integral part of American life.

Like baseball, newspapers were transformed by the urbanization of the 1850s. What had begun as a method of communicating information soon became a means of explaining the new phenomenon of city living to readers. Like baseball, newspapers fostered a sense of stability and community in a rapidly changing world, and these parallels created a deep bond between the two institutions. But, as we shall also see, as baseball and the newspapers came of age together, familiarity often bred contempt.[18]

The Franklins soon began to engage in practice games. On Saturday, August 15, the members of the new club played two games of "base" on a vacant lot on Beaubien Street above Adams Avenue. The first game was played to 75 runs, with Henry Starkey and Jonas H. Titus acting as "leaders" of the two sides. It took twenty-two innings (with no record of the number of outs per inning) for Starkey's side to win, 75-40. In a second game, George Atkins and Michael Dempsey acted as leaders, and the game was played to 40. Atkins' squad won, 40-12, but this second contest took thirty-two innings, suggesting that the fielding was improving with practice.[19]

Two more practice games were played the following Saturday, and each side won one, the second by a score of 21-19. How closely the players adhered to the rules they had spent one dollar to procure is questionable, as the squads played with ten to a side. One side was composed of Edward and John Atkins, Titus, Eddie, Plantz, Ross, and four new recruits named Rousseau, Knapp, Taylor, and Patten. Their opponents were Walker, Foster, McMillan, Starkey, Phillips, one of the Robinsons, and newcomers named Scovel, Grieve, Moore, and McLogan.[20] After the two games, the club enjoyed a "generous repast" at the home of Theodore Robinson. A third practice was scheduled for the grounds of the Detroit Cricket Club on August 29, but there is no record of whether it took place.

No contemporary sources listed the new club's name as the Franklins during 1857, the *Free Press* referring to the new group as the Detroit Base Ball Club. But by the time the club re-formed for the 1858 season, its members had evidently seen the need for a name that better identified them and selected the name the Franklin Club, in honor of Ben Franklin, who, in addition to all his distinctions, was a printer by trade. (Club names throughout this period were in the form of, for example, "The Franklin Base Ball Club of Detroit." Sometimes this would be simplified to the Franklins of Detroit, or just the Franklins, but the modern nomenclature, of the nickname following the city name, did not appear until the 1870s.)

The Franklin Club reorganized very early for the 1858 season, holding a preliminary meeting on the grounds at the head of Beaubien Street on April 3 and an organizational meeting six days later at the Congress Hall Saloon. Foster and Theodore Robinson were reelected as president and vice president, while Henry Starkey was chosen to serve as secretary and treasurer and Eugene Robinson and George Atkins were elected captains. The club was described as being in a "very prosperous condition," with twenty-four active members and many new applicants for membership.[21] While no one had tried to justify the existence of a club of men playing a boy's game the previous summer, the *Advertiser* now published two defenses.

The first one stressed that the strict code of rules and the professional class of men playing were transforming the child's game into an adult sport:

The game of base ball is an American game, and that it is one of healthy and manly exercise as well as one of many excitements, no one who ever played it will deny. Last year, for the first time, we believe was there a regular organized club formed and conducted upon regular rules, and by-laws, in this city, and as far as we know in the State. It has had one preliminary meeting this season, and we understand will have regular meetings throughout the season. When governed by strict rules, it is a beautiful game. It has become very popular about New York City, and the highest classes of professional gentlemen—Doctors, lawyers, and clergymen—engage in it. There was recently a large convention held, composed of delegates from the various clubs on Manhattan Island, to revise and adopt rules governing the game. The rules and constitution, &c., may be found in *Porter's Spirit of the Times* of April 3, (for sale by Ross,) which will be useful to those contemplating the formation of clubs.[22]

The players and supporters of what had once been a boy's game were beginning to pride themselves on exactly the kinds of adult concerns—meetings, rules and bylaws, class distinctions—that are anathema to children. Baseball was starting to develop its unique texture of a boy's game peeking out from behind an elaborate adult superstructure.

Five days later, the *Advertiser* supplemented its first argument by citing the unhealthiness of city living and depicting baseball as an appropriate way to get the exercise necessitated by slothful urban lifestyles:

The general neglect of healthful and recreative out-door exercise among us, strikes us as demanding the serious attention not only of the *savans* [*sic*] and philosophic advisers of the public, but of the people at large, and for this reason we regard the establishment in our midst of this really scientific and natural game—base ball—as a harbinger of renewed attention to the culture and development of muscular superiority. In New York, we see it stated, a proposition has been made to the Commissioners of the Central Park, that a portion of that ground be laid out for the use of the various base ball clubs of that city. If such a disposition were made by the Committee on Parks, of this city, it would be a much more rational way of disposing of the small amount which would be required for the purpose, than the present mode adopted, of fencing them in, and announcing by large signs and placards, that *"No one is allowed on these grounds, under penalty of the laws."* We hope that some movement of the kind suggested, will be adopted here, so that this club, and others which are soon to be formed, may have a suitable place for their field exercise.[23]

It is noteworthy that this argument depicts baseball as an inclusive activity by opposing it to the exclusionary message of the placards.

In spite of the newspaper's eloquent support and its hints that more clubs would be welcome, no other clubs were formed, and soon the absence of outside competition took a toll on the Franklins. When a second cricket club was formed in Detroit, the *Advertiser* once again suggested that "there should be a rival base ball club here," but none was forthcoming.[24] There's no way to know whether the Franklin Club's practices stopped or whether the newspapers simply saw no reason to continue devoting space to scrimmages.

Either way, any further activities the club may have had were not reported, and sometime during the 1858 season Michigan's first club apparently called it quits. Starkey's reminiscences seem to suggest that the Franklins and the Detroit Club existed contemporaneously, but he may have been thinking of the 1860 reincarnation of the Franklins, as there is no record that the Franklin Club of 1857–58 ever faced another club. As the *Free Press* later wrote, Michigan's first organized baseball club arrived "unheralded and departed unwept."[25]

NOTES

1. *Flint Wolverine Citizen*, August 29, 1857.
2. A sermon by Rev. Sidney A. Rorey of New York City entitled "Representative Young

Men in Folly and Vice"; reprinted in the *Grand Rapids Daily Morning Democrat*, May 19, 1869.

3. Walt Whitman had once been a baseball reporter for the *Brooklyn Eagle*.

4. "Saints, and their Bodies," *Atlantic Monthly*, March 1858, 582–95, quoted in Stephen Fox, *Big Leagues*, 182. The article was published anonymously, but Fox attributes it to Thomas Wentworth Higginson.

5. *Detroit Free Press*, June 14, 1903.

6. The first such tournament in Michigan seems to have taken place in Kalamazoo as part of the July 4 celebrations of 1857.

7. *Detroit Free Press*, December 26, 1884. The City of the Straits was a common nickname for Detroit in the nineteenth century, *détroit* being the French word for strait.

8. *Detroit Free Press*, April 4, 1884.

9. At least one original member of the Franklins, Marsh D. Robinson, was working for the *Free Press* when this article was published, and at least six other original members— McMillan, Walker, Durney, Folsom, and Charles and Eugene Robinson—were still in Detroit in 1884.

10. When trying to locate Starkey on the 1860 census, I was surprised to discover that Starkey himself had enumerated Detroit's Sixth Ward.

11. Muffin games, described at greater length in chapter 14, featured unskilled or inexperienced players. The name reflected the prevalence of muffing.

12. See the *Detroit Free Press*, September 29, 1888, for the Knight Templars game. Much of the information on Starkey comes from obituaries in the *Detroit Free Press* and the *Detroit Tribune*, October 29, 1888.

13. George Catlin, letter to Clarence Burton, October 17, 1927, in the Burton Collection, Detroit Public Library. Catlin claimed to be the first reporter to send a detailed report of a baseball game via telegraph. George W. Stark's article "George Byron Catlin: The Story of a Rolling Stone," *Michigan History* 25 (spring 1941): 143–67, is an excellent source of information on Catlin.

14. *Detroit Daily Free Press*, August 15, 1857. Many newspapers published both daily and weekly editions during this period, with the weekly editions reprinting only the biggest stories. Thus the newspaper being cited here is the *Detroit Free Press*, but the edition is the *Detroit Daily Free Press*. Where appropriate, I include the words "Daily" and "Weekly" in footnotes for the benefit of anyone wishing to trace the original source, but I refer to the newspaper in the text by the generic name, as was invariably done at the time.

15. *Detroit Daily Advertiser*, August 25, 1857; *Detroit Daily Free Press*, August 26, 1857.

16. Eddie was the secretary, according to the *Daily Free Press* and the *Daily Advertiser*. Catlin, however, listed Marsh Robinson as the club's secretary.

17. Steven A. Riess, *City Games*, 17.

18. Gunther Barth's chapter "Metropolitan Press," in *City People*, further develops these ideas.

19. *Detroit Daily Advertiser*, August 17, 1857.

20. Robinson's initial was given as "F," so this was probably Eugene, but obviously it could have been Theodore, Marsh, or a newcomer. "Moore" is probably William F. Moore, another printer; "Scovel" is likely Henry Scovel, the *Free Press* editor after whom Henry Starkey named his son, Henry Scovel Starkey (b. Detroit, April 26, 1858). The rest cannot be positively identified based only on their surnames.

21. *Detroit Daily Advertiser*, April 7, 1858.

22. *Detroit Daily Advertiser*, April 7, 1858.

23. *Detroit Daily Advertiser*, April 12, 1858. The ambitious and farsighted plan to create Central Park in New York City was proposed in 1858 by Frederick Law Olmsted. It was the crown jewel of a "parks movement which, like the new game of baseball, sought to alleviate the deleterious effects of city living by consecrating prime land as a reminder of the rural past. Olmsted described one of the main purposes of the park as being 'to supply to the hundreds of thousands of tired workers, who have no opportunity to spend their summers in the country, a specimen of God's handiwork'" (Barth, *City People*, 38). For more on the parks movement in New York and other large cities, see Barth, *City People*, 36–41; and Melvin L. Adelman, *A Sporting Time*, 274–75. Note, however, that Detroit's Campus Martius, discussed in chapter 3, had been designed by Judge Augustus Woodward for a similar function half a century earlier.

24. *Detroit Daily Advertiser*, April 27, 1858.

25. *Detroit Free Press*, December 26, 1884.

3

"GENTLEMEN OF RESPECTABILITY AND STANDING"

MICHIGAN'S FIRST BASEBALL MATCHES

Detroit was not without a baseball club for long. Preliminary steps toward forming a new one were taken in the fall of 1858. Advertisements in the *Detroit Tribune* and the *Free Press* announced a meeting at Edward Orr's dry-goods store on October 5 to form a baseball club that would play by the rules of the National Association of Base Ball Players, an innovation that was described as "a great improvement on the ordinary play of base ball."[1] The meeting produced over thirty members, who were described as "gentlemen of respectability and standing."[2] A game was scheduled for October 7 at the Cass Farm on what was then the outskirts of town, but no account of it appeared. That seems to have been the end of the club's activities for that fall.[3]

On May 25, 1859, the club prepared for its first full season with a meeting at the Michigan Exchange Hotel. The main activity was to elect officers, who included John S. Newberry as president; William S. Biddle as vice president; David R. Peirce as secretary; Edward Orr as treasurer; and George A. Baker, Dr. Justin J. Dumon, and Frank Folsom as directors. The club scheduled its first practice for June 3 at the Cass Farm and decided that it would be known simply as the Detroit Base Ball Club.[4]

While the Franklins had been craftsmen, the Detroit Base Ball Club was made up predominantly of young professionals. Many of them came from Detroit's best families, and their status as "gentlemen of respectability and standing" is inextricably linked with the history of the club. Newberry was a lawyer, Dumon a dentist, Peirce a daguerrotypist (an early photographer), and Folsom's father, Simeon, a wool merchant and alderman. The other three officers were local businessmen, nonplaying members whose presence lent much-needed dignity to a club dedicated to playing what so recently had been considered a boy's game.

Historian Clarence Burton later described the Detroit Base Ball Club as "a club of sixty young businessmen . . . composed largely of young attorneys and clerks in stores and people who had a little leisure time to play ball among themselves. They practiced occasionally and became somewhat proficient. . . . It was a social club for their own entertainment and those not belonging were not allowed to play."[5] The exclusivity introduced by the Knickerbockers was becoming part of Michigan baseball.

The higher class status of the members of the Detroit Base Ball Club did not necessarily entail their having more money, but there were critical distinctions between them and the Franklins that shaped the new club. While the antebellum United States lacked the rigid class structure of Great Britain, it nonetheless retained some of its elements. A traditional English gentleman was someone who owned land, and therefore his own time, since he could rent his lands if he didn't wish to cultivate them himself. Over time the idea of the gentleman expanded to include a code of behavior designed to prevent exploitation of the privilege of land ownership.

Many settlers of the United States were escaping from the reality of the limited amount of land in Great Britain, which meant that land ownership was mostly inherited. The new country's vast terrain made it possible for anyone to own land, but land maintenance was time-consuming. So owning one's own time remained an elusive ideal, and this was one of the many factors that brought Americans to the cities. As Americans again became clustered in close

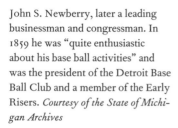

John S. Newberry, later a leading businessman and congressman. In 1859 he was "quite enthusiastic about his base ball activities" and was the president of the Detroit Base Ball Club and a member of the Early Risers. *Courtesy of the State of Michigan Archives*

proximity with each other, elements of the British class system became more apparent.

Gentlemen's clubs, for example, were borrowed from the British class system, using exclusive admission standards to foster pride in belonging. Like other early baseball clubs, the Detroit Base Ball Club was first and foremost a social entity, with athletics of only secondary importance.[6] Such clubs were expected to take their play seriously, but not to the point of competitiveness. As gentlemen, their members were bound by chivalric ideals and viewed a discourtesy as a far greater disgrace than losing a ball game.

The structure of the gentlemen's club gave baseball a solemnity that again helped to underline the game's break from its juvenile past. Early baseball clubs had elaborate business meetings where the nature of their enterprise was carefully concealed beneath a veneer of procedure. The minutes of three Michigan clubs of the period that have been preserved, for example, show an amazing attentiveness to the rules of order. Formal resolutions were made, seconded, and passed for such trivial items as buying a ledger book, accepting a member's resignation, and changing the practice time.[7] The Kent Base Ball Club of Grand Rapids nevertheless decided at one point that its meetings were too informal and passed a motion that they be conducted in a more businesslike manner. Clearly, baseball clubs were distancing themselves from the days when the score was kept by making notches on a stick.

Businesslike meetings probably didn't do much to inspire club loyalty and enthusiasm, but early baseball clubs did incorporate three elements that proved very effective in creating identity and inspiring a sense of belonging. The first was a grassy ball field, which evoked memories of the rural past for city dwellers, as shown by one player's nostalgic description of the Elysian Fields (see chap. 1). The "hacking and hewing" necessary to subjugate the remnants of a wilderness to the uniformity of a baseball field also indicated that Americans no longer had to scrabble for the necessities of existence. What better way to symbolize the triumph of owning their own time than by consecrating arable land to the guilty pleasure of playing a boy's game? The second element, the uniforms of the players, provided a powerful way of asserting status and belonging amid the challenges to identity presented by urban living. The final element was the team's name. Most of the earliest clubs were known simply by the name of the town they represented, which conferred on their members the obligation of representing their whole community. Later, with more than one club in most towns, nicknames became a way of creating a more specific identity. All three elements played an important role in shaping the identities of early baseball clubs, and they still inspire allegiance and nostalgia in modern baseball fans.

As had the Knickerbockers, the Detroit Base Ball Club took advantage of the comparatively high status of its members to hold its practices at 4:00 P.M. on weekday afternoons. But by July 1859, a club known as the Early Risers had been formed by Detroiters with less flexible schedules.[8] Like the Franklins, the new club derived its name from that quintessential American Ben Franklin, one of whose proverbs counsels that "early to bed and early to rise makes a man healthy, wealthy, and wise."

The Early Risers took this advice to extremes even Franklin might have found startling, as this description suggests:

A Base Ball Club has been organized by some of our enterprising young men, which meets every morning at four o'clock in front of the Russell House for practice. It is very fine exercise, and most emphatically causes those who enter into the arrangement to comply with one of the conditions given as requisite by Dr. Franklin to become healthy, wealthy and wise, viz. "early to rise." We have it from good authority that it is exceedingly beneficial to rise early and take exercise before one takes his matutinal meal. If any one wishes to make the experiment an opportunity is afforded them, by joining this Club, to do so. Applications for membership will be received by Frank Folsom, at Raymond's bookstore.[9]

The Early Risers' practices took place on the diagonal pavement on Fort Street at the corner of Woodward, adjoining the Campus Martius. The location was an appropriate one. After Detroit was destroyed by fire in 1805, Judge Augustus Woodward created an ambitious plan for redesigning the city. At the city's center was the Campus Martius, a large, open green space for public assemblies.

Much of Judge Woodward's plan was thwarted by landowners, but the Campus Martius became a hub for the city's activities throughout the nineteenth century. In the twentieth century, rapid development made the site begin to appear obsolete. However, in 2000, plans were unveiled to restore the Campus Martius to correspond to Judge Woodward's original vision. Another part of the effort to rebuild the same area was the opening that year of the Detroit Tigers' new home at Comerica Park.

Even in 1859, the location's proximity to nearby development caused problems. The players batted so many balls through the windows of the Russell House that the hotel's proprietor finally began charging them a flat rate. The club stored its bats and balls in a large box situated behind a grocery store. A local marketwoman, Nancy Martin, "established her quarters on our playing grounds every morning and furnished us coffee and light refreshments which very often was our only breakfast." Three members of the Detroit Base Ball Club also became members of the Early Risers—Luther S. Trowbridge; Frank Folsom, who had earlier been a member of the Franklins; and John S. Newberry, the attorney who had recently been widowed and who had become "quite enthusiastic about his base ball activities." Newberry was boarding at the Russell House, so perhaps he found it easier to join the practices than to be awoken by balls coming through his window.[10]

In 1860 the Campus Martius in Detroit was the site of the early-morning practices of the Early Risers Base Ball Club. But a year later this crowd gathered there on May 11, 1861, to bid farewell to the first regiment of Michigan troops as they left for Washington to fight in the Civil War. *Courtesy of the Burton Historical Library, Detroit Public Library*

As their practice habits suggest, most of the members of the Early Risers were not yet established in a social class and were eager to prove themselves. While many came from well-to-do backgrounds (such as Heber LeFavour, the nephew of former Michigan governor Henry Baldwin), they were only beginning to make a name for themselves. More significantly, they belonged to the rapidly expanding class of white-collar workers who relied on the written word to communicate. The *Free Press* described the Early Risers as "young men employed in stores and offices, whose occupations prevent their taking any recreation during the day."[11] Many had recently been lured west by tales of prosperity and were willing to follow Ben Franklin's homespun advice in hopes of realizing their own rags-to-riches story.

No one could have better exemplified that dream than Richard Henry Fyfe, the catcher and first president of the Early Risers, whose life story reads like that of a Horatio Alger hero. Fyfe was

The Early Risers hit so many balls through the windows of the neighboring Russell House that the hotel proprietor finally began charging them a flat rate. *Courtesy of the Burton Historical Library, Detroit Public Library*

Richard Fyfe, the first president of the Early Risers. A real-life Horatio Alger character, he rose from humble beginnings to operate the world's largest retail shoe store. *Courtesy of the State of Michigan Archives*

born on January 5, 1839, in Oak Orchard Creek, New York, to well-to-do parents, and his family moved to Kalamazoo when Richard was a boy. But Fyfe's father suffered a series of financial reversals, and at eleven Richard was sent to work. He decided to try his luck in Detroit in 1855, but at first could not find work in spite of searching diligently. Finally a shoe-store owner named T. K. Adams hired Fyfe to sweep his store for the sum of two dollars a week. Fyfe was also allowed "the privilege of sleeping on the second floor of the store," his "room" nothing more than a small area of the warehouse that he denoted as his by "piling up empty boxes."[12]

Fyfe applied himself to learning every aspect of the shoe business and economized in order to obtain independence. In 1865, he borrowed one thousand dollars to buy his own store, but continued sleeping over it to save money until he felt that it had a sound financial footing. His early days in business were humble ones, with customers trading eggs and other products for shoes, one even being followed into the store by his horse. But the store successfully made the transition from bartering to modern business techniques and began a series of expansions. Eventually, R. H. Fyfe and Co. became Detroit's biggest shoe store; by the twentieth century it was the largest retail shoe store in the world.

Even after becoming a millionaire, Richard Fyfe attributed his success to appropriately Franklinesque principles, relentlessly preaching the value of selling an honest product and dealing squarely with customers, his motto being, "Never tell the customer something that isn't so."[13] After finally moving from over his store, he continued to walk the twenty blocks from home to work twice a day regardless of weather until shortly before his ninetieth birthday. He believed that "nothing will keep a man in good health like having his mind occupied" and treated his business as a recreation: "I am not a slave to my business. Rather, business is my slave."[14]

Richard Fyfe's Early Risers faced the Detroit Club on August 8, 1859, the first-ever match in Detroit between regulation baseball clubs. The historic match took place on the grounds of the Detroit Club, which were located on King's Fair Grounds, a part of the Cass Farm that Lewis Cass had leased to Harvey King. The Detroit Club won the game, 59-21.[15]

The *Free Press* remarked that the Early Risers "were offered odds in the match by the other club on account of their inexperience and acknowledged inferiority, but with the true Young America spirit they declined accepting the offer, and went in on equal terms. They were of course beaten, but, as they expected this they took it in good part, consoling themselves with the recollection that they had had an even share of the sport, as well as the opportunity of practicing with superior players." The paper added: "The more such games are patronized and the greater zest and spirit with which they are entered into, the better it will be for the young men of this city. Those who hang around the billiard saloons and liquor shops will do well to join one of these regular ball clubs and take regular exercise with them."[16]

The 59-21 score will no doubt raise eyebrows, but it is indicative of the role of the pitcher in early baseball. The pitcher was required to literally pitch the ball like a horseshoe, underhanded, without spin or velocity, while the batter could wait for a pitch of his liking, as there were no balls or strikes. With barehanded fielders, a lively rubbery ball, and uneven grounds, the game was a paradise for hitters, even though they were out if a hit was caught on the first bounce.[17] Captain W. V. James served as umpire of this first match, but this was still a largely ceremonial position, and he was probably called on to settle few if any disputes.

Detroit used David Peirce as pitcher, Justin J. Dumon as catcher, Jim Craig at first base, George Niles at second base, E. R. McDonald at third base, John S. Newberry in short field, Robert H. Anderson in center field, Frank Folsom in right field, and Morgan Fellers in left field. The Early Risers countered with Henry G. Field pitching, Richard Fyfe catching, Charles S. Wright at first base, Morton H. Hawley at second base, Heber LeFavour at third base, Elisha B. Gorton in short field, Benjamin Rush Young in center field, John C. Pierce in right field, and Joseph Winter in left field.[18]

The success of the match prompted plans for a return engagement on August 19.[19] The rematch saw the Detroit Club again emerge triumphant, by a score of 51-30. The Detroit Club used the same players as in the previous game, although McDonald and Peirce changed positions, but the Early Risers used two new players, Frank J. Phelps and Luther S. Trowbridge.

Other clubs were now getting excited about the new game. The Brother Jonathan Wicket Club, a "club of young lads in the upper part of the city," voted unanimously on September 1 to change sports and rechristen themselves the Brother Jonathan Base Ball Club. Like the Franklins and the Early Risers, the club chose a name that paid tribute to an American patriot. The term "Brother Jonathan" had originally been used by George Washington to refer to Connecticut governor Jonathan Trumbull but had gradually expanded to become "a designation for the whole country, as John Bull has for England."[20] The *Advertiser* expressed the hope that the young members of the new club would "be successful in enjoying themselves in their manly game."[21]

Employees of the Michigan Central Rail Road also formed a

club and challenged the Early Risers to a match. The clubs met on September 30 on the grounds of the Detroit Base Ball Club at the Cass Farm, and "notwithstanding the unpleasant nature of the day, the match was spirited and close."[22] The game ended in a 23-23 tie, a result neither side saw any need to settle by playing extra innings.[23] This demonstration that winning and losing were still relatively unimportant brought a fitting conclusion to the season that had seen the start of match play in Detroit.

NOTES

1. *Detroit Daily Tribune*, October 4, 1858; *Detroit Daily Free Press*, October 5, 1858.
2. *Detroit Daily Tribune*, October 7, 1858.
3. The Cass Farm was a large piece of land willed to the city by Lewis Cass, Michigan's most famous nineteenth-century politician.
4. *Detroit Daily Advertiser*, May 26, 1859; *Detroit Free Press*, May 26, 1859.
5. Letter to the *Detroit News*, October 1, 1927, in the Burton Collection, Detroit Public Library.
6. While most of the social aspects of the club are lost to history, a few hints of this important element are preserved. For example, Early Risers' member George L. Field, a dentist and the brother of Henry, married Frank Folsom's sister Sarah in 1861.
7. *Kent Base Ball Club By-Laws and Constitution; Aetna Base Ball Association Constitution and By-Laws;* minutes of the Washtenaw Base Ball Club of Manchester, Bentley Library, Ann Arbor, Michigan. Newspapers also frequently summarized such business meetings.
8. The *Free Press* stated on June 14, 1859, that there were two baseball clubs in Detroit—one was the Detroit Base Ball Club, but it's not clear what the other one was. Possibly the Franklin Club was still practicing, or perhaps the Early Risers or the Brother Jonathans had begun playing. The Brother Jonathans had been formed in early May, but as a wicket club (*Detroit Daily Advertiser*, May 3, 1859).
9. *Detroit Daily Advertiser*, July 7, 1859. Alexander Cartwright, one of the leaders of the Knickerbockers, was also a bookstore clerk, another coincidence suggesting a connection between baseball and the country's transition from an oral to a written mode.
10. Richard Fyfe, letter to Clarence Burton, Burton Collection, Detroit Public Library. This letter is the source of most of the information in this paragraph.
11. *Detroit Free Press*, May 20, 1860.
12. Richard Fyfe, letter to Clarence Burton.
13. *Detroit Free Press*, October 28, 1931.
14. *Detroit News*, January 5, 1929 (Fyfe's ninetieth birthday). Also see the *News, Times,* and *Free Press* of October 27 and 28, 1931, following Fyfe's death.
15. The score was given as 60-21 in some accounts and as 59-23 in others. With the players yelling "tally" after crossing home, discrepancies were common. Both clubs had an official scorer at games, and they apparently did not reconcile their scores if the game did not hang in the balance, as slightly different scores were often reported for games. In general, I do not note such discrepancies.
16. *Detroit Free Press*, August 9, 1859.

17. The Knickerbockers favored the abolition of the "bound rule," but the NABBP did not adopt it until 1864.

18. Box scores for this game, as with virtually all box scores of this period, gave only the surnames of most of the players. Identification of the players is largely from contemporary accounts, my own research, and an article in the *Detroit Advertiser and Tribune* on May 2, 1867, giving a history of baseball in the city. Also of some help was Richard Fyfe's letter to Clarence Burton. However, Fyfe was nearly ninety at the time and was shaky on the identity of several players. In an article in the *Detroit Free Press* on March 25, 1928, Burton misidentified John C. Pierce as Albert D. Pierce, J. J. Dumon as E. E. Dumon, and Robert Anderson as C. A. Anderson. The correct identities of all three are very clear from contemporary sources.

19. The Detroit Club prepared for the match with a game between their first and second nines; the first nine won 25-11 in spite of being two players short.

20. *Ionia Sentinel,* September 28, 1877. A caricature of "Brother Jonathan" became closely associated with the American identity.

21. *Detroit Daily Advertiser,* September 3, 1859.

22. *Detroit Free Press,* October 1, 1859.

23. In 1870 the celebrated winning streak of the Red Stockings of Cincinnati ended in extra innings after their manager, Harry Wright, insisted on playing until a winner was decided. At the end of the ninth inning, the other team and most of the spectators began to leave, showing that even at this much more competitive time it was not standard to play extra innings. However, Wright pointed out to the umpire that he had the option to demand extra innings, and so the game was played to its conclusion.

4

"HAVE A GOOD TIME, BOYS, BUT DON'T HURT THE TREES"

BASEBALL SPREADS

Quite independently of what was happening in Detroit, versions of the game of baseball incorporating some of the new rules began to make their appearance in western Michigan in the late 1850s. In a 1901 *Kalamazoo Telegraph* article, an early settler, Oscar F. Coleman, provided an interesting account of the origins of baseball in Kalamazoo:

> It was some time before the Civil war that Mr. Coleman and Judge W. W. Peck organized the first team that ever played "hard" baseball in Kalamazoo. Previous to that the boys had played a form of cricket with a big soft ball as large as a modern football, but round and made at home of twine and leather and bowled over a level field to knock down wickets less than its own height from the ground. A meeting was held one evening at the Cummings' cigar store located at the corner of south Burdick street and Exchange place, now occupied by the Caryl book store, and an unnamed club was formed with Judge W. W. Peck as secretary and treasurer. Pick-up nines were played for a number of years in Bronson Park until during the term of

Latham Hull as president of the village an order was secured from the village council prohibiting it for fear of injury to the trees from the hard baseballs which had then just come into use. Mr. Coleman recalls how President Hull would pass through the park when they were playing and tell them to "go on and have a good time, boys, but don't hurt the trees." The balls were tossed, not pitched, then, and much of the danger of the game lay in the rocks which were used for bases and gave Mr. Coleman, among others, a badly sprained ankle.[1]

Five years later, the *Kalamazoo Gazette* gave a rather different version of apparently the same events. It identified four members of the first club who were still living in Kalamazoo: Judge Ez White, Judge William W. Peck, Charlie Rice, and Jerome B. Trowbridge (Oscar Coleman had died in 1904). According to Trowbridge, the players had long played patch ball, a game with a flexible number of players in which a runner was out if he was "patched" (hit with a thrown ball). But then John McCord, one of the players, went off to New York to attend school and came back enamored of regulation baseball:

> John used to play the old game of patch ball with us when he was here, but he went down to Poughkeepsie to school and when he came back to Kalamazoo he told us of the other game and prevailed upon us to try it. We tried it and were thoroughly disgusted with the whole thing and wanted to go back to the old game, but John kept at us telling us that this would soon be the only game that would be played and he was right. We kept at it but there were a great many things that we could not get used to. We still wanted to patch a man and some way we could not get used to this new way of putting a man out.[2]

The earliest reference to baseball in a Kalamazoo newspaper appeared on April 20, 1859, when the *Telegraph* wrote: "As dry times approach, base ball comes in order. One club has already been formed, but there is plenty of material for a dozen more. Come, join, and practice, and steal a march on Time and the doctors."[3] The

Kalamazoo newspapers recorded quite a few games of baseball played in 1859 and 1860, but the accounts of these games suggest that McCord's innovations were still being resisted. Although McCord played in many of these games, most were played to a pre-determined score rather than for nine innings, and with only one out constituting an inning.

The earliest recorded game was "a trial at base ball" that took place in Galesburg on May 27, 1859, more than two months before the first match between the Detroit Base Ball Club and the Early Risers.[4] The two clubs played two games to 50, with the visitors from Kalamazoo winning by margins of 8 and 12 tallies. A rematch

Judge William W. Peck in his later years. Peck was a founding member of the first Kalamazoo club to play with a hard ball. *Courtesy of the Western Michigan University Archives and Regional History Collections*

was scheduled for June 10, but there is no record of the result. On June 29, Kalamazoo took on Schoolcraft, winning two games played to 30, 30-19 and 30-20.

In 1860, the Kalamazoo ball players formalized their organization into the Champion Base Ball Club, which included twenty-two active members and ten honorary ones.[5] Perhaps the most important member was L. F. Andrews, who, as editor of the *Kalamazoo Gazette,* provided considerable free publicity to the efforts of the new club. The club claimed that it was playing by the "National Rules," but the New York game was still far from universal in 1860, and the Champion Club seems to have deviated from some of its rules.[6]

Indeed, several elements of these matches suggest that the Champion Club was still playing by the flexible rules of the past. Up to twelve players played on each side, and some games were played to a predetermined score, while others continued until darkness or rain intervened. References to the number of players being "killed while making their runs" or lost "on the goals" suggest that, in spite of McCord's efforts, "patching" may have remained in vogue in some of these games, although it's possible that these terms referred to tagging.[7]

This loose structure ran smoothly in intersquad games but created problems against outside clubs. The first of two matches against the Prairie Club of Schoolcraft was marred by the "incessant remarks of outsiders" and "the impudent interference of outsiders with the duties of the judges," and the *Gazette* complained that the Schoolcraft club took "advantage of a supposed change in the game allowing them to strike from any point."[8] After the rematch, the paper again complained that "the playing was too lawless for [the Champion Club], and they suffered justly from the rules of the National game."[9] Although the Champion Club probably didn't play by the "National Rules" either, the call for standard rules is an important indication of the changing way the game was being played.

While these games sometimes lacked adherence to the new rules of play, they did demonstrate the players' understanding of gentle-manly behavior. In spite of the problems in the first match against Schoolcraft, the "affair ended with a fine supper at the Burdick House."[10] Following the return game at Schoolcraft, the clubs "repaired to the hotel where F. DALE served up an excellent supper, and to which ample justice was done. On going to the office to 'set-tle' the Champion Club found all bills had been generously paid by the Prairie Club."[11]

Baseball also made an appearance in Grand Rapids in 1859. An advertisement in the *Grand Rapids Eagle* on May 7 announced a meeting at Withey's Hall to form a "Bass Ball" club. The news-paper added: "In to-day's paper will be found a call to organize a Base Ball Club, similar to those now so much in vogue in all the eastern cities. *There is not a Base Ball Club in Michigan* governed by the 'National Association of Base Ball Players,' now adopted by all Base Ball Clubs throughout the Union. Let the Valley City be the first to organize."[12] The *Grand Rapids Enquirer and Herald* asked a question on the same day: "There are quite a number of young peo-ple in this city, that are anxious to organize a base ball club. Who will take the lead?"[13]

It was not long before the gauntlet was taken up. After several meetings, the Pioneer Base Ball and Wicket Club was formed on May 17 at the office of local dentist Joel Parker. By the end of the month a second club, the Valley City Wicket Club, was formed. The *Enquirer and Herald* wrote: "Just now, the popular game is Ball Playing. Every evening, after 6 o'clock, the Park is visited by a large number of performers and lookers on, and 'Wicket Ball' played with much vigor and some dexterity. All avocations are engaged—mechanics, doctors, tradesmen, reporters, lawyers, mer-chants, clerks, students, & c., all mix in, and perform to the best of their ability. The sides are generally made up of married and single men, opposed to each other."[14] Soon there were plans for a third club on the west side of town, prompting one of the papers to note that "games and amusements, like diseases, are epidemic in their character."[15] The comparison of the spread of baseball to an epi-

The Pioneer Base Ball and Wicket Club—Grand Rapids' first baseball club—was formed in the dental office of Dr. Joel C. Parker in 1859. *Courtesy of the Local History Department, Grand Rapids Public Library, Grand Rapids, Michigan*

demic would prove an enduring one, with the phrase "base ball fever" and similar metaphors quickly becoming popular.[16]

The Grand Rapids newspapers welcomed the new clubs, one writing that "the pursuit of athletic sports renovates and invigorates the body, and has no deleterious effect upon the morals."[17] Another commended the "invigorating and lively sport afforded by ball playing."[18] This support was undoubtedly increased by the distinguished makeup of the officers of the Pioneer Club. The club's president, Byron D. Ball, was a prominent lawyer and businessman and the son of Daniel Ball, a shipping magnate who had founded the town of Owosso. Byron Ball would later become prosecuting attorney of Kent County, a state senator, and attorney general of Michigan, all in a life of only forty-one years.

The club's vice president was Dr. Joel Parker, who had become Grand Rapids' first full-time dentist five years earlier. Parker was also a distinguished amateur naturalist and inventor, and it was later claimed that he had discovered the principles of the telephone before Alexander Graham Bell.[19] Other officers included Dr. James

Byron Ball, president of Grand Rapids' first baseball club and later attorney general of Michigan.
His sudden death at forty-one fueled a controversy
about the dangers of too much exercise. *Courtesy of
the State of Michigan Archives*

Joseph Herkner was also a member of Grand Rapids' first baseball club. After serving in the
Civil War, he founded a jewelry
store that is still in business. But
he didn't entirely forget about
baseball—he donated a silver ball
that became the symbol of Kent
County's baseball supremacy.
Courtesy of John Gelderloos

H. Morgan, another dentist; Arthur Wood, who would become a
wealthy carriage-factory owner; O. H. Dean; and Joseph Herkner,
who would become a prominent Grand Rapids jeweler. In spite of
these credentials, or possibly because its founders had too many
other things to do, the Pioneer Club was short-lived.

Other towns were also joining the fun. A club was formed in Ypsilanti in April 1859 that included state senator Chester Yost and "other prominent citizens." The game was hailed as being "good for exercise and innocent amusement."[20] In Ann Arbor, a baseball and wicket club was formed on April 14, 1860.[21] On that same day, clubs from Hillsdale and Reading played in the latter town, with the visitors winning 40-18. A student at Hillsdale College reported shortly afterward that baseball was "the principle [sic] game" being played on campus.[22]

Undoubtedly, the citizens of many other Michigan towns were experimenting with more formal rules for the game they had played as boys. The parallel but not entirely simultaneous development of the game in so many different towns would play an important role in its history. As one village tired of the excesses that baseball fever could engender, another would experience a first or renewed rush of enthusiasm for the game, thus keeping baseball's pulse beating even at its bleakest hours.

NOTES

1. *Kalamazoo Telegraph*, December 10, 1901.
2. *Kalamazoo Gazette*, February 11, 1906. A man named Merritt Griswold described the introduction of regulation baseball to St. Louis in strikingly similar terms. Griswold had played regulation baseball in Brooklyn before moving in 1860 to St. Louis, where a club called the Morning Star Club was playing town ball. According to Griswold: "After considerable urging and coaxing on my part they passed a resolution at one of their meetings that they would try the national rules for one morning if I would . . . teach them, which I consented to do if they would agree to stick to it for the full hour without 'kicking,' for as I told them they would not like it until after playing it for a sufficient length of time to be familiar with some of its fine points, all of which they agreed to and kept their words like good fellows as they were, but in ten minutes I could see most of them were disgusted, yet they would not go back on their word and stuck to it for their hour's play. At the breaking up of the game to go home they asked me if I would coach them one more morning as they began to 'kindy like it' " (quoted in Alfred H. Spink, *The National Game*, 406).
3. *Kalamazoo Telegraph*, April 20, 1859.
4. *Kalamazoo Gazette*, June 3, 1859.
5. The active members were Albert H. Randall, H. M. Brown, C. C. Dolloway, S. R. Wheeler, L. C. Tuttle, C. Tuttle, Frank Burlingham, Jerome Trowbridge, William E. White, Horace L. Church, John McCord, William W. Peck, C. M. Randall, J. Doody, George N. Ives, J. A. Robinson, George Dodge, O. H. Brusie, B. Seeley, Clark L. Mott,

and Peyton Ranney. The honorary members were Dwight May, J. P. Woodbury, E. C. Brownell, H. E. Hascall, A. Cameron, Allen Potter, O. N. Giddings, Oscar F. Coleman, D. T. Fox, and L. F. Andrews.

6. *Kalamazoo Gazette,* October 5, 1860.

7. *Kalamazoo Gazette,* June 23, 1860.

8. *Kalamazoo Gazette,* June 23, 1860.

9. *Kalamazoo Gazette,* October 5, 1860.

10. *Kalamazoo Gazette,* June 23, 1860.

11. *Kalamazoo Gazette,* October 5, 1860.

12. *Grand Rapids Daily Eagle,* May 7, 1859.

13. *Grand Rapids Daily Enquirer and Herald,* May 7, 1859.

14. *Grand Rapids Daily Enquirer and Herald,* May 25, 1859.

15. *Grand Rapids Daily Enquirer and Herald,* May 25, 1859.

16. This phrase was revived in the early 1990s by a television marketing campaign that used the slogan, "Baseball Fever—Catch It."

17. *Grand Rapids Daily Enquirer and Herald,* May 25, 1859.

18. *Grand Rapids Daily Eagle,* May 25, 1859.

19. *The City of Grand Rapids and Kent County, Michigan,* (Logansport, Ind.: A. W. Bowen & Co., 1900), 212–14, contains a letter from Professor E. A. Strong of the State Normal School (now Eastern Michigan University) attesting that Strong had failed to encourage Parker to continue work on a design for a telephone that Parker had made in 1874 and had thereby kept him "out of a great world fame and the triumph and profit of a great invention."

20. *Eaton County Republican,* April 9, 1859. State senator Chester Yost (ca.1806–74) was about fifty-three at the time, so it seems safe to assume that he was a nonplaying member of the club.

21. *Ann Arbor Local News,* April 17, 1860.

22. Newell Ransom Dunn papers, entry for May 11, 1860, in the Michigan History Collection, Bentley Library, Ann Arbor, Michigan; reprinted in Arlan K. Gilbert, *Historic Hillsdale College,* 147. Dunn, the son of the president of Hillsdale College, died during the Civil War.

5

"ADAPTED TO THE WANTS OF
YOUNG MEN GENERALLY"

Back in Detroit, the 1860 season saw the new game continue to gain in popularity and increase its level of organization. Toward this end, in March the Detroit Base Ball Club was admitted to membership in the National Association of Base Ball Players, the New York–based governing body for the regulation game.[1] The Detroit Club was very much at the forefront of the game's expansion. J. W. Tomes and J. S. Davies attended the NABBP's convention in New York City, making the Detroit Club the only club west of New York represented. Indeed, fifty-seven of the sixty-two clubs that attended the convention were from New York or New Jersey.[2]

By early April, four Detroit clubs had organized for the new season—the Detroit Club, the Early Risers, the Brother Jonathans, and a new club called the Excelsiors, which had split off from the Brother Jonathans. The Michigan Central Rail Road Club also soon re-formed, as did the Franklins, after having been inactive the previous summer. The Detroit newspapers welcomed the prospect of another summer of baseball. The *Tribune* noted, "We are glad to see this healthy and manly game so popular. It furnishes capital exercise and should be largely engaged in by our young men."[3] The *Free Press* echoed these sentiments, observing that "base ball is strictly an American game, and is fast becoming popular, as it well deserves.

There is no healthier amusement in vogue, and the time spent in practice is so much taken from pursuits that may be far less moral in their tendencies."[4]

A few weeks later, the *Free Press* wrote at much greater length about the sport that was suddenly enjoying such popularity:

> There has no game been introduced to the American people—as fond of novelty and pleasure as they are—that has so rapidly and yet so permanently won their favor as that of base ball. And yet this is not a new game. It has been played in this country for years and years, and has always been a favorite with school boys. But recently it has been reduced to a system, rules have been prescribed for playing it, and the game has been adapted to the wants of young men generally. Three years since the Detroit Base Ball Club was established, followed two years since by the Early Risers, then by the Michigan Central Railroad Club, since which a host of less pretentious organizations have arisen in the city, under the particular patronage of the younger portion of a community. The former clubs are all composed of young men, are fully organized, have strict rules for their government, and meet regularly for practice and exercise on specified days. Base ball is conceded to be one of the most healthy and harmless of field sports. The most rigorous exercise of all the muscles of the body is effected by it, with the double advantage of the fresh air. In this respect it surpasses in merit, by great odds, the most perfect gymnasium that can be devised. It induces activity and strength, and is precisely the game adapted to the wants of the effeminate young men of the present day and generation.
>
> The season for the practice of this sport is just opening and, we believe, all the clubs have already commenced operations. The Early Risers practice every morning, from five to seven o'clock, on the Campus Martius. The Central Railroad Club have grounds in the lower part of the city, where they meet evenings after working hours. They are composed exclusively of the employes of the railroad, and are a fine athletic set of men, and, with a little more practice, will be hard to beat.
>
> The Detroit Club, which is the oldest organization, is composed

of business and professional men mainly. They have grounds on the Cass Farm, near the intersection of George street, where they assemble three times a week for practice. It is stated that they have invited one of the most noted clubs in the State of New York, resident in Brooklyn, to visit this city during the present season and play a match with them. This would be an interesting game, and would attract much attention, from the known accomplishments of the two organizations. Should this purpose be accomplished, it is proposed that the Brooklyn club shall remain in the city several days, during which time the public will have a fair opportunity of witnessing this exhilarating and manly game, which may commend itself, by the exhibition, more fully to their favor.[5]

While the Brooklyn club did not end up visiting Detroit, the attempt to arrange such a match was one of many signs of new ambition on the part of the Detroit Base Ball Club. The club began to search for a new home field, first practicing on the grounds of the Peninsular Cricket Club, near the corner of Grand River and Third Streets, and then settling at the corner of George and Second Streets. The club now included over sixty members, which allowed it to hold a series of intersquad games in May, most of them featuring a nine of married members against a nine of single members.

While baseball grounds brought up memories of an idealized rural past, these games between married and single men also carried symbolic weight. As sports historian Allen Guttmann has observed, grouping players by marital status was a throwback to fertility rituals, in which participants were sometimes divided along the same lines.[6] Such games would become a common feature of early baseball and sometimes elicited revealing commentary. A married-single game in Jackson, for example, prompted the local paper to note, "We would advise all unmarried young ladies, who are now searching for husbands, to be present, as in case the single men are worsted in the game, in order to save their reputation in the next match, they may wish to enter the ranks of married life."[7] The married nine did prevail, but no resultant weddings were reported.

A Hudson newspaper's remarks after another match were more provocative:

> We thought we noticed a marked difference between the players in respect to their observance of the rules of the game—the married men, from the effect of home training, coming down as meek as lambs on a cry of "foul," when the only foul seemed to be in the iteration. Again they would be "put out" on a base without protest—the shaking of a ball at them from a distance doing the business—a gentle reminder of the "broomstick" at home, you know. However, had the game been longer, it is likely the married men would have come out ahead. Their long familiarity with "opposition" and "defeat" would have been of immense advantage in the long run.[8]

Softball games between teams of married and unmarried players later became a popular feature of company picnics, another indicator of baseball's facility for incorporating ritual elements.

The Detroit Base Ball Club took advantage of its status by playing its "bachelor versus benedict" games on weekday afternoons and was therefore able to attract a "large number of spectators" to watch its games.[9] For a game on June 8, the club announced that seats would be provided for women.[10] The Early Risers also advertised an intersquad game, but the 5:00 A.M. starting time must have limited the number of spectators.[11] Nonetheless, the new sport's potential to attract spectators was becoming apparent, a development that would eventually transform baseball.

The Early Risers' predawn practices were beginning to pay benefits. They warmed up by beating the Brother Jonathans 41-10 on June 30. When the Early Risers met the Detroit Club for the first time on July 17, Detroit eked out a 25-22 victory over the club it had easily beaten the previous summer. Three days later, the Daybreak Club of Jackson played the Detroit Base Ball Club in the first match between the two cities that would dominate Michigan baseball over the next two decades. This game showed that Detroit was the superior club, as it won 62-38. Such matches between rival towns would soon become the staple of competitive baseball.

After their close loss, the Early Risers eagerly awaited a rematch with the Detroit Base Ball Club. On August 6, in nearly one-hundred-degree heat, they finally beat the Detroiters 39-32 in "one of the most interesting and closely combated games of base ball ever witnessed in Detroit."[12] The *Free Press* commemorated the first-ever defeat of the Detroit Base Ball Club with an elaborate box score far surpassing any other of the period. In contrast, most other antebellum box scores only gave runs scored and "hands left," a cricket term signifying outs.

The Early Risers next traveled to Jackson, where the Daybreaks showed that they too were improving by beating their guests 21-20. The result of the match still seemed much less important than the camaraderie occasioned by the game. The *Free Press* praised the "gentlemanly manner in which the game was conducted" and the "gentlemanly courtesy and generous hospitality" of the Daybreak Club.[13] The Daybreaks returned the visit in September, and this time the Early Risers pulled off an 18-16 win. There were plans to play a "conquering game" in Jackson, but the game never came off.[14]

While the Early Risers were tangling with the Daybreaks, the Detroit Base Ball Club split two games with the reborn Franklin Club. The stage was now set for the third and deciding match between the Detroit Base Ball Club and the Early Risers. The game was scheduled for Saturday, September 27, and was moved back to Cass Farm to accommodate the expected crowd. The *Daily Advertiser* noted that the sense of equality that had once characterized the players was being transferred to their supporters: "Spectators are welcome, of course.—No reserved seats for any amount of money, and *squatter* sovereignty the style."[15] The game was somewhat of a disappointment, however, in part because the Early Risers had to play a man short during the early innings when one of their players failed to appear on time. The match proved "not very spirited," with the Detroit Base Ball Club winning 34-19 and the game being called in the seventh inning due to darkness.[16]

While most of the matches of 1860 stayed true to the gentlemanly ideal that values good conduct more than winning, there was

Base Ball.

One of the most interesting and closely contested games of base ball ever witnessed in Detroit was played yesterday between the Early Risers and Detroit Clubs, both of this city, on the grounds of the latter, at the corner of George and Second streets, resulting in a victory for the Early Risers by three runs. This is the first defeat of the Detroit Club, and is, in consequence, the more creditable to their more juvenile competitors. The game was played under the rays of a scorching sun, the thermometer marking nearly one hundred degrees on the ground. A very large assembly of spectators, including a number of ladies, were attracted to the grounds to witness the sport, and were detained, by the excitement of the game, until it was finished. The playing was remarkably good on both sides, that of the Early Risers showing the benefit of frequent practice. We append the full score and analysis of the game:

EARLY RISERS.	H.L.	R.		DETROIT.	H.L.	R.
Phelps p	5	3		Anderson p	3	4
Moberly c f	1	8		Dumon c	4	2
Fyfe c	1	5		Newberry s s	3	3
Smith 3d b	3	4		Crage 1st b	4	3
LeFavour 2d b	5	3		Folsom 2d b	1	6
Field 1st b	3	3		Parcher 3d b	3	4
Younge r f	2	5		Niles r f	4	2
Wright s s	4	3		Sines c f	2	5
Pierce l f	3	5		Robinson l f	3	3
Total	27	39		Total	27	32

RUNS MADE EACH INNINGS

Innings	1	2	3	4	5	6	7	8	9	
Early Risers	6	9	3	11	3	0	3	2	2	–39
Detroit	3	3	4	7	9	5	1	0	0	–32

ANALYSIS OF BATTING

Detroit	Fly.	Bound.	1st Base.	2d Base.	3d Base.	Early Risers	Fly.	Bound.	1st Base.	2d Base.	3d Base.
By Phelps	1	3	1	..	..	By Anderson	..	1	1	..	1
Moberly	..	1	..	..	..	Dumon	2	..	1	..	..
Fyfe	1	..	..	..	..	Newberry	1	1	..	..	..
Smith	1	..	2	..	..	Crage	..	1	1	..	..
LeFavour	1	1	1	..	..	Folsom	..	1	..	..	..
Field	..	..	3	..	..	Parcher	..	..	..	..	..
Younge	..	1	..	1	..	Niles	..	..	1	..	..
Wright	..	..	1	..	1	Sines	1	..	..	..	..
Pierce	1	..	1	..	1	Robinson	..	1	2	..	..
Total	5	6	9	1	2	Total	4	5	6	..	1

Wright was put out once by three strikes, and once on the home base. Niles was put out once on the home base.

ANALYSIS OF FIELDING – HOW PUT OUT.

Early Risers.	Fly.	Bound.	Bases.	Foul.	Detroit.	Fly.	Bound.	Bases.	Foul.
Phelps	1	4	..	..	Anderson	3	2	1	..
Moberly	1	..	..	..	Dumon	1	1	2	..
Fyfe	..	..	..	9	Newberry	..	..	..	..
Smith	1	..	1	..	Crage	..	..	9	..
LeFavour	1	..	..	..	Folsom	2	..	..	..
Field	..	..	6	..	Parcher	..	..	1	..
Younge	..	1	..	..	Niles	..	1	..	..
Wright	1	..	..	..	Sines	..	..	1	..
Pierce	..	..	..	..	Robinson	..	3	..	..
Total	4	5	7	9	Total	6	7	14	..

SUMMARY OF EACH INNINGS.
Detroit.

Balls Pitched.	1	2	3	4	5	6	7	8	9
By Anderson	47	49	27	27	38	6	43	20	20
Foul balls struck	7	6	1	6	0	0	0	2	1
Balls passing catcher	8	3	0	5	8	1	7	2	2

Early Risers.

	1	2	3	4	5	6	7	8	9
By Phelps	26	17	18	26	39	22	15	15	16
Foul ball struck	6	1	3	1	3	7	0	1	0
Balls passing catcher	3	0	2	1	1	2	3	3	3

Home runs—Younge 1.
Umpire—Edward Orr.
Scorers—Early Risers, Geo. L. Field; Detroit, William Hull.

This astonishingly detailed box score appeared in the *Detroit Free Press* on August 7, 1860, to commemorate the first-ever defeat of the Detroit Base Ball Club.

at least one early sign of the competitive spirit that would become a major part of the game. The *Detroit Tribune* mistakenly wrote after the third game between the Detroit Club and the Early Risers that "the 'Detroiters' have never been beaten in any match game."[17] An unidentified member of the Early Risers wrote to the *Advertiser* to point out the mistake and to complain that the third game "reflects doubtful credit upon the 'Detroiters,' as they played the early part of the game against eight men, and through the whole game against three of the 'Early Risers' second nine. The 'Detroit' club had two practiced pitchers, while the 'Risers' had to fill that post by their first base man, thus disarranging the whole field, their regular pitcher being unavoidably absent."[18]

Surprisingly, the *Advertiser* responded by counseling the Early Risers regarding "the propriety of never going into the field without a full complement of good men, for people will excuse inactivity, or apparent cowardice even, sooner than a defeat, no matter how well accounted for the defeat may be."[19] Evidently, the "Young America" spirit that had led the Early Risers to play on even terms a year earlier was already going out of favor.

Also that year, a novel experiment pitted the new game of baseball against the more established sport of cricket. In June, Detroit Base Ball Club secretary Dr. Justin J. Dumon issued a challenge to any club in the state to play in a regulation match of base ball.[20] To his surprise, he received a response from the secretary of the Detroit Cricket Club, challenging the club to a baseball match followed by a cricket match. The Detroit Base Ball Club initially accepted the challenge, prompting the *Free Press* to write, "This will be an interesting game, as, while both clubs are experts in the use of the ball, neither are supposed to be familiar with the peculiar game of the other."[21]

However, the baseball players reconsidered after discovering that cricket "is far more intricate and requires more skill and practice than [baseball]. A good cricket player can very readily learn the game of base ball, but a base ball player finds more difficulty in mastering cricket."[22] The cricket club nonetheless sportingly agreed to play the baseball match and was beaten 56-24. After the game, the cricket players "expressed themselves very much surprised at the amount of labor required in playing the game, admitting it was more athletic and spirited than cricket."[23]

By the close of 1860, the continued spread of the game across the state of Michigan seemed inevitable, until history intervened.

NOTES

1. *Detroit Daily Advertiser*, March 23, 1860.
2. Preston D. Orem, *Baseball (1845–1881) from the Newspaper Accounts*, 26. The other four were from Boston, Baltimore, Washington, D.C., and New Haven, Connecticut.
3. *Detroit Daily Tribune*, April 3, 1860.
4. *Detroit Free Press*, April 10, 1860.
5. *Detroit Free Press*, May 5, 1860. In stating that the Detroit Base Ball Club was formed three years earlier, the account confuses the Detroit Club with the Franklin Club.
6. Allen Guttmann, *From Ritual to Record*, 30.
7. *Jackson Daily Citizen*, August 2, 1866.
8. *Hudson Gazette*, June 16, 1871.
9. *Detroit Free Press*, May 26, 1860. "Benedict" was a popular term for married men, derived from the character Benedick in Shakespeare's *Much Ado about Nothing*.
10. *Detroit Daily Tribune*, June 6, 1860.
11. *Detroit Free Press*, May 20, 1860.
12. *Detroit Free Press*, August 7, 1860.
13. *Detroit Free Press*, August 31, 1860.
14. *Detroit Free Press*, September 19, 1860.
15. *Detroit Daily Advertiser*, September 27, 1860.
16. *Detroit Free Press*, September 29, 1860.
17. *Detroit Daily Tribune*, September 28, 1860; reprinted in the *Detroit Daily Advertiser*, October 1, 1860.
18. *Detroit Daily Advertiser*, October 1, 1860.
19. *Detroit Daily Advertiser*, October 1, 1860.
20. *Detroit Daily Tribune*, June 11, 1860.
21. *Detroit Free Press*, June 13, 1860.
22. *Detroit Free Press*, June 20, 1860.
23. *Detroit Free Press*, June 22, 1860.

6

"THEIR RANKS BECAME SO THINNED THAT DISRUPTION FOLLOWED"

BASEBALL DURING THE CIVIL WAR

The 1861 season got off to a flying start. The Detroit Base Ball Club and the Early Risers couldn't even wait for spring to renew their rivalry. On February 21, the two clubs met at a local skating park to participate in Michigan's first game of baseball on ice skates. The play was somewhat lackluster because of a stiff breeze and the fact that the best ball players were novice skaters, while the best skaters were fledgling ball players. Nonetheless, a significant number of spectators enjoyed the novel spectacle.[1]

By April 9, the Detroit Base Ball Club and the Early Risers were ready to renew their rivalry on firmer footing, both clubs having already met and elected officers. But history intervened before either club could make it to the playing field. On April 12, the first shots were fired on Fort Sumter, beginning a war that would change the country fundamentally and put all thoughts of baseball out of young men's minds.

Popular histories of baseball often attribute the spread of baseball to the Civil War, claiming that soldiers learned the game during the war and brought it back home with them.[2] Baseball was still in its infancy in the South and there is evidence that the Civil War did help the game to catch on there.[3] However, extending this conclusion to the North is problematic at best. The prime spokesman for this belief was the man most responsible for popularizing the myth that Abner Doubleday invented baseball—Albert Goodwill "A. G." Spalding.[4] Spalding was one of the most important figures of nineteenth-century baseball, as a player, owner, and sporting-goods magnate, but he was more interested in a good story than in accurate history.

One chapter of Spalding's history of baseball, *America's National Game*, is devoted to the Civil War. Regrettably, his eagerness to depict baseball as a game of American origin leads him to hyperbolize:

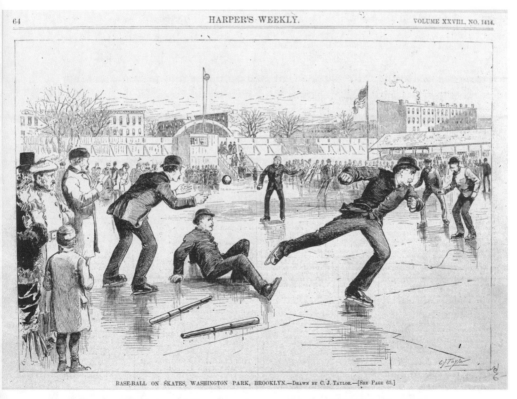

Baseball on ice skates was a popular winter activity in the 1860s. The first such game in Michigan took place in Detroit on February 21, 1861. *Courtesy of Transcendental Graphics*

A National Game? Why, no country on the face of the earth ever had
a form of sport with so clear a title to that distinction. Base Ball had
been born in the brain of an American soldier [i.e., Abner Double-
day]. It received its baptism in bloody days of our nation's direst danger. It had its early evolution when soldiers, North and South, were
striving to forget their foes by cultivating, through this grand game,
fraternal friendships with comrades in arms. It had its best development at the time when soldiers, disheartened by distressing defeat,
were seeking the solace of something safe and sane; at a time when
Northern soldiers, flushed with victory, were yet willing to turn from
fighting with bombs and bullets to playing with bat and ball.[5]

The evidence with which Spalding supports these claims is flimsy.
He does document a few incidents of baseball being played by
troops, but even he acknowledges that baseball was "held in
abeyance" during the war.[6] And while he mentions rumors of
games being played between Union and Confederate soldiers during cease-fires, he admits that he could not find a single soldier to
confirm such games.

Unfortunately, the scrutiny that has been directed to other
aspects of early baseball history has not been applied to the Civil
War. The claim that the Civil War was largely responsible for the
game's spread is repeated as fact in many histories, usually without
evidence. The few shards of evidence that have been produced have
been similarly accepted at face value even when highly implausible.

For example, a game played on Christmas Day of 1862 on the
island of Hilton Head, South Carolina, is invariably described as
being witnessed by forty thousand soldiers. While the game is well
documented, no explanation is given as to how such an extraordinary number of people could watch a game. Baseball historian
William J. Ryczek cites reports of games being played in the Confederate prison camp at Salisbury, North Carolina, but notes that
these stories "apparently stem from a drawing depicting such activity which found wide distribution. Many writers have questioned
this assertion, given the high death rate among the prisoners in the

camp. By the war's end, most of the incarcerated soldiers were incapable of walking from the camp unaided, let alone executing a snappy double play."[7]

There are of course some reliable reports of baseball being played by troops and some documented instances of soldiers bringing the game back home with them after the war.[8] For example, Jim "Deacon" White noted that both he and his great batterymate A. G. Spalding learned the game from disabled veterans. According to White, "previous to the Civil War, it was played almost entirely in New York and Boston and their vicinities. Those players introduced it to the camps. The South's army learned it from captured Union soldiers. At the close of the war, soldiers of both armies carried the game to every city, town, and hamlet."[9]

Without dismissing such anecdotal evidence, there is not nearly enough of it to support the claim that the Civil War had a causative effect on the postwar spread of baseball in the North. Given the enduring interest in both the Civil War and baseball, it seems likely that conclusive evidence would have been found if it existed. Accordingly, it seems most appropriate to regard the belief that the Civil War played a major role in the spread of baseball as an unproven theory or even as part of a legend that may have been specifically designed to ensure baseball's status as the national game.

The spread of the game occurred very differently in Michigan. The regulation rules had been rapidly catching on before the war, although activity slowed dramatically during the war and resumed only after its end. Also, with some exceptions, most of the players after the war were not Civil War veterans. Thus it seems much more accurate to view the Civil War as having temporarily arrested the development of the game in Michigan. Still, although baseball's spread in Michigan was not aided by the Civil War, the war did shape the game in many important ways.

It might be expected that popular sentiment would be against frivolous activities like baseball during a war, but this does not appear to have been the case. Undoubtedly, the Duke of Wellington's belief that the Battle of Waterloo was won on the playing fields of Eton helped baseball to be viewed sympathetically. In describing the founding of the Detroit Gymnastic Association, the *Free Press* wrote, "We wonder that in these times of our country's need, all our young men do not qualify themselves for military life, by increasing their strength and activity through the means offered by this association."[10] The British novelist Anthony Trollope toured the war-torn country and was impressed by Americans' "persistence in the ordinary pursuits of life in spite of the war which was around them. Neither industry or amusement seemed to meet with any check."[11]

However, the Civil War was responsible for the sharp decline in baseball activity for the more practical reason that so many players volunteered for service. This was particularly true during the first year of the war, when a quick end to the hostilities was still anticipated. In Detroit, the Early Risers broke up when half their members joined the Union cause, including the club's president and its vice president, Edwin Barbour and Heber LeFavour, who would both attain high ranks. The Franklins also "succumbed to the war" after a large portion of their membership went into military service.[12] The Brother Jonathans were a little younger and survived for a few years, but before the war had ended, "their ranks became so thinned that disruption followed."[13]

The Detroit Base Ball Club, its members being older, lost fewer players to active duty and could have fielded a team, but many of its members assumed important responsibilities on the home front that left little time for baseball. Charles Vernor served in the office of the Detroit district quartermaster. John S. Newberry, the newly elected president of the Detroit Base Ball Club, took on numerous commitments, including serving as captain of the Witherell Guards, as secretary for the United States Sanitary Commission, and as provost marshal of the state of Michigan.

Accordingly, only one game seems to have been played in Detroit in 1861. In late August, the Burlington Club of Hamilton, Canada West, paid a visit to the Detroit Base Ball Club. The *Free Press* reported that "the game throughout was the most exciting one that has ever been played in this city," but it ended on a down note

Heber LeFavour of the Early Risers commanded the Twenty-second Michigan Voluntary Infantry and later joined Sherman's March to the Sea. *Courtesy of the State of Michigan Archives*

for the home side when the Canadians rallied with 18 runs in the bottom of the ninth inning to win 55-52.[14]

The war did provide a boon to baseball in Marshall, where the formation of a new club called the Red, White, and Blue was linked to the military cause. In addition to the patriotic name, the club rose at 4:00 A.M. for practices that were described as "field exercise."[15] Forty members had soon joined the club, and they invited the Daybreak Club of Jackson to visit on June 17 for the first match ever played in Marshall. The Daybreak Club squeaked out a narrow 24-23 win, but the result was still considered secondary to the ritual surrounding it. Before the game, the Marshall club's president gave a speech welcoming the visitors to the city, and the Daybreaks' president responded in kind. At the game's conclusion, there were more ceremonies, and the Jackson players presented their hosts with a baseball bat.

A second club, called the Pastimes, was soon formed in Marshall, and the new club beat the Red, White, and Blue Club 30-18 on September 6 in the Capitol Square. The game was interrupted in the fourth inning by "a certain old woman's *confiscating* and *burning* a couple of the best base balls to be had in these regions."[16] Obviously not everybody shared the enthusiasm for the new game!

While seventeen of the thirty-four members of the Daybreak Club of Jackson enlisted in the war, the club was able to play six games in 1861, winning all of them.[17] An intersquad game in late July saw the club's single members beat its married ones.[18] In August, the Continental Club of Kalamazoo was scheduled to visit Jackson for a match, beginning a long rivalry between the baseball clubs of the two cities.[19] The score of the game is not extant, but Jerome Trowbridge of the Continentals was probably referring to this game when he later recalled:

> At the time we started to play the new game there were but three teams in the west who played as we did. There was a team in Chicago, one at Jackson and one at Rockford, Illinois. . . . We did not play professional ball at that time. When we went to an outside town to play we paid our own expenses. There was no admission fee charged. I remember the first game we played with Jackson. We played for the supper and we also paid for the supper. But it was a good one, I tell you. They had to play hard to win and they deserved a good meal.[20]

While the spread of the game to new cities slowed for the most part during the war, Monroe was an exception. The *Monroe Commercial* reported in 1862:

> A club of young men mostly of the Union School, is being formed for the purpose of base ball playing, upon each Saturday afternoon. The American game of base ball, as played by clubs in nearly all the cities of the north, is quite a scientific, as it is a very popular game, for summer amusement. It affords a healthful exercise and enjoyment, which is particularly necessary to students. Two or three games have already been played, and we expect before long to witness something expert in the way of base ball playing.[21]

Baseball was also being introduced for the first time in Chelsea, where the Union Base Ball Club was formed on July 20, 1861, soon boasting thirty members. The club's first intersquad game on July 26 was "conducted with strictness according to the code."[22] However, the usual tendency of wartime baseball was to revert to less formal versions of the game, because of the difficulty of finding enough players.[23]

By thus reverting to simpler times, baseball initiated a pattern of returning to its sources to replenish itself whenever necessary. As the following account makes clear, such games provided a much-needed respite from the horrors of war:

> On Tuesday last, the Kalamazoo National Ball Club paid a visit to the pretty little village of Dowagiac to meet a club of the latter place in a friendly match for superiority, according to arrangements previously made by Capt. Brown of Kalamazoo, and Capt. Palmer of Dowagiac. Besides the Kalamazoo nine, some thirty other of our citizens went along to see the sport and to participate [sic] the fate of our boys whether 'twere victory or defeat. The train that bore them was the 12:12 lightning express, and after a delightful and exhilarating trip through verdant valleys, o'er the flowered plains, by still waters, lovely meadows, and through the green palisade of forest trees, forty miles of summer scenery were left behind us, and we had reached our destination. Here we were met by a deputation from the Dowagiac Club and escorted to the hotel, where we soon found a host of friends and a kind reception.
>
> About 3 o'clock the preliminaries having been made the men of both companies, with a large body of spectators, proceeded to the grounds, which are close to the Railroad and West of the public square. Mr. STRAWTHER BOWLING, of Dowagiac, was selected by Capt. Brown, (the choice being accorded to him) as umpire, and M. A. Allen of Kalamazoo, and Ezra Jones of Dowagiac tallymen and Byron Beach caller. Best two in three, Kalamazoo first innings.
>
> At a little after past [sic] 3 o'clock the game commenced. The sun was pouring down its hottest rays, but the wind was high, and the

increasing number of heavy clouds indicated wet weather approaching. The following is the score of the first game which was played with much spirit on both sides and in which our boys never performed better.[24]

Indeed, baseball's ability to return to the country to "[pour] new life into its veins" is why sports historians like Allen Guttmann have argued that "baseball has retained something of the primitive connection between sports and the sacred."[25]

Kalamazoo won the game 32-12, but the account makes clear that the score was only a minor point of interest:

Four home runs were made by the Kalamazoo boys, viz: Trowbridge, White, Burlingham and Doody. The fielding of A. H. Randall was admirable. The wind made a number of foul balls, and was decidedly "in the way" of both parties.

Before this game was half up, rain began to fall, accompanied with a driving wind.—Nevertheless the game went on with just as much zeal as though the heavens had been more propitious.

The game through, the boys went to the hotel and prepared for the next part of the programme. This was THE SUPPER, which the generous Dowagiacans had determined to bestow upon us, whether they lost or won.—At a little after 5 o'clock, we were escorted to the Rochester House, near the R.R., where MRS. BANNARD had prepared for our consideration a most elegant and bounteous supper, which not only did credit to her surpassing qualities as hostess, but to the Club at whose request it was gotten up. It was a most successful and satisfactory achievement, and the Kalamazooins who sat down to it (to the number of about thirty) will not soon forget Mrs. B. nor the tasteful manner in which she ministered to our creature wants on this occasion.

The rain did not "dry up" until after six, and then a promiscuous game was made up and played on the grounds, which resulted in favor of Alward's party, as follows: H. M. Brown's party, 21; Alward's party, 25.

Just as this was concluded the Stock train from the west arrived, and after taking leave of the Dowagiac boys, with mutual expressions of good feeling, we left for home, arriving at 11 P.M.

The visit was a most delightful one, and not a member of the excursion hesitated to accord the Club and Citizens of Dowagiac, the warmest praise for their generous hospitality, their kind and gentlemanly conduct, and their efforts to make our visit pleasant. *They know how to be hospitable.*

Our boys are loud in their commendations of Mr. STRAWTHERS [*sic*] BOWLING, who acted as Umpire, for the excellent manner in which he discharged the duties of that important position. Not a question was raised on the ground, not a word of dispute occurred, and a more harmonious match is not often played. The thanks of the company are especially due to him; as also to Mr. W. H. Campbell, of the *Republican,* Mr. A. N. Alward, Jones and others for many favors. They are all good fellows, and "long may they wave."[26]

Clearly baseball was already being viewed as a source for nostalgia.

By 1862, as it became clear that the war wouldn't be a short one and that life on the home front had to return to some semblance of normalcy, baseball activity began to pick up a bit. In Detroit, because most members of the Brother Jonathans were too young for military service, the club was able to field both first and second nines. After four intersquad games, the Brother Jonathans played a series of matches with a new club called the Unions. The Brother Jonathans also beat the Detroit Base Ball Club in early August, in the second and final game the Detroit Club would play during the war.

On July 4, the Brother Jonathans traveled to Ann Arbor and played the Monitor Club of that city in the University Square, in what may have been the first Independence Day game ever played in Michigan. The Monitors won that game but lost a couple of weeks later to a club from Ypsilanti, which in turn lost to the Brother Jonathans.

Meanwhile many members of the Daybreak Club of Jackson

had been discharged from military service, and the club again became active. The Monitors of Ann Arbor beat them on June 23, the Daybreak Club's first-ever loss on their home grounds. The *Jackson Eagle* noted that the Monitors had proven "fully able to sustain the saucy name they have adopted."[27] But after getting into practice, the Daybreaks avenged the loss in Ann Arbor by a 40-2 score and also beat Dowagiac and the Hickory Club of Howell.

Still, the only campaigns that excited general interest were the ones being fought in the South. Competitiveness was nowhere to be found—not only was there no clearly best team in the state, but it appeared that no one much cared. This philosophical attitude toward wins and losses was about to change.

NOTES

1. *Detroit Free Press*, February 23, 1861.
2. See, for instance Connie Mack, *My Sixty-Six Years in the Big Leagues*, 65–66.
3. See, for example, *Ball Players' Chronicle*, June 27, 1867: "During the war the many games of base ball played by the Northern soldiers on the camp fields and on some of the prison grounds, led to the introduction of the game among Southern soldiers, and 'when the cruel war was over' the game was generally adopted throughout the South." Several other quotations cited later in my text also suggest that the spread of baseball by returning soldiers was a Southern phenomenon.
4. Peter Levine's *A. G. Spalding and the Rise of Baseball: The Promise of American Sport* is the standard biography of Spalding.
5. Albert G. Spalding, *America's National Game*, 92–93.
6. Spalding, *America's National Game*, 92.
7. William J. Ryczek, *When Johnny Came Sliding Home*, 15, 270. Unfortunately, the title of this otherwise excellent study of post–Civil War baseball implies a relationship that the author does not attempt to prove.
8. Allison Caveglia Barash, "Base Ball in the Civil War," *National Pastime* 21 (2001): 17–19, does document half a dozen examples of troops playing baseball during the war. However, like many others, Barash treats the Salisbury prison camp and the spread of the game in the North by returning soldiers as facts without citing any documentation for either claim.
9. From a 1932 interview, reprinted in Martin Quigley, *The Crooked Pitch*, 44.
10. *Detroit Free Press*, August 8, 1862.
11. Anthony Trollope, *An Autobiography* (Oxford: Oxford University Press, 1980), 163.
12. *Detroit Advertiser and Tribune*, May 2, 1867. Members of the Franklin Club formed a "Ben Franklin Guard" (*Detroit Daily Advertiser*, September 23, 1861).
13. *Detroit Advertiser and Tribune*, May 2, 1867.
14. *Detroit Free Press*, August 23, 1862. In early baseball, the home team did not necessarily bat last; this was usually determined by a pregame coin toss.

15. *Marshall Democratic Expounder,* May 16, 1861.

16. *Marshall Statesman,* September 11, 1861.

17. *Jackson Eagle,* June 7, 1862. The seventeen included one captain, four lieutenants, three orderly sergeants, one hospital steward, two corporals, and six privates. For the club's record, see the *Jackson Eagle,* June 28, 1862.

18. *Grand Rapids Weekly Enquirer,* July 31, 1861.

19. *Grand Rapids Weekly Enquirer,* July 31, 1861; *Kalamazoo Gazette,* July 26, 1861.

20. *Kalamazoo Gazette,* February 11, 1906.

21. *Monroe Commercial,* May 1, 1862.

22. *Ann Arbor Peninsular Courier,* July 30, 1861.

23. In addition to Monroe and Chelsea, other Michigan towns to which baseball spread with some degree of formal organization during the Civil War included Niles, Marshall, Concord, Dexter, Lodi, and Howell.

24. *Kalamazoo Gazette,* June 14, 1861 (signed REF).

25. Allen Guttmann, *From Ritual to Record,* 108.

26. *Kalamazoo Gazette,* June 14, 1861 (signed REF).

27. *Jackson Eagle,* July 20, 1862. The *Monitor* was the Union's first ironclad, built in response to fears that the Confederacy had gained a naval advantage by building the *Merrimack.* There was an Ann Arbor baseball club named the Ericsson Club in honor of the inventor who created the *Monitor,* but it seems to have disbanded not long after it was formed on July 8, 1862.

7

"The Squabbles of Rival Clubs"

With so little competitiveness apparent in 1862, it came as quite a surprise when the Brother Jonathans reorganized for the 1863 season and the *Advertiser and Tribune*'s account of their initial meeting announced, "The members of this club *claim* the championship of the State."[1] This boast elicited an immediate response from the Daybreak Club of Jackson: "I noticed in your issue of the 8th inst., that the Brother Jonathan base-ball club 'claim' the championship of the State. Now, I do not propose to dispute in the least their right to this assertion, or their ability to establish it, but I would merely like to enquire through the columns of your paper upon what *grounds* this said *claim* of championship is made. Yours truly, JACKSON."[2] Two days later, the Brother Jonathans replied: "The reason the B. J. Base Ball Club claim the championship of this State, is this: They have beaten the principal clubs in the State, including the Ypsilanti club and the Detroit club, this latter club, by the way, having always been considered up to that time the champions."[3]

The dialogue continued in private until June, when the *Advertiser and Tribune* published a lengthy resolution by the Daybreaks alleging that the Brother Jonathans were refusing to play them after having claimed to be state champions. The rejoinder from Frederick M. Delano, president of the Brother Jonathan Club, was conciliatory this time:

It is true we claim the championship, and for reasons too numerous to mention here, we think, rightly and properly. It was not, however, the intention of the club to publish those articles referred to in their so-called challenge, which was done through the thoughtlessness of a member who has since resigned. But not to enter into detail, suffice it to say that if the Daybreaks see fit to issue a formal challenge, without any attempt at chicanery, either by a letter to our Secretary or through the columns of the papers (which they seem to prefer) they may rest assured that it will be gladly accepted. And here let me say to these lovers of notoriety, in behalf of the Brother Jonathans, they need not feel the slightest compunction in making their blustering challenges as public as possible and if we are beaten in the coming match—of which there seems to be a strong probability, if they are what they profess to be—then we resign all claims to the championship against which they so earnestly and sincerely protest.[4]

But the matter was still far from over, and the sniping continued until the *Advertiser and Tribune* finally declined to publish another lengthy letter from the secretary of the Daybreak Base Ball Club of Jackson, adding, "We would suggest that the less of the squabbles of rival clubs that appear in print the better."[5]

Next to jump into the fray was a nine from the University of Michigan, where regulation baseball was being played for the first time. Organized sports were still unknown on the Ann Arbor campus as late as 1861, according to the president of that year's class: "There were no athletics in those days, no foot-ball, no base-ball, no track-teams, no regents' field, no set games of any kind. The favorite play-ground was back of the North College, where the noble game of wicket was much in evidence. But there were no 'clubs' or 'teams,' no match games, just a little plain, country play for fun."[6] This changed when John Marshall "Jack" Hinchman, one of the stars of the Brother Jonathans, enrolled in 1862.

Hinchman came from one of Detroit's most distinguished families. His father, Theodore, was a prominent businessman and later a state senator. His maternal grandfather, Dr. Marshall Chapin, had come to Detroit to fight a cholera outbreak in 1814 and stayed, opening the city's first drugstore and serving as mayor in 1824. Dr. Chapin fought heroically against a second cholera epidemic that devastated the city in the 1830s. He eventually succumbed to the disease in 1838, but not before preventing the epidemic from becoming far worse than it might have been. Dr. Chapin's house was located directly across the street from that of Lewis Cass and later became one of the city's landmarks.

In the spring of 1863, Jack Hinchman and fellow freshman Emory Grant from Wisconsin helped introduce baseball to the University of Michigan campus for the first time. With an enrollment of about one thousand from all over the country, it was not difficult to find young men interested in playing. The students met on April 20 and elected William D. Hitchcock as club president; Edward C. Page as vice president; Sanford B. Ladd as secretary; Joseph V. Quarles as treasurer; and Hinchman, Louis Stoskopf, and Carroll Fraser as directors.[7] They soon laid out the campus's first regulation diamond to the north of the medical building.[8]

Hinchman's letters to his parents during his first spring were full of references to the sport. On April 26, he recorded, "I played Base Ball yesterday," and asked his younger brother Ford, also a member of the Brother Jonathans, to send him a box of his "Base-Ball things." A week later, he indicated that he was getting plenty of exercise by playing baseball in the mornings. On May 10, he noted, "I play Base Ball two or three times every week."[9] The *Monroe Monitor* mentioned the new club and wrote, "Let the young men of Monroe who are unable to find work for exercise, follow the example."[10]

By mid-June, the new club on campus had a first nine of Hinchman, Page, Grant, Fraser, Ladd, Oscar P. Bills, Charles M. Goodsell, Edmund Adams, and James P. Nixon. Club president Hitchcock now entered into the dispute between the Brother Jonathans and the Daybreaks by writing to the *Detroit Advertiser and Tribune,* announcing the club's formation and claiming that its members were state champions and were willing to defend their claim against any challengers.[11] The Daybreaks responded by specifying the time and place for a match, but Hitchcock stated that it was his club's prerogative to make challenges and that his players would not be able to play the Daybreaks because of final examinations.[12] It was becoming clear that such challenges were not an ideal way to determine the state's best baseball club.

Another dispute ensued after the Monitor Club of Niles hosted the Daybreak Club on Independence Day, the terms in which it was couched revealing the increasing tension between gentlemanly conduct and competitiveness. The Monitors were anxious not to be perceived as caring about the result: "We do not claim [the game], nor do we care for it, but we have made these statements for the purpose of showing that if we *were* beaten, we were not beaten by the Day Breaks [*sic*] as a club *but by a single member of the club and that member the Umpire.*" The Daybreaks responded in similar fashion: "We cared very little at that time to win the game . . . [and] regret exceedingly that anything occurred to mar the pleasure of the game."[13] But it seems more likely that both clubs were protesting too much and that they did care considerably about the result.

Early clubs at the University of Michigan played on a diamond on the northeast part of campus. The batter faced the medical building, and long drives sometimes threatened its windows. *Courtesy of the Bentley Historical Library, University of Michigan*

Eventually, arrangements were made for the debate that had raged so long in the newspapers to be settled on the field. However, the Brother Jonathans were now losing players to the war and to college, and their weakened status soon became evident. In contrast, Jackson was flush with players, and the city was now home to a second club, the Defiance, captained by a man with the fortuitous name of Walter Johnson. The Daybreaks warmed up for the showdown with easy wins over Concord and Dowagiac. The Brother Jonathans prepared with a July 14 match against the Young Canadian Club of Woodstock, champions of Canada West, and were soundly beaten, 29-6.

The Daybreak Club of Jackson arrived in Detroit on August 5 for the first match in a best-of-three series to determine the state's best club, accompanied by nearly one hundred supporters. In spite of the spirited correspondence that had preceded it, the visit was conducted in accordance with traditional gentlemanly customs. As they had with the Young Canadian Club, the Brother Jonathans provided the visiting players with rooms at the Michigan Exchange Hotel, and good sportsmanship prevailed throughout the game.

The game was played in front of a large crowd that included players from clubs throughout the state. The contest was close in the early going, with the home side clinging to a 16-15 lead after five innings. But the absence of three of the Brother Jonathans' key players—John McMillan and Jack and Ford Hinchman—took its toll. Poor fielding by the home side enabled the Daybreak Club to score 14 runs in the seventh inning and open up a commanding lead. The outburst demoralized the Brother Jonathans, who began playing wildly and were blanked in each of the last four innings, the visitors continuing to score easily and winning 43-16.

Newspaper coverage of the game reflected the emerging competitiveness. The *Detroit Advertiser and Tribune* blamed the loss on some "wretched '‘muffing'" by the Brother Jonathans' substitute first baseman, Dr. Jonathan Van Norman.[14] The *Free Press* also chastised Van Norman for "not do[ing] his duty as he should have done," making no allowances for the fact that the forty-year-old physician had been pressed into action by the absence of the regulars.[15] Meanwhile the *Jackson Eagle* gloated, "We trust that Detroit will fling out no more champion banners until she has earned the right to do so."[16] The result was becoming at least as important as the spectacle.

A rematch took place in Jackson on September 3, the Daybreak Club prevailing by a narrow 23-22 margin in what was described as "the most interesting and closely contested game of base ball ever witnessed in this State." The game was again characterized by goodwill, the Daybreak Club hosting its visitors at the Marin House: "Everything passed off in the most pleasant manner, and at the conclusion of the game three rousing cheers were given by the Detroit boys for their conquerors."[17] The Daybreaks of Jackson, who had also swept a home-and-home series with Dowagiac, had earned the right to call themselves state champions.

While examinations prevented the University of Michigan nine from competing for the state championship, the team's players remained active. Over the summer, Jack Hinchman traveled to Chicago to visit classmate Ed Page and played for Page's home club against another city club, which caused him to miss the Brother Jonathans' first game with the Daybreaks. On returning to Ann Arbor for the fall term in 1863, he took part in a match in Ypsilanti on October 17.[18]

The spring of 1864 saw the members of the University Club begin looking for outside competition, but with the war continuing to rage, the only clubs they could find to play were from Ann Arbor High School and the State Normal School in Ypsilanti (now Eastern Michigan University). On May 28, the University Club faced a nine organized by the freshman class and beat them 47-18. The game ended after seven innings by mutual consent, and the Class of 1867 gave "three rousing cheers . . . for their conquerors."[19] Once baseball was established on the campus of the University of Michigan, it established a hold it never relinquished. While formal varsity teams were not organized until the 1880s, clubs organized at the university would play a major role in the development of baseball in Michigan long before then.

But while the game was catching on at the University of Michigan, activity virtually ceased in the rest of the state in 1864. In June, the *Detroit Advertiser and Tribune* reported that "the numerous Base Ball Clubs that formerly existed in this city having all died out, we are glad to see a movement on foot to organize a new club."[20] However, nothing seems to have come of this movement. It is reasonable to assume that, given the scarcity of young men, anyone wishing to play ball found it easier to revert to earlier versions of the game that did not require eighteen players.

The only account of a game in Grand Rapids during the war shows the rules of regulation baseball being abandoned: "A big game of ball came off on the hill, yesterday afternoon. The party consisted of about 100 men, 50 on a side, lead [*sic*] by P. W. Sprague on one side, and L. Buck, on the other, the stake being a keg of lager. Sprague's side won, and the winners had a gay old time in the evening drinking their beer."[21] Similarly, Louis Ives, brother of Butler Ives of the Detroit Base Ball Club, would later recollect games of "Round Ball"—in which batters were out if hit by a thrown ball—played on Washington Avenue in the early 1860s, long after regulation baseball had become established in Detroit.[22]

Meanwhile, the fates of the men who had helped introduce baseball to antebellum Michigan were being directed into a myriad of courses by the war. In 1862, John S. Newberry, the first president of the Detroit Base Ball Club, received a government contract to supply rail cars to the army that would prove highly remunerative. His energies were soon channeled into industry, and in 1864, with partner James McMillan, he opened the Michigan Car Works to manufacture railroad cars.

The factory burned to the ground within three weeks of opening, but the partners immediately rebuilt it, and Newberry was soon established as one of the country's leading industrialists. In a diverse and distinguished life, he would, among many accomplishments,

become a U.S. congressman and host a visit by President Ruther-
ford B. Hayes and General William T. Sherman to Detroit during
the 1879 state fair. While his interest in baseball never entirely vanished, the refocusing of the talents of a leader who had recently been
"quite enthusiastic about his base ball activities" was a major loss to
the state's baseball scene.

The lives of the men who enlisted also took a wide variety of
paths. Luther S. Trowbridge, who had graduated from Yale Law
School in 1857 and was practicing law in Detroit before the war,
fought alongside George Custer at Gettysburg against J. E. B.
Stuart's men and had his horse shot out from under him. He later
walked over two thousand miles behind Southern lines on missions
to sabotage rail transport and was breveted major general. Eugene
Robinson served as captain general of the Detroit Commandery and
became known as one of the best drillmasters in the country. Upon
the death of former governor Moses Wisner, Heber LeFavour was
placed in command of the Twenty-second Michigan Voluntary
Infantry. LeFavour was wounded at Williamsburg and captured
when his regiment was massacred at Chickamauga. He was held
captive for six months but was exchanged in time to join Sherman's
March to the Sea. He was eventually promoted to general.[23] The
marked accomplishments of all three led to lives that remained
closely tied to the military after the war.

Less satisfactory was the experience of Hooker DeLand of the
Daybreak Club of Jackson. DeLand was an officer in the First
Michigan Sharpshooters, a regiment led by his uncle C. V. DeLand,
the editor of one of the local papers. Hooker, however, was accused
of retreating to the rear during battle and court-martialed for cowardice. He was eventually given a dishonorable discharge. Part of
his punishment was having the accusations published in his hometown newspaper.[24] DeLand spent his later years trying unsuccessfully to clear his name.[25]

A few Michigan baseball players even made the supreme
sacrifice. Malachi O'Donnell, one of the original members of the
Franklin Club, wounded at an earlier battle, left the infirmary to

fight at Gettysburg, where he met his death.[26] Samuel Newberry, of the Detroit Club, was killed by a Confederate soldier near Petersburg in 1864.[27] George N. Ives, one of the founding members of the Champion Ball Club of Kalamazoo, died in 1863 of a disease contracted during the war. Henry W. Shipman, of the Daybreaks of Jackson, died on September 11, 1864, of injuries sustained in battle two months earlier.

Others returned to Michigan in no shape to resume their baseball careers. While David B. Harbaugh, an original officer of the Brother Jonathans, overcame illness and a bullet wound in his arm and joined Sherman's March to the Sea, the war ruined his health, and he remained an invalid until his death in 1873.[28] Charles Dupont, of the Detroit Base Ball Club, who commanded over fourteen hundred men, lost his right eye in the war. Although he occasionally played for the club's second nine, his postwar baseball duties were largely administrative. Other veterans, including Henry Starkey and Michael Dempsey of the Franklins, suffered less calamitous injuries, but their days of playing competitive sports were nonetheless over by the time they returned to Michigan.

By the end of the long and dreadful Civil War, the game of baseball, like every other aspect of American life, had been irrevocably changed. Before the war, variant forms of baseball, most notably the Massachusetts game, were being played in several areas of the country. During the war, there was a reversion to disorganized ways of playing. By the war's end, however, the New York version of baseball had almost entirely vanquished its rivals as the regulation game of choice. This pushed New York City to the forefront of the game, and developments in that city were already beginning to push the game toward professionalism.

Perhaps the single most significant step in this direction took place on May 15, 1862, with the opening of Brooklyn's Union Grounds, the first enclosed playing field to be regularly used for baseball.[29] The owner of the Union Grounds was a businessman named William Cammeyer, who needed a way to earn revenue from his skating pond during the summer months.[30] His initial plan was simply to rent the grounds to baseball clubs, but when he decided instead to charge a gate fee, he changed the game forever. While admission fees had been charged at baseball games as early as 1858, enclosed grounds allowed money to be collected from everyone, thereby making professional baseball possible.

While many modern fans feel a deep reverence for outfield fences such as the Green Monster in Boston's Fenway Park and the ivy-covered fences in Chicago's Wrigley Field, it is interesting to note that when baseball's first outfield fence was created, "there was no intention to make the outfield barrier a target for home run hitters, its primary purpose being to keep non-paying spectators from sneaking in to watch the game."[31] At least one early fence was even erected to keep cattle out.[32] Whatever group was being kept out, there was no mistaking that the main function of these fences was exclusion.

Enclosed grounds and paid admissions enforced a distinction between players and spectators that served as a reminder that all were no longer "on a level," as in Judge McGee's day. Paradoxically, however, the exclusivity of enclosed grounds also began to confer on the paying spectator a sense of status, of belonging to the game even without participating. After all, walls that are built to keep things out end up keeping things in as well. Journalist Henry Chadwick concluded that admission charges were regarded "by the respectable portion of the community . . . as a considerable improvement, as by means of the increased price hundreds of black-guard boys and roughs generally are kept out."[33] Eventually the fences helped turn baseball into what F. Scott Fitzgerald aptly described as "a boy's game . . . bounded by walls which kept out novelty or danger, change or adventure."[34]

More practically, enclosed grounds provided a basis for professional baseball, and as soon as businessmen like Cammeyer had the means to profit from the game, players began to expect a share. Before the war was over, many of the top players were illicitly receiving money or other compensation for playing.[35] The modes of competition were changing accordingly, with clubs beginning to

tour and contest for formal distinctions, including a national championship. As the dispute about the championship of Michigan in
1863 had demonstrated, what had so recently been simply a game
for boys was now being "played for keeps."[36]

As competitiveness drove out many of the gentlemanly customs
that had earlier predominated, there were dramatic changes in the
way the game was played, most obviously in the role of the pitcher.
Even before the war, pitchers had rejected the expectation that they
lob up fat pitches, trying instead to make batting more difficult in a
variety of ways. By thus defying the rules, pitchers discovered a
number of the techniques that would eventually enable the game's
least important player to become its most important one.

Some began to experiment with windups that generated greater
speed or perplexed hitters. The first game ever played in California
by New York rules ended in a dispute over the legality of a pitcher's
delivery.[37] Pitchers began to adopt the elaborate windups of cricket
bowlers, a New Jersey pitcher unveiling a particularly convoluted
delivery in an 1862 game: "Their pitcher seized the ball and swinging his hand behind him as if in an effort to dislocate his shoulder,
put his head between his legs—almost—and running furiously, discharged the ball some yards away from home base."[38] Jim "Deacon" White got around the requirement that a pitcher "stand flat-
footed in the box and swing his arm perpendicular without bending
his wrist" and achieved greater speed by "[getting] my shoulder
behind my heave . . . [so that] my knuckles almost touched the
ground."[39] While the rules made a proper curve ball impossible, the
rule against snapping the wrist was much harder to enforce, and
many pitchers were able to make the ball spin.[40]

The simplest and most popular pitching stratagem was to deliberately throw wide pitches in hopes of luring the batter to swing at a
bad pitch. Since there were no balls or called strikes, batters
responded by playing "waiting games," letting hittable pitches pass
until they got one perfectly to their liking.[41] According to player
Bob Ferguson's later description, games accordingly ground to a
halt: "A pitcher had the prerogative of sending as many balls as he

wanted to across the plate until the batsman made up his mind to strike at one. In an ordinary game, forty, fifty and sixty balls were considered nothing for a pitcher before a batsman got started."[42]

In a legendary game between the Atlantic and Excelsior Clubs of Brooklyn to decide the championship of the 1860 season, pitchers Jim Creighton and Mattie O'Brien both threw over 330 pitches before the game was abandoned in the sixth inning.[43] During another heatedly contested 1863 game between the same Atlantic Club and the Mutuals of New York, a single at bat lasted for sixty-eight tedious pitches.[44] As a result of such abuses, an interim measure was adopted by which an umpire could warn a pitcher against wild pitching and then call "unfair" balls, with a base on balls eventually resulting.

Batters had previously simply tried to hit the ball as far as they could, but they soon responded to the new pitching strategies by inventing bunts and "fair-fouls."[45] Baseball historian Robert Smith notes that such tactics were, "in the minds of the original sponsors of the game, just half a step from plain deceit. The Knickerbockers had taken it for granted that any red-blooded man would want to take a healthy cut at the ball to see how far he could drive it."[46] Base runners, who would previously have thought it unmanly not to let themselves be tagged if beaten to a base, began to make evasive slides.[47]

Within years of the adoption of regulation rules, baseball was leaving the child's game far behind. Epitomizing this change, the bound rule finally succumbed to years of being maligned for its childishness and was officially abolished at the NABBP convention in December 1864. A fair ball would now have to be caught on the fly to register an out, although fouls caught on the first bounce would continue to be outs until the 1880s.

While some of these changes to the game of baseball only gradually made their way from New York to Michigan, the state's newspapers were changing in ways that were more immediately apparent, and this affected how baseball was reported. Antebellum Michigan newspapers had been modest single sheets, consisting almost entirely of secondhand national and international news items, partisan politicking, and advertisements. Local news was usually restricted to the doings of a few leading citizens and to puffery for local businesses. In an 1859 issue of the *Battle Creek Journal*, for instance, the local section consisted of four items: one praising the sermon of Reverend Jones; one remarking that Dr. Cox's new building was progressing nicely; one recommending the purchase of Mr. Witter's plants; and one noting that Charles Hubbard, "prince of good fellows," had arrived in town.[48]

During the Civil War, however, the abundance of war reports, and the importance those on the home front attached to them, rapidly increased the amount of news: "In the old times the size of the papers was just 4 pages, whatever happened. . . . During the civil war the papers began to print 'double sheets' and 'triple sheets,' that is to say, eight and 12-page papers. Thus 8 pages became the accepted size."[49] The war also had a major democratizing effect on newspapers, as any local soldier, whether the son of the mayor or of the lowliest resident, became newsworthy.

Additionally, the war helped newspapers to develop an independent voice, and they increasingly supplemented reportage with commentary. With more people reading the papers, their editors became less indebted to wealthy subscribers and advertisers and gained more freedom to express independent views. Boosterism did remain common, especially in baseball reporting, prompting one exasperated reader to write, "Please let a poor, ignorant subscriber know where there is a base-ball park which is not 'without exception the finest base-ball grounds in the United States.'"[50] Still, while "local papers almost universally laud[ed] to the skies . . . doings in their own town whether . . . worthy of laudation or not," major strides toward critical detachment were made.[51]

The end of the war left newspapers with large amounts of space to fill, and the stories chosen were often less than newsworthy. In an extreme example, the *Pontiac Bill Poster* reported that a young boy's cap had been blown into the river by a gust of wind.[52] The reemergence of the sport whose first regulation Michigan club had been made up primarily of newspapermen proved a godsend, and several postwar newspapers provided much more tangible encouragement for "base ball fever."

Thus, the Civil War ended with a number of factors in place that would encourage baseball to reemerge with renewed vigor. But there were also signs that many elements of the game would be very different from this point forward.

NOTES

1. *Detroit Advertiser and Tribune*, April 8, 1863.
2. *Detroit Advertiser and Tribune*, April 14, 1863.
3. *Detroit Advertiser and Tribune*, April 16, 1863.
4. *Detroit Free Press*, June 14, 1863.
5. *Detroit Advertiser and Tribune*, June 23, 1863.
6. Henry Munson Utley and Byron M. Cutcheon, *The Class of Sixty-One: University of Michigan and Something about What 'the Boys' have been Doing during 40 Years from 1861 to 1901* (Detroit: J. Bornman and Sons, 1902), 38. Byron Ball, who had been the president of Grand Rapids' first baseball club in 1859, was a law student at the University of Michigan in 1861 but apparently did not introduce the game there.
7. *Ann Arbor Peninsular Courier*, April 23, 1863.
8. *Inlander* 2 (1892): 320–21, Bentley Library, Ann Arbor, Michigan.
9. Hinchman's letters are at the Bentley Library, Ann Arbor, Michigan.
10. *Monroe Monitor*, April 29, 1863.
11. *Detroit Advertiser and Tribune*, June 15, 1863.
12. *Michigan State News* (Ann Arbor), June 23, 1863.
13. *Niles Republican*, July 25, 1863.
14. *Detroit Advertiser and Tribune*, August 7, 1863.
15. *Detroit Free Press*, August 8, 1863.
16. *Jackson Eagle*, August 8, 1863.
17. *Detroit Advertiser and Tribune*, September 5, 1863.
18. Jack Hinchman, letter to his mother Louisa, October 18, 1863.
19. *Detroit Free Press*, May 31, 1864.
20. *Detroit Advertiser and Tribune*, June 17, 1864.
21. *Grand Rapids Daily Eagle*, May 7, 1864.
22. Louis Ives, letter to Clarence Burton, December 15, 1927, in the Burton Collection, Detroit Public Library.
23. *Detroit Advertiser and Tribune*, October 17, 1865.
24. *Jackson Eagle*, July 23, 1864.
25. Raymond J. Herek, *These Men Have Seen Hard Service: The First Michigan Sharpshooters in the Civil War* (Detroit: Wayne State University Press, 1998), 195–200, 378–80.
26. *Detroit Free Press*, March 10, 1902, in an article on the golden anniversary of the Typographical Union. One member of the Franklins, James Walker, president of the club in 1860, attended the ceremonies.
27. *Detroit Advertiser and Tribune*, August 26, 1864.

28. *Detroit Daily Post*, July 11, 1873.

29. Enclosed fields had occasionally been used earlier. There were enclosed cricket grounds in Philadelphia that were sometimes used for baseball. At an all-star game between Brooklyn and New York City players held on July 20, 1858, at Long Island's Fashion Race Course, a grandstand and the remote setting made it practical to charge admission for the first time.

30. William J. Ryczek, *When Johnny Came Sliding Home*, 29–33, gives a very thorough account of the opening of the Union Base Ball and Cricket Grounds.

31. Ryczek, *When Johnny Came Sliding Home*, 29.

32. William Humber, *Diamonds of the North*, 32

33. Quoted in Michael Gershman, *Diamonds*, 16.

34. Quoted in Gershman, *Diamonds*, 191.

35. Albert Reach was the first openly professional player, in 1863, but earlier players were paid under the table. Jim Creighton, the game's first superstar, was probably paid for playing prior to the Civil War. See Robert F. Burk, *Never Just A Game*, especially 23–30, for more on early professionalism.

36. See Warren Goldstein, *Playing for Keeps*, 60, for more on the rise of competitiveness in New York during the war.

37. Preston D. Orem, *Baseball (1845–1881) from the Newspaper Accounts*, 35–36. The game took place at Centre's Bridge in San Francisco on February 22, 1860.

38. James M. DiClerico and Barry J. Pavelec, *The Jersey Game*, 173. This took place in a game on October 11, 1862, between the Stars of New Brunswick and the Nassau Club of Princeton University. The Stars' pitcher understandably had difficulty attaining accuracy with this delivery, as he had to repeat it "an indefinite number of times" before the Princeton batter got a pitch that "suited him."

39. Quoted in Martin Quigley, *The Crooked Pitch*, 45, as part of an excellent history of the curve ball.

40. Several pitchers experimented with curve balls in the 1860s, but the pitch could not be thrown properly until delivery rules were liberalized in the 1870s. But spinning the ball was another matter. The *New York Clipper* stated on June 29, 1861, that an essential part of pitching was "the capacity to pitch a swift ball, with even and regular delivery, and with a bias or twist imparted to it." On July 20, 1861, the *Clipper* opined that "speed alone is of no advantage unless accompanied with regular delivery and considerable twist to the ball."

41. Old Peto Brine [Pete O'Brien], "Ball Talk," *American Chronicle of Sports and Pastimes*, January 9, 1868.

42. In an interview published in the *St. Louis Post-Dispatch*, July 10, 1884.

43. Ryczek, *When Johnny Came Sliding Home*, 4–7, describes this August 23, 1860, game as the swan song of the gentleman's era in New York City. The genteel Excelsior Club withdrew in the sixth inning due to the rowdy behavior of the pro-Atlantic crowd of over fifteen thousand and vowed never to play the Atlantics again.

44. Goldstein, *Playing for Keeps*, 53–54; Ryczek, *When Johnny Came Sliding Home*, 45. Al Smith was the Atlantics' pitcher and William McKeever the Mutuals' batter.

45. Dickey Pearce of the Atlantics of Brooklyn played a role in the development of both strategies, perhaps because at five feet three inches tall he was undersized even for the period. Fair-fouls were hits that took advantage of the rule that a ball was considered fair if it struck first in fair territory. Pearce became very proficient at hitting the ball with

backspin, so that it hit in fair territory and then spun foul, enabling him to reach first base before it could be retrieved. See Robert H. Schaefer, "The Lost Art of Fair-Foul Hitting," *National Pastime* 20 (2000): 3–9. The bunt's history is more complex. Tom Shieber has found what appears to be the first description of a bunt in the *New York Clipper* of July 14, 1860: a player named Brown, "in bringing his bat down . . . hit with the bat in a similar manner to that in which a cricketer blocks a straight ball." Dickey Pearce modified the technique and used it as a companion to the fair-foul. In the early 1870s, a player named Tommy Barlow used a two-foot-long bat to deliberately bunt the ball. But ridicule caused the strategy to disappear and it did not become a permanent feature of baseball until the mid-1880s.

46. Robert Smith, *Baseball*, 42.

47. There are several references to earlier instances of sliding, but the first documented use of the term *slide* came when the *Detroit Advertiser and Tribune* reported on October 18, 1866, that "[Butler] Ives obtained his run by a tremendous jump and slide on to the base under the pitcher's hand."

48. *Battle Creek Journal*, May 6, 1859.

49. Frederick J. Haskin, "Newspapers in the United States," *Detroit Free Press*, March 14, 1907.

50. *St. Louis Post-Dispatch*, March 17, 1884.

51. *Howard Record*, July 10, 1878, in a very candid article that calls such boosterish practices "one of the veils which threaten to destroy the power of the press" and states that "we do not propose to run our paper in that way."

52. *Pontiac Bill Poster*, August 4, 1869. The item had actually appeared a few issues earlier; in this issue they defended the item against a Mt. Clemens paper that had mocked it.

8

"THE PATIENCE OF HOPE"

THE POSTWAR BOOM

When Confederate general Robert E. Lee surrendered to Ulysses S. Grant on April 9, 1865, bringing the Civil War to an end, the minds of young men began to return almost immediately to the ball field. The Capital Base Ball Club was formed in Lansing the day after Lee's surrender. The club included twenty-five members and moved quickly to lay out grounds and obtain equipment. The *Lansing State Republican* remarked that "something of this kind has long been needed, and it is really surprising that it has not been taken hold of heretofore."[1] As an indication of how new baseball was to the capital area, seven members of the first nine had "never played the game before this season."[2]

The Detroit Base Ball Club re-formed in early April, and the officers it elected were mostly longtime members: Robert H. Anderson as president; Ford Hinchman as vice president; W. H. Baxter as secretary; Butler Ives as treasurer; and Eugene Robinson, John Clark, and Dr. Justin J. Dumon as directors.[3] Nearly thirty members signed up at the initial meeting, and they were joined by quite a few more at subsequent ones. Club fees were set at three dollars for initiation, with monthly dues of fifty cents. A first nine was soon chosen, consisting of Henry Burroughs pitching; Frank J. Phelps catching; John Clark at first base; Frank Folsom at second base; Ford Hinchman at shortstop; David Barry at third base; and Butler Ives, John Horn, and John McMillan in the outfield, with Arthur Van Norman and Charles Vernor available as substitutes.

With the New York City area regarded as the pinnacle of baseball, ambitious clubs from other regions sought to narrow the gap by recruiting New York players. Harry Wright was lured to Cincinnati to act as an instructor for the local cricket club at a salary of twelve hundred dollars, where he would earn fame as the first true manager of a baseball club. More New Yorkers were attracted to Washington, D.C., by the promise of civil service jobs for baseball players. This same trend brought a new captain to the Detroit Base Ball Club in twenty-year-old Henry Burroughs of Newark.

Burroughs had taken a job as a "professor" at the Detroit Gymnasium, where he did give instruction. However, he had no family or other obvious connections to Detroit, so it is very likely that his income was supplemented by under-the-table payments to play baseball.[4] A club's hometown newspapers almost never explicitly acknowledged professionalism, but an Ann Arbor paper later described Burroughs as a "professional player."[5] Although this assertion cannot be positively proven, it seems very likely.

The club's other recently transplanted Easterner was first baseman John Clark, a native of Brooklyn. Although there is less reason to suspect that Clark was paid for his services, he did work as a proofreader for the *Detroit Advertiser and Tribune,* a newspaper that relied heavily on baseball coverage. Did the newspaper recruit him specifically to improve the club and sell more papers? That is only conjecture, but one can at least surmise that it was easier for Clark to get time off from work for a match than for a typical worker.

Its players selected, the club next turned its attention to the always crucial issue of finding suitable grounds. Several possible sites were considered, including a very desirable piece of land on the Brush Farm, behind Harper Hospital. But the search was no longer just a matter of finding flat terrain. It seems reasonable to assume

OLYMPICS, WASHINGTON, D. C.

A. J. Leonard, l.f. G. W. Hall, c.f. H. W. Berthrong, r.f.
F. A. Waterman, 3 b. C. J. Sweasy, 2 b. E. Mills, 1b.
D. W. Force, s.s. Asa Brainard, p.
H. F. Borroughs D. L. Allison, c. J. W. Glenn

Henry Burroughs, of Newark, New Jersey, was most likely Michigan's
first professional player. The *University Chronicle* wrote of him: "If he
returns to Detroit it will be only because he can *do better* there than where
he is. We don't blame Detroit for thus holding out inducements to good
players: she must do it to keep pace with her sister cities. But it is somewhat difficult for us to distinguish between these men and 'professional
players,' or those who play for 'place or emolument.'" *Courtesy of Transcendental Graphics*

that the Eastern transplants made sure their fellow members were aware of William Cammeyer's success with his converted ice rink in Brooklyn and lobbied for a similar enclosed location that would enable the club to charge admission.

Eventually, the club did indeed select the enclosed Woodward Avenue Skating Park, reaching an agreement to rent the park on April 14. The next day the *Free Press* announced that play would commence as soon as the weather permitted, "which, from present appearances will not be long."[6] But in the adjacent column came tidings that would again direct attention to more serious matters than baseball—the breaking news of President Lincoln's assassination. A country too accustomed to sadness was once again plunged into mourning, just when normalcy seemed to have returned.

For the next month, the country was entirely focused on the pursuit, capture, and trial of assassin John Wilkes Booth and his accomplices. But eventually interest in baseball began to pick up again, the first hotbed forming in mid-Michigan. The Capital Club got its first rivals when Monroe Diver introduced baseball at the Agricultural College in Lansing (now Michigan State University) and the collegians formed a club called the Stars.[7] The Stars won the first match between the two clubs on May 10 on the college grounds, but the Capitals evened the series two weeks later. A third game was scheduled for Owosso on June 3, but the game did not come off, prompting the Capitals to allege that the college club had "unceremoniously 'flunked' entirely out of their challenge—preferring to give up their ball without a 'pitch,' than play for it as *a club*."[8]

The matter was cleared up, however, and the clubs played again on June 23, with the Stars winning 34-27. No hard feelings were manifested during the game, and, in accordance with custom, the members of the Capital Club treated their vanquishers to supper at the Edgar House that evening. Still, the *State Republican* did report that "much fault was found with the umpire [A. C. Prutzman], who was a member Star Club [*sic*]. It was thought he allowed partiality to govern many of his decisions, instead of justice and fair dealing."[9]

The Capitals soon had other rivals. On July 7, the newly

formed Sheridan Club of Mason hosted the Capitals in front of a
large crowd. The Capitals won 13-6 and in the evening were furnished with "a bounteous supper" by their hosts.[10] A rematch in
Lansing saw the Capitals win by a much more convincing 39-7 margin. Soon yet another club formed in Lansing, the Lansing Base Ball
Club of Lower Town. Michigan was beginning to discover just how
contagious baseball fever could be.

Further north, the Washington Base Ball Club of Bay City had
been formed on April 27 at the office of local lawyer A. C.
Maxwell.[11] Not finding any local rivals, the Washingtons finally
challenged the Capital Club, and a game was scheduled in Lansing
for July 19. In a game marred by a heavy rain that made the ball and
grounds very slippery and led to numerous misplays, the visitors
won 42-31.

A rematch was scheduled for August 24 in Bay City. When the
Capitals discovered that their travel plans would include a three-
hour stop in Holly, they challenged the Detroit Base Ball Club to
meet them there for a game. While the Detroit Club had to decline
the invitation, the game in Bay City proved to be a memorable one.
The Capitals came up in the bottom of the ninth, trailing 30-29.
However, the Washingtons managed to retire them without a run, a
result that the Lansing paper attributed to the batters becoming
"nervous" and that the Bay City paper credited to "admirable fielding" by the home club.[12] On their way home, the Capitals stopped
in Owosso, where they easily beat another newly formed club.

Other towns had also begun to join in the fun. On June 14, two
ambitious new clubs, the Star Club of Monroe and the host Anchora
Club of Adrian, squared off. It initially appeared that a delay would
be inevitable: "The prospect in the morning was anything but invit-
ing. Black clouds generally bring rain, and there were plenty of
black clouds and some to spare. But Monroe telegraphed to know if
they should come, and Adrian, undaunted, flashed them back the
answer 'yes.' And in preparation for their coming the Anchora boys
sheared the grass of their grounds, got up a fine tent, painted the
bases, and then sat down in the 'patience of hope' and their new uni-

forms until afternoon."[13] That same spirit, of the "patience of hope," would enable the new regulation game to be introduced all over the state in the next two years and help it become a permanent part of the national identity.

A midgame shower did indeed force the teams to retreat under the tent, but eventually they were able to complete the game, with Adrian winning 14-10. Both teams adjourned to the Lawrence House for supper, and a rematch in Monroe six days later was agreed on. The return game on June 20 saw the Anchoras post an easy 47-15 victory. The home field actually proved a disadvantage to Monroe, if one accepts the explanation that "the Monroe men were all tired out by their efforts in preparing the grounds for the match."[14] Both clubs again enjoyed supper together, this time at Strong's.

While the spoils of victory went to Adrian, the Monroe players were also buoyed by the "patience of hope." One Monroe newspaper confidently wrote that the loss was "owing to the greater skill which *experience* gave the Anchoras in throwing, catching and handling the ball. The Stars have pluck, for a new club, or they would never have challenged a better and longer drilled club."[15] This faith that the game would reward hard work proved to be one of the greatest boons to the surge of interest in the game in 1865.

A new club could always take comfort after a loss in the belief that it would get better in time. Owosso's lopsided loss to the Capital Club was greeted with optimism: "As a matter of course [the Capital Club was] the winner of the game by 35 runs, being an old club, while the Owosso club has only been in practice about three weeks."[16] With no fear of failure, clubs had the confidence to challenge far superior clubs, regarding the inevitable loss as a learning experience and not as an embarrassment.

A team sport was a new phenomenon to most Americans, and, in a country just ending a war, military concepts and terminology were used to render it familiar. It quickly became accepted wisdom that a club's success was based not on the individual skills of the players but on teamwork and discipline. This in turn allowed baseball to be depicted not just as a harmless activity, as had been the case before the war, but as a test of character. The role of the captain was particularly important, the best clubs having "one captain, whose name is law."[17] Further attention was drawn to this analogy when baseball appropriated such military terms as *battery, veterans, drills, conquerors,* and *home base.*[18]

Baseball derived additional credibility by becoming associated with the growing belief in science. In the 1860s and 1870s, scientific breakthroughs provided Americans with a tremendous number of labor-saving devices, and *science* became a magic word to Americans. This new faith in science crept into baseball terminology, with an Adrian supporter boasting, for example, that his team would "show the Centrals that New York Base Ball is really a scientific game, and that they will require some years of practice before they can hope to be the second club of the State."[19]

This supporter's team must have deserved his boast. The Adrian club's second game against Monroe had been umpired by Frank Folsom of the Detroit Base Ball Club, and he was sufficiently impressed with the Anchoras for the Detroit Club to issue them a challenge. On July 8, the Detroit Club traveled to Adrian for the opening game, but due to illness and other engagements, only three members of the first nine were able to make the trip. The club fielded eight players by adding five members of the second nine, but for unknown reasons, A. R. Linn, another member of the second nine, acted as scorer for the game rather than playing. The upstarts from Adrian beat the makeshift lineup 27-20. In the return match in Detroit three days later, the Detroit Club was back at full strength and provided "a courteous return for the drubbing the Eight" had received in Adrian, winning 46-19.[20]

With baseball now solidly established in several parts of the state, an intriguing and historic announcement was made in Adrian on July 26. Adrian was to be the host of that year's Michigan State Fair in late September. The state fair had been initiated in 1849 by the State Agricultural Society as an exhibition of crops and livestock, but manufactured items and horse races had been added in

recent years. Now a new attraction was proposed—a baseball tournament that would determine state supremacy. Interested parties
were advised to make a five-dollar deposit by August 15. The *New
York Clipper*'s notice of the event suggests that this may have been
the first baseball tournament ever held: "We have had almost every
other kind of tournament but base ball, but this exception, it
appears, is not to be for long."[21]

The trend toward more ambitious modes of competition continued when the Michigan State Base Ball Association was formed in
late August at a meeting in Jackson. The officers represented a
cross-section of clubs in the state—Dr. Jonathan Van Norman of
Detroit, president; George M. LeVan of Salem in Washtenaw
County, vice-president; Willard Stearns of Adrian, secretary; and
B. J. Billings Jr. of Jackson, treasurer.

More details about the state tournament were also announced.
The entry fee had been increased to ten dollars, the additional
money being needed to purchase a silver goblet that would be
awarded to the champion. That club would be expected to accept all
challenges from clubs belonging to the state association, with a limit
of two challenges per club per year. If any club retained the goblet
for two years, it would become that club's property.

The goblet, valued at eighty dollars, was manufactured by
Detroit jeweler Charles Ward and bore a distinctive baseball theme:
"It consists of a silver cup, mounted on three miniature bats. The lid
of the cup is of oval shape, and in a depression carries a silver ball,
the emblem of success. Between the bats, constituting the standard,
are also placed *fac similes* of the square and circular bases. The prize
is thus very appropriate, in addition to being of a novel model."[22]
Prior to the tournament, the champion cup was displayed at the
Detroit drugstore of Frederick Stearns, whose son and namesake
would serve as president of the world champion Detroit National
League team in the late 1880s.

The tournament organizers optimistically made plans to play
simultaneous games on two fields in the event of a large number of
entrants. But the number of clubs in the state was still limited, and

no quantity of the "patience of hope" could persuade many of the new clubs to part with ten dollars and traveling expenses, just to be trounced by the Detroit Base Ball Club and their Eastern imports. Only six clubs paid the entry fee—Detroit, the Anchoras of Adrian, the Centrals of Jackson, the Capitals of Lansing, the Washingtons of Bay City, and the Salem Club. However, the last two dropped out for unknown reasons, leaving only four entrants.

While the number of participants was disappointing, having four clubs greatly simplified the format of the tournament. In an unseeded, single-elimination tournament, the ideal of fairness can only be satisfied if the number of entrants is a power of two (two, four, eight, sixteen, etc.). But limiting the number of entrants was not considered an option by most tournament organizers during the 1860s, since it would have conflicted with the still-fundamental principle of inclusiveness. In the years to come arranging tournaments involving inconvenient numbers of entrants would become a major problem, but in 1865, with the field reduced to a handy number, the pairings were drawn at random, pitting Jackson against Lansing and Adrian against Detroit.

On the morning of September 20, Jackson and Lansing squared off in a rather lackluster opening game. The correspondent for the *Detroit Advertiser and Tribune,* accustomed to watching better exhibitions of the sport, wrote that the game "was not a very interesting one, the play being of a very ordinary character."[23] Jackson led 30-3 after six innings and won 45-14. A few years later, such a game would have received considerable praise because of the low score of the Capital Club, but the *Advertiser and Tribune*'s correspondent just blamed Lansing's poor hitting.

That afternoon Detroit faced the Anchoras and won 35-21 in front of more than one thousand spectators. The *Advertiser and Tribune* attributed the result to superior teamwork by the Detroiters; while the "Detroit nine played together admirably," it explained, Adrian suffered from "a large number of good balls being missed at first through confusion among the fielders."[24]

The clubs representing Detroit and Jackson were now left to

play for the championship the next morning. The Central Club, already a heavy underdog, was further weakened when several of its best players failed to appear for the game. Detroit claimed the championship with an easy 31-13 victory, but no sooner had Dr. Jonathan Van Norman accepted the championship cup on behalf of the Detroit Base Ball Club than the Salem Club issued a formal challenge to contest its ownership.

In addition to Detroit's victory, the tournament saw another meeting of the Michigan State Base Ball Association, at which new officers were elected. Dr. Jonathan Van Norman remained as president, but Nelson B. Jones of Lansing was elected as vice president; Stephen A. Welling of Jackson as secretary, and William D. Ramsdell of Adrian as treasurer. In addition to the clubs that were already members, Three Rivers was represented at this meeting, and Monroe and Dowagiac expressed interest in joining the next year. While this boded well for the future, and the tournament was in most ways a ringing success, the competitive imbalance demonstrated by Detroit's easy victories was an ominous sign.

The new state champions' match with Salem was scheduled for October 4 on the Detroit Base Ball Club grounds. It was announced beforehand that an admission fee would be charged, which would have made this the first game in Michigan history with a paid audience.[25] But if a fee was in fact collected, it is doubtful that many of the spectators felt they got their money's worth. Game time had been announced as 10:00 A.M., but there was a misunderstanding, and the Salem nine didn't arrive until noon. The spectators had a long wait on a cold day before the game finally got under way at 1:00 P.M.

Salem had never previously faced any of the clubs in the association, and not surprisingly the game was a mismatch. Detroit won 46-19, although the cold adversely affected play. By the time the game ended at 5:00 P.M., any spectators who remained had been outside for seven hours on a day when "watching the game was about as comfortable as dropping brass keys down one's back."[26]

In spite of the lateness of the season, the Detroit Base Ball Club accepted yet another challenge, from the Anchoras of Adrian, and obligingly scheduled the game for October 13. The match was played in front of a large crowd on the Detroit Club's grounds. Detroit presented a makeshift lineup because of the absence of the Hinchman brothers, but at first it didn't appear that this would make much difference. The home team grabbed an early lead, and shaky defense by the visitors helped the Detroiters build on it steadily. The Anchoras' shortstop, Decker, had a particularly rough day, "hardly stopping a single ball."[27] After six innings, Detroit held a commanding 37-20 lead.

But as the *Free Press* observed, "in base ball, as in everything else, there is a 'glorious uncertainty' which sometimes turns the tables, and reduces the assured winners to discomfited losers. Adrian took the bat and commenced knocking the leather about in all directions."[28] The worried Detroiters moved several players to new positions and finally managed to retire the Adrian men, but not before they had outscored Detroit 14-0 in the inning, narrowing the lead to 37-34.

With its hold on the champion cup suddenly in jeopardy, the Detroit Base Ball Club regrouped. Several daring base-running gambles were successful by the narrowest of margins. A particularly close play saw David Barry make a dash for home, where he arrived at the same time as the pitcher and the ball. After a lengthy argument, the Anchora pitcher acknowledged that he had not tagged Barry. While the dispute was raging, Frank Folsom stole around from first base to count another run. Sparked by the aggressive play, Detroit pulled out the game by a 55-41 count and retained the state championship.

The Adrian men took the defeat gracefully and gave the customary cheers for the winners, but the good feeling did not last long. The *Albion Expositor* published an article charging that Detroit's win could be attributed to the biased umpiring of Dr. Jonathan Van Norman, of the Detroit Base Ball Club, who had officiated in the absence of any member of a neutral club.[29] Accord-

ing to the *Expositor*, Van Norman had allowed Detroit to score 11
runs in the critical final two innings after three men were already
out.

The *Detroit Advertiser and Tribune* responded by attacking the
Expositor correspondent, accusing him of "knowing nothing of
grammar, and but little of base-ball." It added that such charges
revealed a "lack of that honorable spirit that can bear defeat without
a loss of temper, as well as carry off victory without boasting." The
article addressed the specific charges and pointed out that Detroit
would still have won even if all the disputed runs had been removed.
Finally, it counseled the Adrian players that they "had better procure a different representative on the occasion of their next game, or
they will mar the effect of their really good play by more babyish
proceedings afterward."[30]

Baseball's long and important association with the agricultural
fairs that marked the end of the Michigan harvest, which had started
at the state fair, now continued at county fairs. In Monroe, the first
and second nines of the Star Club played on September 29 as part of
the county fair.[31] A match between the Washington Club of Bay
City and the Chippewa Club of Portsmouth was also scheduled for
a county fair sponsored by the Bay County Agricultural Society,
but no report of the game exists.[32] The inclusion of baseball alongside the traditional displays of crops and livestock was another
indication of Americans' growing comfort with the game.

Meanwhile, competition continued in the capital area. The Capital Club beat the Star Club of the Agricultural College on September 16 in the fifth and deciding game of their prolonged series. The
Sheridan Club of Mason and the Lansing Club squared off in a
three-game series that began at the county fair in Mason. The Sheridans won the first match 21-19, Lansing tied the series with a 33-28
triumph, and then the Sheridans captured the decisive match by a
51-46 margin. The *Detroit Advertiser and Tribune* published an
account of the closely contested series, erroneously identifying the
Lansing Club as the Capital Club.[33] This irritated the Capital Club,

whose members hastened to point out that they had already beaten the Sheridans twice and then offered to play the Sheridan Club with only six men.[34]

Even though some feathers were now being ruffled by the once-dignified game, 1865 was a most successful season for baseball in Michigan. Notwithstanding the breaches in decorum that were beginning to appear, many clubs still hewed to the old ethos, preferring being outdone on the ball field to being surpassed as hosts. This was particularly noticeable in the Bay City–Capitals series. When the Capital Club visited Bay City its members found that "Lansing money would not pass in Bay City at all."[35] A Lansing correspondent wrote that "the excursion on the bay was a rare treat to our boys, who live here in this inland city."[36]

While the number of clubs was still limited, generous coverage in the newspapers was sparking interest in the sport. The *Detroit Advertiser and Tribune* wrote near the end of the 1865 season that "boating, base-ball, cricket and all that class of out-door sport have received far more attention than usual the present season."[37] Much of this added attention came from newspapers like the *Advertiser and Tribune* itself, since they needed material to fill the large amount of space previously devoted to coverage of the war. Dailies were particularly hard-pressed to fill the void, causing one Michigan newspaper to observe that "since the rebellion has 'played out,' the dailies seem to be making rather dull music."[38] Most newspapers relied heavily on material reprinted from other papers, and original news items with local interest were at a premium.[39] This shortage caused one newspaper to embark on an ambitious course.

Some of the most dramatic coverage of the war had come from letters home from local soldiers, and the *Detroit Advertiser and Tribune* hit on a logical extension of that form of reporting. The *Lansing State Republican,* in the same April issue that announced Robert E. Lee's surrender, noted that the *Advertiser and Tribune*

has added another feature of improvement, which, so far as we know, is entirely new in journalizing. We allude to the establishment of a corps of correspondents, so numerous that there shall be one in every place where there can be any business or news, who are able to write so frequently that every event worth chronicling at all in any paper, shall be published in the *Tribune* in forty-eight hours after its occurrence. . . . [T]he idea of going over a whole state topographically and gathering and reproducing ALL the news the next day after it occurs, is something that we believe has not been before attempted.[40]

The correspondent system was soon copied by other newspapers, and it caused a significant increase in baseball coverage, many correspondents devoting much of their space to the exploits of the local nine. It also led to many disputes, because correspondents all too often told only one side of a story.

But even this dramatic increase in coverage was not always enough to satisfy players. The *Detroit Free Press*, for example, published a letter from a member of the Central Club of Jackson who wrote, "In consequence of our *Daily Citizen* failing to give an account of the base ball match that took place here on Monday . . . I enclose it believing you think enough of the fraternity to give it a place in your columns."[41]

In addition to the increased exposure that the newspapers provided, a solid structure for the game was now in place in Michigan. A championship cup emblematic of state supremacy had been created, along with an undisputed champion and eager challengers waiting in the wings. With one exception, the championship games played in 1865 had excited spectators without sacrificing decorum. A state association had been formed and that winter would see an effort toward further organization.

On December 6, 1865, fourteen clubs representing the states of Indiana, Michigan, Illinois, Missouri, Iowa, Ohio, Wisconsin, and Minnesota met in Chicago and formed the Northwestern Association of Base-ball Players.[42] Robert H. Anderson and Henry Burroughs represented the Detroit Base Ball Club at the convention, both assuming prominent roles. Anderson acted as chairman pro tem of the convention and was elected treasurer of the newly formed organization, while Burroughs sat on the committee that drafted a constitution and bylaws and was appointed assistant vice president for the state of Michigan.[43] Although this new association was never very active, the meeting did pave the way for considerably more interstate competition in the region in the ensuing years.

The *Detroit Free Press* commented near the close of the 1865 season that "there is every prospect that the next season will be the liveliest one ever known in the State at this exciting game." This prediction would come true. The 1866 season brought the organization of an unprecedented number of clubs, with the *Detroit Advertiser and Tribune* looking forward to even bigger and better things:

> Base-ball has become *the* national game—as distinctly American as cricket is English, or curling Scotch. It is played in every town in the North, and is rapidly spreading throughout the South, whence it has hitherto been blockaded by the war. Its clubs must now be numbered by the hundred, and their delegates constitute a National Association, whose rulings and decisions are binding throughout the land. Separate organizations have also been formed, this State being included within the Northwestern Association, two of the officers of which are residents of our city. The game possesses permanent elements of popularity. For proficiency as a player, a quick intellect and cool judgment are as requisite as physical strength and agility. The attendant exercise is not exhausting nor severe, but harmless and invigorating. The progress of the game is always exciting and varied, and the spectators share in the enthusiasm and hopes of the eager participants. The Base Ball Club of our city is one of the finest in the West. It now owns the Champion Cup of Michigan, and for two seasons yet must hold the same against all challenges from members of the State Association. It possesses also the advantage of fine grounds, large membership, and an admirable *esprit de corps*. Its picked "nine" are all superior players, and two or three of them deserve to be ranked among the best in the land, whether professional or *amateur*. Baseball will undoubtedly be active in this region during the coming summer. Our exchanges have announced the formation of fully a score of

new clubs in the interior towns of the State, and the old Associations have all organized anew for the season. The Detroit Club will be often called upon to maintain its title to the championship, and the public will enjoy the opportunity of witnessing a number of exciting matches upon their grounds in our city. It is also probable that the Atlantic Club, of Brooklyn, N.Y.,—*the* champions—will visit Detroit in a general trip through the West this summer—a circumstance which will serve to intensify the general interest in this popular game. Believing Base-Ball to combine to an unusual degree the advantage of exercise and recreation, and being desirous that Detroit shall excel in the minor as well as more important points, we shall gladly promote by all means in our power the welfare of its clubs in our city and State.

After a discussion of cricket, croquet, horseback racing, and calisthenics, the editorial concludes: "In the point of physique, the American people have been always open to attack from the English, whose love of out-door sports has constituted one of the finest of their national traits. The day when rebuke upon this score shall be possible is rapidly passing away—a fact which is a great matter for self-congratulations."[44]

NOTES

1. *Lansing State Republican,* April 19, 1865.
2. *Lansing State Republican,* July 19, 1865.
3. *Detroit Advertiser and Tribune,* April 6, 1865.
4. See chapter 2 of Robert F. Burk's *Never Just a Game* for a description of some of the ways clubs found to pay players under the table.
5. *Ann Arbor Peninsular Courier and Family Visitant,* June 20, 1867. See also the comments of the *University Chronicle* (Ann Arbor) of June 22, 1867, which appear in the caption under Burroughs's picture.
6. *Detroit Free Press,* April 15, 1865.
7. This may not have been the first club at the Agricultural College. According to Lyman L. Frimodig and Fred W. Stabley's *Spartan Saga* (East Lansing: Michigan State University Press, 1971), 155, "President Frank S. Kedzie (class of 1877) once recalled that there had been a team in the early 1860s for which Joseph W. Gunnison was the catcher and William W. Daniels was the pitcher. Both were of the class of 1864."
8. *Lansing State Republican,* June 7, 1865.
9. *Lansing State Republican,* June 28, 1865.

10. *Lansing State Republican,* July 12, 1865.

11. *Bay City Journal,* May 4, 1865. The club took its name from the park in which it practiced.

12. *Lansing State Republican,* August 30, 1865; *Bay City Journal,* August 31, 1865.

13. *Detroit Advertiser and Tribune,* June 16, 1865.

14. *Detroit Advertiser and Tribune,* June 23, 1865.

15. *Monroe Monitor,* June 21, 1865; my emphasis.

16. *Detroit Advertiser and Tribune,* August 30, 1865. The *Lansing State Republican* denied this, stating on July 11, 1865, that the Capitals were themselves a new club.

17. *Detroit Free Press,* August 4, 1868.

18. See chapter 3 of Joel Zoss and John Bowman, *Diamonds in the Rough,* for more examples of baseball's terminology borrowing from the Civil War.

19. *Adrian Expositor;* reprinted in the *Jackson Daily Citizen,* August 23, 1866.

20. *Detroit Free Press,* July 12, 1865.

21. *New York Clipper,* August 8, 1865.

22. *Detroit Advertiser and Tribune,* September 13, 1865.

23. *Detroit Advertiser and Tribune,* September 23, 1865.

24. *Detroit Advertiser and Tribune,* September 23, 1865.

25. *Detroit Advertiser and Tribune,* September 29, 1865.

26. *Detroit Advertiser and Tribune,* October 5, 1865.

27. *Detroit Advertiser and Tribune,* October 14, 1865.

28. *Detroit Free Press,* October 14, 1865.

29. The *Expositor* itself is not extant; the purport of the article has been gleaned from the response in the *Detroit Advertiser and Tribune.*

30. *Detroit Advertiser and Tribune,* October 19, 1865.

31. One of the players in the game was named Custer, and George Custer grew up in Monroe, but as far as I can tell, it was a different Custer. Custer's Seventh Cavalry had a baseball club during the 1870s, but Custer is only known to have attended one game, preferring his favorite sport of hunting (see Tim Wolter, "Bats and Saddles," *National Pastime* 18 [1998]: 25–28).

32. *Bay City Journal,* September 28, 1865.

33. *Detroit Advertiser and Tribune,* October 20, 1865.

34. *Detroit Advertiser and Tribune,* October 23, 1865.

35. *Detroit Advertiser and Tribune,* August 28, 1865.

36. *Detroit Advertiser and Tribune,* August 28, 1865.

37. *Detroit Advertiser and Tribune,* September 26, 1865.

38. *Monroe Commercial,* July 27, 1865.

39. The *Grand Rapids Daily Morning Times* went so far as to claim sarcastically on July 26, 1877, that it had swallowed the *Lowell Journal* whole by reprinting the only eight original items that had appeared in one of that paper's issues.

40. *Lansing State Republican,* April 12, 1865.

41. *Detroit Free Press,* August 15, 1865.

42. The region now usually referred to as the Midwest was then known as the Northwest.

43. *Chicago Tribune,* December 7, 1865.

44. *Detroit Advertiser and Tribune,* April 17, 1866.

9

"ALMOST PERFECT"

THE DETROIT BASE BALL CLUB LOOKS FURTHER AFIELD

The 1865 season had focused around the battle for the state championship, but this would prove to be a relatively minor point of interest in 1866. The Detroit Base Ball Club met in early April, reelecting Robert H. Anderson as president and again arranging for the use of Captain Ives's skating rink as a field. The first challenge for the right to hold the cup was soon received, and Detroit played host to the Washington Base Ball Club of Bay City on June 8. A large crowd was in attendance, the gentlemen paying a ten-cent fee to enter the grounds while the ladies were admitted free.[1] As with the Salem match, through no fault of the Detroit Base Ball Club, the game gave the paying spectators little reason to think they had spent their money wisely.

The day was miserable, the play being disrupted by high winds and the grounds still wet from a heavy rainfall that had prevented the game from being played on the previous day. In addition, the members of the Bay City club were ill-prepared for the match—the rain had disrupted their practice schedule; several members of their first nine were absent in Canada; and their shortstop, W. H. Fennell, had accidentally been shot in the hand a few days before the game.

Detroit had an easy time of it, winning 40-13 with courtesy prevailing. This marked the Detroiters' third successful defense of their title in the eight months since winning the cup, but it would be the last time they would have to defend it before it became their permanent possession sixteen months later.

One reason for this was that both of Detroit's closest challengers in 1865, the Anchora Club of Adrian and the Central Club of Jackson, had fallen into disarray. One of Jackson's regular players, Francis Sharpsteen, had died over the winter of tuberculosis, and several others had not returned. On May 25, Jackson was trounced 41-25 by the Sheridan Club of Mason—the same team that the Capital Club of Lansing had offered to play with only six men. The team apparently took the loss hard: "The Jackson Club commenced with good spirits, high in the hope of success, but as the game progressed, and they were falling in the rear, they became disheartened and careless."[2]

The Central Club continued to play throughout the summer but seems to have never seriously considered challenging the Detroit Base Ball Club. It avenged its loss to the Sheridans but was beaten 61-41 by the club representing the students at the University of Michigan. Any aspirations to prominence the Central Club may have had vanished after it was beaten by the brand-new Peninsular Club of Albion in late August. The Peninsulars were then soundly beaten by a juvenile club from Jackson called the Stars, showing that the Central Club was probably no longer the best club in Jackson.

The Anchora Club of Adrian also had troubles reorganizing, the nucleus of the 1865 club being "scattered around throughout the country."[3] On June 12, a makeshift Anchora nine squeaked out a 1-run victory over the Stars of Monroe—a team they had beaten by 32 runs the previous season. Then the club lapsed into inactivity, failing to respond to Monroe's challenge for a rematch. On August 9, the Anchoras' second nine issued a rather impertinent challenge, saying that they would "play any junior or second nine of any other club in the State; also the first nine of the clubs at Monroe, Hudson, Hillsdale or Albion."[4]

Needless to say, this perturbed the Monroe club, which immediately responded:

> We most decidedly decline stooping so much as to play with the second nine of a club whose first nine we can beat. The last time we played them they beat us one run, in which game the umpire played better than any of their nine. The Stars challenged them to play in a game in Monroe, and the Anchoras have used every means in their power to keep from accepting it, saying that they had no club, etc. Will some Adrian friend be so kind as to inform us how they can have a second nine without having an organized club. If the Anchoras have finally "organized" and are very anxious to play, we would like to have them accept our challenge given them June 12th.[5]

The Detroit Base Ball Club also received a surprising response when its second nine challenged the Anchoras' first nine: "In answer to the challenge they say that their second nine have issued a challenge to any other second nine in the State, therefore they evidently consider that the first nine should not bother their heads about the matter."[6] The *Detroit Post* was more caustic: "What connection this answer has with the challenge it is difficult to say, but it seems as if the Anchora men think it a satisfactory reply."[7]

Then, on September 7, the Anchoras lost to a new team from tiny Wolf Creek in Lenawee County, an upset only partially mitigated by the fact that many of the Anchoras' first nine were absent. At last, the Anchoras issued a challenge to play Detroit for the state championship, and a match was arranged for September 28. However, on the day of the game the Adrian club telegraphed its regrets because several of its players were unable to attend. This appears to have been the end of the club that had brought so much energy to the baseball scene in 1865 and had hosted the first state championship tournament.

The cancellation was another setback to hopes of establishing baseball as a spectator sport in Detroit. The Detroit Base Ball Club had anticipated a sizable attendance and had gone to special lengths to make sure that ample seating was available, putting up a "semi-circular row of seats similar to those in a circus . . . so that all can see and not be in the way of the players."[8] A large crowd had assembled by the time word came of the Anchoras' cancellation, and it had to be satisfied with a hastily arranged exhibition in which the Detroit Club's first nine trounced the second nine 84-39.

With its main in-state rivals inactive, and none of the many new clubs bold enough to challenge it, the Detroit Base Ball Club began looking elsewhere for competition. It entered a tournament in Rockford, Illinois, at the end of June for the championship of the Northwest. Preparations for this tournament were elaborate, and the prizes announced beforehand were particularly impressive. Dr. Joseph P. Norman, a retired Rockford dentist, offered as prizes for the first-place club a ball "of full regulation size, two and three-quarters inches in diameter, of eighteen carat gold, and put up in a satin-lined Morocco case," and a bat "of solid rosewood, elaborately mounted with the same quality of gold, and cased the same as the ball."

These prizes alone were valued at $225, but the Rockford business community contributed additional prizes. Local hotels recognized that they would be prime beneficiaries of the tournament and accordingly led the way. The Holland House offered a silver pitcher to the best thrower, White's Hotel donated a silver goblet for the second-best thrower, and the American House offered the fastest base runner a silver-mounted belt with the image of a man running for dear life on the buckle.

The rest of the community chipped in as well. The women of the east side promised to present a bouquet to the best batsman, while the women of the west side had a floral wreath for the batter who hit the most home runs. A local auctioneer named J. M. Hodge offered a silver tea set (or thirty dollars, if preferred) to the club that played most gracefully.[9] The Rock River Insurance Company donated a silver ice pitcher and goblet for the best catcher. Even the weakest club was not overlooked—the team that lost by the widest margin would receive a silver horn with a green cord, tassels, and a pendant with a ball inscribed "practice."[10]

In preparation for the tournament, temporary bleachers made of bridge planking and capable of holding up to five hundred spectators were erected along the first-base line of Fairgrounds Park. Spectators were charged twenty-five cents for admission and could purchase refreshments from several temporary grocery stands. The refreshment options included lemonade (at five cents a glass), peanuts, and gum made from spruce and white wax, a derivative of kerosene oil.[11]

Unfortunately, not all aspects of the event received as much attention. The playing field was particularly poor, prompting one observer to claim many years later that

> a poorer field, to my mind, has never been known. There was a cluster of five trees around third base. The catcher was hemmed in by trees with the exception of a space about 30 by 50 feet. The umpire could not see a foul unless it was hit back of the plate or a few feet on either side of the base lines.
>
> Between the plate and second base the terrain was fairly level, but approaching third base there was a notable rise. From third to the plate there was a depression. The baserunner had to dig in for life.
>
> At the edge of the outfield was a deep gutter that drained a nearly quarter-mile track. Only Providence's protection kept more players from breaking legs in that trap.[12]

Additionally, little forethought seems to have gone into determining how to pair the teams. Ten clubs had entered, including the Cream City Club of Milwaukee; the Julien Club of Dubuque, Iowa; and six strong Illinois teams. The tenth entry, a new club from tiny Pecatonica, Illinois, stood no chance of competing against the big-city clubs. A proposal to divide the clubs into classes was defeated, so the first round was paired by lot.

Detroit drew the club from Pecatonica and beat it by the extraordinary score of 49-1. Margins of victory in the nineteenth century were usually judged by the number of times the loser's score could be divided into the winner's, so this was deemed "a victory . . . only to be equaled by the Athletics of Philadelphia."[13] The game quickly passed into legend and would end up being the best-remembered aspect of the tournament. One particularly unreliable account, which identified the Red Stockings of Cincinnati (not yet even in existence) as the tournament champions, nonetheless accurately described the Pecatonica Club as winning the horn for losing by the biggest deficit.[14]

References to the Pecatonica game appeared for years afterward, the contrast between the rural nine and their big-city rivals giving the story its enduring appeal. An 1878 account described a Pecatonica farmer wagering three loads of hay and a yearling calf on the outcome, then sitting down to watch the game with a stick on which he planned to notch the runs of the two sides. After his initial high hopes had given way to a mixture of surprise and resignation, an explanation finally occurred to him and he exclaimed, "Why the goldarned fools are after the horn!"[15] In a 1914 story by Finley Peter Dunne, an old-timer reminisces in an exaggeratedly rural dialect about having watched Harry Wright, Cap Anson, Jim White, and "th' Forest Citys bate th' Pecatonica Blues be a scoor iv two hundhred an' eight to nawthin.'"[16]

The other first-round winners were the Excelsior Club of Chicago; the Cream City Club of Milwaukee; the Bloomington Club of Bloomington, Illinois; and the host Forest City Club of Rockford, whose pitcher was the fifteen-year-old A. G. Spalding. At this point, the captains decided to scrap the random draw and have a committee determine the second-round pairings. With five teams still alive in the single-elimination format, there was no fair way to do this. Detroit and Chicago were paired for the second round, with the winner going straight to the finals. Rockford and Milwaukee would meet in the second round, but the winner would then have to play Bloomington to earn the other spot in the finals.

The Detroit Base Ball Club's match with the Excelsiors was

tightly fought, with Chicago rallying with 7 runs in the bottom of the eighth inning to pull out a 16-10 win. *Detroit Advertiser and Tribune* reporter H. D. Griswold believed that Detroit was the superior team and attributed the loss to overconfidence.[17] Griswold claimed that the Detroit players had watched the Excelsiors' previous game and concluded that they would be easy to beat. Accordingly, Detroit agreed to everything the Excelsiors requested during the game's preliminaries, including an umpire who favored them.

Griswold further claimed that McNally, the Excelsior pitcher, illegally used the elaborate windup and overhand motion of a cricket bowler rather than pitching normally.[18] He criticized the Detroit hitters for not asking the umpire for a ruling on the delivery and for not showing any patience at the plate.[19] While they were swinging at McNally's high pitches and popping them up or hitting them foul into one of the temporary grocery stands, the Chicago players were waiting until they got a good pitch to hit.[20]

Griswold's commentary is very telling, because the conduct that he was condemning would once have been considered gentlemanly. The Detroiters' amicable consent to the Excelsiors' choice of an umpire was being construed as overconfidence instead of sportsmanship. Their adherence to the old-fashioned practice of swinging at what was offered was now denounced as impatience, while the Excelsiors' once-unsporting tactic of taking questionable pitches was earning praise. Obviously, a new standard of behavior in baseball was beginning to emerge.

While the batting of the Detroit Club drew criticism, the nine's fielding evoked much admiration. The method used by pitcher Henry Burroughs, catcher Frank J. Phelps, and first baseman John Clark to hold a base runner close was particularly impressive, and demonstrates that modern pick-off techniques were already being used:

Never was better work done by the pitcher, catcher, and baseman than by the Detroit nine in the match. In the sixth innings of the Excelsiors when McNally was on the first base . . . McNally endeavored to "steal," but he was so closely watched that he dared not move his length from the base. The ball would pass with the rapidity of a cannon shot from the hands of Burroughs to Phelps, who stood close to the batsman and received it firmly in his hands, and if McNally was off the base the ball would fly to Clark so quick that one would think it had actually bounded from Phelps' hands in that direction. Clark caught it with the same precision, and not merely caught it, but with the same motion brought it in contact with McNally. The latter soon learned not to leave his base further than his length, and as soon as he saw Burroughs or Phelps make the least motion towards the base, he would drop flat with his hands on it. This interesting scene was finally brought to a close by Burroughs getting the ball into Clark quicker than McNally could drop, and thus putting him out.[21]

Also noteworthy in this account is the positioning of catcher Frank Phelps close behind the batsman. Because catchers were not yet wearing protective equipment, this stratagem did not become common until ten years later.

The Cream City Club defeated Rockford but was defeated by Bloomington the following morning. The Bloomington Club was now scheduled to play the Excelsiors for the championship, but having just finished one game, its members pronounced themselves too tired and conceded the championship to the Excelsiors. Bloomington suggested that Chicago and Detroit play a friendly match, but the Excelsiors demurred. Like so many other baseball tournaments around this time, this one, which had begun with so much anticipation, ended with a whimper. The *Advertiser and Tribune* placed the blame on the "incomprehensible" method of pairing the clubs.[22]

While the tournament revealed a shift in emphasis from pageantry to competition, there were still indications that spectacle remained important. One later account of the tournament evoked memories of the raisin' games by claiming that "the true trophy was the keg, and everyone was a winner. In fact, there was so much beer that the police department and volunteer firemen had to be called to help finish the celebration, which they did without complaint."[23]

There were also individual contests of skill, in which Detroit players distinguished themselves. Ford Hinchman won the long-distance throwing contest with a throw of 299 feet, all three of his attempts surpassing the best throw by the second-place finisher. Charles Force overcame adversity to capture the title of fastest base runner. With the best time standing at 15¾ seconds, Force circled the bases in 15½ seconds. However, the time was disallowed because he had missed third base. After catching his breath, Force again posted a time of 15½ seconds, this time making certain to touch every base.

The Detroit players thus did not return home entirely empty-handed. However, hometown supporters had raised a sizable amount for a reception to welcome the club home as champions, and the individual prizes were little consolation. Disappointment increased when allegations surfaced that the umpire—H. G. Teed of the Laporte, Indiana, club—was actually a former member of the Excelsiors.[24] Thirty-seven years later, Detroit third baseman David Barry was still bitter that Teed had "robbed us of that game. . . . That old grudge rankles deeply in our hearts yet. He was supposed to be from Laporte, Ind., but in reality was a member of the Chicago club."[25]

Fortunately, the members of the Detroit Club soon had another challenge to take their minds off of the Rockford tournament. A group of citizens, eager to see a top-notch challenger play the Detroit Base Ball Club as part of the July 4 festivities, offered a one-hundred-dollar purse to be contested for by the Detroit Club and a "picked nine" (an all-star team) of the state's best players. This innovative idea captured the imagination of the state clubs, which were soon busily corresponding to select players. The final lineup consisted of Hooker DeLand, George Kassick, Stephen Welling, and Thomas Conely from the Central Club of Jackson; F. A. C. McManus and William Cocker from the University of Michigan nine in Ann Arbor; a player named Brock from Salem; John Powell from the Anchoras of Adrian; and Matt Sines from Denton's Mills.

An enthusiastic crowd of fifteen hundred turned out, but hopes of a hotly contested match were again disappointed. Detroit proved vastly superior, winning 45-12. The newspapers saw the result as evidence of the "difficulty of strangers working together."[26] The point was reinforced when the beaten picked nine called Frank Crittenden of Bay City "a cowardly poltroon" for agreeing to play in the match, only to back out at the last minute when he thought there would be no way to replace him.[27] But even the newspapers, which were increasingly depicting baseball as a test of character and teamwork, acknowledged that a difference in skill was also a major factor in the lopsided score.

After this blowout, the Detroit Club found that no state club was willing to play them, even when offered five outs to three. Finally the Detroit Base Ball Club challenged the up-and-coming Ann Arbor Club, traveling to Ann Arbor on September 14 and posting an easy 65-22 victory. The Ann Arbor players were at pains to point out that they had no pretensions to the state championship and that they had merely played to help the Detroit Club keep in practice. The local paper commended the Ann Arbor boys for their pluck in agreeing to play the Detroit juggernaut.[28]

The Detroit Club continued to pursue a rematch with the club that had beaten them at the tournament in Rockford. The *Advertiser and Tribune* carried frequent excerpts from the often heated correspondence. The exchange illuminates the difficulties of translating the intense interest in baseball into a competitive format that was both fair and affordable—a problem that would haunt Michigan baseball for years to come.

The Detroiters wrote and challenged the Excelsiors to a home-and-home match to determine supremacy. The Excelsiors responded that they had already beaten the Detroit Base Ball Club once and saw no reason why two more matches were necessary, but offered to play one game in Chicago. They pointed out that they were amateurs and could not be expected to travel to play every club that challenged them. The Detroiters replied that the match in Rockford could hardly count as a home match for Detroit and began implying that the Excelsiors were afraid to meet them.

The correspondence degenerated into ad hominem attacks and sniping in the newspapers, but it is important to note that both sides had valid points.[29] The Detroit Club could hardly be blamed for wanting a chance at revenge and the opportunity to finally offer its supporters a first-rate game at its enclosed ballpark. Equally unassailable was Chicago's contention that it was unfair to expect an amateur club to travel to play its challengers. Detroit finally responded with an offer to cover all expenses incurred by the Excelsiors and by an umpire from New York, but even this generous proposition was only a partial solution. With Sunday still a day of rest and transportation still primitive, road games meant missed days of work.

After it became evident that no match with Chicago could be arranged, Detroit visited the Forest City Club of Cleveland and won 36-18 in six innings. While the ease of the win might have proved disappointing in Detroit, the Cleveland spectators enthusiastically applauded the play of the visitors. The Cleveland papers wrote that the local club was lucky to have had the chance to play with so experienced a team. The *Leader* described the Detroit Base Ball Club as "confessedly the best club in the West . . . and one whose members by long practice under a most excellent drill master have become almost perfect." The *Herald* praised the Detroiters for their judgment, confidence, knowledge, ability, and even their prudence in not making "any more steps than were strictly necessary, thereby husbanding their strength throughout the game."[30]

This brought the Detroit Base Ball Club's season to a close. Its hold on the state championship had gone virtually unchallenged, and the club had narrowly missed becoming the champions of the Northwest, yet its success was tinged with disappointment. The competitive imbalance of 1865 had now widened to such an extent that there was no meaningful competition for the Detroit Club in the state of Michigan, and sustaining such a club by means of interstate rivalries was not yet practical. The club's enclosed field served as an ironic reminder that nobody would pay to see it play unless it had a worthy rival.

In December, the second annual meeting of the Northwestern Base Ball Association took place in Chicago. The number of member clubs had more than doubled, from fourteen to thirty-two, and Detroit's Jonathan Van Norman was elected president. However, there were obvious indications that all was not well. There was considerable resentment of the Eastern bias of the NABBP, the most heatedly debated issue being whether the Northwestern Base Ball Association should disband in favor of state associations. While this resolution was narrowly defeated, that there was a vote at all made it clear that such governing bodies were losing their ability to control the rapidly changing game.[31]

NOTES

1. Many histories of early baseball try to pinpoint the first "Ladies' Day." However, since women were invariably exempt from paying admission to early games, this is a meaningless distinction. The *Detroit Evening News* of August 28, 1875, for example, noted that the free list was suspended, with the "exception of ladies, who are always free." The practice of admitting women free was adopted because it was believed that women ensured better behavior from the male spectators.

2. *Detroit Advertiser and Tribune*, May 25, 1866.

3. *Adrian Weekly Times*, July 13, 1866.

4. *Detroit Advertiser and Tribune*, August 9, 1866.

5. *Detroit Advertiser and Tribune*, August 11, 1866.

6. *Detroit Advertiser and Tribune*, August 21, 1866.

7. *Detroit Post*, August 22, 1866.

8. *Detroit Post*, September 28, 1866.

9. *Detroit Advertiser and Tribune*, June 21, 1866.

10. The *Detroit Advertiser and Tribune* claimed on July 2, 1866, that the inscription read "out at the little end." However, a resolution by the Pecatonica Club (whose members should have known, since they "won" the horn), printed in the *Chicago Tribune* on July 31, 1867, gives the inscription as "practice."

11. Michael Benson, *Ballparks of North America*, 343.

12. Quoted in Benson, *Ballparks of North America*, 343.

13. Reprinted in the *Detroit Advertiser and Tribune*, June 28, 1866.

14. Quoted in Benson, *Ballparks of North America*, 343.

15. Reprinted in the *Detroit Post and Tribune*, October 12, 1878.

16. Finley Peter Dunne was a former sportswriter who became a popular syndicated columnist; this piece appeared in the *Detroit Free Press* on March 8, 1914.

17. Griswold's articles were not signed, but he was identified by an article in the *Detroit News-Tribune* on March 15, 1903. Griswold must have left Detroit shortly thereafter, as the article states that "the oldest newspaper men in the city have no recollection of him."

18. This claim was also made by Detroit third baseman David Barry, who recalled for the *Detroit News-Tribune*, in an interview published on March 15, 1903, that the umpire

"allowed the Chicago pitcher to 'bowl'—that is, the pitcher would use a slight overhand motion in delivering the ball. Of course, everyone knows how we had to deliver the ball underhand in those times, and the advantage that their pitcher had over us was enough to win the game."

19. Players customarily requested the umpire to rule by calling out "judgment."

20. *Detroit Advertiser and Tribune*, July 3, 1866.

21. *Detroit Advertiser and Tribune*, July 3, 1866. The term "innings" was borrowed from cricket and was commonly used at this time to denote a single inning.

22. *Detroit Advertiser and Tribune*, July 3, 1866.

23. Quoted in Benson, *Ballparks of North America*, 343.

24. *Detroit Post*, October 10, 1866.

25. *Detroit News-Tribune*, March 15, 1903.

26. *Detroit Advertiser and Tribune*, July 6, 1866.

27. *Jackson Daily Citizen*, July 6, 1866.

28. *Ann Arbor Peninsular Courier and Family Visitant*, September 13, 1866.

29. *Detroit Advertiser and Tribune*, September 29, October 10, and October 16, 1866.

30. Both the *Leader* and the *Herald* quotations were reprinted in the *Detroit Advertiser and Tribune*, October 19, 1866.

31. *Detroit Advertiser and Tribune*, December 21, 1866.

10

"A PERFECT FRENZY OF BALL-PLAYING"

THE GEOGRAPHIC EXPANSION OF THE GAME IN 1866

In 1865 and 1866 a perfect frenzy of ball-playing swept over the United States. Old and young took part or interest in the game. Every village and hamlet boasted its nine, and in the cities the list of clubs rivalled the Homeric catalogue of the ships. The game as played then had a breezy range and flavor. The ball, charged to its full with rubber, bounded among the fielders with the ricochet of a cannon ball. One country nine, famous for prowess in hitting, had its bats made of huge square pickets "whittled" down at one end. Another team bore vast round beams of bass-wood as large as a man's thigh, bored out and charged with cork to make them light. The lookers-on invariably constituted themselves a sort of high court of appeal without any legal delicacies of language. Occasionally, in more exciting contests, a stone or brickbat projected from the crowd emphasized its opinions, and sometimes it seemed as though the umpire would have to qualify for a mediaeval suit of armor to hold his place. As for the nines, an epigrammatic phrase by which I once heard a player describe his team, may suffice. Said he: "Our nine can't bat much, or throw much, or catch much; but they're first-rate talkers."

—NEW YORK EVENING POST, 1883

While the 1866 season saw a decline in competition for the state championship, in every other respect baseball activity in Michigan increased dramatically. New clubs sprang up in small towns all over the southern half of the Lower Peninsula, and new rivalries quickly developed. In no time, there were reports that "almost every wide-awake town in the State boasts one or two clubs."[1]

In addition to the clubs mentioned later, the Excelsior Club of Dentonville squared off against the Wolverine Club of Wayne; the Eagle Club of Fowler's Corners met the Superior Club of Russell's Corners; clubs representing Lyons and Saranac crossed bats; the National Club of Adrian played the Atlantic Club of Marshall; the Plymouth Club matched up against the Union Club of Wayne; the Peninsular Club of Battle Creek did battle with the Battle Creek City Club; and the Maseppa Club of Lansing faced the Academy

Among the many clubs formed as part of the postwar boom were the Wahoos of Dexter. *Back row, left to right:* W. Irving Keal, right field; George Hostler, catcher; Ed K. Appleton, third base; George Smith, second base; Byron C. Tyler, first base; George Presley, center field; Eugene Beal, shortstop; Henry Ewing, pitcher; and Ed Haigh, left field. *Courtesy of the Bentley Historical Library, University of Michigan*

Club of the Lansing Academy. Other new clubs included the Schoolcraft Club, the Cliquer Club of Vienna, and the Maple Valley Club of Ovid. If not quite rivaling Homer's catalog of ships, the list was still an impressive one. For all the activity in 1865, there had been only 16 documented clubs in the state. That number ballooned to 102 in 1866, with fifty-nine different cities represented.

The game's rapid spread eliminated the need for elaborate justifications of men spending time playing a boy's game. The *Tecumseh Herald* announced the formation of that town's first baseball club by reasoning that "our young men are determined to be up with the times. Amusements of some kind are necessary to complete development of man's physical and intellectual nature, and hence all innocent amusements should be encouraged.—Among such we class a Bass [*sic*] Ball Club."[2] This is not a particularly compelling argument, but no one really needed convincing anymore, and most newspapers stuck to reporting the activities of the new clubs. Carefully reasoned arguments were replaced by pragmatic ones, a St. Clair paper arguing vaguely that "amusements and social gatherings must and will exist, if not healthful and manly, then some other, perhaps, of a pernicious character and tendency is liable to be substituted. As we must have amusements let us endeavor to have them of the most befitting character."[3]

As it had in Grand Rapids in 1860, the speed with which the game spread now prompted comparisons to a "mania" or "contagion." While very apt, this baseball-fever metaphor was an ambiguous one, particularly since the country was threatened by a cholera epidemic in the spring of 1866. Just as important, a fever usually didn't last very long. In the years to come, the negative connotations of the metaphor would often be pointed out, but they were not yet attracting attention.

Regulation baseball was primarily introduced to new areas by games between neighboring towns. In Saginaw, a baseball club was organized by boys "ambitious of imitating the doings of other towns."[4] The members of a new club in Okemos invited the Capital Club of Lansing "to play a friendly game with them for the purpose of instructing them in the rules and regulations of the game."[5] Members of the White Pigeon Club attended a meeting in Constantine to assist with the formation of that town's first baseball club.[6] The Wolverines of Wayne played a friendly game against the Detroit Base Ball Club, not expecting to win but hoping to "learn some of the 'points of the game.'"[7]

The rapidly expanding railroad system made it easier to develop the friendly but heatedly contested rivalries between neighboring towns that were becoming the basis of competitive baseball in Michigan. When the Three Rivers Club played in Schoolcraft, an extra train was run to accommodate the many friends wishing to travel with the players.[8] Spectators who accompanied a club added to the perception of games as events that could improve commerce and other mutually beneficial relationships between two towns.

Just as settlers from New York had helped introduce the game to Michigan, urbanites settling in rural areas enhanced its further dispersal across the state. For example, Henry Field, who had pitched for the Early Risers in the state's first regulation match back in 1859, completed his medical studies and began a practice in Paw Paw. There Dr. Field helped establish that area's first club, the Lafayette Base Ball Club of Paw Paw, in 1866.

Boarding schools and universities also contributed significantly to the spread of baseball, as students learned the game and then brought it home with them. In Kalamazoo, a rivalry developed between the Burr Oak Club of the Union School and the Gymnastic Club of Kalamazoo College. In Ypsilanti, nines from the State Normal School (now Eastern Michigan University) and the Union Seminary squared off. A club formed at Detroit High School played several games against other local clubs. A nine called the College Pills was organized at Hillsdale College. At the Michigan Agricultural College in Lansing (now Michigan State University), a club was formed that included both students and faculty members. The students didn't always appreciate having their professors as teammates; one student later remembered that "[Alfred N.] Prentiss, Professor of Botany, often played with us, but was so awkward that

most of us preferred that he should play on the side of our opponents."9

As has been suggested, the newspapers also played a major role
in the growth of the game. This created a potential conflict of interest, as the papers not only reported the games but could profit if the
local club galvanized the community and helped sell papers. This
was particularly evident in Ionia, where the second issue of the new
Ionia County Sentinel announced that a meeting would be held in the
newspaper's office to organize a baseball club.10

The new club was named the Custers in honor of Michigan's
Civil War hero, and membership filled so quickly that a second
club, the Ionias, was formed. The Custers procured uniforms of
blue shirts, red caps, and black pants and busied themselves both on
and off the field. Virtually every issue of the *Sentinel* that summer
chronicled the club's doings—not surprisingly, since editor J. C.
Taylor was the club's third baseman.

The fledgling journal's enthusiasm for baseball paid off, as the
community soon had baseball "on the brain."11 The club's secretary
wrote "for information in regard to certain disputed points" of the
rules.12 When a group of boys aged sixteen to eighteen formed a
club, the *Sentinel* remarked that this would be "more beneficial than
loafing on the street corners or around saloons."13 Baseball's potential to create a sense of belonging that involved an entire community
was shown by the Custer Club's forty honorary members, including
five clergymen and George Custer himself.

National publications about baseball also helped to spread the
game. *Beadle's Dime Base Ball Player*, a guide written by Henry
Chadwick, offered step-by-step directions for forming a baseball
club. The City Base Ball Club of Marshall followed Chadwick's
instructions exactly and formed the first club in Marshall since
1861.14

It bears repeating that for all the methods of spreading baseball
in Michigan that can be documented, there are no accounts of the
one method that is sometimes claimed to have been the most important. There are no references to be found to a Michigan community

discovering baseball because a soldier returning home from the war brought the new game with him.

While most baseball activity was in the southern part of the state, outbreaks of baseball fever occurred as far north as the Upper Peninsula. In early May, a club was formed in Marquette that included nearly all the young men of the town. The club met daily in the public square, exhibiting a "keen relish" for baseball that had been nurtured by the "compulsory abstinence" from exercise over the "long and severe winter."[15]

This tremendous upswing in the game's popularity meant that baseball was being played by a whole new class of Americans. Clerks and artisans were now among the game's most avid participants, and baseball was beginning to be viewed as competing with work. If baseball were detached from the gentlemanly customs that had nurtured it, what would become of the feverish emotions it produced? What would happen if it were played by people who were more interested in winning the game than in partaking in a social ritual? The answers to these questions were starting to emerge.

In the hotbeds of baseball—the greater New York City area, Philadelphia, and Washington, D.C.—the desire to win was manifesting itself in a variety of ways, with money featuring prominently in most of these. An increasing number of players for the top clubs were receiving compensation for playing baseball. This in turn led to the practice of "revolving"—players jumping from club to club whenever a more lucrative offer was forthcoming. And the friendly wagering on games began to attract serious gamblers, who had their own sections at some New York ballparks. Inevitably, baseball's first game-fixing scandal occurred in 1865, involving the Mutuals of New York, who had close ties to Tammany Hall.[16] Similar scandals would plague the game for years to come.

However, such serious abuses had not yet reached Michigan, where most of the matches played in 1866 exhibited a high level of sportsmanship. At a match between the Bawbeese Club of Hillsdale and the Wolverine Club of Hudson, for example, "the best of good feeling prevailed."[17] When the Custer Club of Ionia hosted the

Monitor Club of St. Johns, the "utmost good feeling prevailed during the game, both clubs being composed of gentlemanly fellows."[18] The Stars of Niles were "regaled" by their hosts with oysters and peaches and cream after a game in St. Joseph.[19]

After the Battle Creek Club traveled to Marshall, the grateful visitors noted that "where the Marshall Club failed in making tallies, they more than made up in the reception and hospitable manner in which they treated the Battle Creek Club."[20] The Marshall players "allowed no thought of defeat to embitter the hospitalities" that followed the game.[21] After a match between Schoolcraft and Three Rivers, "the members of the winning club proposed three cheers for their visitors, which were heartily given. A bountiful supper closed the festivities of the day."[22]

Following a 52–52 tie between the Wolverines of Wayne and the Wahoos of Dexter, "the Dexter boys were handsomely entertained by the Wolverines and went home in the best of spirits."[23] A match between the Pinckney Club and the Wahoo Club of Dexter on July 23 concluded with umpire F. A. C. McManus of the University Club being "loudly cheered by both clubs for his promptness and justice."[24] The *Detroit Advertiser and Tribune* observed that at a match between Hudson and Hillsdale, "it is a noticeable fact that not a vulgar or profane word was heard from either party. It is safe to say these clubs are composed of *gentlemen* in the strict sense of the word."[25]

That the absence of cursing was worthy of comment suggests that new forces were entering Michigan baseball. Whereas before the war it was pro forma to note that good feelings had prevailed during a game, this was now pertinent information, since the opposite was sometimes true.

NOTES

1. *Hudson Gazette*, July 28, 1866.
2. *Tecumseh Herald*, June 14, 1866.
3. *St. Clair Republican*, July 3, 1866.
4. *Saginaw Weekly Enterprise*, June 7, 1866.
5. *Detroit Advertiser and Tribune*, August 11, 1866.

6. *Constantine Weekly Mercury and St. Joseph County Advertiser,* August 9, 1866.

7. *Detroit Post,* September 10, 1866.

8. *Detroit Advertiser and Tribune,* September 19, 1866.

9. *M.A.C. Record* 21, no. 32 (May 23, 1916).

10. *Ionia County Sentinel,* May 8, 1866.

11. *Ionia County Sentinel,* July 24, 1866.

12. *Ionia County Sentinel,* July 3, 1866.

13. *Ionia County Sentinel,* July 24, 1866.

14. *Marshall Statesman,* July 18, 1866.

15. *Detroit Advertiser and Tribune,* May 7, 1866. The club's name was not given, but it was likely the Superior Club, which two years later was described as the "oldest organization" in the Upper Peninsula (*Lake Superior Mining Journal* (Marquette), September 26, 1868).

16. David Q. Voigt, *American Baseball,* 18.

17. *Detroit Advertiser and Tribune,* August 15, 1866.

18. *Detroit Advertiser and Tribune,* August 24, 1866.

19. *Niles Weekly Times* September 27, 1866.

20. *Detroit Advertiser and Tribune,* August 28, 1866.

21. *Marshall Statesman,* August 29, 1866.

22. *Detroit Advertiser and Tribune,* September 19, 1866.

23. *Detroit Post,* August 21, 1866.

24. *Detroit Advertiser and Tribune,* July 23, 1866.

25. *Detroit Advertiser and Tribune,* July 27, 1866.

11

"Too Much Talking on Both Sides"

Growing Pains

All the rapid growth brought with it reports of growing pains from all over Michigan. While many of the incidents might appear minor to modern readers, for a game that had gained support by aligning itself with gentlemanly conduct, they held significance.

For example, in South Bend, Indiana, the Rough and Ready Club issued a challenge to any under-twenty club to play for the championship of junior clubs of Indiana and Michigan. The Star Club of Niles accepted the challenge and won the game 71-41 on August 2. After the game, foot races and a ball-throwing contest added to the festive atmosphere. However, the *Niles Republican* lectured the players that "both clubs should improve upon . . . the language used while playing. If ball players wish to have lady spectators they must treat them with respect."[1]

And controversy flared between the Wolverine Club of Hudson and the Bawbeese Club of Hillsdale when Hillsdale claimed to have won their match two games to one, while Hudson contended that one of the games was a friendly one between the Bawbeese first nine and its second nine. Hillsdale also alleged that some of the Hudson players were imports from other towns but withdrew the claim when the Wolverines' president, whom the Hillsdale club acknowledged to be "a gentleman of truth and veracity," stated that all the club's players were locals.[2] Unfortunately, the principals in such disputes were rarely willing to make such concessions.

A series between the Three Rivers Base Ball Club and the Wolverines of White Pigeon led to Three Rivers accusing the Wolverines of being "slippery."[3] According to Three Rivers, after the White Pigeon club won the first game of the best-of-three series, it demanded the ball that was to go to the first club to win two games. Then the Wolverines, in the Three Rivers version, insisted that the second game also be played in White Pigeon, contrary to the prearranged conditions of the match. The Wolverines countered by claiming that, as winners of the first game, they should hold the ball until defeat. The squabbling was all the more unfortunate as two trainloads of spectators from Three Rivers had accompanied the club and the entire town of White Pigeon had turned out for the game. Seeing a day that could have brought the two towns closer together degenerate into ill will over a mere baseball game must have disgusted cooler heads.[4]

Further east, after losing to the Ann Arbor Club 43-29 on August 14, the Hercules Club of Howell cried foul. It claimed that Ann Arbor had gained an unfair advantage by using a substitute pitcher in midgame. (The rules permitted substitutions only in the event of serious injury.) Additionally, members of the Hercules Club alleged that the Ann Arbor players had taunted them with "jeers, epithets and hard names." The Howell men asserted that citizens of Dexter and Pinckney and even some Ann Arbor residents who had attended the game would vouch for their claims. Indeed, these spectators, they continued, had been so disgusted by the Ann Arbor Club's behavior that they hosted the Howell players for supper afterward to apologize.[5]

These charges brought an immediate response from the president of the Ann Arbor Base Ball Club, William V. Richards, who termed the Howell story a "low, scurrilous, whimpering account." Richards countercharged that Howell had insisted on playing by the old bound rule, although it had been abolished nearly two years earlier. Ann Arbor had finally consented to play a bound game only because the Howell players vowed that they would get back in their wagon and go home rather than play a "fly game." He argued that the player who had been removed had received a terrible blow in the leg earlier in the game and was replaced when he could no longer play.

Richards also strongly disputed the claim that neutral parties had sided with Howell and challenged Howell to give their names. He conceded that there had been "too much talking on both sides" but claimed that

> the first ungentlemanly remark that was made on the game was made by a prominent member of their club, on being told by the umpire that he must not get on the third base with his men and run in with them, thus hindering the play of their opponents, which latter they attempted to do throughout the game. We can say, what they cannot, that the ungentlemanly remark of our man, made in the heat and excitement of running bases, was expiated by a quick and ready apology, which was accepted. How manly it is to refer to such things, after accepting an apology, we leave the readers to say.

Richards closed by alluding caustically to the childishness of the bound game: "It recalls the old adage 'Remind a child of his misfortune and he will be sure to cry.' Better luck next time, 'Howell boys!' Remember when you meet men you should be men."[6] Not surprisingly, no rematch was forthcoming, though supporters of both clubs offered to wager fifty dollars or more on the outcome.

A match between the Continentals of Kalamazoo and the Central Club of Jackson in mid-July elicited a similar barrage of allegations about umpire Howard H. Gridley of Jackson. The Kalamazoo club charged that the Jackson players had deliberately taken good pitches while batting so that the base runners could steal bases and that Gridley had aided this unfair tactic by neglecting to call balls and strikes. It also alleged that Gridley had taken the word of a Jackson player when he hadn't seen the play. The *Jackson Citizen* responded by pointing out that the Continentals had selected Gridley to umpire, that the Kalamazoo player himself had acknowledged the justice of one disputed call, and that the Continentals had not questioned other rulings at the time.

The Continentals countered by mocking the latter argument: "The Jackson *Citizen* thinks the decisions were just simply because the Kalamazoo players did not get angry, dispute the umpire's decisions to his face, and end the game in a general row. The *Citizen*'s opinion of gentlemanly conduct on a ball field seems to differ from that opinion held by the Continentals."[7] The *Citizen* replied: "This perpetual harping about a victory gained simply by superior playing, will be frowned upon by all lovers of the game. It certainly shows bad taste, to say the least, to exhibit such chafings under defeat, and we would recommend our disappointed friends to practice the golden rule."[8]

Such bickering was especially unseemly because the two cities' fire departments had just pledged to cooperate in fighting the fires that could devastate nineteenth-century cities. Ironically, the slogan the two fire departments had agreed on was, "Jackson and Kalamazoo—Near enough to be friends—too far apart to be rivals."[9] Several incidents on the baseball field in the ensuing years would disprove the latter part of the slogan.

Adrian also experienced difficulties with the Central Club. After the Anchoras' close win, they expressed disgust that a "scribbler" in the *Jackson Citizen* had "tried to gloss over a fair defeat by abuse of their opponents, our city and the ladies present as spectators at the game."[10] Obviously, it was easier to adhere to the golden rule after a victory than after a defeat.

Such squabbles also demonstrated the problematic nature of the correspondent system initiated by the *Advertiser and Tribune* and now being imitated by other papers. Whereas earlier newspapers had been able to show discretion and decline to print unseemly bickering, once a correspondent from one town began a dispute, the matter inevitably snowballed. The editors would then feel obliged to let the other town respond, and neither side would be happy until it had gotten the last word. Molehills were frequently turned into mountains in this way.

An extreme example came after an August match between the Tiger Club of Lapeer and the Flint Base Ball Club. An earlier match in Flint had passed off very pleasantly, in spite of the hosts' lopsided 98-37 win. Both clubs had exhibited "gentlemanly deportment and friendly intercourse during the progress of the game," and afterward, the Lapeer club had been "entertained in a handsome manner by the Flint club" at a newly opened restaurant on Union Street.[11]

The rematch saw a surprising victory by the Lapeer club, but the *Advertiser and Tribune*'s Lapeer correspondent reported instead that "quite a large number of loafers and rowdies came over from Flint with the ball players, got drunk and acted in the most disgraceful manner, leaving with all their bills charged to the Tigers. Time will show whether they will pay such rowdy bills or not. If they do, it will probably break up the Lapeer Club, as the best man of the club will not sanction any such course."[12] Both clubs denounced the account as a vile slander, and the Tiger Club vowed to expel the correspondent when his identity became known.[13]

Many of these wrangles can be attributed to the growing pains of a sport whose rules and structures were slow to adapt to its rapid growth. But to many of the players from the prewar days, the unpleasantness was a sign of the "lack of that honorable spirit that can bear defeat without a loss of temper, as well as carry off victory without boasting." Understandably, many of the leading citizens who had lent respectability to baseball before the war now began to drift out of the game, devoting their attentions to their business and civic activities and to less contentious forms of recreation. Their defection further accentuated the game's association with nostalgia for an irretrievable past.

Even with tensions mounting, most new clubs were still looked on indulgently. The minimal expectations imposed on fledgling clubs had aided the beginning of the postwar boom, and they continued to foster its growth in 1866. The now-veteran Owosso Club beat the newly formed Monitors of St. Johns 18-9, with a St. Johns newspaper attributing the loss to Owosso's "more experienced players" and "better knowledge of the rules of the game."[14] An Albion loss was greeted with the commendation that "the Albion boys play well for new beginners."[15] And after Plymouth was beaten 103-73 by the Unions of Wayne, an account noted that "the Plymouth club did some fine batting, and with practice will make good players."[16]

Coldwater's first club was formed in May, and after the club's match on October 16, the local paper was similarly indulgent: "It is but fair to state that the Coldwater Club is a new one, while the Burr Oak Club is one of a year or more standing, and all things considered, our boys made a much better showing than could reasonably have been expected under the circumstances."[17] When the Spear Club of Niles lost to the Continentals of Kalamazoo, the result was credited to the Continentals' "discipline and drill, the different players yielding implicit obedience to every suggestion of their captain," while Niles's loss was attributed "not to want of skill, but to a lack of practice."[18]

After the Wolverines of Hudson were trounced in their first match, they were assured that "all that is necessary to make the Wolverines a 'crack' club is for the members to keep up the interest."[19] Another one-sided loss was described as "a blessing in disguise—a Bull Run, to stimulate them on to greater efforts and skill."[20] The almost universal belief that skill was the result of practice rather than innate ability created a patient, nurturing atmosphere for new clubs.[21] One newspaper even described an 89-40 game as "closely contested."[22]

Such patience, however, was not unlimited. In time, clubs found out the hard way that a lack of speed, strength, and athleticism could not always be overcome by practice. When this happened, clubs often plunged rapidly from the "patience of hope" to the state newspapers usually described as discouragement or demoralization. For example, when the Spear Club of Niles surrendered 26 runs to Dowagiac in an inning, this "seemed to discourage the Spears, at whose request the game was called at the close of seven even innings."[23] As baseball historian Robert Smith wryly observes, demoralization was "a state that the amateur-professional teams of that era seemed especially susceptible to."[24]

This demoralization put increased stress on the club structure, as players relegated to the second and third nines of a club began to feel slighted. After a Three Rivers club picked a first nine, the players who had not been chosen challenged the first nine to a match and beat them.[25] After the Wolverines of Hudson's third match produced a worse defeat than the first two, the local paper suggested that the club needed "a partial change of men and more practice."[26] Such developments were serious threats to the sense of belonging that clubs were supposed to create.

Another increasingly common manifestation of growing pains was the accusation that ringers had been inserted into a lineup. The *Niles Republican* complained after the Spears' loss to the Continentals that "there was one thing we did not like to see. The 'Continentals' . . . sent to Ypsilanti for Mr. Wheeler, to Augusta for Mr. McCord . . . and sent to Wayland for Mr. White. . . . [I]f the Niles boys had been allowed to drop three of their poorest players and send to Dowagiac or some other place, the result might have been different."[27] The Wolverines of Hudson discovered prior to a match with the Junior Club of Adrian that some of their opponents were actually members of other clubs and complained that they did not "feel competent to play the whole State without a special understanding to that effect."[28]

Youth games were particularly vulnerable to such manipulation. The Lansing correspondent to the *Advertiser and Tribune* stated that his town's club of "little boys" had found their counterparts from Mason to be a little "long between the joints."[29] The juvenile Stars of Hudson groused after a loss to the Young Americas of Hillsdale that "some of the *Young* Americas were rather large for their age."[30]

The role of money was also becoming evident. When the Stars of Monroe met the Quicksteps of Toledo, "several heavy and numberless minor bets were made upon the result of the game."[31] A ten-cent admission was charged to men (but not to women) attending a match on August 25 between the Athletic Club of Detroit and the Peninsular Club of Ypsilanti. While Michigan had no professional players, with the possible exception of Henry Burroughs and John Clark, some were beginning to view the game as more than a hobby.

The close connection between baseball and the newspapers was again emphasized by an advertisement in the *Kalamazoo Telegraph:* "WANTED—By a base ball pitcher, a 'sit' as a compositor on a weekly paper."[32] The *Telegraph* recommended him both as a ballplayer and as a baseball reporter, calling him "a young gentleman thoroughly conversant in all the mysteries of 'The Art.'" It seems reasonable to infer that he viewed his playing ability as a marketable commodity.

The same newspaper's complaint about the public's lack of support for the Continentals the following month was much more explicit:

> The ball-players of this place have never received assistance or encouragement from the citizens, in the way of defraying expenses on match days or providing them a uniform, as almost every town is doing or has done. On the contrary, the citizens seem so much opposed to the necessary physical exercise that the players receive more curses than blessings, and on leaving town to take part in a match, receive the encouraging assurance "that they will get cleaned out this *time* for certain."[33]

The days of playing for ham and eggs were gone forever!

Money was even a factor in the ball games played as part of Independence Day celebrations. As noted earlier, the Detroit Club played against a picked nine in 1866 for the considerable sum of $100. To the southwest, the Lafayette Base Ball Club of Paw Paw and the Decatur Club were scheduled to meet in Lawrence and compete for a purse of $10. Upon arriving at the Lawrence Driving Park, however, the players discovered that they were expected to pay a twenty-five-cent admission fee. Both clubs indignantly refused to pay, arguing that more people were there to see the baseball game than the horse races (for which premiums totaled $370). Eventually they were admitted for free. After the Lafayette Club won the game, it headed to Dowagiac, where, in front of another large crowd on the fairgrounds, Dowagiac defeated the Spear Club of Niles 57-27 to win a purse of $20. The Lafayettes and the Cassopolis Club then concluded the day's activities by playing a short match, which the Lafayettes won.

The establishment of baseball as a staple of Independence Day was a most significant development. It helped solidify the game's status as the national pastime and enabled it to survive after initial enthusiasm had subsided. In many succeeding seasons, interest in baseball would be on the wane in a community until a traditional game on July 4 helped spark a revival.

Indeed, even while baseball was encountering significant growing pains, it was forging the alliances that would help it endure tough times. The *Clinton Republican* explained the important benefits the game was already deriving from its link with nationalism: "The game of base ball, which has assumed the dignity of a national game throughout the country, has made especial progress not only in this village but in the entire State. In fact everywhere it is a decided institution, and we may safely say a beneficial one, as, apart from the muscular exercise necessary to the game, it tends to keep young men away from places where far more objectionable sports are indulged in."[34]

Another indication that the game was becoming an institution was the emergence of routines. A calendar was developing that accommodated Michigan's still largely rural population—baseball season began in spring with the planting and climaxed with tournaments in September after the harvest had ended. Sports historian Allen Guttmann emphasizes the importance of such patterns, arguing that part of baseball's appeal is derived from the way the game evokes the changing seasons and speculating on a relationship between the four bases and the four seasons.[35] Modern baseball remains, in both obvious and subtle ways, a game obsessed with routines.

Michigan's baseball calendar became more firmly established in the autumn of 1866 as a result of several tournaments that attempted to capitalize on the fever for baseball. Unfortunately, planning was often characterized more by enthusiasm than by forethought. In this respect, a tournament in Pokagon in September merits a special place in Michigan baseball history. A baseball club called the Comets had been formed in Pokagon earlier that season, and the citizens had taken a great interest in its exploits. To give the players the opportunity to face first-class competition, one hundred dollars was raised for prizes and a tournament open to clubs in Michigan and Indiana was announced. Fifty dollars of the prize fund would go to the best club, twenty to the second-place finisher, and thirty to the best club formed that season. Ten clubs made plans to attend.

The first day of the tournament was cancelled due to steady rain, an omen of things to come. Dark clouds the next morning prompted talk of abandoning the entire tournament, but eventually the sun came out. However, the threatening weather had kept five clubs away, leaving the Dowagiac Club; the Cassopolis Club; the junior Stars of Niles; the Diamond Club of Mishawaka, Indiana; and the home club.

That afternoon the Stars of Niles beat the Indiana club 26-15, and the Cassopolis Club defeated the Comets of Pokagon 55-24. The next morning the two winners from the previous day squared off, and Cassopolis emerged victorious, 37-27. This left Cassopolis with two wins, but Dowagiac had still not played. With time for only one more game before dark, the tournament committee announced that Dowagiac would play . . . Pokagon! Dowagiac won 55-20 in a game called early on account of darkness.

The Cassopolis players, who earlier in the year had lost decisively to Dowagiac, sportingly conceded the title to that club. The committee announced the prizes: first prize and fifty dollars to Dowagiac; the award for best new club and thirty dollars to Cassopolis; and, to the amazement of everyone, second prize and

twenty dollars to Pokagon, although the Comets had been soundly
defeated in both their games. The *Detroit Advertiser and Tribune*
tactfully noted that the tournament "can hardly be termed a success."[36] The *Post* more bluntly characterized it as a "muffin game, in
a muffin town, with a muffin set of players."[37] Nevertheless, the
organizing committee blithely announced plans for another tournament in 1867.[38]

Tournament organizers were beginning to discover that even
an impeccably run event elicited complaints from the losers. The
Spear Club of Niles, which earlier in the year had been content to
attribute losses to want of practice, was beaten in the championship
game in a tournament in South Bend, Indiana, and pronounced it "a
cheat and a swindle."[39] However, their complaint that the game had
been called in the eighth inning due to darkness, with the LaPorte,
Indiana, club leading 31-29, had no merit.[40]

A much more successful tournament took place in Lansing in mid-
September during a fair sponsored by the Central Michigan Agricultural Society. On the first day, the Monitor Club of St. Johns defeated
the Farmers of Okemos 54-12, while the Capital Club of Lansing beat
the Star Club of the Agricultural College 65-48. The next day the
Monitors of St. Johns defeated the Capital Club 43-42 to win the cov-
eted prize—a solid silver goblet with a gold lining; an engraving of a
ball, two bats, and a medallion; and the inscription, "The Champion
Prize of the Central Michigan Base Ball Association."

Several individual prizes were also awarded. Rush J. Holmes of
the Capital Club was selected as best batter; C. H. Watrous of the
Star Club won the base-running contest with a time of sixteen seconds; and Henry H. Turner of the Farmers had the longest throw,
of 271 feet. A meeting was also held to form a permanent Central
Michigan Base Ball Association, with Stephen D. Bingham elected
president. The association drafted a sixteen-article constitution that
was published as a supplement to the *Lansing State Republican*.[41]
After the tournament ended, the Capital Club challenged the Monitors to an October 17 rematch, but St. Johns prevailed 61-47 on the
public square in St. Johns and retained the trophy.[42]

At this time, the relationship between baseball players and the press was already starting to change. Instead of writing to the newspapers to request space, players were beginning to take the coverage for granted or even try to avoid it. The *Detroit Advertiser and Tribune* wrote sarcastically: "On Saturday we presume a base ball match was played in this city between the Athletics and the second nine of the Detroit Club. Notwithstanding explicit promises from four members of the Detroiters that the score should be handed in, it has not yet reached us. We therefore conclude that the Detroit nine was badly beaten—probably did not make a run. Such a victory for the Athletics, which is a juvenile club, is most creditable to their skill, and we congratulate them upon their success."[43]

In the ensuing years, players started to view good publicity as an entitlement. This was evident across the country, not just in Michigan. Jimmy Wood of the White Stockings told a *Chicago Tribune* reporter in 1875 that "there are thousands of people who buy the papers simply for the reports of the games . . . who would not otherwise think of looking at a newspaper."[44] But when a club lost, it preferred no coverage. The *Jonesville Independent* reported after an 1875 game, "We made inquiries as to the result and received this intelligence: Aughhellwedontwantanypuffonthat."[45] In 1879, a Grand Rapids newspaper noted sardonically that "the Hastings base ball club played a game yesterday. A Grand Rapids nine was present, but it is understood that they took no part in the game, as they refuse to say anything about the score when approached on the subject."[46] An 1868 article showed that players were already reading and resenting criticism in the newspapers by concluding, "The exquisitely sensitive members of the Detroit Club will doubtless take exception thereto."[47] Sometimes hostilities between players and newspapers were more overt. In 1870, Bob Ferguson of the Atlantics of Brooklyn "threatened to knock every tooth out of the head" of a *New York Herald* reporter who questioned his competency as captain.[48]

Newspapers understandably resented these contradictory expectations. In 1867, the *Chicago Tribune* offered an apt summary of the state of affairs:

The journalists initiated a rage for base ball in this city, and the fever is spreading throughout all circles of society. To the journalist the extent of this fever is becoming positively alarming. If the base ball players would rest content with enjoying their game, and the health which the exercise is sure to bring, it would be well enough. But they will not let well alone. . . . If the Muffins challenge the Ragamuffins to play, and beat them, the whole world must hear of it, else the victory is not worth having. . . . Amateur clubs have started up in every direction, and now base ball threatens to absorb every other theme of public interest. It is base ball for breakfast, base ball for dinner, and base ball for supper. The number of Corresponding Secretaries who are instructed to furnish to the morning papers reports of their proceedings, and the results of their little games, is quite amazing. From bootblacks and other small gentlemen in tattered shirtsleeves, who have meetings to announce and business to transact, up to Excelsiors, there is a wondrous variety of sportsmen, and from morning till night the cry is still they come. Were we to publish the scores of scores with accompanying descriptive sketches of the "spirited games" which have been played in this city for the past week, it would furnish not very instructive reading for another week to come. But we can't. . . . It is questionable, after all, if the public are so profoundly interested in the result of all these games as the players are apt to imagine. It is quite natural that every young man who hits a ball well should look upon himself as a hero, and it is also natural that he should like the public to know it. But it is quite as likely that the public will become bored with base ball, and there is much danger that the present excessive rage for this excellent game may result at length in playing it out altogether. Probably the majority of our citizens will be perfectly content to know that all good boys are enjoying themselves with the bat and ball without caring to inquire how.[49]

This growing tension between players and reporters is one of the numerous examples of problems that modern fans think of as recent developments but that have actually been around nearly as long as the game itself.

Lester Goddard, president of the University of Michigan Base Ball Club in 1867, had to write apologetically to the student newspaper because evergreens and elms had been cleared from the club's playing field "by some one who had more in mind the interests of ball players, center fielders in particular, than the worth of the trees or the feeling of the authorities." *Courtesy of the Bentley Historical Library, University of Michigan*

People were also growing increasingly alarmed about the injuries that resulted from the game. (This was, after all, a public unaccustomed to strenuous leisure activities; at one point, the *Detroit Advertiser and Tribune* published a lengthy warning to croquet players after a near-fatal accident in that game!)[50] And there were certainly injuries associated with baseball. A collision between two players at the Agricultural College left one missing two teeth and the other with a broken arm and a gash on his forehead.[51] A similar accident knocked a player senseless in a match between Adrian and the Wolverine Club of Hudson. When the Star Club of the Agricultural College met the Capital Club of Lansing, nearly all the players insured themselves with an accident company before the match, and eight of them did indeed suffer injuries.[52]

It is fair to say, then, that the first great explosion of baseball fever in Michigan brought many new challenges. Many of the problems that began to surface at this time would take years to adequately address, and some continue to plague the game today. But the enthusiasm created was equally powerful, carrying with it the impetus to find solutions and forge alliances to help effect those solutions. Emblematic of this enthusiasm, the 1866 season continued well into November. After the Wolverine Club of Vermontville won a narrow victory over the Olivet Club on November 8, a rematch was scheduled for November 18. But inclement weather foiled these plans and brought this season of great growth, but also considerable growing pains, to a close.

NOTES

1. *Niles Republican*, August 4, 1866.
2. *Hillsdale Standard*, August 21, 1866.
3. *Detroit Advertiser and Tribune*, August 15, 1866.
4. *Detroit Advertiser and Tribune*, August 9, 15, and 27, 1866; *Detroit Post*, August 7 and 13, 1866.
5. *Detroit Advertiser and Tribune*, August 22, 1866.
6. *Detroit Advertiser and Tribune*, August 25, 1866.
7. *Detroit Post*, July 21, 1866.
8. *Jackson Daily Citizen*, July 23, 1866.
9. *Detroit Advertiser and Tribune*, July 16, 1866.
10. *Detroit Post*, August 21, 1866.
11. *Detroit Advertiser and Tribune*, July 6, 1866.
12. *Detroit Advertiser and Tribune*, August 23, 1866.
13. *Flint Wolverine Citizen*, September 1, 1866.
14. *Clinton Republican* (St. Johns), June 15, 1866.
15. *Detroit Advertiser and Tribune*, July 26, 1866.
16. *Detroit Advertiser and Tribune*, July 26 and November 6, 1866.
17. *Coldwater Sentinel*, May 11 and October 19, 1866; *Coldwater Republican*, November 3, 1866.
18. *Niles Weekly Times*, May 24, 1866.
19. *Hudson Gazette*, July 14, 1866.
20. *Hudson Gazette*, July 28, 1866.
21. Warren Goldstein, *Playing for Keeps*, 21, discusses this issue at greater length.
22. *Detroit Post*, August 3, 1866.
23. *Detroit Advertiser and Tribune*, August 30, 1866.
24. Robert Smith, *Baseball in America*, 22.
25. *Detroit Post*, July 28, 1866.
26. *Hudson Gazette*, August 4, 1866.
27. *Niles Republican*, May 19, 1866.
28. *Detroit Advertiser and Tribune*, July 13, 1866. A friendly game was played instead of a match.
29. *Detroit Advertiser and Tribune*, June 14, 1866.
30. *Hudson Gazette*, September 1, 1866.
31. *Detroit Advertiser and Tribune*, August 22, 1866.
32. *Kalamazoo Weekly Telegraph*, September 5, 1866.
33. *Kalamazoo Weekly Telegraph*, October 3, 1866.
34. *Clinton Republican* (St. Johns), September 7, 1866.
35. Allen Guttmann, *From Ritual to Record*, 100–108.

36. *Detroit Advertiser and Tribune,* September 15, 1866.

37. *Detroit Post,* September 17, 1866.

38. Even more incredibly, there were reports in the *Detroit Post* of September 19, 1866, and the *Jackson Daily Citizen* of the next day that Pokagon players had suggested to Dowagiac players that the two clubs pull fingers for the fifty-dollar first prize. Not surprisingly, the 1867 tournament does not appear to have occurred.

39. *Niles Weekly Times,* October 11, 1866.

40. The Spears felt that the game should have been continued the next day, but this rule did not apply to such games, as LaPorte captain H. G. Teed pointed out in a letter to the *Weekly Times.* Teed is the same man who umpired the Detroit-Chicago game at the Rockford tournament and whom the Detroit players later claimed was a member of the Excelsiors.

41. *Lansing State Republican,* October 17, 1866.

42. The centennial edition of the *Clinton County Republican-News* on June 28, 1956, carried a summary of the Monitors' exploits. It stated that the whereabouts of the trophy were unknown but that the centennial committee was hoping to locate it.

43. *Detroit Advertiser and Tribune,* October 15, 1866.

44. Quoted in Larry Names, *Bury My Heart at Wrigley Field,* 104.

45. *Jonesville Weekly Independent,* May 13, 1875.

46. *Grand Rapids Daily Leader,* August 31, 1879.

47. *Detroit Post,* June 23, 1868.

48. Quoted in Preston D. Orem, *Baseball (1845–1881) from the Newspaper Accounts,* 105.

49. *Chicago Tribune,* August 24, 1867. Ironically, the *Tribune*'s parent company is the current owner of the Chicago Cubs.

50. *Detroit Advertiser and Tribune,* May 20, 1867. Even more incredibly, an article in a London, Ontario, newspaper warned that excessive croquet playing could cause curved spines, disproportionate arm length, painful bunions, permanent lameness, and even consumption (tuberculosis) due to constraint on the chest (reprinted in the *Kalamazoo Daily Telegraph,* August 24, 1872). Obviously, limited understanding of health issues made people susceptible to extreme ideas about the possible side effects of physical exertion.

51. *Detroit Advertiser and Tribune,* July 19, 1866.

52. *Detroit Advertiser and Tribune,* September 17, 1866.

12

"NOT THE DETROIT FIRST NINE"

A SEASON OF CHANGE

After the success and growth of 1866, there was considerable optimism that the 1867 season would see more of the same. The *Detroit Post* offered this rosy preview:

> Base ball is now accepted as the national game, and is yearly growing in importance. We hail its popularity as an omen that the young men of this country are discarding effeminate sources of enjoyment, and find in physical cultivation a higher and more permanent pleasure. The friendly contests between rival clubs and rival cities have awakened a general interest in the game, and have set all the young men practicing in a way which must result in great benefit to them. Numerous clubs have been formed, and every village and hamlet in the country now boasts its club, which looks forward to a championship over the club of some neighboring village, if it does not aspire to be the champion of its county or State.
>
> The Detroit Club has won an enviable reputation on many a hard contested field. It is still alive and vigorous, and instead of evincing a disposition to allow its laurels to wither, it proposes to gather fresh ones during the coming summer.[1]

The article also enumerated the players likely to make up the Detroit Base Ball Club's first nine—the Hinchman brothers, Frank Folsom, Butler Ives, Arthur Van Norman, John Horn, Frank Phelps, and John McMillan. Conspicuously absent were Henry Burroughs, who had returned to Newark when the Detroit Gymnasium closed in February, and John Clark (who did rejoin the club later in the season). The *Post* was nonetheless optimistic that the club would be able to fill the vacancies with "men who are scarcely less proficient." While there is no way to be certain why the two Easterners departed, it seems likely that the failure of the club's efforts to attract worthy rivals to their enclosed playing field might have been at least an indirect cause.

However, the club was not abandoning aspirations to compete nationally. There was speculation that Fred Crane, "the celebrated second base of the Atlantics" of Brooklyn, would be relocating in Detroit. More significantly, the club had also arranged matches with the Forest City Club of Cleveland, the Niagaras of Buffalo, and the Ontarios of Rochester (New York) and was negotiating with such national powers as the Excelsiors of Chicago, the Atlantics of Brooklyn, the Athletics of Philadelphia, and the Nationals of Washington. Finally, the club announced its intention to host a grand Northwestern baseball tournament.

The tournament would begin on August 18 and continue until all the prizes had been distributed. The generous prize fund totaled nearly $2,000, encompassing three classes and numerous special prizes. In the first class, where the entrance fee was $15, first prize was $300 cash and a gold-mounted bat valued at $75, second prize was a silver tea set and urn offered by local jeweler M. S. Smith and Co. and valued at $250, and third prize was a gold ball worth $75.[2] In the second class, with a $10 entrance fee, first prize was $200 cash and a gold-mounted bat valued at $75, second prize was a creation of local jeweler John H. Morrison valued at $150, and third prize was a silver ball worth $25. Entrance fee in the third class was $5, and first prize was $100 in cash and a gold-mounted bat valued at $75, second prize was a design of Morrison's partner James S. Conklin worth

$100, and third prize was a silver trumpet worth $75. Special premiums ranging from $25 to $50 were offered to the best captain, pitcher, batter, runner, and thrower; to the batter making the most home runs; to the club with the best uniform; and to the club coming the greatest distance. Many of the prizes were displayed in advance at M. S. Smith's jewelry store.

Special $200 premiums were offered to the Athletics of Philadelphia and the Atlantics of Brooklyn to induce them to attend. The Detroit Club—"in order that no dissatisfaction may ensue"— would not compete but instead would play the first-class winners for a special purse of $100.[3] The Detroit Base Ball Club put $1,200 into getting its grounds ready for the tournament. The ground was plowed, rolled, and seeded until it was "as level as a floor," and seats were constructed to accommodate two thousand, with special elevated seating for women and a nook for scorers. Buildings and tents were erected for the clubs.[4] Expectations for the grand event continued to build all summer.

Meanwhile, the University of Michigan's nine had started out the 1867 season with convincing wins over Ann Arbor (30-26), Ypsilanti (42-12), and the once-mighty Central Club of Jackson (43-15). With school about to adjourn for the summer, the team scheduled a game on the grounds of the Detroit Base Ball Club on June 15. Legend has it that "on their way to the grounds the boys were met by an old base ball enthusiast who asked them with whom they were going to play. 'The Detroit Club,' they answered. 'What,' he rejoined, 'not the Detroit first nine?' Receiving the assurance that such was the fact, he turned and looked the speaker full on in the face, and after a moment's silence, gravely remarked, 'Well, boys, you'll be sick enough before night.'"[5]

Just the opposite happened. The university's nine pulled off a stunning upset, not only winning but drubbing the state champions by a 70-18 score. The star for the students was catcher George Ellis Dawson, later principal of Flint High School, who hit four home runs and scored 11 runs without once being retired. Dawson's catching and Julius A. Blackburn's sharp pitching handcuffed the Detroit

When the University of Michigan's nine were on their way to play the state champion Detroit Base Ball Club on June 15, 1867, a passerby told them they'd be "sick enough before night." Instead the collegians pulled off an amazing 70-18 upset, sparked by the baffling pitching of Julius A. Blackburn. *Courtesy of the Bentley Historical Library, University of Michigan*

The other star of the University of Michigan's upset over the Detroit Base Ball Club was catcher George Ellis Dawson, who hit four home runs and scored eleven times without making a single out. Dawson spent the summer of 1868 "interning" with the Detroit Base Ball Club and receiving seventy-five dollars a month for his services. He later was principal of Flint High School and a lawyer in Chicago. *Courtesy of the Bentley Historical Library, University of Michigan*

Club. Several excuses were offered for the rout, including the Detroit players' lack of practice and the departure of Henry Burroughs, but nothing could diminish the accomplishment of the college students. An Ann Arbor paper pointed out that the club from the university had even played several players out of position, including Eugene Cooley, son of famed lawyer Thomas Cooley, who had never before played shortstop in a match.[6]

The win created quite a stir on campus: "The University boys are feeling jubilant over the success of their first nine. A large crowd met the nine at the depot on their return, and gave them a hearty and clamorous welcome, though the train did not come in until after midnight."[7] It did not, however, make the club state champions, presumably because it was agreed beforehand that the game was not a championship match. The university's nine were invited to play against an Eastern squad during the Harvard-Yale regatta but were not able to attend and did not play again before school let out for the summer.

Nonetheless, the stunning upset sent shock waves through the world of Michigan baseball. It was already understood that the Detroit Club could not hope to compete with the best clubs from New York and Pennsylvania.[8] However, it was one thing to acknowledge inferiority to distant professionals and quite another to be humbled by a club of local college students. The victory of the University of Michigan nine made it evident not only that the Detroit Base Ball Club was not the national power it had once aspired to become but that it was going in the wrong direction.

Another upset helped reinforce the message sent by the university's triumph. The Capitals of Lansing were getting a bit long in the tooth, with several members in their thirties, but they were still considered "the best ball-players in the city." However, when they played the Union Club, composed of "lads under seventeen years of age," they were trounced 75-38.[9] And the players on the university's team were scarcely older: Blackburn was twenty, Dawson only nineteen. Such results again raised the issue of inclusion by prompting older clubs to reevaluate whether the game was worthy of their continued efforts. They also suggested that youth and agility were at least as important as experience—a reality at odds with the effort to depict baseball as a test of character.

The end of the dominance of the Detroit Base Ball Club and other established clubs sent an encouraging message to aspiring baseballists around the state. Players envisioned themselves pulling off the next great upset, and their ambitions were accordingly

In the outfield the day of the university's upset over Detroit was Albert H. Pattengill, who stayed on at the university as a professor of Greek until his death in 1906. He served as chairman of the Board in Control of Athletics for the last twelve years of his life and was credited with persuading football coach Fielding Yost to stay. His obituary noted: "To this day the students relate a tradition as to how he batted a home-run once from a point 100 feet south of North University avenue, so that the sphere landed on the skylight on top of the old medical building. Professional baseball players have looked at the distance and disputed it, but the tradition stands, nonetheless." *Courtesy of the Bentley Historical Library, University of Michigan*

raised. The Olivet Club won its first five matches and announced its desire to play for the county championship. The Oakland Club of Holly opened with a string of victories and crowed, "Our club has not yet been beaten in any match."[10] The Defiance Club of Saranac formed for the season, claiming to have "magnanimously" allowed itself to be beaten in 1866 but stating that its members "unanimously resolved to wear the championship of the Grand River Valley before the close of the season."[11] The Wolverines of Ionia responded by passing a similar resolution; after their victories over the Custers of Ionia and the Kents of Grand Rapids, a correspondent wrote that the Wolverines "seem bound to make good their claim to the championship of the Grand River Valley, and they may extend their claim further."[12]

By this time, however, a positive attitude—the "patience of hope"—no longer compensated for winning. After beating the Eagle Club of Fowlerville, the Union Club of Wayne issued this challenge: "The Unions have a ball for any village or country club in the State that will come and capture it in nine innings."[13] But the "village or country" specification in this challenge signifies that the "Young America" spirit of the Early Risers had been succeeded by a more pragmatic outlook. A similar message was sent when the State Normal School accepted the offer of the Peninsulars of Ypsilanti of a five-outs-to-three handicap. And the familiar mantra that the Mayflower Club of Maple Rapids was "a new club, and consequently could not be expected to compete, but have material for an excellent club," rang rather hollow when it lost 138-16 to the Monitors of St. Johns.[14] Although enthusiasm for the game was on the rise again, the desire to win was changing the rules of conduct.

Also changing the rules was the fact that many cities now had multiple clubs, enabling players to gain experience without the expense of traveling. Detroit boasted "no less than twenty *bona fide* base ball clubs," while Jackson had fifteen.[15] Even small towns were beginning to have two or three clubs. Lawton now had the Lawton Club and the Excelsior Club; Dowagiac had the Dowagiac and Fearnaught Clubs; Holly was home to the Oakland, Lightfoot, and Eagle Clubs; Flint had the Ogemas, the Hercules Club, the Independents, and the Wolverines; Tecumseh boasted the Chiefs and the Tecumseh Club. Homer had the Ziskas, plus a team of married men called the Tempest Club and one of bachelors called the Young America Club. Lowell had five different clubs—the Green Club (businessmen), the Forest Club (young men and clerks), the Mechanics Club (laborers), the Star Club (boys thirteen to seventeen), and the Young America Club (boys eight to thirteen).[16] Olivet, Pontiac, and Charlotte boasted two clubs apiece. In most cases at least one of the clubs was a junior club, but the upsets in Detroit and Lansing had shown that this no longer prevented a rivalry from developing.

Another new manifestation of interest was the growing market for baseball equipment. Frank Phelps capitalized on his expertise as catcher of the Detroit Base Ball Club to sell "Base Balls (Ross, Van Horn and Horseman balls), Bats, Belts, Caps, Spikes, etc."[17] In Jackson, Dorrance and Goodman's offered "the National Regulation, Star, New York Regulation, Junior and Young American Base Balls."[18] Hall and Scales in Kalamazoo also offered a wide variety of baseball paraphernalia.

In the meantime, the spread of the regulation game to new locales continued. Since most towns in southeast Michigan had already been introduced to the regulation game, most places in that region where baseball arrived for the first time in 1867 were small villages like Corunna and Dansville. Nonetheless, the number of clubs that can be documented more than doubled, from 102 in 1866 to 241 in 1867, and the number of cities with clubs rose from 59 to 117 (see appendix B).

With the adoption of regulation baseball in rural areas, accommodations often had to be made. Games had to be scheduled around the harvest; one series, for example, was adjourned until the "peaches are ripe."[19] Play often had to be adapted to less than ideal grounds. A report on a game between the Eagle Club of Fowler's Corners and the Banner Club of Cherry Hill observed that "the excellent fielding of Trumbull, who was stationed in r.f., on a side hill, prevented the Banners from making a single home run."[20]

Baseball was also continuing to spread throughout western Michigan. Ionia remained in the forefront, with John H. Mitchell even starting a weekly called the *Umpire* to report on the area's baseball news.[21] Hastings and Greenville also formed ball clubs for the first time in 1867. In Grand Rapids, the game's first period of sustained enthusiasm began when the Kent Club was formed on April 4, 1867, at Perkins' leather store. Silas K. Pierce, who had captained the Custer Club of Ionia in 1866, moved to the "Valley City" and served as the Kent Club's president. Its secretary was Lawrence C. Earle, who would later establish himself as one of the country's best-known painters. But while Earle would eventually become a distinguished portrait and landscape artist and paint the logo of the Dutch Boy Paint Company, in 1867 he was caught up in the fever for the new game and was drawing sketches of "base ball players in different attitudes."[22]

The Kent Club's initial practice on a hill east of the city

While most Civil War veterans did not play baseball after the war, a notable exception was Silas K. Pierce. This photo of the captain of the Custer Club of Ionia and the Kent Base Ball Club of Grand Rapids was taken by the legendary Mathew Brady. *Courtesy of the Clarke Historical Library, Central Michigan University*

Seven of the original members of Grand Rapids' Kent Base Ball Club. Second from the right is club secretary Lawrence C. Earle, who would become one of the country's finest landscape painters and painted the logo of the Dutch Boy Paint Company. In 1867, however, he was caught up by "base ball fever" and was drawing sketches of "base ball players in different attitudes." *Courtesy of the Local History Department, Grand Rapids Public Library, Grand Rapids, Michigan*

prompted one reporter to observe that he hadn't noticed who won, "nor do we care muchly, and that, in our opinion, is about as deep an interest as our readers or the boys themselves have in the result. They want exercise and fun and that they get in this athletic game."[23] But baseball fever soon broke out, and by the end of May half a dozen clubs were thriving in Grand Rapids. A more organized competitive environment began to emerge as a result of a donation from Joseph Herkner, who had been an officer in Grand Rapids' first club eight years earlier. Herkner and his business partner offered a silver ball to the city's best baseball club and a silver cup for the best local junior club.

The silver ball generated great interest, as a reporter later recalled:

> Grand Rapids' first glory in the base ball profession was radiated from the Peninsulars and the Kents, which were formed about 1867. The ball grounds were all of the "green" or open field between Lyon and Bronson streets which had been the camping ground of the old Tenth cavalry under Col. Foote. The present residence of Mr James A Rogers on Lyon street was then the last house on the east of the city settlement, the grove which surrounded his house ceasing just beyond. The ground was admirably adapted for any sort of field sport and there was room for a dozen ball diamonds. This place was the scene of many hard fought contests on emerald aceldama. Often during the period following the organization of these clubs a number of games would be going on especially during practice hours. A silver ball suitably engraved was "hung up" as a gift of the citizens to the champion club and this ball was many times transferred to a different nine which had been compelled to work hard for its possession.[24]

The ensuing years would see spirited but friendly competition for the silver ball and silver cup, with the most substantial bet on the outcome reported to be "a box of Ayer's pills against a copy of the Plymouth *Collector*."[25]

The perpetual optimism produced by a new season made many Michigan newspapers willing to give baseball another chance. The *Jackson Citizen* urged the public "to visit the grounds and see what a game of base ball is. It will be worth your time and trouble. It also gives the boys more confidence, and they exert themselves more to do fine playing than if no one were present."[26] A month later the same paper gushed:

The American chivalry are found in the base ball clubs. The game unites with sport enough of danger to keep the pusilanimous [*sic*] and effeminate out of the field. No *roue* billiard match or tournament, played all night long to spectators in a close room filled with the fumes of tobacco and whiskey . . . nor any horse race, where you meet jockeys, gamblers and thieves, possesses half the interest, or stirs the blood as much. . . . We want our boys to learn base ball, and keep away from billiard saloons. The clubs are always temperate. No bad language is used by the players. The exhibition of muscle, of activity, grace—unaffected grace—is beyond all the circus performances we ever witnessed.

The article also noted the presence of many distinguished gentlemen at the matches and advised women to join them: "Ladies, we assure you that you will enjoy a game of base ball, and any young man that plays this manly game is a safer husband, or will make one, than those who find amusement in the ways we have indicated in contrast."[27] It is significant, however, that the emphasis was now less on baseball's virtues than on the vice of rival activities.

The *Charlotte Republican* more overtly presented baseball as a test of character:

The National Game of Base Ball is an invigorating exercise and manly sport. Perhaps no game yet devised is so well calculated to develop body and mind. It gives exercise to all parts of the body, and inures to labor, so the "hard work" is readily borne by those unaccustomed to it. It requires close attention, quick perception, prompt decision and action. It also brings out the peculiarities of individual players and reveals their real characters. The gentleman will be more than ever a gentleman, whether at bat or base, or in the field; and faults of character will be distinctly seen. While the game gives the most complete bodily exercise, it thus by strengthening the good and exposing the bad traits of character, improves all who play—except only the few whom nothing can benefit.[28]

Tournaments were the next logical consequence of this increased interest, but as in previous years, their execution did not always live up to initial enthusiasm. Plans for a tournament in Romeo were announced, but a few days beforehand it was reduced to a match game for a fifty-dollar purse. Finally, "owing to some misunderstanding," only a match between the Inland City Club of Romeo and the Welkin Club of Port Huron took place.[29]

A tournament advertised as a grand Horse Fair and Base Ball Tournament at Park Grove in Dowagiac on July 3 and 4, with over five hundred dollars in premiums, was also scaled back. The Continentals of Kalamazoo played Battle Creek on July 3 for a purse of seventy-five dollars and won 19-5, beating Battle Creek's pitcher A. N. Ball, who was billed as "probably [having] no equal in the state."[30] The second division of the tournament was to see Pokagon, a Battle Creek club, and the Fearnaught Club of Dowagiac compete for thirty dollars, but Battle Creek walked out in the middle of their game against the Fearnaughts in protest of the umpiring. What happened to Pokagon is unclear. Kalamazoo players won prizes for best general player, best base running, and best pitcher.

Another tournament was held in Lapeer, on June 27, with two Flint clubs and one from Almont competing. Resentment still festered over the previous year's libelous account of a game between clubs from Flint and Lapeer, so "reporters were not invited."[31] Details of the tournament are therefore sketchy, but the Ogemas of Flint won first prize (a silver ball worth fifty dollars), and the Almont nine took home second prize, a rosewood bat valued at twenty-five dollars.

Independence Day and baseball were also becoming an increasingly popular combination. In 1867, the Detroit Base Ball Club hosted the Forest City Club of Cleveland, with proceeds going to the Soldiers' Monument Association. The game was postponed by a rainstorm and was finally completed on a wet field in near darkness, with Cleveland winning 49-23 in seven innings. Many factors were blamed for the loss, the chief being the lack of a good pitcher, as no adequate replacement for Henry Burroughs had emerged: "The pitching was a failure, much of it being wild and often lacking speed. This defect, it is absolutely necessary for the club to remedy before they can hope to compete successfully with first class opponents. . . . The services of a first-rate pitcher should be secured as soon as possible, and then a few weeks practice would bring the club into the old form."[32]

The national holiday also provided other opportunities for showcasing what was now widely acknowledged as the national game. In Battle Creek, "the Agricultural and Mechanical and Ladies Industrial Associations will celebrate the Fourth on the fair ground, with a festival and speech by ex–Lieutenant Governor May, of Kalamazoo, by a ball play, in which the 'old boys' will take 'front seats,' and other amusements."[33] The Ziskas of Homer played the Peninsulars of Albion, with the home club winning 64-25. The Star Base Ball Club of Jackson and the Unions of Lansing squared off to settle the claim both had made to the state junior championship.

Inevitably, the increased competition brought some hard feelings. After Jackson beat Battle Creek 27-20 on July 19, the *Advertiser and Tribune* reported: "There were players of both sides not *bona fide* members of the respective clubs, but who had been surreptitiously introduced. This is wrong and should not be tolerated."[34] A. N. Ball, now established as the best pitcher in western Michigan, was soon moonlighting for clubs in Marshall, Battle Creek, and Kalamazoo.

The importing of this East Coast practice of "revolving" was incompatible with the nature of the gentlemen's clubs that had been essential to the sport's development. In early May, the *Kalamazoo Telegraph* reported that the Pine Browse Club of Wayland had defeated the Island Club of Plainwell 86-41. However, a week later the paper noted: "There is no such club as the Pine Browse of Wayland. There were nine men, *saying* that they belonged to such an organization. . . . They can claim no victory, not only for that reason, but because the pitcher of the Pine Browse and the pitcher of one of the Kalamazoo clubs are one and the same person."[35] And the following week the paper advised, "If you have any consideration for the honor of your club among the ball fraternity, do not try to palm off players belonging to other clubs as members of your nine."[36]

The fight to retain traditional clubs was ultimately a losing battle, as the temptation to improve a nine with outside members proved too great. A Charlotte paper criticized its local clubs for admitting each other's members but then wrote: "There are four or five players of acknowledged skill,—say, Turner, Shepherd, Johnson, Dwinell, Lacy. Let these fill up the *nine* and organize a new Club. *If they should beat all others,* they will then become the pet club of the public and will excite a special public interest in their games. There is undoubtedly material in Charlotte for a first class Club."[37] Such reasoning doomed traditional clubs, since as soon as one club succumbed to the temptation to import outsiders "with the especial object of beating all other Clubs," its rivals were forced to do the same in order to remain competitive.

This transformation of baseball clubs from social to competitive organizations was a fundamental change. As the basis for inclusion shifted from common values to athletic skill, more and more of the young men who wished to participate in the game found out the hard way that no longer was everyone "just as good as any other." Baseball was now facing a crucial challenge: Could it retain the loyalty of this growing group of disaffected ex-players by transforming them into spectators?

In order to reinvent itself as a spectator sport, baseball needed to find a sound economic basis. Many obstacles remained, however, as was shown when the Athletic Club of Detroit hosted the Peninsulars of Ypsilanti on July 20. The game was advertised beforehand, with an admission fee of twenty-five cents for men, women free. But once again the product being offered did not justify such a price: "Seats were erected for the benefit of spectators, who were present in large numbers to witness the match, and among them were many ladies. The game was commenced at half past 2 o'clock, and was long and tediously drawn out until half past 7 o'clock, when, at the close of the eighth innings, it being nearly twilight, the game was called. . . . Both clubs were deficient in fielding, the Athletics particularly so, and although a large number of fly balls were batted into the field by the Peninsulars, not one was caught."[38] The Peninsulars won 100-57.

As the game was being passed on to a new generation, many of the traditions of the gentleman's era of baseball were falling by the wayside. Previously, even if the games themselves produced some acrimony, the home club took pride in being generous hosts. But after the junior Peninsulars of Detroit hosted another junior club, the Lively Club of Monroe, the *Advertiser and Tribune* reported, "The Monroe lads complain, and with seeming entire justice, of rather shabby treatment on the part of the Detroiters—the latter neither meeting them at the depot nor offering them anything to eat either before or after the game."[39] Following a loss, the junior Active Club of Marshall handed the requisite ball to their rivals only "after much hesitation."[40]

Even when the customs were observed, the gentlemanly spirit was sometimes lacking. A letter from J. Ginns, the secretary of the Wolverine Club of Ionia, to the Eagle Club of Greenville read: "We are sorry to inform you that we do not care about playing with you it would be only childs Play you could not give us any practize if you at any time Should challenge us we of course would feel duty bound to play with you but on no other account would we ever think of playing with you."[41] Both the sentiments and the grammar would have shocked the Knickerbockers!

A few baseball players were violating more than the abstract ideals of gentlemanly behavior and syntax. In Detroit, a group of boys was arrested for playing baseball on Sunday, beginning a long controversy over this issue.[42] When the junior Excelsior Club of Jackson visited Mason, the local paper alleged that the players "carried bottles of liquor in their pockets, and would frequently stop on the field to take a suck."[43]

It is important to note again that the general level of conduct remained very high, as is indicated by the trivial infractions that attracted comment. The *Charlotte Republican,* for instance, reported these breaches of conduct: "Stephen Pierce, of Benton, persisted in remaining within the lines [i.e., on the playing field] until the Plains Club, who were batting, started for him in a body and he quickly vamoosed. Morgan, the captain of the Prairie Club, got off a foul word during the game, for which the Club do not wish to be held responsible—he has since left the Club."[44]

While many of these infractions might appear trivial to modern readers, the declining standards of behavior represented a major challenge for a game that had derived so much of its early support from its alliance with traditional values. And the increasingly youthful makeup of the game's players left little hope of a return to earlier customs. By the middle of the 1867 season, the game had alienated many of its most important supporters, raising major questions about its future. In order to win them back, baseball would have to achieve a delicate balance between spectacle and competition. The grand tournament in Detroit thus loomed as a critical opportunity for baseball to recapture public favor.

NOTES

1. *Detroit Post,* April 12, 1867. The article goes on to describe the Woodward Avenue Skating Park as the club's "new grounds," a most puzzling statement since the club had played there since 1865. Perhaps the reporter had not covered the club previously and was misinformed. The next few quotations are from this same article.
2. William Humber, *Diamonds of the North,* 28, reports that the gold-plated ball became a prized possession of Bill Shuttleworth of the Maple Leafs of Hamilton.
3. *Detroit Post,* June 15, 1867.
4. *Detroit Post,* August 9, 1867.
5. Edwin H. Humphrey, *The Michigan Book* (Ann Arbor: Inland Press, 1898), 144.
6. *Ann Arbor Peninsular Courier and Family Visitant,* June 20, 1867.
7. *Detroit Advertiser and Tribune,* June 19, 1867.
8. The *Detroit Advertiser and Tribune* stated on May 26, 1867: "It may be well here to explain that these famous clubs, together with many others of note in the East are made up not only of gentlemen who are members from the love of exercise and sport, but in a large degree of professional base ball players who do but little save practice their favorite game, and who in matches make up the bulk of the first or playing nine. In the West no such body of men is or can be gathered at present, and these facts will explain the disparity in power existing between the majority of the Western clubs, and their experienced and professional rivals of the metropolitan cities."
9. *Detroit Post,* May 7, 1867.

10. *Detroit Advertiser and Tribune*, June 18, 1867.

11. *Ionia Sentinel;* reprinted in the *Grand Rapids Daily Eagle*, April 6, 1867.

12. *Detroit Post*, June 21, 1867.

13. *Detroit Advertiser and Tribune*, July 12, 1867.

14. *Clinton Independent* (St. Johns), June 5, 1867.

15. *Detroit Post*, August 8, 1867; *Jackson Daily Citizen*, August 14, 1867.

16. *Grand Rapids Daily Eagle*, July 19, 1867.

17. *Detroit Advertiser and Tribune*, June 19, 1867.

18. *Jackson Daily Citizen*, June 8, 1867.

19. *Charlotte Republican*, June 27, 1867.

20. *Ypsilanti Commercial*, August 31, 1867.

21. *Grand Rapids Daily Eagle*, April 6 and 12, 1867. The first issue of the *Umpire* appeared on April 8, 1867, but does not seem to be extant; no record of any additional issues could be found.

22. *Grand Rapids Daily Eagle*, July 25, 1867.

23. *Grand Rapids Daily Democrat*, April 13, 1867.

24. *Grand Rapids Daily Democrat*, May 18, 1883.

25. *Grand Rapids Daily Eagle*, July 31, 1867.

26. *Jackson Daily Citizen*, June 18, 1867.

27. *Jackson Daily Citizen*, July 22, 1867.

28. *Charlotte Republican*, July 18, 1867.

29. *Detroit Advertiser and Tribune*, June 18, 1867.

30. *Detroit Advertiser and Tribune*, July 8, 1867.

31. *Flint Wolverine Citizen*, June 29, 1867.

32. *Detroit Advertiser and Tribune*, July 6, 1867.

33. *Detroit Advertiser and Tribune*, July 2, 1867.

34. *Detroit Advertiser and Tribune*, July 22, 1867.

35. *Kalamazoo Telegraph*, May 15, 1867.

36. *Kalamazoo Telegraph*, May 29, 1867.

37. *Charlotte Republican*, July 25, 1867.

38. *Detroit Advertiser and Tribune*, July 22, 1867. However, a very different account in the *Detroit Post* on the same day called the game "in every respect the best which has been played in the city this season."

39. *Detroit Advertiser and Tribune*, August 30, 1867.

40. *Marshall Democratic Expounder*, June 20, 1867.

41. *Greenville Independent*, July 23, 1867. All mistakes are from the original.

42. *Detroit Free Press*, October 29, 1867.

43. *Ingham County News* (Mason), August 21, 1867.

44. *Charlotte Republican*, June 27, 1867.

13

"ONE HEARS LITTLE ELSE ON THE STREET"

The approach of the great tournament in Detroit in 1867 focused the energies of clubs across the state. The Creightons of Detroit, a juvenile club that included future star Tommy Shaughnessy, showed that the Young America spirit of the Early Risers was not dead.[1] Undeterred by losing their first game 104-17, the Creightons entered the tournament.

In Jackson, meanwhile, with many newer clubs rivaling the Centrals, there was no clear consensus on how to best represent the city. When the August 1 deadline for entries arrived, the name "Unknowns" was submitted to allow more time to select the nine players. This fateful decision would reveal much about the changing nature of baseball clubs.

Other clubs were just aiming to put a full nine together. The Oakland Club of Holly ran off a string of victories and had high hopes for the tournament when they received a shock:

> The Oakland Club has recently been sorely crippled by the pitcher, Robinson, surreptitiously leaving town. He was becoming a fine pitcher, and the club are at a loss to know what to do to supply his place. Robinson is a dentist, and some recent reports from his former residence relating to ungentlemanly proceedings with ladies under

the influence of chloroform, undoubtedly caused him to think that the people of Holly would not appreciate his professional services. The Oakland Club hold [*sic*] a festival on the 8th inst. for the purpose of raising money to defray expenses of the coming tournament.[2]

The Ogemas of Flint lost one of their players, George Flanders, when he tripped and broke his collarbone and shoulder. Even worse off were the longtime Canadian champions, the Young Canadians of Woodstock, Ontario, whose pitcher died a week before the tournament was to start.

On August 12, the hotels of Detroit began to fill with "congregations of the faithful—in base ball—all eager and anxious" for the grand tournament.[3] The efforts to attract such famous clubs as the Athletics and the Atlantics had failed, but twenty-three clubs had entered, including the Alleghenys of Allegheny City, Pennsylvania, and three from the newly formed dominion of Canada.

Many elements of the tournament's organization reflected the gentlemanly customs that were rapidly losing their hold on the game. The deadline for entries was pushed back twice, and even after the deadline had finally passed, places were saved for well-known clubs. Additionally, clubs were allowed to enter any division they chose, with no effort being made to assure a convenient number of clubs in each class. This leniency would have significant repercussions.

The emphasis of the tournament was very much on spectacle. The beautiful grounds made quite an impression, and stands offered "a stock of eatables and drinkables to meet the wants of the expected multitude."[4] One of the suppliers of drinks was local pharmacist James Vernor, the brother of Charles Vernor of the Detroit Base Ball Club. James Vernor had recently perfected a recipe for ginger ale that would eventually make him rich, and it seems reasonable to assume that he served what would become known as Vernor's Ginger Ale at the tournament.[5]

Even though a second field had been readied so that two games could be played at once, it was decided to play tournament games

At Detroit's grand baseball tournament in 1867, one of the concessionaires was local pharmacist James Vernor, whose brother played for the Detroit Base Ball Club. In all likelihood, the thirsty baseball spectators were among the first to sample Vernor's Ginger Ale. *Courtesy of the State of Michigan Archives*

exclusively on the primary field. As a result, the tournament stretched luxuriantly over eight days, causing great inconvenience for working men. One of the players for the Monitors of St. Johns did return home during the tournament; the game started without him when the train bringing him back to Detroit was late. Undoubtedly other working men had to forgo the tournament althogether, making it inevitable that this would be the last planned on so grand a scale.

There were other signs that this tournament would be a swan song for the gentleman's game of baseball. Betting was prohibited, and police were present to discourage intoxication. While plans were made for a grand parade of the nearly three hundred players in their uniforms accompanied by a band, they had to be abandoned due to the difficulty of getting all of the players together. A photograph of ten of the clubs was taken, however.

And many of the clubs did get into the old chivalric spirit. The Maple Leafs of Hamilton, Ontario, for instance, declined to accept a forfeit they could have claimed and instead agreed to reschedule the game. The spectators got in the spirit by applauding both sides, although there were some imbalances when, as one newspaper diplomatically put it, "one club had more friends present than the other."[6]

The umpires also reflected the gentleman's game rather than the competitive sport baseball was becoming. They encouraged debate of their calls and frequently reversed them, which naturally stimulated further questioning of their rulings. Arthur Van Norman of the Detroit Club umpired one game and "was either very nervous or not fully conversant with the duties of his position. . . . As soon, however, as convinced of errors he had made, he took the earliest opportunity to correct them, and we will also give him credit for making impartial decisions. He no doubt aimed to do what was right, but failed to evince any remarkable knowledge of the rules of the game."[7]

Weather could ruin the most well-planned tournament, so there was reason for concern when overnight rain delayed the first match for an hour. But the skies were clear for the remainder of the tournament, and the organizers had to scramble to put awnings in place to protect spectators from the scorching sun. The beautiful weather attracted crowds of up to five thousand spectators each day, who paid twenty-five cents a head to witness the festivities. The whole city was caught up in the tournament: "One hears little else on the street than discussions on the merits or demerits of clubs, umpires, &c, &c."[8] It started to seem as if "every second person one met on the street had on either a red cap, blue pants or carried over his shoulder a murderous looking club."[9]

The tournament received generous attention in the newspapers. Even the *Detroit Free Press,* which had cut back on its baseball coverage considerably that season, devoted most of its front page to the tournament. Many out-of-state newspapers featured the tournament prominently, and the *Chicago Tribune* sent a special correspondent. While the *Tribune* correspondent complained that "the most splendid arrangements are made for everybody except the reporters of the press," he had high praise for the tournament's organizers.[10]

One noteworthy feature of the tournament was observed by a *Free Press* reporter: "We have noticed in all the matches played thus

far that the use of gloves by the players was to some degree a customary practice, which, we think, cannot be too highly condemned,
and are of the opinion, that the Custers would have shown a better
score, if there had been less buckskin on their hands."[11] It seems safe
to assume that these were thin gloves that only cushioned the blow
of the ball, but their use is historically significant, as most histories
state that gloves originated no earlier than 1869. Early glove wear-
ers wore flesh-colored gloves to avoid appearing unmanly, which
may account for why no one has claimed the distinction of being
their originator.[12]

The tournament's third class comprised ten clubs, most of them
juvenile or newly formed. The first round saw fairly close games, as
the Commercials of Detroit topped the Oaklands of Holly 52-42,
the Alerts of Detroit beat the Diamonds of Fenton 27-21, the Monitors of St. Johns stopped the Nationals of Parma 61-34, the Unions
of Wayne beat the Creightons of Detroit 41-27, and the Victorias of
Ingersoll, Ontario, defeated the Ann Arbor Juniors 39-23.

Unfortunately, in subsequent rounds, the Victorias of Ingersoll
would demonstrate the need for some criteria for determining what
class a club should play in. In a class made up mostly of schoolboys,
the Victorias were "hard-fisted laboring men" in their mid-twenties,
some of whom had been playing since the 1850s.[13] The club romped
through the field by increasingly lopsided margins, trouncing the
Unions of Wayne 40-18, the Monitors of St. Johns 41-15, and the
Alerts of Detroit 63-19 to claim one hundred dollars and the gold
bat. After four innings of the championship match, the Victorias led
the hopelessly overmatched Alerts 39-1. The ease of the Ingersoll
club's victories understandably prompted complaints that the Canadian club belonged in the second or even the first class. The Alerts
were awarded second prize and the Monitors of St. Johns third
prize.

Eight Michigan clubs were entered in the second class, eliminat-
ing the need for byes. The Champions of Olivet did not appear for
their match against the Athletics of Detroit and thus forfeited. The
Ann Arbor Seniors, an entrant that included Julius Blackburn and

Alfred Wilkinson from the University of Michigan nine, routed the Tecumseh Club 50-11, with the Tecumseh players resigning after six innings. However, the other two first-round matches proved much more competitive.

When the Battle Creek Club and the Peninsulars of Ypsilanti were paired, it delighted both clubs, as there was "a great strife" between the two. The Peninsulars were "very confident of an easy victory" and did quite a bit of boasting before the game, but Battle Creek won 45-37.[14] The game was ended after seven innings so that another game could be played, and the Peninsulars were understandably aggrieved at being deprived of the opportunity to overcome the 8-run deficit. In the final first-round match, the Custers of Ionia jumped to a 24-8 lead over the Ogemas of Flint after two innings. However, the Ogemas staged a furious comeback and led 62-50 after eight innings, with darkness beginning to fall. The Custers counted 12 runs in the top of the ninth to tie the score, but with one out in the Flint half, Ogema captain E. W. McIntyre scored the winning run. (With the result no longer in doubt, the game was called; by the custom of the day the final score reverted to that of the previous inning.)

The semifinals in the second class saw the Ann Arbor Seniors beat the Battle Creek Club 46-37 and the Athletics of Detroit top the Ogemas of Flint 41-40. The latter game was particularly dramatic, as the Athletics had to shut out the Ogemas in the ninth inning to hold on to their 1-run victory. Once again the championship game proved anticlimactic, as the Ann Arbor Seniors massacred the Athletics 66-27. A third-place match between the Ogemas and Battle Creek was scheduled, but the Ogemas did not appear, and Battle Creek was declared a winner by forfeit.

The entrants in the first class were four first-rate nines and the overly optimistic Welkins of Port Huron. The Welkins missed their match, but the Maple Leafs of Hamilton sportingly refused to accept a forfeit, so the game was rescheduled for the next day. On the second try, with the Maple Leafs ahead 19-10 in the third inning, the Welkins' pitcher was injured, and the club withdrew rather than try to go on without him. This reduced the field to four candidates for the top honors—the Maple Leafs, the Young Canadians of Woodstock, the Unknowns of Jackson, and the Alleghenys of Pennsylvania.

The first semifinal featured the Young Canadians and the Alleghenys, the two clubs generally regarded as the favorites. The Young Canadians had been considered the champions of Canada since wresting that title from the Maple Leafs of Hamilton in 1861. It was reported that their only loss in seven years had come at the hands of the mighty Atlantics of Brooklyn.[15] However, the death of their pitcher a week before the tournament proved too much to overcome, and the Alleghenys won 55-35. Henry Burroughs, back in town to witness the great tournament, umpired the game. In the other semifinal the Maple Leafs jumped to an early lead, but the Unknowns outscored the Canadians 11-0 in the fifth inning to grab the lead and cruised to a 55-39 win.

The Alleghenys were heavily favored in the championship match. They started quickly and had built a 16-10 lead after five innings. When the Alleghenys scored 7 runs in the top of the sixth, the game looked all but over. But the resilient Jackson club mounted another rally, scoring fourteen times in the bottom of the sixth to grab a 1-run lead. The Alleghenys reclaimed a 26-25 lead after the eighth but were blanked in the top of the ninth, meaning that the Unknowns would need only 2 runs in the bottom of the ninth to claim the championship. Melville McGee, who had been playing ball since the raisin' games of the 1830s, scored the tying run, and William Cocker followed him to score the winning run, as "cheer after cheer went up until all Jackson, or at least that part that was present, was hoarse with the effort."[16] The Unknowns counted 2 more meaningless runs, making the final score 29-26.

The champion Unknowns were supposed to play the Detroit Base Ball Club for a special purse of one hundred dollars. However, ill will between the Unknowns and the host club had been building throughout the tournament, and the Unknowns declined to play. The Alleghenys agreed to play Detroit instead, and they won easily,

31-16. The Detroit Club again demonstrated its lack of practice, the new shortstop fumbling chances until he was exiled to right field, while Jack Hinchman, at third base, "instead of attending to his business, tried to make fancy catches with one hand and never succeeded."[17]

This left the special prizes. Frank Burlingham of Battle Creek, one of the original members of the Champion Club of Kalamazoo, outraced a dozen rivals to win the base-running contest in 16½ seconds. One of the runners-up was William C. Maybury of the Athletics of Detroit, who would later be mayor of Detroit. Eight men entered the long-distance throwing contest, Freeman S. Porter of the Custers of Ionia winning with a throw of 290 feet, 7 inches. Ford Hinchman of the Detroit Club did not enter, but he made a practice throw of 312 feet, 4 inches, that easily bested the other competitors.

The awards ceremony gave further evidence of the antagonism between the Unknowns of Jackson and their hosts. Though most prizewinners were "cheered lustily," the Unknowns' captain, John McCord, accepted first prize to an "absence of all applause."[18] The captains of the second- and third-place clubs made speeches thanking their hosts, but McCord apparently had nothing to say.

Other prizewinners included Milo Shaffer of the Peninsulars of Ypsilanti as best captain, Ambrose Lynch of the Alleghenys as best catcher, his batterymate Albert Pratt as best pitcher, William F. Rathbun of the Alerts of Detroit as best batter, Frederick Marker of the Unions of Wayne for most home runs, the Alleghenys for having come the greatest distance, and the Custers of Ionia for best uniform (as selected by a group of women on the basis of beauty and serviceability). A final, previously unannounced prize of a pint of peanuts, donated by the reporters who covered the tournament, was awarded to the Tecumseh Club for having suffered the most lopsided loss.

The Detroit papers proudly announced that the tournament had been "a decided success" and that "everything has passed off with the utmost good feeling on all sides."[19] However, the *Post* was clearly incorrect when it claimed that it was "but speaking the unanimous sentiment to say the success of the tournament was due in a great measure to their untiring efforts to make it such. . . . [A]ll return to their homes well satisfied."[20] While the tournament was a success in many ways, the hard feelings between the Unknowns of Jackson and the Detroit Club were a major blemish.

Contradictory accounts make it impossible to definitively ascertain the roots of the animosity, and the underlying dispute inevitably degenerated into an array of charges and countercharges. The *Detroit Post* alleged that the Unknowns had "received their wages, and scattered to their several places of residence in different parts of the State."[21] The *Chicago Tribune* went further, claiming that "the Unknowns are well named, for, if report be true, they are a lot of players collected from all parts of the country."[22] Such rumors of course were wild exaggerations; all but three of the Unknowns were longtime Jackson residents. Still, the innuendoes were not entirely baseless, since the Unknowns weren't a regularly formed club and since three of their members—John McCord and University of Michigan students William Cocker and Lester Goddard—were not from Jackson. To Detroiters it must have seemed that Jackson had put together an all-star contingent that ruined the gentlemanly spirit of the tournament.

It is equally easy to see why the matter was perceived very differently in Jackson, where memories of the Detroit Base Ball Club using Eastern imports to defeat Jackson at the state tournament two years earlier were still fresh. It accordingly now seemed very hypocritical for Detroit to quibble about Jackson's use of a couple of Michigan collegians. Other clubs in the tournament were guilty of similar tactics: the Ann Arbor Seniors, for example, had used two students in dominating the second class, while the Maple Leafs of Hamilton included two players from Guelph.[23]

Moreover, many of the members of the Unknown Club were respected citizens whose age and accomplishments hearkened back to baseball's gentlemanly days. Thirty-nine-year-old first baseman Melville McGee was a judge of probate, while thirty-one-year-old Thomas J. Conely was the city recorder and a Civil War veteran.

Three other players—John McCord, Hooker DeLand, and Stephen Welling—had also been playing the game since before the war.

The *Jackson Citizen* thus complained bitterly of the attempts to "deprive the Unknown Club not only of the honors of their hard earned victory, but also at the same time of reputation as individuals, and of trustworthiness as gentlemen."[24] It further accused the Detroit press of jealousy and blamed the unpleasantness on Detroiters who had bet on the Alleghenys. The *Pittsburgh Chronicle* stirred the pot by accusing umpire J. L. Haynie of deliberately favoring the Unknowns.[25] Increasingly outlandish charges succeeded these, creating an enmity between Jackson and Detroit that would not soon abate. Undoubtedly this contributed to Melville McGee's belief that the spirit in which baseball was played had changed dramatically from his childhood.

The Unknowns were not the only dissatisfied club. Battle Creek players understandably complained bitterly about their game ending after seven innings.[26] The Juniors of Ann Arbor were also reported as being "not *loud* in their praise of the treatment received at the hands of those having control of the tournament."[27] The *Jackson Citizen* cited the Chief Club of Tecumseh as "yet another club that are *not* loud in their praise of the way in which the late tournament was conducted," an opinion that would have carried more weight had the Chiefs actually played in the tournament.[28] Perhaps the paper was confusing the Chief Club with the Tecumseh Club.

Nonetheless, the many positive elements of the tournament prompted imitators. It became especially popular to present tournaments as social affairs by combining them with ice-cream festivals, picnics, and dances. In Homer, a baseball tournament and ice-cream festival was held on August 27. Ice-cream tables were set up, a baseball dance was held, and the club cleared a ten-dollar profit. Decatur hosted Lawton on August 31, and after the game "the ladies of Decatur . . . provided a picnic supper in a grove hard by the grounds to which the tired gamesters were invited."[29]

The Superior Club of Russell's Corners held a baseball picnic on August 23, with games against the first and second nines of the

Peninsular Club of Ypsilanti followed by a dance. However, one attendee complained that the picnic was characterized by a "profusion of base ball, and a lamentable absence of everything in the shape of edibles."[30] Combining the social realm with baseball, and its tendency to produce feverish enthusiasm, required a delicate touch.

A tournament in Tecumseh on September 4 and 5 attracted the champion Unknowns of Jackson, but very little competition for them. Although the Unknowns were missing some of the players who had competed in Detroit, they easily won the tournament and a tea set valued at one hundred dollars. They took the opportunity to aim another barb at the organizers of the Detroit tournament, claiming that they "returned home with infinitely more satisfaction than they felt on their return from Detroit . . . simply because they were treated from first to last at Tecumseh like gentlemen."[31] There was competition in two other classes, with the Stars of Clinton winning the second class and the Caledonians of Blissfield capturing the honors in the third class.

The Unknowns of Jackson soon became aware of the unreasonable expectations that come from winning a title. The Monitors of Chelsea held a baseball picnic on September 14 and invited the Unknowns. When they did not come, a correspondent to the *Advertiser and Tribune* wrote, "Some surmised that they did not care to hazard the reputation they gained at Detroit as the successful competitors for the first prize in the first class."[32] The paper's Jackson correspondent justifiably complained, "It is a great hardship if the Unknowns are bound to accept every invitation hither and yon throughout the State, or be subject to this babyish sneer."[33] The Unknowns played little the rest of the season, giving their detractors further reason to claim that the collegians were essential to their success.

The Detroit tournament also spurred the Detroi[t] into renewed activity. The club's commitment to [w]as lacking when only five of its first nine played in a 2[ ] Quickstep Club of Toledo on August 29. But four[ ]

Detroit Club notched a significant win when it beat the Niagara Base Ball Club of Buffalo 26-19.[34] The Detroit Club followed up on this victory by traveling to Cleveland and beating the Forest City Club 37-27 on September 18.

These impressive victories were followed by the exciting news that the Detroit Club had finally arranged a home-and-home match with the Excelsior Club of Chicago. Like the Detroit Base Ball Club, the Excelsiors were experiencing a tumultuous season. Hopes had been high after the previous season and had increased when the club beat its chief in-state rival, the Forest City Club of Rockford, in two close games at a July 4 tournament. With the great Nationals of Washington scheduled to arrive in Chicago at the end of the month, the Excelsiors would get a chance to find out how they compared with a top Eastern nine.

The players on the National Club of Washington were mostly New York natives who had been lured to the capital by offers of clerkships in the treasury and other government departments.[35] The star player was twenty-year-old George Wright, who was probably paid exclusively for his baseball skills. The rest seem to have had actual responsibilities, but they were excused from them long enough to embark on a twenty-four-hundred-mile, three-week tour of what was then known as the West.

The Nationals beat all their opponents by lopsided margins until they arrived in Chicago for the last stop on the tour. The Nationals had originally invited the Detroit Base Ball Club to travel to Chicago so they could play both the Excelsiors and the Detroit Club. When the Detroit Club declined, the Nationals scheduled a preliminary battle with the Forest City Club of Rockford instead. Rockford pulled off a stunning upset, defeating the "invincible" Nationals 29-23 and marking the first time that a Western nine had ever beaten a top Eastern club.[36] The hero of the game was Rockford's sixteen-year-old pitcher A. G. Spalding, who, although his heart was beating "like a trip-hammer," subdued the club that had been averaging over 80 runs a game.[37]

In light of this shocking result, it was assumed that the Excelsiors stood an excellent chance against the great touring club on the following day. But the Nationals took out their frustrations on the Excelsiors, thrashing them by a 49-4 margin. Following this embarrassing loss, the Excelsiors received a package from the Pecatonica Club that included the now famous horn it had acquired at the Rockford tournament and a note commending the Excelsiors for having "fairly taken from us our hard-earned laurels."[38]

This turn of events took a lot of the luster off the Excelsiors, but the Detroit Club was thrilled by the opportunity for a rematch with even a diminished Excelsior Club. To prepare, the Detroit Club tried to find local clubs willing to play exhibition games with it—no easy task now that the "Young America spirit" was waning. The first such game was on September 21, Detroit easily beating the Regulars of Mt. Clemens 95-23. The game fell on the second anniversary of the day the Detroit Club had won the state championship, which caused some of the Detroit papers to mistakenly assume it was a title game and to deride the Regulars for their hubris in challenging so superior a club.

This understandably angered the Regulars, who pointed out that they had agreed to a practice game to help Detroit prepare for the Excelsiors and to improve their own play. Instead of being applauded for their efforts—they had left before daylight and traveled twenty miles in a lumber wagon to play—they were being mocked. It was no wonder that the Young America spirit was now in short supply.

The Detroit Club continued its preparations for the rematch with the Excelsiors by beating the University of Michigan Club 26-23 on September 28 in what was carefully billed as a practice game. The informal nature of the game was reinforced by some light moments, such as when Samuel Hayes reached base for the college squad and "caught sight of a pretty Detroit lady in the gallery, and fell into a trance, from which he was awakened by having Clark, first base, catch a ball suddenly sent in by Kelly, putting him out amid general laughter."[39] Another practice game on October 3 saw Detroit beat the Quicksteps of Toledo 71-18. The Quicksteps played without four of their best players, just as Detroit had in the first match between the two sides. The sloppy play of the Detroit players caused the *Advertiser and Tribune* to observe that "it has become almost a proverb that the Detroit Club never plays closely until compelled to."[40]

The first game of the long-anticipated rematch with the Excelsiors was scheduled for October 5 in Chicago, and nearly a hundred supporters accompanied the players on their train ride. But instead of getting revenge, Detroit was again soundly beaten by the Excelsiors, 49-20. The *Post*'s reporter felt that the Excelsiors had benefited from the umpiring of Ambrose Lynch, the Allegheny player who had won the best-catcher award at the Detroit tournament. The reporter claimed that Lynch let the Excelsiors' pitcher get away with deliberate wild pitching while being so strict about the delivery of Detroit Club pitcher M. M. Kelly that he had to be replaced. To its credit, the Detroit Club refused to use this as an excuse, and Frank Folsom made a point of stating that "Mr. Lynch fulfilled his duty promptly, and very satisfactorily."[41] The *Post*'s description of the crowd suggests that another element of the gentleman's game was dying; with only one policeman and few women present, the spectators engaged in "betting, hissing the umpire, getting in the way of Detroit players, and oaths and loud talk."[42]

The next stop for the Detroit Base Ball Club was Ann Arbor, for a formal match against the University of Michigan nine that had thrashed it so thoroughly and unexpectedly in the spring. On October 17, in front of a large and exuberant crowd, the Detroit Club got its revenge, winning 36-20. The spectators in Ann Arbor were similarly accused by the *Post* of engaging in behavior "not consistent with those professing to be gentlemen. But then it must be borne in mind that they are students, that they must feel their ignorance, and are attending the colleges for the purpose of learning something. One crew, especially, immediately in rear of the catcher and those on the fence endeavored to get off little jokes and puny sarcasm on every occasion."[43] The university's student newspaper responded in kind, counseling the *Post*'s reporter that "a deference for grammar, veracity, and common politeness, if not essential, are, at least, accessory to a successful literary career."[44] The third and deciding game in the series between the Detroit Base Ball Club and the University of Michigan was scheduled for November 2, but was postponed due to bad weather and never played.

Two days after the match in Ann Arbor, the Detroit Club hosted the Excelsiors of Chicago. The Excelsiors had been "reorganizing" since the debacle against the Nationals of Washington, adding players from the Mutuals of New York and a club in Bloomington, Illinois. Most important, they had recruited A. G. Spalding, the star teenaged pitcher of the Forest City Club of Rockford, who had accepted a forty-dollar-a-week job with a wholesale grocer in Chicago that required minimal duties as long as he pitched for the Excelsiors. (That would prove to be not for very long, as the grocer soon went bankrupt. The game against Detroit was Spalding's only appearance for the Excelsiors.)[45]

The Excelsiors' supporters came prepared for a celebration, bringing with them the Pecatonica horn and blowing loudly on it to cheer on their side. The game was very close throughout, and Detroit clung to a 24-21 lead after five innings, with darkness rapidly descending. But then poor defense by Detroit allowed the visitors to take the lead. After falling behind, Detroit's fielders started intentionally muffing the ball and allowing Chicago to score runs, hoping that the game would have to be called and that the score would revert to the last completed inning. Finally, the strange inning was concluded, and the game was called with Chicago victorious by a 36-24 score.

As usual, the Detroit Base Ball Club treated its guests with consummate courtesy: "The Excelsiors held a meeting, after leaving the city, and adopted a resolution thanking Mr. H. C. Wentworth, General Ticket Agent of the Michigan Central Railroad for his kindness in placing at their disposal, for the trip, the magnificent sleeping car 'Kalamazoo,' and in other ways enhancing the pleasure of the otherwise tedious journey. They also expressed their obligations to the proprietors of the Russell House, Detroit, for the sumptuous manner in which they were entertained while at that worthy hotel, and declare that they will also remember with pleasure the kindly treatment received at the hands of the Detroit Base Ball Club, on the occasion of their visit to this city."[46]

The season's final tour was made by the Eureka Club of Detroit, which traveled to Hamilton, Ontario, where it was beaten 39-37 on October 29. Several members of the Eureka Club were no-shows for the train, and the club had to borrow four players from Hamilton to fill out its nine. Nonetheless, the trip was a success. The behavior of the spectators was exemplary: "These people indulged in no demonstrations that might interfere with the playing. They cheered alike the good points on both sides, and while it must naturally be expected, they secretly hoped for the success of the Maple Leaf Club, yet they exercised good discretion, and did everything they could to make their visitors feel as comfortable as possible."

There was similar praise for the treatment the players received: "The Detroit players . . . arrived in Hamilton early Tuesday morning, and found a committee of reception awaiting them, and they were escorted to comfortable quarters at Cort's Hotel on King street west, where every possible attention was shown them, and nothing was left undone to make their visit agreeable in every respect. The members of the Maple Leaf Club were constant in their attentions, and the Detroit players feel that they are unable to repay them for the many kindnesses shown."[47]

While games continued into November, those sentiments afford an appropriate conclusion to a season that would be baseball's last as a gentleman's game in Michigan.

NOTES

1. The Creightons were named after baseball's first superstar, James Creighton of Brooklyn, who died in 1862, shortly after his twenty-first birthday. Legend attributes his untimely death to his rupturing an internal organ while hitting a home run, although the authenticity of this story is questionable.

2. *Detroit Advertiser and Tribune*, August 8, 1867. The abbreviation "inst." means "of this month."

3. *Detroit Free Press*, August 13, 1867.

4. *Detroit Free Press*, August 15, 1867.

5. According to the company, James Vernor left a barrel of his recipe for ginger ale to age while he fought in the Civil War. After his distinguished service culminated in his helping to capture Jefferson Davis, Vernor returned home and found the beverage even better than he expected.

6. *Detroit Post*, August 19, 1867.

7. *Detroit Advertiser and Tribune*, August 14, 1867.

8. *Detroit Free Press*, August 18, 1867.

9. *Detroit Post*, October 21, 1867.

10. *Chicago Tribune*, August 16, 1867.

11. *Detroit Free Press*, August 15, 1867.

12. There is evidence that gloves were being used even earlier than 1867. Frank E. Knappen reminisced some forty years later about his days at Kalamazoo High School, writing, "I remember seeing George C. Winslow during those years, play first base on a large common just south of the Old Union with buckskin gloves on." Knappen graduated from the high school in 1868, and Winslow in 1866, suggesting that gloves were being used at least that early (*Delphian* 4, no. 7 [April 1909]: 40). According to the *Sporting News* of June 28, 1886, "Delavarge, the catcher of the old Knickerbockers, an amateur club of Albany, used gloves when playing behind the bat in the sixties." There are other references that suggest that players were experimenting with gloves in the early 1860s, but the indication that their use had become common makes this article especially significant.

13. William Humber, *Diamonds of the North*, 28.

14. *Detroit Post*, August 17, 1867.

15. The Atlantics trounced the Young Canadians by a 75-11 margin in 1864. The statement that this was their only loss since 1861 was made in the Detroit papers. William Humber's *Diamonds of the North* does not refute the claim, but it appears that the team did not face much competition.

16. *Detroit Free Press*, August 18, 1867.

17. *Detroit Post*, August 21, 1867.

18. *Detroit Post*, August 21, 1867.

19. *Detroit Post*, August 19, 1867.

20. *Detroit Post*, August 21, 1867.

21. *Detroit Post*, August 22, 1867.

22. *Chicago Tribune*, August 17, 1867.

23. Humber, *Diamonds of the North*, 28. The players were Jim Nichols and Bill Sunley.

24. *Jackson Daily Citizen*, August 28, 1867. The article claimed that Conely was the club's captain, although McCord had accepted the award at the tournament.

25. Reprinted in the *Detroit Post*, August 21, 1867. Haynie was a reporter for the *Chicago Republican* and a member of the Excelsior Club. He would later umpire an 1871 National Association game between Cleveland and Chicago in which Cleveland walked off the field, forfeiting after claiming that Haynie had favored Chicago. The Cleveland papers alleged that Haynie had done the same in a game between Chicago and Philadelphia the previous season (*New York Clipper*, May 20, 1871, quoted in William J. Ryczek, *Blackguards and Red Stockings*, 104–5).

26. *Detroit Free Press*, August 23, 1867.

27. *Ann Arbor Peninsular Courier and Family Visitant*, August 22, 1867.

28. *Jackson Daily Citizen*, September 9, 1867.

29. *Detroit Advertiser and Tribune*, September 5, 1867.

30. *Ypsilanti Commercial,* August 31, 1867.

31. *Jackson Daily Citizen,* September 9, 1867. The Unknowns also swept the individual prizes, with John McCord winning a silver cup as best pitcher, Thomas Conely winning a silver goblet as best catcher, and Walter Johnson also winning a silver goblet for being the fastest base runner.

32. *Detroit Advertiser and Tribune,* September 18, 1867.

33. *Detroit Advertiser and Tribune,* September 20, 1867.

34. The Niagara Club would beat the Atlantics of Brooklyn the following season. Two of the Niagara players later settled in Michigan, Stanley Cowing in Kalamazoo and Myron Holly in Monroe. Cowing reminisced in 1906 about a game on June 6, 1869, when the Niagaras beat another Buffalo club called the Columbias by the record score of 209-10 (*Kalamazoo Evening Telegraph,* March 26, 1906). In spite of the score, the game took only three hours to complete.

35. Stephen Fox, *Big Leagues,* 184–96, gives an excellent account of the Nationals. The *E. F. French Baseball Scrapbook* (microfilm, the Historic Society of Washington, D.C.) gives additional details.

36. *Chicago Tribune,* July 26, 1867.

37. Albert G. Spalding, *America's National Game,* 109. This particular chapter contains many details about the Nationals' tour. However, Stephen Fox's account (in *Big Leagues*) is much more reliable than Spalding's rather self-serving one.

38. *Chicago Tribune,* July 31, 1867.

39. *Detroit Post,* September 30, 1867.

40. *Detroit Advertiser and Tribune,* October 4, 1867.

41. *Detroit Post,* October 8, 1867.

42. *Detroit Post,* October 8, 1867.

43. *Detroit Post,* October 18, 1867.

44. *University Chronicle* (Ann Arbor), October 26, 1867.

45. Spalding, *America's National Game,* 119–22.

46. *Detroit Advertiser and Tribune,* October 24, 1867.

47. *Detroit Advertiser and Tribune,* October 31, 1867.

14

BREAKING "FINGERS AND THE THIRD COMMANDMENT"

How Muffin Games Helped Renew a Sense of Belonging

The closing of the gentleman's era left baseball at a critical juncture. Prior to the war, regulation baseball had been played in Michigan only in a few large cities and primarily by middle- and upper-middle-class white men. This allowed the disorganized, all-inclusive version of the game to retain a substantial base. However, in the immediate aftermath of the war, the organized version of the game broke social barriers as it swept across lower Michigan and essentially drove the disorganized game into hiding.

As the burgeoning of competitive fervor began to limit the playing field to the young and athletic, elitism based on social class was succeeded by a new type of exclusivity. From clubs across the country came complaints that the first nine had a virtual monopoly on the practice field while the majority of club members paid their dues faithfully but rarely got the opportunity to play. When the *Detroit Post* had to apologize for accidentally describing original Franklin Club member Eugene Robinson as a "second-rate man" instead of as a "second nine man," many members of second nines must have found the mistake symbolic of their role.[1]

This new development represented a very grave threat to baseball's future. Could those disenfranchised from participation due to age or physical limitation continue to feel the sense of belonging that the game had once engendered? If this problem wasn't solved, baseball could prove to be just another fad.

A critical part of the solution was the advent of "muffin games," baseball games contested between club members or community members with no claim to athletic prowess and so named because of the amount of muffing that characterized the fielding. These games became immensely popular, and clubs began to boast a muffin nine in addition to a first and second nine. The games also served several important functions.

First, they kept club members who lacked the skill to play on the first nine happy and even conferred on them a special distinction. Second, they reminded spectators and players of the sheer fun of playing ball games. Third, they showed that society no longer frowned on displays of unalloyed pleasure. Fourth, they reminded spectators of the skill level of the best players by demonstrating the difficulty of plays that the best players made routinely. Fifth, they allowed a variety of new groups based on occupation, hobbies, and marital status to experience the camaraderie that had been so essential to building baseball's first clubs. Finally, they provided reporters, who described match games in deadly serious tones, with an opportunity to unleash their creative powers. These factors contributed to reviving the sense that everyone was on the same side.

The most celebrated of these matches took place on October 29, 1867, between nines representing the Russell and Biddle Houses, two of Detroit's principal hotels.[2] The game was heralded for days before, with the players preparing by dining exclusively on muffins and the newspapers contributing jocular notes, such as one that read, "All who have any knowledge of the game are to be excluded from the nines."[3] Richard Fyfe's experience as catcher for the Early Risers before the war must have been overlooked, but otherwise, as this account in the *Advertiser and Tribune* indicates, those responsible for enforcing this precept were very thorough:

The honors of the day were borne off by Mr. Taber, the proprietor of the Biddle House, who succeeded most of the time in striking out in a style that evinced the thoroughness of his training, as well as innate adaptation to the game. Mr. Baker, of the Russell House, was about equally lucky at the bat, but his game was marred by a propensity on his part to stop most of the balls that came into his section of the field. With practice, however, he will be able to break himself of this bad habit. Both these gentlemen made the handsome score of five outs, leading all others. Mr. Tinker's game, on the Russell House side, was also worthy of notice. A run to the third base, when there was a man already on it, who was thereby put out, was received with great applause, and in the field he displayed much skill in letting go "hot" balls that came to him, and much assiduity in nursing his hands thereafter. The finest running of the day was done by Mr. Cobb, of the Biddle House, who ultimately put in a substitute, to the disappointment of the crowd. In the matter of "flies" the honors are divided between Mr. LeFavour and Mr. L'Hommedieu. The former missed the largest number, while the latter let go of them with a neatness that astonished even himself, as well as his numerous admiring friends. Mr. LeF. excelled in quantity, and Mr. LeH. in quality. Mr. Bacon, amid other weak points of his play, made his crowning misplay by holding the only high "fly" that was caught during the game. The worst score was made by Mr. Fyfe, of the Russell House. He opened nobly, going to the bat first, hitting the first ball pitched, and immediately thereafter placing himself flat on the ground; but he degenerated from this excellent beginning. He did not succeed in making a single out, while his score was further marred by two home runs and five catches of foul balls. . . . Book opened promisingly by striking out twice in the first innings, but failed to keep it up. Hotchkiss and Rutter also commenced with a handsome series of outs, but they finally gave in, and notwithstanding their earnest endeavors made seven runs each.[4]

A later account gave the attendance at this game at over thirty thousand, clearly an impossible figure (the *Advertiser and Tribune* put the number at one thousand).[5] This account also detailed numerous highlights, including the injury to banker E. M. Cobb, who collapsed of exhaustion while running the bases. While Cobb's teammates were attempting to carry him off the field on a wooden shutter, the contraption broke and he fell to the ground again. Another mishap occurred when Mr. Langdon of the Biddle House nine put the wrong end of his meerschaum pipe in his mouth.

The dapper outfits of the two sides also contributed to the fun. The Russell House players were attired in nankeen pantaloons and knit jackets, while those representing the Biddle House sported nankeen pantaloons and brown linen dusters. When one player attempted to celebrate a base hit by turning somersaults on the way to first base, "a seam burst in his nankeens, . . . which sadly marred the effect."

Base-running errors afforded the crowd additional merriment. A. B. Taber, the proprietor of the Biddle House, was standing on second base when "a note was handed him, stating that he had neglected to leave orders with the steward whether there should be baked potatoes for supper or not, which in his excited state caused him to leave his base, and was thereby put out." L. W. Tinker created an even greater commotion with his ill-advised dash for third base: "When Tinker struck for his third base, coming in contact with Baker, who was already there, a shout went up from the immense throng that almost rent the earth. Cries of 'Beautiful!' 'Splendid!' came from the ladies; but Baker, when he arrived home, could not see it." The Biddle House won the game 72-70, but the score was barely noticed amid all the other features of the game.

Games like these have received little attention, since such buffoonery appears to defy analysis. Nonetheless, it is important to note that the parody was directed at precisely the characteristics that distinguished the man's sport from the boy's game, particularly the competitiveness. By incongruously juxtaposing childish actions with adult rituals, these muffin games offered both a belly laugh and a reminder that, in spite of the excesses of professional baseball, the game itself still belonged to everyone.

This parodic approach characterized coverage of many muffin games in Detroit. When the Biddle House played another local hotel, the Michigan Exchange, it was reported that both clubs prepared by dining on "fly" soup.[6] Prior to a game between the city's editors and reporters and the Atheneum Theatrical Company, special rules were announced, including one stating that "not more than one-quarter of an hour will be allowed any player to run from one base to another, unless he stops to tie his shoe."[7]

The *Free Press*'s account of a game between employees of two rival Detroit companies, the Merchants' Union and American Express, began with the words, "we hardly feel like criticizing the playing of muffins," but the opportunity proved irresistible:

> In the game of base-ball as played now-a-days we might regret that three men are not allowed on one base at the same time. It isn't necessary in such case that in order to get one of the men out the pitcher should run over and pound a man on the back. . . . Two men rushing to the same base are not safe from being put out, even if they both climb up on top of the sand bag and balance themselves. If the pitcher takes the ball on the bound direct from the bat, he should throw it to first base instead of holding it till the man runs the whole distance and lots of time to spare. In fielding, don't throw yourself on the ground and shut your eyes till the ball strikes and then pick it up as though it was a spherical shell with a lighted fuse attached. Stand up manfully and take it, it won't explode. . . . Calling "tally" on the third base is not available in the score, unless you afterwards reach the home base.[8]

Another muffin game, between officers of Wayne County and their counterparts from the city of Detroit, prompted this account:

> All of the players proved their right to the title of first class muffins, some of them by hard knocks and harder tumbles.
>
> Each side had nine captains, and it would be difficult to say how many umpires there were. Several times the whole field came in to argue the case with the official umpire, and only by great exertion

were they driven back. . . . The record of passed balls and missed flies was kept until the close of the fifth innings, when the scorers ran out of paper and gave it up. Four flies were caught and one home run made. As such play was out of order the names are suppressed.[9]

Such muffin games between civic officials became a regular feature of Detroit baseball. By 1870, the games had developed into a series with its own mock history in which a lazy city official who had been sitting at his desk swatting flies proudly announced that he'd caught eight flies in succession just when a county official appeared at his door. The county official assumed he was referring to baseball and bet him a bottle of wine that he couldn't catch a single fly, and the series ensued.[10]

The city officials won in 1868, prompting the county officials to engage in some practice before the 1870 game. Meanwhile their city counterparts, "not anticipating the return game at so early a date, were not in playing condition." Henry Starkey led off for the city officials, and the *Detroit Post* gave this uproarious account of his at bat:

Circuit Court Commissioner Prentis was the first pitcher of the county nine, and not having played in that position since he left the Red Stockings, his first ball was a fly, reaching its greatest altitude when above the striker's head. Starkey struck at it, however, but it wouldn't come down or stop, probably because it didn't see him motion to it with his bat. The umpire instructed the pitcher to "get his balls down," but meantime it had come down and been thrown back to the catcher. Three or four more balls were then pitched, which Starkey didn't strike at, and then put in a claim of foul pitching, alleging that the balls were thrown so near his feet and so close to the ground that they were not within his range of vision while passing. The claim was allowed, and the pitcher was directed to pitch the ball within sight of the batter. Two more balls were then pitched in close proximity to the striker's head, and he struck at both of them, such as little boys cuff at bumble bees that have got into their hair. At the third strike he dropped his club, as directed by the captain, and ran for the first base, but it was such a run as would have reminded Gordon Cumming of nothing in the world but a thirsty elephant getting under locomotion for a pool of water. The catcher had kindly let the ball go past him, however, and though he had ample time to send it to first base by freight, he miscalculated the distance or direction, or both, and sent it to the right fielder, thus giving Starkey his base.[11]

Other highlights that the *Post* recounted with pleasure involved the players' unfamiliarity with the basic rules of the game. These included "a slight error by Eaton, who mistook the third base for the first, and didn't deem it necessary to touch [the base runner] with the ball. He made amends for his mistake, however, by throwing it so accurately that he hit the base-runner squarely in the back." There was "a similar error on the part of De Foe, who thought it only necessary to lay the ball on the home base before the runner arrived." All of these anecdotes evoked nostalgia for the days when rules were loose or nonexistent.

As usual, the players' ineptitude also provided great amusement: "Not a fly was caught in the outfield, but the fielders invariably held up their hands, stumbled and rolled over the ball. Spectators, out of sympathy, rolled upon the grass." The game nearly had to be abandoned when the ball was hit into a neighboring potato patch and an elderly lady sicced her dog on the players who went in search of the ball. But one of the searchers fortuitously stepped on the ball while retreating, allowing the game to be completed with the county avenging their earlier loss by a 39-37 count.

These civic muffin games usually began with good-natured debate about who was eligible to play, as if in parody of the underlying issue of inclusion. In 1870, the county officials argued that street superintendent Bob Reaume of the city officials had such a fine physique that if he "should chance to hit the ball while batting, it might not come down this side of Dearborn, or perchance go much further," and that the game would never end.[12] A substitute replaced Reaume, and the county officials beat Henry Starkey and the city officials. In 1879, George H. Lesher, clerk of the recorder's court, showed up for a game between local aldermen and city officials wearing a boating hat and shirt and was promptly deemed a professional and ruled out of the game.

That so many of these games featured public officials suggests another reason for their popularity. Humor usually derives its force from what people feel most deeply. While the hilarity evoked by the muffin games seems disproportionate, it suggests that the games had become rituals offering catharsis for the pain of being excluded from participation. Watching distinguished members of the community act out this exclusion helped to assuage that pain and transform it into a renewed sense of belonging.

The muffin games offered biting parodies of the increasing tendency of players to take themselves and the game too seriously, especially the growing abuse of umpires. One game featured all the players rushing en masse to argue calls with the umpire. After a game between the employees of the *Detroit Post* and the *Detroit Tribune*, the *Post* wrote of the umpire that "the decisions of that functionary were never questioned. . . . [H]e was never called a 'lunkhead,' either publicly or privately, and . . . no one of the players recommended that he 'go home and soak his head.' All these omissions are, of course, attributable to the fact that the players were green at the business."[13]

Other games parodied players' priorities by raising a simpler question: did winning a baseball game really justify all that running? The answer was a decided "no." After a game between the No. 46 Lafayette Avenue Amateurs and Farrand, Williams, and Company, F. S. Lewis was commended for "repeatedly avoiding the labor of running around the bases under an uncomfortably hot sun."[14] The *Detroit Post* similarly wrote in mock praise of the strategy employed by a team of *Tribune* employees in a game against a nine of chair-factory workers. With the temperature reaching ninety-four degrees in the shade, the *Tribune*'s club kept

> their deluded victims running the gauntlet of bases all the afternoon, until they were nearly melted. . . . The whole catch of the trick is, not

to catch the ball. Run for it as hard as you like, put up your hands, and adroitly let it slip through your fingers. The *Tribune* nine have reduced this to a science, and in the game of Saturday the skill with which they executed the trick evoked roars of laughter. In a game of only seven innings they made their opponents run around the in-field 54 times, and were sent around but five times themselves.[15]

Quite a variety of other muffin matches soon surfaced in Detroit. Men working in the dry-goods trade played men employed in the book industry. Two literary societies met on the ball field, as did two of the local boat clubs. A group of fire-insurance salesmen squared off against life-insurance salesmen. In Fort Wayne, infantrymen faced members of the battery for a barrel of ale. Employees of H. P. Baldwin played workers for A. C. McGraw. Various groups had games between married and single members. After a game between two dispatch companies, the box score was prefaced with the observation, "For about two hours the carnage was dreadful, and when the smoke of battle cleared away the following were discovered to be the casualties."[16] A game between law clerks was scheduled "unless an injunction should be issued by the clerk of the weather."[17]

The development of more segmented groupings was an important indication of Detroit's transition into a modern city. As Detroit's population continued to grow, identifying oneself as a resident of Detroit was no longer specific enough to confer a sense of identity. These games allowed fraternal groups to be established that reflected more nuanced elements of identity.

Muffin games soon spread outside of Detroit. Two fire companies played in Muskegon in 1870; the prizes awarded at the game's conclusion included a cabbage, nine red herrings, a pumpkin, and Mrs. Winslow's soothing syrup.[18] City versus county muffin games also soon caught on in Adrian and Ann Arbor. A tongue-in-cheek account of one in Adrian parodied the increasing abuse of umpires:

The *umpire* was against [the City nine]. We shall not give this umpire's name, we will not do him that honor; but Ed. Crane didn't do the fair thing. He called the City boys out when they were not out at all; and he wouldn't call the County boys out, if he could help it. Ed. Crane can't umpire a game of base ball right. He don't know the game. He can't tell a foul, from a second base. He decided a "city" man out because he wouldn't run the bases backwards, and called Sim Babcock out, because he wouldn't let him wear his policeman's star. He made Tynan lose a tally, because he ran with his boots off, and called Dan Anderson out, because he put both hands in his pocket, and yelled "butter-fingers" to Ed. Sayers, when he dropped a ball. Of course no one could play against an umpire, and we ought to give his name, so that clubs hereafter won't get deceived, but we will not do Ed. Crane the pleasure of mentioning him as umpire. We have no doubt that he was bought, yes *bought*, and that his pockets are now lined with County gold.[19]

Three years later, the same newspaper wrote before another muffin game that "the decisions of the umpire are to be received in humble submission when they are in your favor. If he decides against your club, an intimation that he has been paid may prove effectual."[20]

A game in Hudson featured local lawyers and doctors whose outlandish attire heightened the inherent incongruity of dignified gentlemen playing a boy's game. The "grave-looking members of each distinguished profession marched through the gates and a shower of garlands of choice flowers. . . . [Some] were accoutred after the oriental manner, and others wore sandals and knee-bands. Some again wore Turkish turbans, while a few had donned naval attire, and one or two had on regular's uniforms."[21] The contrast between the grave manner of the players and their comical outfits suggests the reaction to the men who had dared to play baseball in Philadelphia thirty-five years earlier.

The game prompted the lawyers of Adrian to challenge the attorneys of Hudson. The highlight of that game came when George Whitbeck of Hudson wandered off base on a foul ball. The rules of the day required him to return to the base before the ball got there, and his teammates yelled at him to remind him of this fact.

Unfortunately, "he did not get under motion easily, and once being under way was difficult to stop. At last the whole club incontinently went for him, picked him up and amid much rough treatment carried him back to his base. But it was too late."[22] Three years later, the lawyers of Adrian challenged their Hudson counterparts to another game. Parodying the increasingly litigious approach to the rules, Willard Stearns of Adrian specified that the match was "to be played by the rules of the National Base Ball Association—and Bouvier's Law Dictionary. You may select an umpire, provided he be not over seven feet high or under three, and is not blind in both eyes."[23]

A game in Grand Rapids featured an intermission whenever one of the players felt a whim to take a drink, perform a balancing act, or buy a hat.[24] Another game, in Hudson, saw one of the players "run whenever he felt it in his bones, foul or otherwise, and it took all the force of Captain Jo.'s lungs to recall him to his proper position."[25] In Adrian, one outfielder started to chase a long hit but "inadvertently forgot what he went for, and stopped near the race track to applaud the winner of the race then in progress."[26] The captain of a Saginaw muffin nine had trouble aligning his fielders, "as most of them wished to be stationed near the brewery on Hamilton street."[27] After a game in Ann Arbor, the *Detroit Post* noted, "It was rare sport for the lookers-on to see grave old men, weighing 200 pounds and upwards, rolling in the sand like babies at every misstep."[28] All of these descriptions bring to mind the impulsive way that baseball was played before the advent of the regulation game.

Other muffin games parodied the pain that had become part of the game since the change to a hard ball. A celebrated game in Flint on September 4, 1874, pitted hardware merchants against members of other professions. A procession to the grounds was led by Gardner's Flint City Band and followed by the players and an ambulance bearing the encouraging inscription, "Ambulance for killed and wounded of Hardware vs. Merchants and Professionals." The ambulance was followed by the mayor, whose function was to take dying confessions, and the brevet surgeon-general, who could barely be seen beneath a pile of scalpels and other medical paraphernalia.[29] A game in Charlotte between the "Scoopers" and the "Hoopers" was prefaced by the announcement that, while no admittance fee would be charged, "a collection may be taken up, to defray the surgeons [*sic*] fees."[30] At a muffin game between Fats and Leans in Kalamazoo on October 20, 1875, to the catcher's immediate left was a table covered with surgical instruments, including a stretcher, a three-foot syringe, and a butcher's saw for amputating limbs.

Muffin games soon prompted many spin-offs. Especially popular were games, such as the one in Kalamazoo, between Fats and Leans, offering a vivid example of reinvolving men otherwise precluded from participation. An 1867 club called the "Never Sweats" of Saranac was made up of men between forty and seventy who weighed over two hundred pounds, with an aggregate of over a ton. The players earned their name because they only batted, hiring boys to run the bases for them![31] The third baseman for the Maumee Street nine of Adrian in 1879 was rumored to have "built a tent around his base and [hired] a boy to get the ball and carry it to him when a base runner is to be put out."[32] Fats and Leans games became so popular in 1875 that one paper estimated that no fewer than 189,645 took place that year.[33]

These exhibitions naturally produced their share of comical moments. One in Jackson was advertised with the promise that "something like three tons of humanity will tread down the grass and break its fingers and the third commandment."[34] The game featured the "Quicksteps" and the "Pounders," both of whose players moved with the "speed of a canal boat."[35] The highlight of a Fats versus Leans game in Niles came when a player named Sam Gunzburg made "the run of three bases in remarkable time. On reaching the first base he fell, striking on his head; at the second base he fell, striking the ground mostly all over, and at the third, he turned a double somersault, when a friend stopped him and told him it was love's labor lost. He had been 'put out' after dropping the bat. Sam remarked: 'Well, so help me gracious. I was bound for that home run if I shoost had to break a leg.'"[36]

Competition between rival companies was another offshoot of the muffin game that developed a life of its own. These games thrived in the 1860s by enhancing workers' identification with their employers but by the 1870s were being replaced by industrial leagues that had a standard of play far eclipsing that of the muffin game. Chicago had more than fifty company-sponsored clubs by 1870, and the practice soon spread to Michigan.[37]

As early as 1872, Nichols, Shepard, and Company, a Battle Creek foundry, was sponsoring one of that city's best baseball clubs. The Yates Club, one of Grand Rapids' best clubs in the late 1870s, grew out of a club of employees of the Phoenix Furniture Company. D. M. Ferry, owner of the rapidly growing seed company D. M. Ferry and Company and a member of the Detroit Base Ball Club, sponsored and umpired games between different divisions of his company. By 1879, the "Seeds," a team made up of Ferry's employees, was competing against top amateur clubs.[38]

Another important offspring of the muffin game was the old-timer's game. These games became especially popular in Grand Rapids in 1879, with a series of games played with "a soft ball, putting out runners by hitting them with the ball, tallying with notches on a stick, etc., etc."[39]

Eventually most offshoots of the muffin game began to be played with more competitiveness and, in another indication of baseball's cyclical tendencies, to assume characteristics of the games they had initially parodied. As early as 1868, prizes were being competed for and ringers were occasionally being introduced. Two members of the Detroit Base Ball Club helped the Celtic Literary Society to an easy win in a supposed muffin game against the Literary Adelphi, causing the *Free Press* to suggest that "as the games between the two societies have hitherto been so close, their next game should be confined to their own members."[40] By 1879, the *Post and Tribune* complained, "Now-a-days rival shops indulge in base ball matches, and, after muffing through nine innings and running the score up into the hundreds, report the score at the newspaper office as 'a closely contested game—score 4 to 3.'"[41]

Dexter M. Ferry of the Detroit Base
Ball Club was the owner of the
rapidly growing seed company
D. M. Ferry and Company, still in
existence today. He understood the
camaraderie baseball could bring
and sponsored and umpired games
between different divisions of his
company. He also sponsored a company team called the "Seeds," one of
whose players graduated to the
major leagues. *Courtesy of the State
of Michigan Archives*

D. M. FERRY.

The desire not to appear risible is understandable, but such self-
consciousness detracted from the entertainment value of the games.
The *Post* wrote of the 1868 game between the Merchants' Union and
American Express that "most of the players are profoundly ignorant
of the laws and science of the game, but all are terribly in earnest."[42]
This earnestness was essential to the appeal of the muffin games—
without the incongruity between that solemnity and the laughable
play, the spectacle would merely be a second-rate game of ball. A
much better understanding of the spirit of such games was shown
when the *Post and Tribune* noted in 1879 that a muffin game between
lawyers and reporters would be "none of your paltry 3 to 0 affairs;
look out for a good old fashioned score—say about 63 to 97."[43]

But such developments were still years away, and at their outset
the muffin games offered a welcome respite from the serious issues
that were beginning to plague the game. When nine members of the
Atheneum Theatrical Company played a muffin game with nine
newspapermen, spectators were invited to attend with the reminder
that "smiles and applause only are required to insure admission."[44]
Another muffin game, between clerks from two rival banks, was
advertised with the words, "Their friends and the public generally

are invited to witness the breaking of fingers, blacking of eyes and bruising of heads consequent on the noble game."[45] It was refreshing to know that all that was being settled was who would pay for the shared supper after the match. At a muffin game in Saginaw, "there was nothing at stake but fun and warmth, and they had plenty of both."[46]

Muffin games thus accomplished the essential feat of allowing baseball fever to again be a shared passion. As one game description noted: "It is not merely 'professional' players that are liable to infection. Base ball spares neither the high or the low, the rich or the poor, the young or the old, but numbers among its victims and devotees representatives from all classes in society. Fat men's clubs are organized, and oleaginous matches played; old gray-headed parties . . . catch the infection, and struggle through antiquated, ossified games."[47] The lineal descendants of the muffin game continue to this day, and the magnitude of their contribution to baseball history is difficult to overstate. At a time when rapid changes to the game were excluding more and more people and threatening its support, the muffin game helped return baseball to the people.

NOTES

1. *Detroit Post*, September 25, 1867.
2. The Russell House had been a major part of the rituals of the Early Risers and would again figure in Detroit baseball history. Before Detroit's first game in the American League in 1900, a parade to the game commenced at the Russell House. (The American League would become a major league the next year.)
3. *Detroit Advertiser and Tribune*, October 26, 1867.
4. *Detroit Advertiser and Tribune*, October 30, 1867.
5. *Detroit Free Press*, December 26, 1884. It erroneously claimed the account was from the *Commercial Advertiser*. Most of the description that follows comes from this reprint.
6. *Detroit Advertiser and Tribune*, November 8, 1867.
7. *Detroit Post*, August 31, 1867.
8. *Detroit Free Press*, August 13, 1868. The last comment was directed at a player named Vail.
9. *Detroit Free Press*, August 14, 1868.
10. *Detroit Daily Post*, August 6, 1870.
11. *Detroit Daily Post*, August 6, 1870.
12. *Detroit Advertiser and Tribune*, August 6, 1870.
13. *Detroit Post*, September 13, 1873.
14. *Detroit Advertiser and Tribune*, June 6, 1874.

15. *Detroit Daily Post*, July 18, 1870.

16. *Detroit Advertiser and Tribune*, August 13, 1877.

17. *Detroit Advertiser and Tribune*, July 30, 1874.

18. *Muskegon Enterprise*, September 30, 1870.

19. *Adrian Daily Press*, August 18, 1873.

20. *Adrian Daily Press*, April 28, 1876.

21. *Hudson Gazette*, August 4, 1871.

22. *Adrian Times and Expositor*, September 2, 1871.

23. *Hudson Gazette*, August 7, 1874.

24. *Grand Rapids Daily Times*, September 4, 1877.

25. *Hudson Post*, July 30, 1874.

26. *Adrian Times and Expositor*, August 18, 1873.

27. *Saginaw Daily Courier*, September 12, 1879.

28. *Detroit Daily Post*, September 1, 1870.

29. *Flint Wolverine Citizen*, September 12, 1874.

30. *Charlotte Leader*, July 30, 1875.

31. *Detroit Advertiser and Tribune*, July 24, 1867.

32. *Adrian Daily Times and Expositor*, August 8, 1879.

33. *Detroit Evening News*, August 24, 1875.

34. *Detroit Evening News*, July 27, 1875.

35. *Jackson Daily Citizen*, July 28, 1875.

36. *Niles Republican*, August 22, 1878.

37. Stephen Freedman, "The Baseball Fad in Chicago, 1865–1870," 54.

38. The pitcher for the "Seeds," a clerk named Frank W. McIntyre, would have a brief major-league career.

39. *Grand Rapids Daily Eagle*, June 4, 1879.

40. *Detroit Free Press*, August 26, 1868. The American Express Club soon began using a first-rate pitcher and catcher who were "hardly attaches of the Express Company" (*Detroit Free Press*, July 12, 1871).

41. *Detroit Post and Tribune*, April 29, 1879.

42. *Detroit Post*, August 12, 1868.

43. *Detroit Post and Tribune*, August 1, 1879.

44. *Detroit Advertiser and Tribune*, August 31, 1867.

45. *Detroit Advertiser and Tribune*, June 10, 1874.

46. *Saginaw Daily Courier*, July 26, 1877.

47. *Detroit Free Press*, July 10, 1870.

15

"ABILITY AND INTELLIGENCE SHOULD BE RECOGNIZED FIRST AND LAST"

WOMEN AND AFRICAN AMERICANS IN EARLY BASEBALL

Unfortunately, at the same time that muffin games were helping to restore a sense of inclusiveness, opportunities to draw new groups into baseball were being missed. Although the long-standing resistance to playing games for pleasure had been overcome, society still allowed only a limited range of acceptable roles for women and African Americans.

The presence of women at early baseball games was strongly encouraged because it improved the behavior of the male spectators. However, it was another matter for women to actually play baseball. Croquet was a popular feminine activity, but competition at a physical sport like baseball represented a serious threat to society's idealized view of the gentler sex. On a practical level, baseball was very difficult to play in the restrictive clothing worn by nineteenth-century women. Perhaps at a deeper level, the immoderate passion that the game produced also made many consider it an unacceptable activity for women.

Nonetheless, in at least five Michigan towns between 1867 and 1880, young women attempted to form baseball clubs. The first two efforts were made in Saranac and Dowagiac in 1867, but no record of the activities of either club exists.[1] A similar club in Kalamazoo the following year received a genial, if rather condescending, reaction: "A number of ladies of this place have organized a base ball and croquet club.—They have secured grounds and are putting themselves through a thorough course of training. The two nines played a spirited little game a few nights ago, and the score showed some good playing. We shall expect to hear shortly of a challenge being given to some of our old clubs. The boys will have to look out for their laurels."[2]

The next attempt came in 1874 when a group of young ladies in East Tawas formed a baseball club. The local newspaper applauded their efforts, but condescension was again evident in remarks like, "with a reasonably gallant umpire they could, even now, knock the spots off the 'Red Stockings,' 'Rough and Ready's,' [and] 'Plug Uglies'" and, "Their poorest playing was at the bat where they will no doubt greatly improve, especially after marriage." The reporter carefully used terms like "fielderesses" and "base women" and noted with amusement that the umpire kept announcing "'two *men* out' 'three *men* out' & c., when he couldn't help seeing they were all women."[3]

Finally, a female baseball club was organized in Bayfield in the Upper Peninsula in 1878. The risqué nature of the enterprise was conveyed by a note in the *Marquette Mining Journal* that, in order to preserve decency, "none but married men are allowed to umpire and watch the girls slide in on the home base."[4] There is no mistaking the hint that a sport like baseball represented a challenge to a society uncomfortable with the idea of women as physical beings.

None of these trailblazing clubs were treated with outright hostility by the local newspapers. Nevertheless, each club either gave up almost immediately or the newspapers ceased to report their activities. It is quite possible that they simply found baseball less enjoyable than they expected and decided to disband, a course pursued by many men's clubs. However, the experience of the few women's clubs of the period who persevered in their efforts makes it very likely that the Michigan women felt some pressure to desist.

In 1879, two clubs of professional women baseball players toured the country and attracted significant crowds. Sadly, however, the crowds seemed to have turned out largely for the opportunity to laugh at the endeavor. As the women toured New England there were reports that "the spectators tease them unmercifully, sometimes trip them up as they run, and even seize and kiss them."[5] Another Michigan paper crowed, "let's have the women here . . . it's better than a circus."[6]

When the women did play in Detroit in front of a large crowd, the *Post and Tribune* made no effort to hide its contempt: "It was the worst burlesque upon the national game imaginable, and not even funny. The females were neither comely, shapely nor graceful, and their awkward antics demonstrated that while there are many things a woman can accomplish playing base ball is not one of them. It is not her great specialty. It does not enable her to do justice to herself. The women of America may do a great many things with impunity, but when she essays base ball she should be kindly but firmly suppressed."[7]

These comments seem wildly disproportionate; nobody was being forced to watch, so why should there be such outrage? Especially significant is the assertion that women who play poorly need to be "suppressed," since muffin games were popular precisely because of the players' ineptitude. The overreaction clearly suggests a much deeper underlying threat: recognition of women's physicality would be a tacit acknowledgment of their sexuality and would lead inevitably to the basic forms of equality already being called for by the women's suffrage movement.[8]

Another effort five years later was condemned just as harshly: "Females can't play base ball even a little bit, and all attempts to organize and run such clubs must end in disaster. Let us hear no more of female base ball clubs. The public wants none of it."[9] A tour by a Philadelphia women's baseball club that same year enabled the press to more openly allege sexual impropriety.

> The girls are from 15 to 19 years of age, jaunty in style, brazen in manner, and peculiar in dress. When they reached [Albany, Georgia]

their agent obtained room for them at the Artesian Hotel. It was not long before the proprietor discovered that the character of his house was suffering. All the swells of the city were around the place like a swarm of bees. The proprietor promptly ejected the ball players, and they had to amuse themselves for several hours at the depot until the train arrived. . . . Their conduct was of such a character that respectable ladies got off the cars and waited for the next train.[10]

And the press took an "I told you so" approach in 1891 when the male manager of a touring female baseball team was sent to Sing Sing for abducting a sixteen-year-old girl and forcing her to travel with the club: "The sentence . . . will likely put an end to all female base ball clubs. For this relief much thanks."[11]

Thus, although the first Michigan women to form baseball clubs appear to have been treated with surface indulgence, it seems reasonable to suspect that they encountered at least subtle disapproval. And, had they persevered with playing baseball, we can be much more certain that the disapproval would have turned to overt pressure.

The prejudice against African Americans took a different form. There was no objection to their playing the game, but there was some resistance to recognizing their activities and allowing them to appear on the same field with whites. In 1867, the Pythians of Philadelphia, an African American club, applied for membership in the NABBP and were turned down because of their skin color. The nominating committee did not elaborate on their reasons, but one reporter wrote that their object was "to keep out of the Convention the discussion of any subject having a political bearing, as this undoubtedly had."[12] The curious reasoning was typical of an era in which white Americans were unwilling to recognize African Americans as equals, yet were too busy patting themselves on the back for ending slavery to admit the extent of their prejudice.

While barriers and indignities confronted African Americans at every turn, many elements of the systematic segregation that later emerged were not yet in place, and baseball is a good case in point. This was especially true in states like Michigan where the small

African American population made racial issues easy to avoid. Michigan was home to fewer than seven thousand African Americans in 1860, with only three counties having more than five hundred African American residents. As a result, the state's first documented African American club, the Rialto Base Ball Club of Detroit, did not appear until 1867.

Unfortunately, the Rialtos had a difficult time getting white clubs to face them. For example, on November 12, 1867, the *Detroit Advertiser and Tribune* published a challenge from twelve grocerymen on Woodward Avenue to any interested club. The next day, the paper published a note indicating that the challenge had been accepted by the Rialtos but that "in order that there may be no misunderstanding, we will state beforehand that the Rialto Club is composed of colored men."[13] This backed the issuers of the challenge into a corner, since the code of gentlemanly conduct required them to stand by their challenge.

The issuers of the challenge took the cowardly way out. Seven grocerymen wrote the *Advertiser and Tribune* to claim that the initial challenge had been a hoax, which they blamed on an "individual styling himself Frank R. Giddy."[14] Giddy, singled out, had no interest in being a pioneer and named the men who were party to the challenge, while repeating their willingness for a match against another club. The *Advertiser and Tribune* pointed out in vain that "if they issue an unconditional challenge, they are honor bound to play any men who accept that challenge. Unless he is willing to do this he must be willing to shut up."[15] The OK Club of Detroit accepted this second challenge and a match was played. In 1870, the Rialtos challenged the city champion Empires but this challenge appears to have fallen on deaf ears.[16] In spite of these disappointing outcomes, the support of the *Advertiser and Tribune* suggests that there was no consensus that African Americans and whites could not compete on the baseball field.

Appropriately enough it was in Battle Creek, hometown of Sojourner Truth, that the state's first documented game between an African American club and a white one took place on June 15, 1871.

The Snowflakes, an African American team, lost to the Battle Creek High School Club by a 24-23 score, ushering in a decade that would see increasing, though by no means unanimous, acceptance of integration on the ball field. Later that year, the *Kalamazoo Telegraph* noted that an African American club from Detroit was planning to tour the rural districts, but no further details appeared.[17]

Another African American club, the Red Stars of Battle Creek, took third at a tournament in Charlotte in 1874 and challenged any club in the county to play them for the county championship and ten dollars.[18] An Ann Arbor club called the Black Stockings faced the old Ann Arbor Club on July 29, 1874, but was trounced 119-18. An African American club formed by the employees of the Northwestern Hotel in Marquette County played three games against white clubs in 1874, and the Emancipation Base Ball Club of Hudson challenged a club of doctors and lawyers that same year, though there is no record of the game being played. Another club, the Uniques of Chicago, tried to plan a tour of Michigan in 1874, but the Mutuals of Jackson declined to play them and the tour seems to have been canceled.[19]

An African American club from Detroit played a club from Ann Arbor on July 26, 1875, at the university. In August 1875, a club of African American barbers was formed in Jackson. The barbers procured grounds between Milwaukee and Francis streets and challenged the city's white barbers to a game, though there is no indication that one was ever played.[20] Emancipation Day, the August 1 celebration of the freeing of the slaves in the West Indies, was commemorated in East Saginaw in 1876 by a game between the African American Unique Club and the white Continental Club. Unfortunately, the opportunity to increase racial harmony was lost when the Uniques claimed that they had won 21-14, while the Continentals contended that they had won by forfeit.

In September 1877, an African American club called the Eckfords of Battle Creek entered a tournament in Augusta. The Eckfords beat Ross Centre 11-8 and a club called the Plow Boys 20-3 to capture first place in the second division. Their presence in the tournament does not seem to have excited any controversy.

In contrast, only five matches in Michigan between African American clubs during the 1870s can be documented. Two of these were billed as championship matches—one between an African American club from Niles and the Red Stars of Battle Creek in August 1874, and the second in Battle Creek on the centennial day of July 4, 1876, between the Red Stars of Battle Creek and the Snow Flakes of Jackson.[21] Did the white newspapers simply ignore many other matches between African American clubs? Or did the size of the African American population and the expense of travel prevent such matches from being anything other than rarities? Unfortunately, there is no way to be certain.

What can be said more definitively is that there were several integrated clubs during the 1870s. In a game in Jackson on September 13, 1875, a team called the Westerns that consisted of two African American boys and seven white boys beat an all–African American club called the Sailor Boys, 16-14.[22] An African American man named John Wesley played in a game between the Stars of Norvell and the Phoenix Club of Brooklyn on June 11, 1875.[23]

Another integrated club was the Wolverine Club of Benton Harbor, founded in 1870. The Wolverines' star player was Luck Hackley, a light-skinned African American man who became renowned for hitting home runs up Hunter's Hill on the club's playing grounds. Even when outfielders positioned themselves at the top of the hill, Hackley was still able to hit the ball over their heads. Hackley became known as "the most popular base ball man in the village. He kept the game alive whenever it showed signs of waning. . . . His barber shop on Pipestone street was base ball headquarters."[24]

Luck Hackley's race was never mentioned in the newspapers, a very suggestive fact. It is quite possible that Luck's light skin allowed him to pass for white in games against outside clubs. However, he had three brothers who had much darker skin, and it seems unlikely that anyone in a small community like Benton Harbor would have been unaware of his race.

Another integrated club was the Courier nine of Saginaw. On

July 4, 1878, the Courier nine put up a tough fight against the Plymouth Club, then considered the top club in the state. However, none of the accounts of the game thought it necessary to mention that Saginaw catcher and club assistant captain Will H. Smith was an African American. His race only emerged when an article six years later casually mentioned that Smith had been playing for the Black Stockings of St. Louis, Missouri.[25]

In light of the fact that both Hackley and Smith were star baseball players and took a leadership role in their communities, it is intriguing that no mention was made of their race. It suggests that, at least on the baseball field, many considered race a non-issue. This raises the possibility that there may have been many other integrated clubs during the 1870s.

A particularly impressive display of racial harmony took place in Flint on September 17, 1877, in a muffin game between white barbers and their African American counterparts. A dramatic prelude to the game was planned: "At 1:30 P.M. the colored nine will assemble on the corner at Fenton Block, and the whites on the opposite corner near the Savings Bank. The drum corps will give a signal, the boys will then fall in in a single file, half face inward, forward, and meet in the center of the street, a colored and a white man together, and march to the Fair Grounds."[26] The account of the game, under the headline "THE COLOR LINE EXPUNGED," reported that "much merriment was indulged in by all present."[27]

The 1880s started with signs that baseball was becoming still more accessible to African Americans. Several played professional baseball in the minor leagues and two former University of Michigan students, brothers Fleetwood and Welday Walker, became the first African Americans to play in the major leagues.

However, as the decade wore on, matters changed dramatically. African Americans faced increasing hostility and eventually were driven out of professional baseball entirely by "gentlemen's agreements" not to sign them. With the opportunity closing, Welday Walker wrote sadly in 1888, "There should be some broader cause—such as want of ability, behavior, and intelligence—for barring a player than his color. It is for these reasons and because I think ability and intelligence should be recognized first and last—at all times and by everyone—I ask the question again, why was the 'law permitting colored men to sign repealed, etc.?' "[28]

But African Americans did not give up baseball easily. Abortive attempts to form professional leagues for African Americans were made in 1886 and 1887. By the 1890s, several African American touring clubs were thriving, with one of the most successful being the Page Fence Giants of Adrian. Eventually the success of these touring clubs led to the 1920 founding of the first of the leagues known collectively as the Negro Leagues.

Why did the color barrier descend in the 1880s, especially when there were such positive signs in the 1870s? Certainly part of the answer to this important question lies in a complex white backlash against African Americans epitomized by the Supreme Court's 1883 invalidation of the Civil Rights Act of 1875. As historian Harold Seymour notes, "It is a well-known historical paradox that, as the Civil War receded, Jim Crowism in America became more pronounced."[29] But likely African American baseball players were also victims of their own success—the better they played, the harder it was to reconcile their accomplishments with racist assumptions of their inferiority.[30] Historian Allen Guttmann notes that fourteen of the fifteen jockeys in the first Kentucky Derby in 1875 were African Americans, but African Americans were soon excluded from that sport as well.[31]

It is equally tempting to speculate about the reasons that led women and African Americans to play baseball. Was it primarily for exercise and relaxation? Did they see it as a means of casting off the bonds placed on them by society? Did they realize the consternation they would cause and sense that provocation was their only form of power? The limited evidence does not permit a definitive conclusion, but most likely all three of these reasons provide at least some measure of truth.

Whatever women and African Americans hoped to access by means of baseball, what they got instead was a reminder of their limited role in society. The experience of immigrants from non-English-speaking countries stands in particularly stark contrast.

Immigrants from the British Isles had been included from the game's earliest days, and by the late 1860s immigrants from non-English-speaking countries were beginning to make baseball part of the process of assimilation.[32] A particularly symbolic instance occurred in Detroit, where a group of young German immigrants formed the Milo Base Ball Club. In order to raise money for uniforms, the new club organized a ball on September 2, 1868, at Woodbridge Grove, which was located at the corner of Michigan and Trumbull, the future home of the Tigers.

During the 1870s, the names of immigrants from non-English-speaking countries gradually became more common in box scores. They faced less direct opposition than did women and African Americans and thus their important story attracted less attention. Ever since then, immigrants have found baseball a potent means of assimilating themselves into American culture. But this highlights an important distinction: most immigrants could choose to eliminate their differences and blend in with their new neighbors, but women and African Americans had no choice about being defined by those differences.

Thus, while muffin games were allowing baseball to become more inclusive, societal pressures did not make it possible to take full advantage of the opportunity. Baseball did gradually incorporate immigrants from non-English-speaking countries and they would become loyal supporters of the game. But the inclusion of women and African Americans was much more conditional. Women were welcomed as spectators, but discouraged from active participation. African Americans were at first welcomed as participants, but then excluded when the possibility that they would outperform whites began to emerge. This was a loss for baseball and, much worse, for the country.

NOTES

1. *Detroit Advertiser and Tribune*, July 22, 1867. Three days later the *Ball Players' Chronicle* reported that a baseball club of women had been formed in Niles, and the item was widely reprinted. However, the *Niles Weekly Times* of September 12, 1867, denounced the story as a hoax. Undoubtedly, the original note had simply been misread.

2. *Kalamazoo Daily Telegraph*, May 29, 1868.

3. *Iosco County Gazette* (Tawas), August 20, 1874.

4. *Marquette Mining Journal*, June 29, 1878.

5. *Muskegon News and Reporter*, August 13, 1879.

6. *Adrian Daily Times and Expositor*, August 18, 1879.

7. *Detroit Post and Tribune*, August 18, 1879.

8. Lucretia Mott and Elizabeth Cady Stanton organized their Women's Rights Convention in 1848. The American Woman Suffrage Association was established in 1869; its ideas began to attract widespread attention after an 1890 merger with Susan B. Anthony's more militant National Woman Suffrage Association.

9. *Sporting Life*, May 28, 1884.

10. *Sporting Life*, December 24, 1884.

11. *Sporting Life*, October 31, 1891.

12. *Ball Players' Chronicle*, December 19, 1867, reprinted in Dean Sullivan, *Early Innings*, 68.

13. *Detroit Advertiser and Tribune*, November 13, 1867.

14. *Detroit Advertiser and Tribune*, November 14, 1867.

15. *Detroit Advertiser and Tribune*, November 17, 1867.

16. *Detroit Advertiser and Tribune*, October 1, 1870.

17. *Kalamazoo Daily Telegraph*, August 21, 1871.

18. *Detroit Advertiser and Tribune*, July 13, 1874.

19. *Jackson Daily Citizen*, May 15, 1874; the *Grand Rapids Daily Eagle* of September 2, 1874, claimed that the Uniques had games arranged in Greenville and Big Rapids, but there is no record that the games were played. The Mutuals' unwillingness to play the Uniques was not necessarily racially motivated, as they frequently declined games if they were not remunerative.

20. *Jackson Daily Citizen*, August 16 and 17, 1875.

21. The other documented games between African American clubs were: an unnamed African American club from Detroit hosting a club from Chatham, Ontario, on July 12, 1871, in front of a large crowd; the Red Stars of Battle Creek beating a club called the Creepers 20-11 on July 27, 1874; an African American club from Ypsilanti beating one from Detroit 19-4 on August 23, 1874.

22. *Jackson Daily Citizen*, September 14, 1875.

23. *Manchester Enterprise*, June 17, 1875.

24. James Pender, *History of Benton Harbor and Tales of Village Days*, 76. Pender is the source for all the information on Hackley. Few box scores from Benton Harbor games of the early 1870s survive, but Hackley's name appears in several game accounts from the late 1870s, including one between Muskegon and St. Joseph on August 22, 1878, in which the St. Joseph club contained several players from South Haven and Benton Harbor.

25. *Saginaw Evening Express*, April 12, 1884.

26. *Flint Sunday Democrat*, September 15, 1877.

27. *Flint Sunday Democrat*, September 22, 1877. The African American barbers were said to show considerable skill, but they lost 31-18 due to inexperience.

28. *Sporting Life*, March 14, 1888, reprinted in David W. Zang, *Fleet Walker's Divided Heart*, 62–63. The immediate cause of the letter was Welday Walker's incorrect belief that the Ohio State League had incorporated a color barrier, but it is obviously an apt response to the broader issue.

29. Harold Seymour, *Baseball: The Early Years*, 334–35.

30. There were also more immediate incidents that contributed to the color barrier, such as Cap Anson's notorious refusal to play against African Americans. For a full description, see David W. Zang, *Fleet Walker's Divided Heart*, 38–44, 52–61.

31. Allen Guttmann, *From Ritual to Record*, 32.

32. There were a few earlier examples as well, such as Joseph Herkner, an officer of Grand Rapids' first club, who was mentioned in chapter 4. Herkner was born in Germany and his letters home during the Civil War were written in German.

16

"LEFT IN THE HANDS OF A FEW OF QUESTIONABLE INDUSTRY"

The muffin games and their offspring played a major role in revitalizing the game. However, their effect was not immediate, and interest began to taper off in Michigan in 1868 after three years of rapid growth. A number of factors contributed to the decline.

Baseball had paved the way for vigorous sports to become an acceptable activity, but its hold on the hearts of the young was now being challenged by a variety of more active sports, such as soccer, rowing, and riding velocipedes (the forerunner of the bicycle). Meanwhile, many older players were concluding that baseball was a young man's game and turning to less vigorous forms of recreation.

However, the success of baseball's competitors was primarily symptomatic of the underlying problem: the game had alienated many of its supporters. The initial hopes that it would reflect gentlemanly principles had long since given way to competitive fervor. And the belief that baseball was a test of character was even less tenable; it was becoming evident that practice and teamwork could not always overcome athleticism and youth. With the linchpins of the game's ideological support tenuous at best, many of baseball's former advocates turned to other leisure pursuits.

Unidentified players from Adrian and Grand Rapids (*opposite page*), ca. 1868 exemplify that baseball was again becoming a sport dominated by boys and young men. *Courtesy of Transcendental Graphics and the Local History Department, Grand Rapids Public Library, Grand Rapids, Michigan*

As a result, Michigan newspapers, once the game's greatest supporters, began candidly reporting the challenges facing it. Baseball's status as "an institution" was a double-edged sword, and it had to accept its share of criticism from the press.[1] A lengthy article in the *Detroit Post* lamented:

Not without cause, the business men of the city, toward the close of last year, became heartily disgusted with every mention of base ball. They found it almost impossible to keep their youthful employes at their respective posts; for, so wide-spread and infective was the mania, and to such extremes was it carried, that the noble pastime which affords such facilities for healthful recreation to the partici-

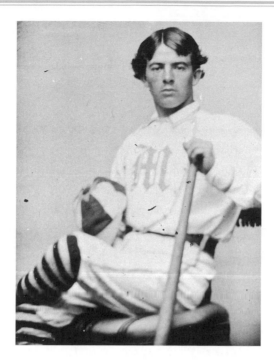

pants and gratification to the spectators, degenerated into a weari-
some bore. . . . It would be well could it be played with more moderation, because few business men can afford to let their employes
absent themselves on an average of twice a week to play in base ball
matches; and if the respectable youth forsake the game, it is left in the
hands of a few of questionable industry, while the former are
deprived of that vigorous exercise which is a sure preventive of
effeminacy.[2]

Newspapers around the state joined in the backlash. An Adrian
daily noted that baseball had initially served as much-needed recreation for men too devoted to their work. But now, the paper argued,
the game was breeding an equally unhealthy devotion:

As an exercise and means of amusement there can be no objection to
Base Ball, the question just here is, is it really conducive to physical
developement [sic] and consequent good health? As it is practiced we

venture that it provokes more ills than it cures. Looking at the game for a very few minutes it will be seen that most violent exercise alternates with bodily quiet at short intervals, while the action is violent from its beginning, and ceases abruptly. Any one conversant with the simplest requirements of physiology and hygiene, will see at once that such exercise is not fitted to secure the result desired. But this objection is perhaps the smallest that can be urged against the game as practised. Just as everything else that has been instituted for some good end, it has become subject to shameful abuse. "Picked nines" go strolling over the land carrying in their wake, if not in their number, professional gamblers whose peculiar talents find ample employment in "backing-up" the muscles of their favorites. This is a shameful abuse of a well meant amusement. Certainly there can be no wrong in friendly matches between neighboring clubs. But, after all, the question arises, is not the whole thing a waste of muscle? We think that it is, and our opinion is founded on the theory that the exercise necessitated by the game is inconsistent with the increased health and strength of the physical system. The ladies have a graceful and healthful exercise in Croquet, and the man who shall invent a game equally well adapted to the physical health and vigor of men will deserve a laurel wreath.[3]

The game's link to gamblers was also a serious concern. The usually supportive *Detroit Advertiser and Tribune* described a particularly sorry spectacle:

Attending a recent base ball match in this city, our attention was diverted before the game commenced, and for nearly two-thirds of its progress, by the performances of a squad of some half dozen young bloods, who managed to monopolize the attention of the spectators within ear-shot throughout the neighborhood of their location. They were fashionably dressed, apparently from 16 to 18 years old, impudent and savvy. They kept up a continual cackle of what were considered smart speeches and repartees, each being accompanied by boisterous laughter over the wit that nobody else could possibly perceive. They proceeded to "bet their pile" upon each particular innings as to which club would score the most, finally making wagers upon the achievements of individual members. They talked learnedly of the defects in play, and discoursed familiarly about "opening pools" for the next innings. They sported little canes, and one of them gravely wore a pair of eye-glasses astride his nose. After continuing this sort of performance till everybody who was compelled to listen to it was nauseated, they finally adjourned for a drink, seriously pondering the question as they went what each should take, whether a "smash," a "cobbler," a "julep" or "the lager." . . . Their whole language and demeanor reeked of the race-course and the saloon. It spoke of the dissolute, the drunkard, the horse jockey and the gambler as their frequent, if not their customary associates. It proclaimed them boon companions of the rowdy and the vile. It showed them destitute of good breeding, and emulous only of that which was "fast" and low, and from which every manly instinct would shrink. It presaged almost certain wreck of hopes, health and life. It was sad to look upon, and a shame to father and son.[4]

In East Saginaw, two young men named James Wilson and Edward Gosler were convicted of breaking the Sabbath-day peace by playing baseball and drinking, and Wilson served a thirty-day jail term after refusing to pay the eight-dollar fine.[5] Baseball was now becoming associated with the same dissolution that its advocates had hoped would be prevented by the arrival of the regulation game a decade earlier.

At the end of the 1867 season, a St. Clair newspaper had fulminated:

Our exchanges, far and wide, come to us full of spun-out details of base-ball matches, in which the mighty doings of undistinguished nondescripts are detailed with puerile minuteness. . . . We do not honestly believe that one twentieth part of the subscribers of any paper other than sporting journals, care one continental about reading column after column of this dreary stuff. Healthful and manly

exercise as the game undoubtedly is, we think the physical improvement of the eighteen participants is heavily overbalanced by the mental nausea endured by the reading public.[6]

Even more damaging than such harsh words was the fact that many
Michigan newspaper editors silently expressed their concurrence by
dropping baseball coverage in 1868.

Another factor in the decline of Michigan baseball was the lack
of a suitable mode of competition. The Champion's Cup was now
the possession of the Detroit Base Ball Club, and no effort was made
to initiate a new system. Tournaments generated great enthusiasm,
but they rarely ran smoothly. While some of the problems could be
attributed to poor organization, many seemed to be insuperable. It
was becoming increasingly clear that the all-inclusive ideal of tournaments was at odds with the expectation that the best club be fairly
determined.

Planning a tournament was a logistical nightmare. The lack of
reliable modes of transportation meant that clubs often were last-
minute no-shows. (A member of the Greenville Stars, for example,
recalled traveling to Ionia for a tournament in the back of a lumber
wagon.)[7] A single match took upwards of three hours, so scheduling
more than two games per day on a field was unrealistic. The number
of games that could be played was further limited by the requirement of daylight and pleasant weather and the need of players to
return to work. Unplanned-for events were the rule rather than the
exception, and they led to improvisations that rarely satisfied anyone.

Also contributing to the decline were the well-publicized
excesses that had overcome Eastern baseball. The competition for
the national championship had become a farce, as the New York
clubs effectively prevented any outsiders from competing for it.[8]
The practice of revolving increased dramatically in 1868, with the
best Eastern clubs now almost entirely made up of professionals that
no amateur club could hope to beat. Moreover, there was an increasing perception that "revolvers" were prone to heavy drinking and

other undesirable conduct.[9] The original concept of a baseball club had become outmoded, and it is no coincidence that the word *team* was first used to describe a baseball club in 1868.[10] Still, the worst abuses of Eastern baseball had yet to make their way to Michigan.[11]

These abuses should have theoretically been tempered by the National Association of Base Ball Players, but the game's governing association had little ability to control the game, since its only recourse was to expel clubs from membership. It was almost comically disorganized, its treasurers losing or absconding with its funds three times in a five-year period.[12] The NABBP finally responded to the evils of professionalism by banning match games altogether. Needless to say, matches continued; the NABBP had lost the limited power it still had.

Thus, ambitious clubs around the country had a choice in 1868—get in the bidding war for the top players or revert to second-class status. For the Detroit Base Ball Club, this was not much of a dilemma. Two years of bad luck and disappointments in trying to create a profitable rivalry left little reason to think that a plunge into professionalism would be supported. Moreover, the members who formed the club's nucleus were getting older and beginning to invest their time in furthering their careers. Detroit Club president Dr. Jonathan Van Norman conceded:

> We lost sight of the best interests and legitimate objects of base ball when we began to have an itching for foreign aid. What we haven't the brain and muscle to accomplish ourselves, by education and practice, we had better leave unaccomplished. So soon as our club becomes possessed with a hankering after professionals, that moment there is danger of its becoming prostituted from its beneficial and noble aims, and thus can no longer either claim or expect countenance from the public.[13]

While the club scaled back its ambition, it still was far from the pure amateurism recommended by Van Norman. A Jackson paper claimed that a player named T. Collins, formerly of the junior

Excelsior Club of Detroit, was paid fifteen dollars a week for his services.[14] Although the Detroit newspapers did not confirm that any Detroit Club players were paid, the *Detroit Post*'s animosity toward the club supports this supposition. Since George Dawson was paid for the 1868 season, there seems little reason to doubt that others were paid as well.[15] The two other players who most likely received some form of compensation were Henry Burroughs, who had returned from Newark, and new pitcher S. C. Lane, who was introduced in the *Post* as a mechanic who had recently moved to Detroit.[16] It does not appear that these deviations from amateurism improved the club much, but they did alienate the press, which blamed every defeat on the imports.

Other clubs around the state were facing similar dilemmas. In Greenville, the Eagle Club decided not to play in 1868 and gave its foul flags to the juvenile Star Club.[17] This symbolic passing of the torch was reenacted around the state. The Continental Club of Kalamazoo lapsed into inactivity because "a greater proportion of the nine are so much engrossed with the cares of business that they cannot leave for practice."[18] In Grand Rapids, the Peninsulars and Kents continued to contest for the silver cup, but many of the previous season's players had "retired on their laurels."[19] For the Central Club of Jackson, just getting a good nine to attend practice was a struggle. After several unsuccessful attempts, a married versus single game was scheduled for May 26, with inducements of a gold badge for the player making the best score, a pair of shoes for the one with the next best score, and a pint of peanuts for the one with the poorest score. But even these incentives failed to attract enough players, and only a practice could be held. As a result, the 1868 season brought a decline in the number of clubs, from 240 to 190, with juvenile clubs making up the vast majority.

Another consequence of the upheaval for the Detroit Base Ball Club was a dramatic shift in its set lineup. The club's first nine added five recent graduates from local junior clubs, but few of them appeared to be improvements on the players they replaced. Henry Burroughs's return did not solve the club's pitching problems, as the forte of the five-foot-eight-inch, 147-pound Burroughs had always been cunning. Now that umpires were being increasingly lenient on deliveries, the emphasis was on speed pitching. As a result, the swift but wild Lane did the bulk of the pitching, with indifferent results.

The Detroit Base Ball Club began the 1868 season with two close-fought games against the University of Michigan. The first game, on May 30, was tied after nine innings, but the university squad finally pushed across the winning runs in the eleventh inning to win 26-24. Five days later Detroit jumped all over Julius Blackburn, the university's swift pitcher, and led 11-2 after two innings. But then the slow "twist" pitching of Alfred Wilkinson shut Detroit down, and the college boys rallied to tie the score at 18-18 heading into the ninth.[20] The collegians then scored 8 unanswered runs in the ninth to win the game 26-18.

The two close losses failed to earn the Detroit Club any sympathy from the press. The *Detroit Post,* intent on blaming all problems on the club's use of professional players, wrote: "They have good material within the Club, but fail to develop it, and, just so long as they blindly overlook this fact and strain for players from a distance, even so long will the public not sympathise with them when they are defeated. A few years ago, when home talent alone was called into play, victory almost unceasingly perched on the banner of the Detroit club."[21] The animosity of the previous season was not forgotten in Jackson, where the *Citizen* gloatingly announced the defeat of the "self boasted 'Champions'" and wrote that the Detroit Club "must now relinquish its claim to the championship."[22] Clearly, the Detroit Base Ball Club was not what it once had been, nor would it ever again enjoy the rose-colored press coverage it had once received.

Ironically, this diminished squad got the opportunity for which the club had so long hoped, to compete against the country's top baseball clubs. Railway travel was becoming cheaper and more convenient, and touring was becoming lucrative. On June 16, the Detroit Club faced the Forest City Club of Cleveland, which was upgrading its talent—its battery consisted of Albert Pratt, selected as best pitcher at the Detroit tournament, and twenty-year-old catcher Jim "Deacon" White, who would become one of the game's greats. However, the Detroit Base Ball Club beat the Forest City Club 45-23.

In the week following this impressive win over the Forest City Club, Detroit hosted two of the country's best clubs—the Atlantics of Brooklyn and the Athletic Club of Philadelphia. The *Free Press* advertised the game against the Atlantics on June 18 by writing, "This of course will be an event in the history of the game in this city, and it is to be hoped that the enterprise of the Detroit Club in bringing the Eastern players here will be amply rewarded."[23] The

In 1866 the Forest City Club of Cleveland had viewed a match with the great Detroit Base Ball Club as a learning experience. But by 1868 the Cleveland club was emerging as a national power, and the Detroiters were scaling back their ambitions. Shown here is the 1870 Forest City Club, which included even more professionals (*standing, left to right*): Jack Ward, Elmer White, Albert Pratt, Art Allison, Ezra Sutton; (*seated*) Gene Kimball, Jim "Deacon" White, Jim Carleton, George Heubel, and Charles Fulmer.) Jim "Deacon" White would help bring a world championship to Detroit in 1887. *Courtesy of Transcendental Graphics*

Detroit Club had gone to great trouble to prepare the field for the game, rolling the grounds repeatedly and erecting a roofed grandstand. A full house of two thousand spectators turned out for the chance to see many baseball greats for the first time: Dickey Pearce, credited with inventing the "fair-foul" hit and the trapped ball and for making shortstop a key position; Bob Ferguson, the first switch-hitter; Al Reach, the first openly professional player; and legendary figures like "Old Reliable" Joe Start, George "The Charmer" Zettlein, "Count" Sensenderfer, and Jack "Death to Flying Things" Chapman.[24]

Only three days before their arrival, the Atlantics had been upset by the Niagaras of Buffalo, a club that Detroit had beaten in 1867. This prompted hopes that Detroit could at least make the

Two thousand spectators turned out in Detroit in 1868 to see the Detroit Base Ball Club host the six-time national champion Atlantics of Brooklyn. But the Atlantics won so easily that their second baseman smoked a pipe while fielding his position. The loss prompted the *Detroit Post* to describe professional players as "drones on the community." The Jackson papers gloated about the lopsided 40-7 score until the Atlantics beat the Central City Club of Jackson 56-8. This photo is of the 1860 club, with the innovative Dickey Pearce (*standing, top left*). *Courtesy of Transcendental Graphics*

game close, but the home club was beaten 40-7. The drubbing was made worse by the nonchalance of the Brooklynites, whose second baseman, Charley Smith, smoked a pipe while playing his position. Much of the considerable crowd left before the end. The *Free Press* called the loss the "total overthrow of any pretensions [Detroit] may have entertained to a rank among first-class clubs."[25]

The *Post* took another swipe at the Detroit Club's use of imported players:

> Their pride has had a collapse, and hereafter good may accrue therefrom. The bitter defeat will have taught them that it is useless for them to presume to rival a really first class club, for a very valid reason. The Detroit Club is mainly composed of young men of honorable connections, with whom aptitude for business is a greater desideratum than unequaled skill in handling a ball and bat. The former requires brains; while a mere clown in education and refinement, so long as he possesses muscle, may be a fine base ball player. For this reason we have always condemned the practice of purchasing the services of professional players. Such men are drones on the community. They have no noble aim in life, and ought not to be tolerated in a thrifty community.[26]

The Atlantics moved on to Jackson, where they played the Central City Club the next day. The game was much anticipated in Jackson, the *Daily Citizen* writing that "our boys stand a poor chance for victory against this crack club of the country, but it is confidently expected that they will make as good a showing as any Western club."[27] To this end, the Central City Club was supplemented with Frank Crittenden, Alfred Wilkinson, and Eugene Cooley of the University of Michigan nine. The Atlantics nonetheless whipped the Jackson club 56-8. Now it was the Detroit papers' turn to gloat, with the *Post* sermonizing:

> Jackson, like all other places of the kind, has ever staggered under a load of egotism which was palpable and unwieldy, and now for once

that overweening confidence has received an overwhelming blow from the bats of the Atlantics. Year after year in our State tournaments and local matches the champion clubs of Jackson have come off with flying colors and many trophies until success had naturally produced a confidence, which any one could have foreseen would be dissipated in a contest with a club of professionals.[28]

The Detroit Base Ball Club then hosted the Athletics on June 22. As the Philadelphia club had just annihilated the strong Forest City Club of Rockford, Illinois, 94-13, another rout was expected. Instead Detroit lost by the respectable margin of 30-17, and the *Free Press* sounded a rare commendatory note in writing that the members of the local club "have reason to be proud of themselves."[29] But the *Post* was upset that the Detroit Club had added George Dawson of the University of Michigan to its roster, paying him seventy-five dollars a month for his services, and launched another tirade against Lane's pitching.[30]

While the Central City Club and the Detroit Base Ball Club were outclassed by top clubs, they were both too good for in-state rivalries to develop. The OK Club was expected to be Detroit's second-best club, but after procuring new uniforms and paying the Detroit Base Ball Club two hundred dollars to use its grounds part-time, the OK Club was massacred by the Detroit Club 76-13.[31] The best opponent the Central City Club could arrange for July 4 was the Valley City Club of Hillsdale, and the Jackson club won 89-41. At the end of the month, the Central City Club beat the Alerts of Grass Lake 104-30. Obviously, meaningful in-state competition would be hard to find.

On July 4, Detroit hosted the Alleghenys of Allegheny City and avenged its loss at the previous year's tournament with a 22-4 triumph. Twelve days later, the Alleghenys hosted Detroit and got even with a 29-18 win. The next day in Cleveland the Detroit Club was trounced 44-7 by the Forest City Club. Back home on July 20, Detroit hosted the Buckeye Club of Cincinnati and lost a 36-35 decision to a club that featured two players, Charlie Sweasy and Andy

Leonard, who would join the famous Red Stocking Club of Cincinnati the next year. But while the score was respectable, the Detroit Club's waning interest was evident. At game time, only seven players had shown up; by the time nine had finally arrived, no umpire was present, and Bob Anderson had to fill that role.

Anderson was the man whom Henry Starkey had credited with forming the Detroit Base Ball Club, and he was still one of the club's directors. Coming from the gentlemanly tradition, Anderson was reluctant to enforce the relatively new balls and strikes rule; he occasionally called balls, but never strikes. The Buckeye batters took advantage of this by standing at the plate for up to fifteen minutes before swinging at a pitch. As a result of the delays, only seven innings could be played before darkness fell, and most of the crowd had departed long before then.

The reigning national champions, the Unions of Morrisania, New York (now a part of the Bronx), were the next club to pass through Michigan.[32] This club featured yet another baseball great in George Wright, only twenty-one years old but already regarded as the game's best shortstop. On August 3, the Unions beat the Detroit Base Ball Club 38-11. The Unions continued on to Jackson the next day, where a fifty-cent admission fee was charged for the highly anticipated game. However, the Central City Club was completely unable to hit the left-handed pitching of Charlie Pabor and lost by the ignominious score of 65-1.

The *Jackson Citizen,* which had earlier lauded the club for its initiative in bringing such a strong opponent to the city, now called the score a "disgrace" and wrote that the club's members, "so long as they cannot make a better display than that of yesterday, should not aspire to compete with clubs so much their superiors."[33] A couple of days later, the *Citizen* published a challenge to the Central City Base Ball Club from the second nine of the Old Ladies Sewing Society of Charlotte, signed by their secretary, Aunt Sally.[34] Other newspapers were quick to rub salt in the wound, and the beleaguered Central City players understandably played no more matches that season.[35]

Things were sluggish around the rest of state as well. Tournaments were rarer than in years past, and the ones that did occur were of limited geographic scope. In Romeo on July 4, the Peninsulars of Ypsilanti beat the Inland Club of Romeo 50-28 to win a purse of fifty dollars, with Ypsilanti captain Frank Emerick winning a silver cup for running the bases in sixteen seconds. A tournament scheduled to be played in Hudson was cancelled without a word of explanation.

The belief that practice would eliminate all shortcomings no longer carried much weight; the "patience of hope" was now in short supply, and clubs that struggled were quick to disband. A player at Adrian College took matters one step further and, in midgame, "observing that his nine were likely to be beaten, shamefully withdrew, for which his party, by a unanimous vote expelled him."[36] As baseball historian William Ryczek concludes, "By 1868 . . . no one was bearing any defeats gracefully."[37]

Even successful clubs no longer exhibited much enterprise. The Emmet Club of Detroit rather underwhelmingly pronounced itself "as good as any fourth-class club."[38] The Stars of the Agricultural College claimed to be champions "of this part of the state" but showed no inclination to look further afield for competition.[39]

Nevertheless, Grand Rapids continued to see competition for the silver cup and silver ball, and extensive rules were devised to ensure fairness. A committee of five citizens, led by Dr. Joel Parker, at whose office Grand Rapids' first club had been formed nine years earlier, was named to adjudicate disputes.[40] However, none of the Valley City's clubs were ready to meet outside competition, and a picked nine of the best players had to be formed to challenge the Custers of Ionia. The Custers beat the picked nine 35-21 in Grand Rapids to remain "the champion club of the Valley," in a game that attracted such interest that the more than two thousand spectators crowded around the players so closely that they impeded play.[41] But even after such a turnout, the Custers played no more games (although they tried unsuccessfully to schedule a rematch with the Ogemas of Flint, who had beaten them at the Detroit tournament).

While baseball was on the decline in southern Michigan, it was beginning to spread into the state's northern regions, and the Upper Peninsula experienced its first epidemic of "base ball fever." A newspaper in Negaunee asked in March: "Can't we organize a base-ball club here this spring? No place can lay claim to any importance until it has its base-ball club, and the metropolis of the Upper Peninsula should not be behind in this matter. Moreover, it is one of the most invigorating and healthful games in which one can indulge."[42]

A club called the Iron District Base Ball Club of Negaunee was formed on June 25, with twenty-two members.[43] As this description suggests, like the earliest Detroit clubs, this club took up the game primarily for the light recreation it provided:

> The Iron District Base Ballists, meet occasionally for exercise. As yet no broken limbs have been reported, though the club took the precaution to include a physician in their list of officers. At the last game the first nine made several runs to the third base, and one of them made a beautiful fly catch on the third bound. The second nine made several fine bats and all congregated on the second base, when the ball got lost in the sand and the game was indefinitely postponed.[44]

Several other clubs were soon formed in the Upper Peninsula. Two nines of the Ontonagon Base Ball Club played a match on July 4. In Marquette, the Superior Club reorganized, and a junior club named the Resolutes was formed. Houghton boasted both a senior and a junior club, and a club was also organized in Ishpeming.

The bounty of new clubs prompted the first fumbling steps toward organized competition. In Marquette, the Superior Club beat the Resolutes, but the local *Mining Journal* found the sight of a group of six-foot-tall men playing against a club of twelve-year-old boys ludicrous. The report of the game sarcastically praised the Superiors for having "mustered up courage enough to challenge the Resolutes, and the act should be recorded on the brightest page of base ball history." It speculated that the Superiors would now be "looking around for a club of boys *smaller* than the Resolutes."[45]

The Superior Club's subsequent efforts to stimulate competition only elicited more ridicule. After beating the Resolutes, the Superiors sent a challenge to the Iron District Club of Negaunee, but that club had already disbanded. They then claimed the championship of the Upper Peninsula, but when they received a challenge from the Independents of Houghton, it "fell like a wet blanket on the hopes of the Superior. They were willing to play boys, and had spunk enough to challenge a defunct club, but to meet a club of men was something they were not prepared for."[46] The Superiors did not show up to play the Independents, and, according to the *Mining Journal*, it became impossible to find anyone who would admit to being a member of the Superior Club.

Baseball also caught on in Tuscola County, where games became a frequent occurrence and attracted many spectators. The Cass River Club of Centreville (the town's name was changed to its present name of Caro the following year) won a series of games against the Stars of Watrousville and the Athletics of Vassar to gain recognition as the champions of the county.

But baseball's success in new areas stood in stark contrast to its bleak prospects in many towns where the game had only recently been very popular. With the Continental Club disbanded, the Unas of Kalamazoo organized early to fill the void. However, after playing a game against a picked nine and losing, the Unas did not play again that season. The make-up of that picked nine afforded particularly striking evidence that inexperience could no longer be used to excuse defeat. The nine players had been members of ten different clubs, with George Scales, a Kalamazoo printer, having belonged to six different clubs—the Continentals, the Burr Oaks and Eagles of Kalamazoo, the Star and Island Clubs of Plainwell, and the Tiger Club of Lapeer.

Near the end of the 1868 season, the interest of even the players began to turn away from baseball and toward the upcoming elections. After the Radicals of Rives Township beat the Lone Stars of Leslie 46-40 on August 15, one of the Radicals proposed three cheers for the Republican presidential ticket of Ulysses S. Grant and Schuyler Colfax and was joined by all the other players except for a solitary holdout from Leslie. Shortly after this, the Excelsior Club of Jackson, a junior club, began playing as the Excelsior Grant Club.

Nevertheless, the Detroit Base Ball Club did have one last hurrah. On September 12, the team traveled to Chicago and finally beat its longtime rivals the Excelsiors by a 15-12 margin. Unfortunately, a victory that once would have provoked wild celebrations was barely noticed. The once-mighty Excelsiors had been humbled by a series of losses and were now viewed in Chicago as a source of embarrassment. One correspondent wrote caustically that the Excelsiors "do not pretend any more to be players, but merely stick together for the purpose of furnishing mild amusement to visitors."[47] The *Chicago Times* chimed in: "Why doesn't somebody get the club to stop? If it insists upon continuing to play, it ought to engage in no matches except those like certain mule-races, in which the slowest mule is the winner."[48] The *Chicago Republican* derisively invoked one of the Detroit Base Ball Club's earlier victims: "Cannot the Excelsior Base Ball Club, of this city, now on its travels, be induced to come home? There is a club down in Pecatonica they can beat, or once could, and if they *must* challenge outside clubs, let them select a set of men who play no better than they do."[49]

Five days later the Excelsiors and the Niagara Base Ball Club of Buffalo came to Detroit for a round-robin. On September 17, the Niagara Club handily beat Detroit 38-17. The next day the Niagaras played the Excelsiors of Chicago and were beaten 31-12. On the following day Detroit hosted the Excelsiors. But, as usual, luck was not on the side of the Detroiters at the gate, as the results of the two previous days severely detracted from what would once have been a tremendous draw. Wintry weather also helped deter all but a few hardy fans. Bettors favored Chicago by as many as 17 runs, but the outcome would demonstrate "the glorious uncertainty of the noble game."[50]

Detroit fell behind 17-3, but then Burroughs replaced Lane in the pitcher's box and the home side gradually gained ground.

Finally an 11-run rally in the bottom of the eighth drew the two clubs even at 31-31. Chicago then counted 8 runs in the top of the ninth, at which point the umpire ruled it too dark to continue. By the rules of the day, the score reverted to the last completed inning, and the game was thus considered a tie. The Excelsiors vehemently disputed the decision and refused to offer three cheers for their adversaries or umpire Eugene Cooley.

The spectators who attended had finally had the chance to witness the Detroit Base Ball Club and the Excelsiors play the kind of exciting game that had so long been anticipated. However, they had also watched the finale for the nucleus of players who had dominated Michigan baseball since the end of the war.

NOTES

1. *Kalamazoo Daily Telegraph*, May 14, 1868.
2. *Detroit Post*, March 17, 1868.
3. *Adrian Daily Times and Expositor*, May 1, 1868.
4. *Detroit Advertiser and Tribune*, July 29, 1868.
5. *Saginaw Daily Courier*, April 28, 1868.
6. *St. Clair Republican*, September 7, 1867.
7. *Big Rapids Pioneer*, August 12, 1902.
8. William J. Ryczek, *When Johnny Came Sliding Home*, 156–61, describes how the New York clubs ensured that the championship would stay in New York City by keeping the champion from completing the obligatory two-of-three series with any outsider until it had played a team from New York.
9. Ryczek, *When Johnny Came Sliding Home*, 144–45, shows that 1868 was the season that revolving became "entrenched." The NABBP tried to prevent revolving with a rule that players had to be members of a club for thirty days before playing for it, but the rule was frequently subverted or ignored.
10. Paul Dickson, ed., *The New Dickson Baseball Dictionary*. The first citation, discovered by E. J. Nichols, appeared in the *New York Herald* on July 24, 1868.
11. The *Detroit Post* noted on March 27, 1868: "It should be added in justice to our clubs in Michigan, that match games have always been conducted fairly and honorably, and in good temper. No betting has ever been allowed on the grounds of any of the clubs in this city, nor have intoxicating drinks been allowed to be sold. Base ball matches in Michigan have not degenerated as they have in eastern cities."
12. Ryczek, *When Johnny Came Sliding Home*, 248–49.
13. *Detroit Post*, April 7, 1868.
14. *Jackson Daily Citizen*, June 5, 1868.
15. *Chicago Tribune*, August 20, 1935.
16. Lane had probably pitched for the Lincolns of Pittsburgh the previous season.
17. *Greenville Independent*, May 5, 1868.

18. *Kalamazoo Telegraph*, August 31, 1869.

19. *Grand Rapids Daily Eagle*, May 29, 1868.

20. *Detroit Advertiser and Tribune*, June 19, 1868. The curve ball was starting to develop by this time, and it is possible that Wilkinson was throwing a rudimentary version of that pitch. However, restrictions on delivery made curves difficult to throw (see chap. 7), and it is more likely that the pitch just spun.

21. *Detroit Post*, June 5, 1868. On June 13 the *Advertiser and Tribune* responded that the Detroit Club "is comprised of only *home talent*," which goes against all the evidence.

22. *Jackson Daily Citizen*, June 5, 1868.

23. *Detroit Free Press*, June 18, 1868.

24. Bob Ferguson is also credited with this nickname, and both seem to have had a right to it, but contemporary sources use it more frequently for Chapman.

25. *Detroit Free Press*, June 19, 1868.

26. *Detroit Post*, June 22, 1868.

27. *Jackson Daily Citizen*, June 19, 1868.

28. *Detroit Post*, June 22, 1868.

29. *Detroit Free Press*, June 23, 1868.

30. The amount is given in Dawson's obituary in the *Chicago Tribune* on August 20, 1935. Dawson was quite a singular man to use as an example of the evils of professionalism. As a schoolboy in Illinois, Dawson had sung in the choir at President Lincoln's funeral. Quiet and gentlemanly on and off the field, he would later be the principal of Flint High School and a lawyer in Chicago. His lifelong interest in literature and the arts led him to become fluent in numerous languages and to go on frequent tours of Europe. For the *Post*'s tirade, see the *Detroit Post*, June 23, 1868.

31. The OK Club had beaten the Detroit Club 38-30 in a game of baseball on ice on January 24, 1868.

32. However, the status of the Unions of Morrisania as national champions was in large part the product of the manipulation of the anachronistic championship series by New York City clubs. The Unions beat the Atlantics 14-13 on October 10, 1867, to capture the official championship, but their overall record in 1867 was less impressive than that of either the Atlantics or the Athletics.

33. *Jackson Daily Citizen*, August 5, 1868.

34. *Jackson Daily Citizen*, August 7, 1868.

35. The *Detroit Post* of August 6, 1868, asked if the Jackson players had been training "for the prize that Horace Greeley (or somebody else) is to offer for the worst players." The *Parma News* of August 8, 1868, took a shot at the Central City Club for having imported pitcher A. N. Ball for the game, writing rather unrealistically that "if the Centrals would be content to play their own men, each in his home position, instead of importing players, and then practice systematically, they would 'raise Michigan ball stock to a premium.'" Another correspondent to the same paper derisively praised the "wonderful skill displayed by the Centrals in 'chasing ball' for the Unions."

36. *Adrian Times and Expositor*, May 4, 1868.

37. Ryczek, *When Johnny Came Sliding Home*, 166.

38. *Detroit Post*, August 10 and September 14, 1868.

39. *Lansing State Republican*, August 3, 1868. A member of the class claimed fifty years later that the Agricultural College and the University of Michigan played an eleven-inning game that was won 2-1 by the university boys (*M.A.C. Record* 21, no. 32 [May 23, 1916]).

The writer, S. M. Tracy, claimed that the score was a "world record" for the lively ball era. I can find no documentation for this claim and find it very hard to believe that such a game, had it occurred, would not have attracted considerable attention. Other obviously exaggerated claims made by Tracy in the article further weaken his credibility.

40. *Grand Rapids Daily Eagle*, May 26, 1868.

41. *Ionia County Sentinel*, August 28, 1868.

42. *Negaunee Mining and Manufacturing News*, March 26, 1868.

43. *Negaunee Mining and Manufacturing News*, July 2, 1868.

44. *Negaunee Mining and Manufacturing News*, July 25, 1868.

45. *Lake Superior Mining Journal* (Marquette), August 29, 1868.

46. *Lake Superior Mining Journal* (Marquette), September 26, 1868.

47. *Lake Superior Miner* (Ontonagon), July 11, 1868.

48. Reprinted in the *Detroit Advertiser and Tribune*, July 8, 1868.

49. Reprinted in the *Detroit Post*, September 24, 1868. Even when they won, the Excelsiors had to read that they had "at length found one nine which it can beat. To get such a nine from any one club was impracticable, so they were picked from several" (*Adrian Times and Expositor*, August 24, 1868).

50. *Detroit Free Press*, September 19, 1868.

17

"PRINCIPALLY CONFINED
TO THE YOUNG AMERICANS"

The reversion of Michigan baseball to a young man's activity continued in 1869. A Saginaw newspaper observed that "the base ball fever here, as nearly everywhere else in the West, has about died out. All the old adult clubs in the three Saginaw cities have lost their organization, and the game is principally confined to the Young Americans."[1] The Exercise Club of Charlotte, formed during the boom of 1867, disbanded and paid off all its bills, donating the $5.55 balance to the local Ladies' Benevolent Society. The decision was a common one, as the number of active clubs plunged to 113, less than half the number of two years earlier.

One reason for this trend was the emergence of openly professional baseball. After years of under-the-table payments, the National Association of Base Ball Players had finally ended the hypocrisy by recognizing professional baseball clubs. One of the clubs to choose open professionalism was the Red Stockings of Cincinnati. The Red Stockings are usually credited with being the only club to take this path, but the evidence contradicts that claim. The Mutuals of New York, for example, joined the Red Stockings in openly paying salaries to all their players; in all likelihood, several of the other professional clubs did the same.[2]

GEORGE WRIGHT.   LEONARD.   GOULD.
SWEASY.   HENRY WRIGHT.   McVEY.
HURLEY (Substitute).   WATERMAN.   BRAINARD.   ALLISON.

THE PICKED NINE OF THE CINCINNATI, (RED STOCKINGS) BASE-BALL CLUB, OF CINCINNATI, OHIO.—From a Photograph by F. L. Huff.—See Page 279.

The 1869 Red Stockings of Cincinnati fashioned an undefeated record and changed the face of baseball. But they weren't the only openly all-professional club that season. *Courtesy of Transcendental Graphics*

The Detroit Base Ball Club announced that it would adhere to a strictly amateur policy and underscored that decision by electing long-time member David Peirce as president. The club initially accepted an invitation to play three games with the Red Stockings of Cincinnati, but the games were later dropped from the schedule. No reason was given for this decision, but the most likely theory is that the club realized that it was no longer competitive with such professional clubs.

Soon it was clear that a massive turnover of the Detroit Club's first nine would take place. Henry Burroughs left to play for the professional Irvington Club of Brooklyn and would eventually go on to have a brief major-league career in the National Association.[3] John Clark joined the Susan Galton English Opera Company. A group of New Yorkers later decided that he was the "great singer of America" and raised a great purse to send him to Italy for voice training. He selected the stage name of Signor Brocolini as a way of giving tribute to his native town of Brooklyn. He would sing Primo Basso for Her Majesty's opera in London, but eventually his singing career would fade, and he would become a reporter for the *Brooklyn Eagle*.[4] Bergen, George Dawson, and the much-maligned S. C. Lane also left town. Ford Hinchman (though only twenty-one) and John Horn retired from baseball, meaning that only J. A. Brown and T. Collins from last year's first nine would return in 1869.

The club showed no inclination to import new players to fill the void. It received a letter from "Horace Van Velsor, a 'rusty player' of Oil City, Pa., who has played none since 1867, and who asked what inducement would be offered him to play with the Detroit Club as left fielder."[5] The offer was referred to the board of directors, which understandably declined to act on it.

Thus, an almost entirely new lineup would represent the Detroit Base Ball Club, most under twenty years of age. Coverage of the club became so perfunctory that even the players' first names are impossible to determine. The first nine now consisted of Charley Ward pitching; T. Collins catching; Joseph L. Hull, Brown, Webster, and Sheeran in the infield; and Bowler, C. Presley, and Milton Ward in the outfield. After an easy 68-5 win over the local Mystic Club, the new players faced their first major challenge with two games against the Forest City Club of Cleveland.

The Forest City Club had opted for professionalism, offering Deacon White a salary to return after a stint in Syracuse and also paying Albert Pratt, Art Allison, and Jack Ward.[6] The Cleveland club pounded Detroit, 25-10 and 54-9. A few years earlier, the Detroit Base Ball Club had given the Forest City Club a valuable lesson in ball-playing, but now the two clubs were headed in opposite directions.

Detroit lost again to Rockford and A. G. Spalding 31-10 on July 29. Two days later, Detroit beat the Central City Club of Syracuse 30-14, but the *Advertiser and Tribune* was more impressed by such a weak team's willingness to tour than by Detroit's victory.[7] At this point, the Detroit Base Ball Club began to change its focus; it would play only two more games against out-of-state clubs. The first came on August 18, as Detroit debuted new white uniforms with red edging but was easily beaten by the famous Eckford Club of Brooklyn, 42-12. Then on September 3, the Alert Club of Rochester, New York, composed primarily of players who had been juniors before this year, came to town and won 30-9. It was the only game the Alerts won on their tour.

In early August, the Detroit Base Ball Club shifted its attentions to trying to revive state rivalries. The team was able to arrange a brief tour in which it beat the Empires of Bay City 37-17, the Athletics of Saginaw 48-11, and the Hercules Club of Flint 20-16. But there was limited enthusiasm among potential in-state rivals about playing a club that was no longer competitive with the country's top clubs yet was still better than they were.

The clubs in the two cities with enough experienced players to be formidable rivals—Jackson and Kalamazoo—had lapsed into inactivity. (One of the few games played in Kalamazoo in 1869 was played on a field with six-inch-high grass and a ditch in the middle.)[8] Few other towns had enough experience to hope to compete with even a significantly weaker version of the Detroit Base Ball Club.

On August 23, a bold move was made to try to reverse this state of affairs. J. M. L. Campbell, the secretary of the Detroit Base Ball Club, announced:

> The Detroit Base Ball Club, having unsuccessfully tried to get up a match with a number of clubs of the State (some of those written to not so much as answering the communications), therefore, on behalf of said Detroit B.B.C., I hereby claim for them the championship of the State, and do herewith challenge one and all of the Base Ball Clubs of this State to play us for the same a single match game, on our grounds (one of the best in the West,) the club accepting said challenge to name the date of playing and also name the Umpire; and the Detroit club further agree to give said club one-half of the net receipts at the gate. Mr. Anderson, the owner of the cup won by the club at the Adrian tournament, and held by them against all competitors for two seasons, has kindly offered it again as a token of championship to any club that can win it from us, the club winning it to be a regular one, not made up with imported players, etc., and any club winning the same to hold it against all competitors for two seasons.[9]

The first club to respond to this offer was the Olympic Club of Detroit, but the August 31 game proved a complete mismatch, as Detroit won 119-12. However, subsequent defenses of the cup would be much more competitive. The Star Club of Lansing came to town on September 21 and jumped out to an 11-2 lead after two innings, before a rainstorm ended the game. On September 25, the Ann Arbor Club came to town and was ahead 18-17 after seven innings. During the eighth inning, rain began to fall, and the game quickly degenerated into "a disgraceful attempt at umpire bullying."[10]

The Ann Arbor players contended that the game should be called immediately, making them the champions. The Detroit players, however, argued that since the inning had begun it should be completed, and umpire J. H. Whiting of Detroit sided with them. The eighth inning ended with Ann Arbor still ahead 21-19 and rain still falling, so Ann Arbor again claimed that it should be declared the victor. But now the umpire ruled that since one inning had been played in the rain the game should be continued. Detroit scored several runs in its half of the ninth, at which point the Ann Arbor players became completely disgusted and walked off the field. The umpire forfeited the game to Detroit.

Two weeks later, a rematch was scheduled. This time Julius Blackburn of the University of Michigan Club umpired, and Ann Arbor held a 19-12 lead after seven innings when rain came once again. This time Blackburn immediately ruled the game over, and the championship cup, for the first time ever, left Detroit. The players who had wrested it away were A. G. Tyng, Frank Bliss, Morris Starne, W. J. Maynard, Wayne Hayman, George H. Winslow, brothers George and Henry Nelson Loud, and an unidentified player named Farmer, most of them University of Michigan students. There were efforts to schedule a rematch later in the month, but the game never materialized.

The 1869 University of Michigan baseball team. That summer a club representing Ann Arbor, but composed mostly of University of Michigan students, captured the state baseball championship. *Courtesy of the Bentley Historical Library, University of Michigan*

This marked the end of the Detroit Base Ball Club. One of the reasons for the decision to make this its final season was related to the changing notion of gentlemanly conduct. The most talented of the club's new players was pitcher Charley Ward, whom the *Post* called "undoubtedly the best pitcher that has ever become identified with the club. It is doubtful if there is a more rapid pitcher in the country, but there are more accurate ones."[11] The players on the Rockford club agreed that Ward was as good a pitcher as they had faced on their tour. But if the club's future depended on Charley Ward, then it was quite literally "in the hands" of a man of "questionable industry."

Charley Ward, nineteen, and his brother Milton, twenty-one, the club's center fielder, were the sons of Captain Eber Brock Ward, a shipbuilder who was the richest man in Michigan.[12] The senior Ward reported an income of over two hundred thousand dollars in 1868, more than twice as much as anyone else in Detroit.[13] One historian described E. B. Ward as being "generally recognized as the first real captain of industry in this state."[14] But he was a despot at home and undoubtedly was affected by the insanity that ran in his family.

After abandoning the mother of his five children, Captain Ward attempted to control the lives of his three ostensibly sane children with threats of disinheritance. He sent both Charley and Milton to the Agricultural College in Lansing. The traditional ideal of a gentleman would have allowed the sons of a wealthy man to lead lives of leisure, but E. B. Ward had other ideas for them. After Charley left school in 1867, his father got him a job in a bank so that he might gain financial experience and eventually take over the business. After a year and a half, Charley expressed a desire to build a ship. His father saw the value of the project and consented to support him for a year.

Charley took shipbuilding very seriously and designed a model for improving a steamboat's propelling system that attracted considerable interest among vessel owners and engineers.[15] But when his father suffered a stroke, the unsupervised Charley wasted eigh-

The bizarre relationship between multimillionaire shipbuilder E. B. Ward and his sons hastened the demise of the Detroit Base Ball Club. *Courtesy of the State of Michigan Archives*

teen hundred dollars on "the usual nonsense a boy indulges in," both he and Milton spending much more time on baseball than their father had intended.[16] When Captain Ward recovered his health and found out how his sons had been spending their time, he sent them up north to get them away from temptation. Thus ended Charley Ward's promising pitching career and with it any hopes of the revival of the Detroit Base Ball Club.

For five years, Ward tried desperately to make businessmen of his sons, but failed miserably. He put Charley in charge of a business in Toledo, and Charley proceeded to run up thirty-seven thousand dollars in debts. Captain Ward bailed him out, and Charley ran up another two hundred thousand dollars in debts that his father again had to make good. E. B. Ward made similar attempts with Milton, with no more success. Milton ran up large bills in Ludington, Milwaukee, and Ripon, Wisconsin, without making much pretense of following his father's instructions. Both sons of the state's "first real captain of industry" became notorious for their "questionable industry," though it's unclear whether this should be attributed to insanity, rebellion against their father, or mere laziness. In

1874, the *Detroit Evening News* announced that "Milt Ward has at last found his strong point. He says that he can sit in a chair, and balance longer on the two hind legs than any man in the West."[17]

By the time the senior Ward died in 1875, he had come to the realization that Charley and Milton would squander any money allotted them and had bequeathed them minimal amounts. The two sons challenged the will on the grounds that their father was incompetent when he made it. The trial produced abundant evidence of their father's mental instability, particularly his dependence on spiritualism. However, the sons' case was doomed by the obvious sanity of their father's decision to leave them out of the will. After a hung jury, a compromise was reached that still left the bulk of Captain Ward's estate to his widow. The two boys continued to pursue dissipated habits and squander whatever money their stepmother gave them. Milton Ward died of tuberculosis in Jamaica on May 26, 1877, having gone there to try to recover his health. Charley finally married, but left his wife without support, and she committed suicide in despair. As of 1893, he was living as "a kind of roving renegade," continuing to fritter away what money he could get his hands on.[18]

Returning to the 1869 season, however, as the Detroit Base Ball Club was sputtering to an end, an important event was transpiring in neighboring Ohio. Three years earlier, the Excelsiors of Chicago had considered long distance travel to be prohibitively expensive and time-consuming. But the railways were making travel faster, cheaper, and, thanks to the introduction of George M. Pullman's sleeping car, more comfortable. The last spike of the transcontinental railroad was driven in 1869. Harry Wright, the capable manager of the Red Stockings of Cincinnati, took advantage of these developments to schedule an ambitious tour of the country.

Harry Wright was a man of great integrity who had played with the Knickerbocker Club on the Elysian Fields. He also understood public relations. Because of the excesses associated with professional baseball, Wright was careful to select players with temperate habits. One Cincinnati newspaper attributed the success of the Red Stockings to teetotaling, and whether that was true or not, the club soon became almost as closely associated with clean living as with winning baseball. Club president Aaron Champion emphasized that the club had "made the word 'Red Stocking' . . . famous throughout the country by . . . gentlemanly qualities, as well as by . . . abilities on the field."[19]

As the tour gathered momentum, the word spread that baseball again could be viewed as a test of character. A California paper wrote that "nearly all the players were first-class ballists before they joined the Cincinnati Club, but the credit of their being nurtured and carefully trained, so as to work together in a faultless manner, solely falls to the steady head-work of Captain Wright."[20] A New York journal credited the club's dominance to "steady, temperate habits and constant training" and to the fact that Harry Wright was the only member of the nine who spoke on the field.[21]

The club also had plenty of talent, including Harry Wright's younger brother George, a brilliant shortstop and an incomparable hitter who had earlier starred for the Nationals of Washington and the Unions of Morrisania. Whether because of discipline or talent, the Red Stockings compiled an undefeated record in 1869 in spite of a grueling touring schedule that saw them cover twelve thousand miles and play in front of two hundred thousand spectators.[22] The Detroit Base Ball Club tried to get back on the club's schedule, but there were too many other suitors, and Harry Wright opted instead for an unprecedented tour of California. Thus, in spite of the agreement in the spring and its proximity, Michigan was one of the few states with established baseball where the Red Stockings did not play.

The business community took note of the Red Stockings' drawing power and ability to generate civic pride. One Cincinnati businessman said gleefully, "Glory, they've advertised the city—advertised us, sir, and helped our business."[23] In turn the newspapers rediscovered the sport they had largely abandoned. Upon reconsideration, the *Advertiser and Tribune* concluded:

> While the system of employing professionals is one that in some respects is injurious and to be regretted, it does not seem likely that it

will cease in the large cities or that its effect will be to engross all the fine players of the country into two or three clubs. There are now by far too many good pitchers, catchers, fielders, etc., to permit of any such result and they will be scattered pretty evenly over the country, while their number and skill will each year increase. We think the game is destined to become a permanent institution in the United States and we do not by any means despair of seeing Detroit turn out a strong nine in the course of another season or two.[24]

Although most of the Red Stockings' players were transplanted Easterners, the fact that a club from the West could not only compete with but beat the top New York teams was a great boon in the Midwest. Their tour soon inspired an imitator in Michigan, where the Clodhoppers of Oshtemo began a tour of southern Michigan on August 19 with more eagerness than forethought:

The party first stopped at Three Rivers, found that place dead on base ball, so they went on to White Pigeon where they met the club of that place. At the close of the game the score stood as follows: Clodhoppers 37, White Pigeon 17. The next day they played the Sturgis club on the Sturgis fairground. There was a horse fair on the ground at the time, and the boys were obliged to pay 50 cents each for the privilege of entering and drawing the crowd away from the grand stand. At the close of the game the score stood, Clodhoppers 36, Sturgis 26. Cheers were given and the Clodhoppers repaired to the hotel, where, they aver, they partook of a dinner fit for a lord. Finding no other clubs ready for the bat, the Oshtemo boys returned home.[25]

Although the Clodhoppers showed that Michigan was not quite ready for touring, there were signs of renewed vitality late in the 1869 season that boded well for baseball's future. In St. Joseph, no doubt aware of the way the Red Stockings had publicized the city of Cincinnati, the editor of the *St. Joseph Herald*, along with twelve prominent honorary citizens, formed the Favorites, the town's first baseball club. The *Herald* commented, "Why such a club has not been organized before is surprising."[26] While it would be unrealistic to think that a small town like St. Joseph could ever sponsor a touring professional team, it is significant that the influence of the Red Stockings extended to towns small and large. After a very slow summer, the fall saw a flurry of activity among the junior clubs.

Such upswings always produced many new clubs, few of which would last very long, but three clubs formed around this time would rise to prominence in the 1870s as their members came of age. The first was the Mutual Club of Jackson, which was formed on April 1, 1869. Several of the members were firemen, so they named their club in honor of the Mutual Club of New York, which also had ties to the fire department. The new club's first president was Robert

The Mutuals of Jackson won two straight state championships and were involved in a heated dispute over a third title. Robert Lake (*back row, second from right*) roamed the outfield for the Mutuals of Jackson, and later founded the Robert Lake Company, which is still in business in Jackson. *Courtesy of the State of Michigan Archives*

Lake, who would be a star player for years to come and later a prominent businessman, founding the Robert Lake Company, which still exists today.[27]

In Detroit, a group of scholars at the private Cass School formed the Hunkidori Club. Joe Weiss recalled in 1889 that the Hunkidori Club

> was organized in John Demass' barn on Elizabeth street west in 1869. This club was composed of Charles Reed, now agent of the American Express Company, as pitcher; John Demass, Jr., catcher; Robert McBride, son of ex-Assessor McBride, and who is now agent of the Lake Shore at West Detroit, first base; myself second base; Ben Briscoe, now running a box factory at Bay City, third base; Alex McDonnell, cashier of the Detroit Fire and Marine Insurance Company, short stop, and Billy Beck, son of the commission merchant, left field. Who played center and right I do not remember. Our grounds were on the corner of Second and Bagg streets. When we played a match an agreement was entered into that each club pay for half the ball, which necessitated the levying of an assessment of about six cents on each player.[28]

The Hunkidoris' first recorded game took place on June 12, 1869, as they beat a club called the Velocipedes 27-14.

The following spring a group of young boys studying at Philo M. Patterson's school, an exclusive Detroit classical and mathematical institution, formed the Nobby Base Ball Club, which would develop into the Aetnas. The Nobbys' field was a vacant lot on Fort Street West between North and Tenth Streets, and their earliest members included Frederick Stearns, later president of the National League's Detroit Wolverines; George Hosmer, later a prominent judge; Charles Dean; Fred Wiley; George Bartlett; Jim Craig; Duncan Stewart; Will Cahoon; the Glover boys; Ed Barrows; and Tom Fraser.[29] The Nobbys played their first game on April 15, 1870, beating the Actives 78-11.

The prosperous backgrounds of these boys and the professional success they would achieve are significant. With the game widely perceived as having slipped into the hands of players of "questionable industry," the example of Harry Wright's club had helped make baseball a respectable pursuit again. Now these two clubs, formed at prominent private schools, would sow the seeds for the eventual reclamation of Detroit baseball from the indolent hands into which it had fallen.

Competition among the junior clubs demonstrated that the earlier "Young America spirit" of the Early Risers was a thing of the past; clubs now sought only to play their equals. A supporter of the junior club of Dexter wrote to the *Dexter Leader* that the first nine averaged fifteen years of age and weighed a total of 920 pounds, issuing a challenge to any club in the state not exceeding them in either height or weight.[30] After the Cupid Club of Kalamazoo, a group of boys aged twelve to fifteen, lost 51-16 to the junior club of Galesburg, its members alleged that their "juvenile" opponents had "cow hide boots and huge whiskers," a charge that was naturally denied.[31] The Cupids also claimed that they had to return home from Galesburg without dinner or supper, to which the Galesburg lads responded that the Cupids had been offered supper but "preferred hanging round the billiard and whisky saloon."[32] Still, the rising level of interest among junior clubs boded well for the future of the game.

While there were some signs of strain, there were still many games being played where camaraderie was exhibited on both sides. When the Union Club of Otsego hosted a Kalamazoo picked nine, the clubs shared a boisterous meal after the game. One of the Kalamazoo players announced loudly that the pies in Otsego were the best he had eaten and that he would like to kiss the cook. Only then did the laughter of his fellow players alert him that the cook was standing right behind him, waiting to claim her reward.[33] Such moments serve as a reminder that even when interest in baseball was at a low point, there was plenty of pleasure being derived from the game.

Notes

1. *Saginaw Daily Enterprise*, July 31, 1869.

2. *National Chronicle*, February 20, 1869: "The [Mutual] Club will adopt a new system this coming year in dealing with their professional members. A stated sum per season is to be given each professional, in lieu of the gate money dividend heretofore awarded." The *National Chronicle* noted on February 27, 1869: "The Mutuals have organized for the campaign in tip-top style, and are in a flourishing condition. They have $15,000 in their club treasury, have twelve picked professional players from which to select their nine, each of whom will not only receive a regular salary to be paid whether games are played or not. . . . Premiums will be paid to those who excel in the special departments of the game as shown by regular statistics at the close of the season."

3. Burroughs would eventually return to Newark, where he died of tuberculosis on March 31, 1878. His death was tracked down by Debbi Dagavarian-Bonar, with help from the author.

4. *Detroit Post*, October 6, 1869; *Kalamazoo Daily Telegraph*, April 17, 1876; *Adrian Times and Expositor*, April 13, 1877; *New York Times*, June 22, 1890; and research by Bob Richardson and Richard Malatzky.

5. *Detroit Advertiser and Tribune*, May 13, 1869.

6. William J. Ryczek, *When Johnny Came Sliding Home*, 152.

7. The Syracuse club lost seven of eight games on the tour, according to Marshall Wright's *The National Association of Base Ball Players, 1857–1870*, 276.

8. *Allegan County Record* (Otsego), June 12, 1869.

9. *Detroit Advertiser and Tribune*, August 23, 1869.

10. *Detroit Post*, September 27, 1869.

11. *Detroit Post*, July 2, 1869.

12. Ward's wealth was estimated to be as high as twenty million dollars (*Big Rapids Magnet*, May 8, 1873). He was also briefly a part owner of the *Detroit Advertiser and Tribune*.

13. *Detroit Post*, June 1, 1869. Such income lists were routinely printed in Michigan newspapers at this time.

14. Kenneth N. Metcalf, "Detroit . . . Steelmaker to the Nation," *Detroit Historical Society Bulletin* 17, no. 9 (summer 1962): 7.

15. *Detroit Post*, October 11, 1869.

16. *Detroit Advertiser and Tribune*, October 27, 1875.

17. *Detroit Evening News*, May 25, 1874.

18. David Ward, *Autobiography of David Ward* (New York: n.p., 1912), 146.

19. Stephen D. Guschov, *The Red Stockings of Cincinnati*, 124.

20. *Daily Alta California*, September 23, 1869; reprinted in Guschov, *The Red Stockings of Cincinnati*, 84.

21. *Spirit of the Times*, June 19, 1869; reprinted in Guschov, *The Red Stockings of Cincinnati*, 60.

22. Numerous win totals have been credited to the 1869 Red Stockings, but reliable ones range between fifty-six and seventy. Fifty-six was the total Harry Wright used.

23. *Cincinnati Commercial*, July 2, 1869; reprinted in Guschov, *The Red Stockings of Cincinnati*, 68.

24. *Detroit Advertiser and Tribune*, August 16, 1869.

25. *Allegan County Record* (Otsego), September 4, 1869.

26. *St. Joseph Herald*, September 25, 1869.

27. Robert Lake also helped with the management of the Jackson club in the Tri-State League in 1888.

28. *Detroit Free Press*, January 13, 1889.

29. *Detroit Free Press*, February 24, 1889.

30. *Detroit Advertiser and Tribune*, July 26, 1875.

31. *Kalamazoo Daily Telegraph*, June 3, 1869.

32. *Kalamazoo Daily Telegraph*, June 7, 1869.

33. *Kalamazoo Daily Telegraph*, May 25, 1869.

18

"BASE BALL IS POPULAR AGAIN"

The example of the 1869 Red Stockings of Cincinnati proved a fruitful one in Ohio's neighboring state of Michigan, and the seeds of revival that had been planted in 1869 blossomed in the spring of 1870.

Red Stockings' leader Harry Wright combined the roles of the modern manager and general manager, diligently handling the club's business affairs and masterminding the team's play on the field. Although the club's profits were actually meager, they sparked exaggerated reports, such as one that stated, "The Red Stockings are worth $200,000 a year to the business men and citizens of Cincinnati, because, whenever a big game is played there, the town is filled to overflowing with visitors from along the lines of the different railroads leading into the city."[1] Other cities accordingly began forming stock companies to finance their own professional baseball clubs in 1870.

Detroit, however, was not one of these cities. The Detroit Base Ball Club made preliminary efforts at organizing in April, but the departure of Charley Ward meant that the club would again have to develop a battery or import one. There was no longer sufficient enthusiasm to pursue either course, and the historic club disbanded. Nor did Detroit see any rush to fill the shoes of the club that had dominated Michigan baseball for most of the last decade. The *Free Press* had become so fed up with the excesses of baseball fever that it expressed the wish that the Red Stockings "could be prevailed upon to have all the games come off at night, or in some hall where secrecy could be observed."[2] And the *Advertiser and Tribune* was still commenting in late June that "there is again a good deal of talk of organizing a good base ball club in the city, but we think nothing definite will be done in the matter until next season."[3]

But elsewhere, clubs were organizing enthusiastically. In Clio, by mid-April, forty members had joined the baseball club, grounds had been secured, and practice had commenced. Several fine players had relocated to Grand Rapids, and the Valley City Club was formed there to represent the city. Other clubs that were active by the end of May included the Alerts of East Saginaw; the Actives of

Michigan and Trumbull was a quiet Detroit corner in 1870, long before the arrival of the Tigers. *Courtesy of the Burton Historical Library, Detroit Public Library*

Saginaw; the Wolverines of Benton Harbor; the Favorites of St. Joseph; the Shoo Flys of Howell; the Empires of Bay City; the Experts of Galesburg; the Spears of Niles; the Stars of St. Johns; the Hurons of Milford; the First Nationals of Hancock; the German Socks of Calumet; and clubs representing the towns of Owosso, Houghton, Hillsdale, and Jonesville.

The First National Base Ball Club of Hancock. *Back row, left to right:* J. Bittenbender, left field; Al Brockway, center field; William Harry, third base; Joe Johnson, right field. *Front row, left to right:* James Trembath, second base; A. J. Scott, catcher; Thomas D. Meads, shortstop; J. V. Trembath, pitcher; Otto Kunath, first base. While a handwritten date of 1868 has been added to the photo, this exact lineup represented the club in a game against the Houghton Base Ball Club on August 11, 1870, so that is probably the correct date. A. J. Scott later became fire chief and mayor of Hancock, as well as vice president of the First National Bank; however, he was said not to make a good baseball captain because "he was too easily excited, and dropped too many balls." *Courtesy of the Michigan Technological University Archives and Copper Country Historical Collections*

In May, the Ann Arbor Club defended the championship cup for the first time, playing the Praktikoi of Hillsdale College in a planned best-of-three series. Hillsdale won the first game 29-28 on May 14 in Ann Arbor in front of a large crowd.[4] The cup was put on display at C. L. Budd's jewelry store in Hillsdale, but Ann Arbor's supporters predicted that it would be "automatically regained" in the rematch.[5] In the second game at Hillsdale on May 28, the Praktikoi led throughout, but Ann Arbor staged a dramatic 8-run rally in the ninth inning to win 28-22. The deciding game was scheduled for June 13, but Hillsdale did not appear. Ann Arbor was again the state champion, but the team lacked the aura of invincibility associated with the Detroit Base Ball Club for most of its reign.

New clubs continued to form, and with the state champions perceived as beatable, the new teams' efforts were characterized by increasing ambition. Burr Oak borrowed three of Sturgis's best players for a game against Coldwater. The Favorites of St. Joseph beat the Fearless Club of New Buffalo to claim the championship of Berrien County. The Huron Club of Milford, after winning match games against Waterford, Commerce, and Fentonville, wondered who would challenge them next. In the Saginaw area, competition was stimulated by handicap games in which one club received up to eight outs per inning. In late April, the *Jackson Citizen* exclaimed, "Base ball is popular again."[6]

The Una Club of Kalamazoo secured pitcher Thomas Dorgan, twenty-one, formerly of the Athletics of Chicago. It is possible that he received some form of compensation for his services, as he was given a job working on the house of Allen Potter (the president of the Continental Club in 1866 and later president of the Unas and mayor of Kalamazoo). But even if Potter did take Dorgan's baseball abilities into account in giving him the job, Dorgan's industry proved to be anything but questionable.

Thomas Dorgan married a local woman and became a highly respected plumber in Kalamazoo. He soon had all the plumbing business he could handle and within two years hired an assistant so he could start a second establishment in Allegan.[7] He would later

Allen Potter, Kalamazoo mayor and
businessman and a prominent sup-
porter of the city's baseball clubs.
*Courtesy of the Western Michigan
University Archives and Regional
History Collections*

branch out into inventing, and in 1891 one of his inventions caused
a local paper to claim that the "world-renowned advocate of the hot
water system of heating, Thomas Dorgan, . . . has conquered the
natural laws and compels heat to fall instead of rise."[8] When Dorgan died suddenly two months later, he was described as "a self-
made man of the truest and best of principles," and his funeral was
one of the largest ever in Kalamazoo.[9]

Dorgan's arrival further stimulated the baseball revival and
eventually Detroit got into the act as well. In late June, the formation of the Mystic Base Ball Club of Detroit was announced. The
Mystics' only import was pitcher George Tremaine, who originally hailed from Smith's Creek, Michigan, and had played for the
Niagara Club of Buffalo, New York. In March, Tremaine had tried
out with the new professional White Stockings Club of Chicago
but, having failed to make that club, had been playing cricket in
Windsor. The rest of the Mystics' nine was composed of some of
the city's best amateur players, including future major leaguer Dan
O'Leary.

On July 4, the new club played its first match game in Chicago,
losing to that city's Aetna Club 31-13. The Mystics announced their

intention to secure enclosed grounds to play in and requested the public's help in locating an appropriate venue. However, they eventually settled for a makeshift location on Baker Street, near the corner of Tenth.

The bounty of new clubs throughout the state renewed interest in competition, which had been rendered more practical by the building of the Air Line Railway line. The new line brought easy, affordable travel to many communities in southern Michigan for the first time, and grateful residents of Pinckney and Tekonsha named their baseball clubs in its honor. On July 4, the new Una Club of Kalamazoo hosted the Eureka Club of Chicago—reputedly the

Allen Potter hired Chicago pitcher Thomas Dorgan to do work on this landmark house in 1870. The appearance that this was another "do-nothing" baseball job was belied, however, when Dorgan became one of Kalamazoo's leading plumbers. *Courtesy of the Western Michigan University Archives and Regional History Collections*

third-best club in that city—and immediately acquired a formidable reputation when they won 22-20.

Another Chicago club, the Potter Palmer Club, announced plans for a tour of Michigan, lining up games in Kalamazoo, East Saginaw, Flint, and Owosso. Several defunct clubs began making noises about reorganizing so as not to miss out on the tour. They learned too late that the club was only named in honor of Chicago millionaire Potter Palmer and not sponsored by him. After a disastrous loss in Janesville, Wisconsin, the Potter Palmers abandoned their tour.[10] Owosso was especially disappointed by their nonappearance, having gone to considerable expense in making arrangements.

Competition was also sparked again by Independence Day celebrations. A tournament in Middleville on July 4 saw the Valley City Club of Grand Rapids beat the Island Club of Plainwell 88-28 to win a thirty-dollar purse. Plans for a tournament in Marshall fell through, but two games were played and enough interest generated that another tournament was planned for August. The St. Joseph Club of Burr Oak defeated the Lively Reds of Sturgis 62-36 on July 11 to claim the championship of St. Joseph County. The Blue Stockings of Clarkston beat the Wolverines of Pontiac 72-18 and challenged any club in the county to play them for the championship.

As competition expanded, stakes rose rapidly. In mid-July, the Dowagiac Club captured a twenty-dollar purse by defeating the Constellation Club of Dowagiac 51-14. Only two weeks later the Dowagiac Club captured a two-hundred-dollar purse in Dexter by beating its hosts 53-18. The *Advertiser and Tribune* described this amount as "perhaps, the largest purse ever contested for in this state."[11]

As summer progressed, the rising stakes and comparative ease of travel stimulated even more activity around the state. The Unas of Kalamazoo followed up their win over the Eurekas of Chicago with convincing victories over the Continentals of Kalamazoo and the Clippers of Decatur and pronounced themselves ready to play the Detroit Base Ball Club, though that club had already disbanded.

A club called the "Unprofessionals" was formed in Battle Creek, causing the *Advertiser and Tribune*'s correspondent to remark that "base ball mania has finally taken possession of the young men of this city."[12] The Ogema Club of Flint "roused itself from its long sleep" and consolidated with the junior Hercules Club.[13] On August 11, the Ogemas hosted the Mystics of Detroit and crushed them 66-18, causing the Mystics to disband and leaving Detroit again without a first-rate club.

Competition for the emblems of Kent County supremacy resumed. The Dexter Club of Grand Rapids defeated the Try Us Club of Muskegon to capture the silver ball but was in turn beaten by the Valley City Club of Grand Rapids. Even the Upper Peninsula was catching the fever, with the First Nationals of Hancock playing tightly contested series with the Houghton Club and the German Socks of Calumet.

The nicknames chosen by the new clubs suggest the critical juncture that baseball had reached. Many of the new clubs hearkened back to the older notion of belonging and sought to give themselves credibility by selecting popular names. Benton Harbor, Williamston, Allegan, Porter, Flint, Bay City, Adrian, Muskegon, Battle Creek, White Lake, and Howell all had clubs called the Shoo Flies, after the popular song. There were Star Clubs in Marshall, Algansee, St. Johns, Fenton, Salina, Rockford, Birmingham, Negaunee, East Saginaw, Flint, Adrian, Muskegon, Kalamazoo, Grand Rapids, Antwerp, and Plainwell and at the Agricultural College in Lansing. Clubs in Newton, Sorter's Corners, Marshall, Grand Rapids, and Fredonia dubbed themselves the Unknowns, while Wolverine Clubs sprang up in Loomisville, Hudson, Galien, Benton Harbor, Vermontville, Lapeer, East Saginaw, Johnson's Hollow, and Pontiac.

Other club names reflected a growing taste for individuality. Some of the more intriguing monikers included the Awkwards of Palo, the Whippoorwills of Carson City, the Water Sprites of Ypsilanti, the Vagrants of Buchanan, the Whitewashers of Ortonville, the Lively Turtles of Coloma, the Mattawees of Leroy, the Light

Foot of Union City, the Rag Pickers of Litchfield, the Lively Reds of Sturgis, the You Bets of Detroit, the Artful Dodgers of Gaines, the Sleeping Beauties of Burr Oak, the Backwoods Refugees of rural Oakland County, the Wild Cats of Algansee, the Light Strikers of Commerce, and even the Dead Beats of North Farmington.[14] The members of a Birmingham club developed quite an appetite during a long trek to a game and upon arriving announced themselves as the Hungry Nine of Birmingham, a name that stuck.[15] By the end of the 1870 season, there were new high-water marks, with 263 active clubs and 129 Michigan cities represented.

The time finally seemed right for major tournaments to again be attempted, and several were proposed. The first began in Fenton on August 23 and, as in the past, ran far from smoothly. The tournament's organizers strove initially to arrange a keynote match between the Red Stockings of Cincinnati and the White Stockings of Chicago. Had this game come off, it would have been a historic moment in Michigan baseball. Although the Red Stockings' extraordinary winning streak had ended on June 14, and although the club was weakened by injuries and internal turmoil, it remained a contender for the national championship and a tremendous gate attraction.

The White Stockings had been formed at great expense in Chicago with a mission to "capture the whole world of Base Ball players, and oh, especially wollop [*sic*] the Red Stockings."[16] The club's formation was a clear indication of the competitiveness bred by city living. As one Cincinnati paper crowed, "It vexes the metropolitan soul of Chicago that a village like Cincinnati should bear off the palm in the baseball world."[17] Accordingly, a stock corporation had been formed with no pretense of the trappings of a club, with eighteen thousand dollars—almost twice what the Red Stockings had earned the year before—allotted to player salaries. Nor did the club's management share Harry Wright's concern for the character of the players, luring several athletes with dubious reputations, most notably the notoriously crooked William Craver of the Mutuals of New York.

Nevertheless, the White Stockings had gotten off to a very slow start and had hit rock bottom with a 9-0 loss to the Mutuals of New York, which earned the White Stockings the kind of abuse previously reserved for the Excelsiors. This was the first time a top club failed to score in a match, and the loss helped popularize the use of the term *chicagoed* to denote a shutout. But the White Stockings expelled Craver, revamped their lineup, and began to compile an impressive record. With several strong clubs in New York and Philadelphia also in contention, all of the clubs suffered enough defeats that the 1870 season ended with no undisputed champion, although some authorities considered the White Stockings the new champions on the basis of a better head-to-head record with the Red Stockings. A game in Fenton, had it come off, could conceivably have altered this picture.

The White Stockings did commit to the game, and hopes were high for a marquee match. But the Red Stockings, reeling from a devastating knee injury to George Wright, opted instead to give their players a week off. The Athletics of Philadelphia also declined an invitation. Alternative plans were made to match the White Stockings against the best available Michigan club, which was determined to be the newly reorganized Ogemas of Flint. But the White Stockings demanded that the guarantee amount be upped from $275 to $300, and when this wasn't agreed to, Chicago's famous nine withdrew.

This left a field of twelve competitors, neatly divided into four clubs in each of the three classes. However, with the exception of the Try Us Club of Muskegon, the field was too geographically narrow for the tournament to be considered much more than a local contest on a large scale. Six of the twelve clubs represented either Flint or Fenton, with the others hailing from Milford, Linden, Lapeer, and East Saginaw. The tournament organizers were therefore happy to permit the last-minute entrance of the newly formed Empire Club of Detroit, which included the Mystics' old battery of M. Kinney and Dan O'Leary.

The Ogema Club of Flint was considerably less satisfied with the late entry and refused to play either the Empires or the Try Us Club of Muskegon, which had also entered after the deadline. While the Ogemas may have been technically correct, their shortsightedness was disastrous for the tournament and the future of the game in Michigan, and a sad reminder of how much the attitude of players had changed from the "Young America spirit" of the Early Risers. When the Ogemas beat the Hurons of Milford 57-50 in a game that attracted few spectators and minimal excitement, the tournament organizers had little choice but to award the Ogemas the first prize of fifty dollars. This gave Flint a clean sweep of the three classes, as the Ogemas' second nine beat the Plow Boys of Linden 38-31 to capture the second class and the Lumber City Club of Flint claimed the honors in the third class with a 35-28 triumph over the I X L Club of East Saginaw.

The tournament organizers attempted to salvage matters by raising a special purse of fifty dollars for a game between the Empires and the Try Us Club of Muskegon, which the Empires won 54-5. The Ogemas were then offered the opportunity to play the Empires for another special purse, but they churlishly declined and went home. Instead, the Empires were matched up with a picked nine from the Try Us, Plow Boy, and Huron Clubs. This game was considered the best of the tournament, with the Empires ending up on the long end of a 35-24 score and earning twenty-five dollars and a silver cup. The beleaguered tournament organizers awarded a special prize of a handsome bat to the Try Us Club of Muskegon for its members' general bearing throughout the tournament. One of the players who represented the Try Us Club on the all-star team, Harry Spence, would join the Empire Club the following season and later manage in the major leagues.[18]

The Fenton tournament also suffered from inadequate facilities. The attendance of over one thousand people was far more than a small town could accommodate, and there were complaints about the low, rickety, and uncovered seats; the uneven field; the shortage of water; and the negligible facilities for the players. Still, in spite of all the problems, the tournament was far from a failure.

While the influx of tourists exceeded the town's capacities, the owners of Fenton's hotels and taverns were happy to have such problems. The town buzzed with excitement during the tournament, and at night the halls and streets overflowed with baseball enthusiasts. Betting was common, even at the third-class games. A ball was held for the players and spectators at the Andrews House that featured three fiddlers and a caller and lasted into the wee hours. All in all, in spite of dissatisfaction with many elements, visitors reported favorably on the tournament. Several other cities took note, and Dowagiac, Marshall, and Kalamazoo all announced plans for major tournaments in the immediate aftermath of the Fenton tournament.

Meanwhile, the Ann Arbor Club defended its state title against Jackson on August 16 with a 50-30 victory and accepted a challenge from the Empires of Detroit. But before this match could come off, the Ogemas of Flint also issued a challenge and began using the newspapers to insinuate that Ann Arbor was afraid to play them. Like other state champions before them, the Ann Arbor Club was beginning to learn that the title conferred more responsibilities than benefits. The club indignantly responded to the charge by pointing out that the Ogemas would have to wait until after the match with the Empires, adding that "we think we can and will relieve the Ogemas of a trifle of their conceit when they do meet."[19]

The tournament at Dowagiac opened on August 31. The prize fund was announced in advance and included a first prize of $150 in the open division and $50 for the second-place finisher, while $75 and $25 respectively would be awarded to the top two junior clubs. Additional $5 premiums to the top base runner, pitcher, catcher, batter, and general ball player brought the total to a hefty $325. Unfortunately, instead of a good turnout, the generous prize fund produced only overheated competitiveness.

The Athletics of Decatur defeated the Constellation Club of Dowagiac and the Mechanics of Buchanan to claim the junior title and $75. In the senior division, the Dowagiac Club beat the Unions of Kalamazoo to set up a championship game with the Favorites of St. Joseph for first place and $150.

The Favorites had added three "revolvers" for the tournament—Thomas Gaskins, Fred Pullen, and Tommy Mackey from the recently disbanded Garden City Club of Chicago. The St. Joseph club justified this as a preemptive strike; it alleged that Dowagiac was planning to import two Chicago players, including recently expelled White Stockings catcher William Craver. The stage was thus set for the rancor that would follow.

The championship game was delayed by rain until it was so late that there was little hope of completing the game before dark. St. Joseph jumped to an 11-2 advantage after three innings and still led 15-11 after four innings as dusk was approaching. But in the bottom of the fifth, Dowagiac scored 9 runs in near darkness to grab a 20-15 lead. The game was halted, both clubs arguing that they had won.

In the version in the St. Joseph newspaper, the umpire eventually ruled in Dowagiac's favor after "the directors and their shoulder-hitters crowded around the poor, trembling umpire, whom they had bullied during the whole game, and declared they would never let him leave the grounds alive if he decided against Dowagiac." The paper further labeled the tournament "a farce" and declared, "If you want to be treated mean go to Dowagiac."[20] It's equally easy to see why Dowagiac resented the Favorites' efforts to win the tournament with imported players. The only undeniable conclusion was that such bickering did the game of baseball no good.

At the Marshall tournament, which ran from September 6 to 8, an attempt was made to avoid the problems that had plagued the Fenton tournament by announcing all pairings and purses in advance. The first day saw matches between two third-class teams, with the Stars of Marshall beating the Unknowns of Newton 36-33 to claim a ball and bat valued at five dollars and the Ziskas of Homer defeating the Air Lines of Tekonsha 55-32 to win a ten-dollar prize. On September 7, the two second-class matches took place, with the Juniors of Marshall routing the Excelsiors of Jackson 66-36 to win twenty dollars and the Pastimes of Marshall trouncing the Unprofessionals of Battle Creek 75-32 for thirty dollars.

In spite of complaints that the field was "unsuited for the purpose, it being a clearing full of stumps, weeds and manure, while the entire ground was an inclined plane from right to left," the tournament did create excitement.[21] On the evening of September 7, a baseball party took place at the Eagle Hall, where the first-class games to take place on the morrow were fervently discussed. In the first game, the state champion Ann Arbor Club would take on the Mutuals of Jackson. Then the winner would face the Unas of Kalamazoo for a seventy-five-dollar purse and the state championship.

The next day, Ann Arbor beat the Mutuals 41-34 in the opening game. But the match between Ann Arbor and the Unas, which should have provided a rousing finish to the tournament, ended prematurely in another dispute. After one inning, the Unas led 8-0. In the Ann Arbor Club's second at bats, its captain began to protest that the Unas' pitcher Thomas Dorgan was not adhering to the rules, which dictated that he deliver the ball in underhand style without bending his elbow.

The umpire, Barney Schaffer of Ypsilanti, agreed and began calling a balk on each pitch. Finally, Johnny McCord, who had been responsible for introducing baseball to Kalamazoo a decade earlier, replaced Dorgan in the pitcher's box but used the same delivery. When Schaffer also ruled McCord's pitches balks, the Unas demanded that Schaffer be replaced with a new umpire. This appeal falling on deaf ears, the game was abandoned, the players continuing to argue while the spectators filed out in disgust. As invariably happened in such situations, the dispute was carried on in the newspapers for several weeks afterward.

Most such quarrels centered around two irreconcilable versions of events and were followed by wild and usually irrelevant accusations that obscured the original issue. This dispute was quite different because all agreed that the only question was whether Dorgan's delivery was legal. The Ann Arbor Club pointed out that in every recent game played by the Unas, including the one at the Dowagiac tournament, the opposing club had complained about the delivery. They noted that Schaffer, an experienced and impartial umpire, as well as most of the spectators, had agreed that the delivery violated the letter of the law. The Unas countered by arguing that Dorgan's pitching style was now acceptable in all the large cities, noting that when the Unas played the Forest City Club of Cleveland, both pitchers used the same style and no objections were made on either side.[22]

Michigan was thus the scene of an important ongoing debate about the direction the game should be taking. According to A. G. Spalding, there were only a few pitchers in this period who could generate speed or curves while adhering to the requirement of a straight elbow. With so few legal pitchers, clubs had to use ones who bent the rules, and "the effect of course was to put the question up to the umpire, and if he ruled against the pitcher there was a disappointed crowd, no game, or an utterly uninteresting exhibition." Consequently, there was "a growing tendency on the part of umpires to be lax in the enforcement of the rule . . . rather than stop the game and disappoint the crowd."[23]

According to Spalding, enforcement of the rules was eventually deemed less important than competitive balance. Another practical consideration was that being lenient on pitching deliveries lowered scores and shortened games, which could be a great boon to tournament organizers. Baseball thus began a long and still-intact tradition of having separate de facto and de jure rules.

The debate about pitching deliveries would rage for another two years until liberalized rules were adopted. But in 1870, Michigan was not yet ready for these rules, and popular sentiment ran in Ann Arbor's favor. The organizers of the tournament wrote to the Ann Arbor Club to thank its members for being "perfect gentlemen" and absolve them from any responsibility for the fiasco. Nonetheless, when the Ann Arbor Club requested that they remit the seventy-five dollars in prize money, they politely declined.[24]

The final big tournament took place in Kalamazoo on the grounds of the National Horse Fair from September 13 to 15. Prizes had been announced at four hundred dollars for the first class, two hundred dollars for the second class, and one hundred dollars for the third class, in order to "giv[e] all clubs a chance to contend for the championship of Michigan."[25] Things went smoothly in the lower divisions, with the Constellations of Dowagiac beating the Stars of Plainwell 40-13 to earn the first prize in the second class and the Hungry Nine of Oshtemo beating the Union Club of Kalamazoo 24-19 to win the top prize in the third class. A dearth of entries in the first class prompted the cancellation of that division altogether, and a match between the Forest City Club of Cleveland and the Unas was substituted. The Forest City Club won 54-5, though Kalamazoo took some consolation from the fact that the Cleveland pitcher used the same delivery as Dorgan.

On September 14, the Empire Club of Detroit met Ann Arbor for the state championship, and Ann Arbor easily retained the title, 37-17. The Empires were without the services of four of their regular players, including their pitcher M. Kinney, causing the *Advertiser and Tribune* to write, "It is difficult to discover the utility of their contesting a match game under such circumstances."[26]

A week later, Ann Arbor played the Ogemas of Flint for the state championship and annihilated them 75-11. The Ogemas' earlier insinuations that Ann Arbor was afraid to play them were not forgotten, and the Ann Arbor correspondent to the *Advertiser and Tribune* contemptuously referred to the inflated reputation that the Ogemas "had obtained newspaperially." Even the enormous margin of defeat did not entirely silence the Ogemas, as following the game "some of the Flint boys loudly asserted the ability of their club to beat the Ann Arbor club for *money*."[27] But the players must have realized the folly of this boast, as they appear to have disbanded soon after the "Bull Run defeat."[28]

Ann Arbor successfully defended the state championship one last time, beating Salem 66-21 on September 26 and even making an unsuccessful attempt to arrange a game against the White Stockings of Chicago. In spite of being widely perceived as beatable after briefly losing the championship cup to the Praktikoi, the Ann Arbor Club was the undisputed state champion at the conclusion of what had been one of the busiest baseball seasons ever.

In Detroit, a city with nearly ten times the population of Ann

Arbor, the Empires had to be content with playing the Eurekas for the city championship. Many of the Eurekas had belonged to the Mystic Club, and they gave the Empires a close game, but lost 15-9. The game was closer than the score indicated, being tied at 9-9 after seven innings. The Empires scored a single run in the bottom of the eighth and then whitewashed the Eurekas in the top of the ninth to clinch the victory. But by the rules of the day, the bottom of the ninth still had to be played, and the Empires pushed across 5 meaningless runs. It was an appropriate coda to a season that had seen a promising start give way to an increasing sense that baseball was becoming irrelevant.

NOTES

1. *Grand Rapids Daily Eagle*, September 2, 1870.
2. *Detroit Free Press*, May 17, 1870.
3. *Detroit Advertiser and Tribune*, June 22, 1870.
4. The spectators included Harvard president Charles William Eliot, but the game could not have made a positive impression on Eliot. He later called baseball a "wretched game" because of its exclusivity ("There are only nine men who can play a game . . . and out of the nine there are only two desirable positions—pitcher and catcher") and tried to prevent its growth as an intercollegiate sport (David Q. Voigt, *American Baseball*, 205).
5. *Hillsdale Standard*, May 24, 1870; *Owosso Weekly Press*, May 25, 1870. One of the members of the Praktikoi was twenty-year-old Clarence Winfield Terwilliger, who would soon establish himself as one of Michigan's best baseball players and then become one of the country's most famous athletes, leading the Hillsdale crew to three consecutive national rowing championships and becoming a boyhood hero of Teddy Roosevelt.
6. *Jackson Daily Citizen*, April 29, 1870.
7. *Kalamazoo Daily Gazette*, May 4, 1872.
8. *Kalamazoo Daily Gazette*, March 4, 1891.
9. *Kalamazoo Daily Gazette*, May 5, 1891.
10. *Chicago Tribune*, July 22 and 23, 1870.
11. *Detroit Advertiser and Tribune*, July 23, 1870.
12. *Detroit Advertiser and Tribune*, August 3, 1870.
13. *Detroit Advertiser and Tribune*, July 18, 1870.
14. The *Coldwater Republican* of August 26, 1870, claimed that the Rag Pickers' name suited "the ridiculous uniforms they wear."
15. *Birmingham Eccentric*, January 15, 1970, centennial edition. Clubs in Walled Lake, Big Rapids, and Oshtemo were soon also using this name.
16. *Adrian Times and Expositor*, July 26, 1870.
17. *Cincinnati Commercial*, from the Chadwick Scrapbooks; reprinted in William J. Ryczek, *When Johnny Came Sliding Home*, 202.
18. Harry Spence's playing career continued until 1884, and he managed Indianapolis of the National League in 1888.

19. *Detroit Advertiser and Tribune*, August 24, 1870.

20. *St. Joseph Herald*, September 10, 1870.

21. *Michigan Argus* (Ann Arbor), September 16, 1870.

22. *Detroit Advertiser and Tribune*, September 14 and 20, 1870. However, when Deacon White had attempted such a windup two years earlier against the Mutuals of New York, umpire Jack Chapman told him, "This is New York, not Cleveland," and threw him out of the game (Martin Quigley, *The Crooked Pitch*, 45).

23. Albert G. Spalding, *America's National Game*, 482–83.

24. *Michigan Argus* (Ann Arbor), September 16, 1870.

25. *Detroit Daily Post*, August 27, 1870.

26. *Detroit Advertiser and Tribune*, September 15, 1870.

27. *Detroit Advertiser and Tribune*, September 23, 1870.

28. *Detroit Advertiser and Tribune*, September 26, 1870.

19

"WHAT USE IS ALL THIS STRAINING OF MUSCLE"

While the 1870 season did see a considerable upswing in baseball interest, it was becoming clear by late in the campaign that the revival would be short-lived. For all the imitators the Red Stockings had inspired, the club's example was not a sustainable one. Train travel had made professional baseball possible, but it was competitive balance that was required to transform the sport into a stable industry.

As much as the newspapers liked to stress the discipline and character of Harry Wright's club, it was the undefeated record that was the team's underlying attraction. This was ultimately a step backward for baseball, since the harsh reality remained that each baseball game produced only one winner and left the other club dissatisfied. Over the next six years, clubs seeking to emulate the Red Stockings' unbeaten record drove potential rivals away. Only with the formation of the National League in 1876 did the issue of competitive balance begin to be addressed.

The more immediate effect of the Red Stockings' undefeated season was to create the impossible expectation that the best club would again win every game in 1870. The numerous emulators of the Red Stockings ensured instead that no club would go undefeated. Every first-class club lost at least six games, prompting one reporter to write that "it would take a Philadelphia lawyer to find out which was the champion club of 1870."[1] Such a closely contested race would cause great excitement today, but in the aftermath of the 1869 season, many were disappointed by the lack of a clear champion.

The Red Stockings felt the pressure, and discipline and drinking problems emerged among the players whose success a year earlier had been attributed to their upstanding character. Things were made worse by the serious knee injury to George Wright, and soon the town that had worshipped the club began to turn on them. The backlash prompted one observer to write, "It's Cincinnati's turn now to say something about their crack club, and the way an infuriated populace are cursing the 'Red Socks' is a caution to all professionals. Verily the way of the base ballist is an extremely dusty one."[2]

The new president of the Red Stockings, A. P. C. Bonte, led the attack on the professional players. No sooner had the season ended than he claimed that "the amateurs at Cincinnati had the pleasure of

In this 1870 game at Brooklyn's Capitoline Grounds, the Atlantics of Brooklyn finally ended the two-year unbeaten streak of the Red Stockings of Cincinnati. Note that the second baseman was positioned on second base. Bob Ferguson of the Atlantics, normally a right-handed batter, batted left-handed in this game to take advantage of the large hole and to keep the ball away from Red Stockings shortstop George Wright. Thus was the switch-hitter born.
Courtesy of Transcendental Graphics

footing the bills and seeing 'Red Stockings' in the newspapers. It was very much as though some old gentleman who had been put upon slim fare by his physician should hire a fellow of large appetite and powerful digestion to go around the country and represent him at public dinners."[3] Bonte announced that the Red Stockings would revert to being an amateur club. Not one to stay where he wasn't wanted, Harry Wright took his favorite players and the Red Stockings name to Boston. (As a result, two current teams, the Boston Red Sox and the Cincinnati Reds, owe their nicknames to Harry Wright's Red Stockings.)

With the Red Stockings of Cincinnati unable to survive as a professional team, it is no surprise that many of the Michigan clubs modeled on them met a similar fate. When they realized that they couldn't attain such a high level of play, most clubs disbanded. In vain, such clubs were urged by one letter writer to aim to raise a banner with the inscription, "The Champion Moral, Social, or Friendly Base Ball Club."[4] A decade ago such a goal would have inspired many clubs, but it no longer generated much enthusiasm in 1870.

The disappointment of falling short of expectations was beginning to manifest itself in behavior that would have been unthinkable ten years earlier. After a picked nine from Big Rapids and Cedar Springs won at Rockford, the "defeat caused no little chagrin amongst the Rockfords, who pride themselves on being experts in this national game, and at the close of the game, they were conspicuously scarce, permitting their visitors to leave town unmolested, and without refreshments of any kind."[5] Four years later, Cedar Springs and Rockford were still at odds over this incident.

In another incident, after the Valley City Club of Grand Rapids hosted the Unas of Kalamazoo, the *Grand Rapids Morning Democrat* launched into a tirade against the visitors. The Unas, it claimed, were "a set of roughs, whose dirty linen does not surpass their ungentlemanly and dirty practice of playing the national game." The players and their friends ("roughs and gamblers") spent the night in Grand Rapids after their victory and, according to the

Morning Democrat, "made last night hideous with their bacchanalian songs."[6]

After the Kalamazoo newspapers and the other two Grand Rapids papers jumped to the defense of the Unas, the *Morning Democrat* became even more outlandish, accusing the Unas of "gambling, insulting respectable people, getting drunk, running in the halls of a hotel naked, visiting gambling houses and houses of prostitution."[7] The Valley City Club passed a resolution condemning the accusations as "unjust and uncalled for."[8] But by now, the Kalamazoo newspapers were alleging that the Valley City Club had failed to pay its bills on an earlier visit to Plainwell, which further poisoned the atmosphere.

In addition, the considerable excitement created by the tournament season proved to be a mixed blessing. Tournaments were even harsher than individual games in that they left one winner and many losers, thereby weeding out many would-be Red Stockings. Typical was the experience in Coldwater, where excitement reached a new high after the Resolute Club won its first eleven games. But after decisive losses to the Pastimes of Marshall and a club from Algansee, interest almost entirely vanished.

New clubs were finding that the patience that had been granted new teams four years earlier was now in short supply. When a newly formed club in Cedar Springs played its first friendly game and was soundly beaten by a more experienced club, the *Grand Rapids Times* described the Cedar Springs Club as being three years old. Their home paper responded in exasperation: "Our boys make no pretentions [*sic*]. They are just learning, and are not even yet perfectly organized. There is nothing to hinder the two Clubs having many friendly games, and by-and-by match games, if the friendship is not destroyed by some brainless scribbler, who mistakes falsehood for shrewdness."[9]

The demise of the Peninsular Club of Grand Rapids was particularly poignant. Since competition for the silver ball emblematic of the championship of Kent County had begun three years earlier, the Penisulars had held the trophy longer than any other club. But when the veteran club lost to the juvenile Dexter Club, the *Grand Rapids Morning Democrat* advised its members never to "appear in the base ball arena again, unless they are challenged by some old woman's club.—With one or two exceptions, the players are worse than bad, and the several defeats they have suffered already this season should convince them that they cannot play base ball."[10] Three days later, the *Morning Democrat* announced unsympathetically, "After their terrible defeat by the Dexters, a lot of small boys, last week, [the Peninsulars] concluded wisely that they could not play the national game and disbanded."[11] Perhaps it is fair to conclude that the success of the Red Stockings had set expectations so high as to virtually ensure the failure of every club in 1870.

The correspondence between W. R. Morrison of the Favorites of St. Joseph and Fred Butler of the Fearless Club of New Buffalo is particularly revealing. In late June in St. Joseph, the Favorites had beaten the Fearless Club, previously recognized as county champion, by a 40-35 margin. The game was an exciting one, and the batting was so heavy that the two clubs "broke all the bats in the field and sent for more."[12] Butler issued a challenge for a return match, for "amusement or *money*," with the now necessary stipulation that both clubs be limited to using established members. Morrison responded that due to "circumstances beyond control," his club would agree to play only in St. Joseph or its twin town of Benton Harbor.

Butler offered to play in any neutral town on the Michigan Central Rail Road line between the two villages. The St. Joseph secretary answered by reiterating his club's inability to travel and asserting that for that reason it had never sought a match with the Fearless Club in the first place. He did offer to pay the rival club's travel expenses to Benton Harbor, but only if the Fearless Club won. Butler declined to play on such terms and admonished the Favorites, "There are occasions when it might be beneficial, even for youthful lads to cut loose from apron strings and exhibit a little self-reliance."[13]

This was not the only warning sign that baseball in Michigan was threatening to revert to the juvenile realm. A match between junior clubs representing Battle Creek and Marshall was tied at 12-12 after eight innings. When Battle Creek scored 11 runs in the top of the ninth inning to break the game open, the members of the Marshall Club expressed their displeasure with the umpiring and literally "seized the ball and went home to their mothers."[14]

Because baseball was now threatened with the loss of its critical association with manliness, it had to withstand another of the periodic backlashes from the newspapers that had once been so supportive. The feverish devotion that baseball tended to inspire was of particular concern. A Hillsdale newspaper noted:

> After a while this continued talk about Red Stockings, and White Stockings, and Empires, and Mutuals, and Key Stones, etc. etc., grows dry, and the question arises in the mind—what use is all this straining of muscle and exercise of perception for the sake of counting the most tallies.
>
> This base ball business is a very good thing in moderation; it improves the health, and develops the muscles of those who take part in it, but like other American institutions, it is run into the ground. It would form a much more interesting and profitable exhibition, if those young men, instead of perambulating the country by nines, and gambling away their muscle on the "national Game" would devote their powers of body and mind to the agricultural, commercial and intellectual development of the country.[15]

Others went much further. A Muskegon newspaper termed baseball "the national nonsense" and suggested that the members of the local Shoo Fly Club "stick to business. Base ball is a base delusion, and beside [sic] it evidently isn't their forte. By the time they acquire sufficient skill to play the game successfully, it will have been numbered among the follies of the past."[16]

The Detroit newspapers—once quick to defend the game for

the exercise and fresh air it provided—were now regularly publishing articles that questioned baseball's value to society. The *Free Press* reprinted a particularly scathing article:

> The American people are perhaps the least practical while the most industrious and enterprising of all the people in the world. We say the least practical because they are the easiest led away in admiration of affairs that have "nothing in them," that are meretricious, silly, even foolish. We are subject to periodical passions for foolish things, and when a thing becomes a fashion, however ridiculous it may be, those who refuse to worship and commend it are at once set down as the ignorant ones. We are led to these remarks by the returning base ball fever, and its counterpart croquet. If a number of genteel idlers organize a base ball club, and engage in other clubs with rivalries which have no meaning, it is expected that business should at once be suspended, that the telegraph and newspapers should yield all their facilities to spread before the public a result that doesn't prove anything. The best base ball players in the world are men who never did an honest day's labor in their lives, yet such fellows will fry what little brains they have, in the best of a summer solstice, competing with bat and ball for a superiority which does not add a feature to society's good, physical powers of usefulness, or moral dignity. But it is fashionable. That's enough. The men or man who does an honest day's work, where genius and art and mechanism contribute to the wealth and glory of the land, are not made half as reputable by the telegraph and the press as is a base ball club. Our city contemporaries would not advertise the most useful invention unless they are paid for it, and yet during the season they do not hesitate to force on their readers columns of stuff about base ball contests which are a bore to all but those whose are glorified thereby. . . . Herein is just where the American people so often render themselves ridiculous before the world. Our amusements are of the impracticable kind; and when we do anything of a sportive character, instead of making it subservient to good sense, we outrage the latter quality and turn our pleasure into dissipation. The base ball fever now amounts to a ridiculous display of petty

vanities which claim to have a monopoly of our attention. American journalism is to blame for this cultivation of a national snobbishness, and it is about time that the telegraph were employed in furnishing newspapers with intelligence of a more useful character than that of reports of base ball contests.[17]

Serious questions were also being raised about whether baseball offered the health benefits once attributed to it. The *Detroit Post* reprinted an article from *Hearth and Home* that deplored professional baseball: "If there were ever a time when the American people were in danger of physical degeneracy from the lack of out-of-door sports, it must have been many years ago."[18] And considerable attention was given to *Man and Wife*, a recent novel by the popular British author Wilkie Collins that depicted sports as having dire consequences for the spiritual and physical man.

Collins's hero describes "the present mania for athletic sports as . . . an outbreak of our insular boastfulness and our insular barbarity, in a new form."[19] One character in the novel, a young man, dies suddenly because of the overexertion of his heart caused by athletics. Many questioned the plausibility of this plot line, but Collins seemed prescient when champion British oarsman James Renforth died suddenly the next year during a race in New Brunswick. Renforth's death was viewed as "a most emphatic protest against all athletic sports that require such an unusual strain of the muscular system."[20] Those who had criticized Collins were forced to "confess that his imagination did not outrun the possibilities of fact."[21]

The following month, another newspaper noted that "the theory delivered by Wilkie Collins, in his story of 'Man and Wife,' that muscular culture is more likely to destroy than promote health, receives confirmation in the case of H. A. Cleveland, a graduate of Yale. He was one of the prominent boating men of his class, and pulled oar in the boat which won the race with the Harvard crew. He was one of the best and most enthusiastic ball-players in the college, and carried off the celebrated wooden spoon, which is given annually to the most popular member of the graduating class. He has just returned from a tour of Europe, in such a low state of health that he can not long survive."[22] Concern grew when Byron D. Ball, who had been president of Grand Rapids' first base ball club in 1859, died of enlargement of the heart at age forty-one. Ball was fond of "violent muscular exertion, gymnasium exercise and heavy lifting," and an autopsy showed that his right auricle was three to four times the normal size.[23]

The *New York Times* fanned the flames by claiming that "fatal accidents on the ball field have become so common of late as to hardly excite remark and maiming is the rule and not the exception."[24] This was a gross exaggeration, but the *New York Tribune* had recently reported that "the violent running incident to home-runs ended in the death of a ball-player in Washington last week, the player falling dead at the home-base from bursting a blood-vessel."[25] In a somber coincidence, a twelve-year-old Grand Rapids boy was hit in the stomach with a baseball, causing the first baseball-related death in Michigan. One account of the event erroneously stated that the boy had been the only support for his widowed mother.[26]

In October, the *Detroit Post* published a long article that described baseball fever in the past tense with no hint of regret. The newspaper continued to advocate moderate exercise but now questioned whether moderation could be practiced by Americans, due to the "proneness of Americans to carry to excess all athletic games and pursuits, until they are satiated." It contended that any benefits baseball had were outweighed by three attendant evils. The first was money, which soon led to the destructive "tendency to convert ball clubs into gigantic stock concerns, and, under the disguise of a 'friendly' or match game, carry on a species of stock gambling." Second was the threat posed to pedestrians by the games played on public streets; the *Post* decried "the dodging and ducking it was necessary to perform while walking through the streets . . . to avoid a 'red-hot' ball."[27] Finally, there was the bad influence the game had on its enthusiasts. In contrast to the Early Risers, who had scheduled 5:00 A.M. practices so as not to jeopardize their employment, "many clerks lost their situations, others failed to obtain them, because the National game interfered with the performance of their duties."[28]

Thus the 1870 season ended with the game of baseball, both in Michigan and across the country, again at a crossroads. Perhaps "the ridicule heaped upon the players for taking part in such childish sports" when men had started playing baseball was warranted? When the Red Stockings of Cincinnati renounced professional baseball, the *New York Tribune* proclaimed, "This is but the beginning of the end of professional ball-playing."[29] Although the conditions to establish baseball as a successful business enterprise were not yet in place, a retreat to the idealized past of carefree play seemed equally impossible. To borrow Matthew Arnold's powerful image, baseball was now "Wandering between two worlds, one dead / The other powerless to be born."[30]

NOTES

1. From the Chadwick Scrapbooks; reprinted in William J. Ryczek, *When Johnny Came Sliding Home*, 231.
2. *Detroit Free Press*, September 10, 1870.
3. *Wilkes' Spirit of the Times*, November 26, 1870; reprinted in Ryczek, *When Johnny Came Sliding Home*, 237.
4. *Berrien County Record* (Buchanan), September 1, 1870, letter from J. O. Baker of Three Oaks.
5. *Big Rapids Independent*, September 24, 1870.
6. *Grand Rapids Daily Morning Democrat*, August 19, 1870.
7. *Grand Rapids Daily Morning Democrat*, August 26, 1870.
8. *Grand Rapids Daily Times*, August 28, 1870.
9. *Cedar Springs Wolverine Clipper*, August 3, 1870.
10. *Grand Rapids Daily Morning Democrat*, August 9, 1870.
11. *Grand Rapids Daily Morning Democrat*, August 12, 1870.
12. *St. Joseph Herald*, June 25, 1870.
13. The entire correspondence was reprinted in the *Berrien County Record* (Buchanan), July 14, 1870.
14. *Marshall Statesman*, October 26, 1870.
15. *Hillsdale Standard*, July 19, 1870.
16. *Muskegon News and Reporter*, October 25, 1870.
17. *Harrisburg Topic;* reprinted in the *Detroit Free Press*, June 27, 1870.
18. *Detroit Daily Post*, July 19, 1870.
19. Wilkie Collins, *Man and Wife*, 193.
20. *Big Rapids Independent*, September 2, 1871.

21. *Grand Rapids Daily Times*, August 27, 1871.

22. *Ionia Sentinel*, October 7, 1871.

23. *Grand Rapids Daily Eagle*, February 5, 1876.

24. *New York Times*, September 11, 1870; reprinted in Ryczek, *When Johnny Came Sliding Home*, 245.

25. *New York Daily Tribune*, August 15, 1870.

26. The boy's death was reported in the *Grand Rapids Daily Times* on August 31, 1870, and the *Grand Rapids Daily Eagle* on August 30, 1870. There are some discrepancies in the accounts: the *Times* gave his name as Robert Cowding, while the *Eagle* had it as Richard Dowding. There is no death record under either name, but there was a widow named Mrs. Jane Dowding in the 1869 Grand Rapids City Directory. The 1870 census, compiled only three weeks before the tragedy, shows a widow named Jane Dowling with five children; the two oldest were Robert, 14, and Richard, 12, both of whom worked in a box factory. Although the newspapers were frequently commenting on the dangers of baseball, this was the only documented death caused by the game in Michigan before 1880. According to the *Detroit Advertiser and Tribune* of September 26, 1871, George Waite of the Plainwell Base Ball Club exerted himself too much during a match at Wayland and died after returning home. However, his death record lists kidney disease as the cause of death.

27. This menace was also prevalent elsewhere. See, for example, the *St. Joseph Herald*, May 21, 1870.

28. *Detroit Daily Post*, October 7, 1870.

29. Chadwick Scrapbooks; reprinted in Ryczek, *When Johnny Came Sliding Home*, 244.

30. Matthew Arnold, "Stanzas from the Grande Chartreuse," stanza 15.

20

"WHERE ARE OUR BASE BALLISTS?"

With the opening of the 1871 season, baseball had a new landscape. The National Association of Base Ball Players, long ineffectual in its attempts to stem the tide of professionalism, had lost what little power it had two years earlier when it authorized professional play. During the off-season it had disbanded and been replaced by two new organizations—the National Association of Amateur Base Ball Players and the National Association of Professional Base Ball Players.

The latter organization oversaw baseball's first professional league, commonly known as the National Association, which began play in April 1871 and was in existence for five years. The player-run National Association, though not officially recognized as a major league, contained all the best players of the era, and historians are in such agreement that it is deserving of that recognition that I will refer to it as a major league.[1]

The new league presented a wonderful opportunity to clubs in a strategically located state like Michigan. National Association clubs set their own schedules and were always looking for ways to offset the considerable expense of traveling by filling in open dates. With Chicago and Fort Wayne both having franchises in the National Association, Michigan was a convenient stopping-off point for many Eastern clubs.

The master business manager continued to be Harry Wright, who was now managing the Red Stockings of Boston. Wright insisted on a cash guarantee for all matches, telling one Canadian club that offered "other attractions," "We are not much on cognac, etc. and I can assure you we prefer a good game and big gate receipts to 'Hail Columbia,' 'Won't Go Home 'til Morn,' and all that sort of thing." Wright typically arranged for a guarantee of one hundred to three hundred dollars, or 60 percent of the gate receipts if greater.[2]

Michigan followed the new league's early days with interest. A party from Grand Rapids traveled down to Fort Wayne, its members among the fewer than five hundred spectators who witnessed the National Association's first game.[3] (The Kekiongas of Fort Wayne challenged the Valley City Club of Grand Rapids to a home-and-home match, though it never came off.) The *Kalamazoo Telegraph* began the season reporting news about the new league with interest and lobbying for the Unas to play the professionals or host a championship game.[4] And a party from Kalamazoo traveled to Chicago in July to watch a game between the top two teams, the White Stockings and the Athletics of Philadelphia.

While the new professional league started strongly, its amateur counterpart did little. As a result, areas without professional baseball saw a serious decline. Nowhere was this more evident than in Michigan, where the game fell into a three-year funk. When a challenge from an East Saginaw club fell on deaf ears, a Bay City paper asked, "Where are our Base Ballists?"[5] The question resonated all across the state.

Signs of life finally emerged in June, when the state championship was again contested. The Empire Club of Detroit traveled to Ann Arbor on June 14 and beat the state champions 32-12 in the first match of a best-of-three series. Ann Arbor paid a return visit on June 29, and the Empire Club again won easily, 43-23.

The nine who had brought the state championship back to Detroit received little respect from the newspapers, which constantly stressed that they were very young men.[6] However, they had their share of talent, including Harry Spence and Dan O'Leary, both of whom would have long careers in professional baseball, first as players and then as managers. O'Leary, the club's catcher, developed the unique "habit of making his right leg go through the swinging motion of the pitcher's arm as the ball was delivered."[7] On July 4, the new champions made their first defense of the cup with a 39-20 win over a local club called the Innocents, apparently a picked nine.

With no other state clubs clamoring to play them, the Empires began to accept challenges from touring clubs. This was a risky move for young players who were still in the shadow of the Detroit Base Ball Club, and the results did nothing to help their image. On August 7, the Empires were thrashed 28-7 by the Active Club of Clinton, Iowa.[8] The Actives had upset the White Stockings of Chicago the previous month, so the loss was no embarrassment, but the *Advertiser and Tribune*'s description of the Empires as "only an amateur organization at the best" was hardly flattering.

Nevertheless, the audience was a bright spot: "The attendance was quite large, and reminded one of old times when base ball flourished in Detroit. It was an enthusiastic crowd, and applauded good play heartily, whether on the home club or the strangers."[9] The *Post* commended the spectators and players for their gentlemanly behavior ("no player demeaning himself even by questioning the decisions of the umpire") but pointed out that due to the absence of seats in the grandstand, no ladies were present.[10]

The Empires soon hosted two more touring clubs, and again, the results did little to enhance their reputation. Before a game with the National Association's Haymakers of Troy, New York, the *Advertiser and Tribune* wrote that the "Detroiters will be troubled to make even a respectable showing."[11] Troy won a rain-shortened five-inning game 33-15. Troy's players included Enrique "Steve" Bellan, the game's first Hispanic player, and Lipman Pike, the game's first Jewish star, but neither this nor any other aspect of the game elicited much comment in the local press.[12] The second game, against the amateur Stars of Brooklyn, did generate a bit of interest

since the Stars featured Arthur "Candy" Cummings, one of the earliest practitioners of the curve ball. An advertisement appeared in
the local papers to publicize the game, but Cummings didn't play,
and the Stars won anyway, 39-16.

Baseball's status as an Independence Day fixture did help initiate a revival in Ypsilanti. The Peninsulars of Ypsilanti beat the
Mutuals of Jackson 21-18 on July 4 (earning them a laurel wreath),
and the game stimulated the Peninsulars to greater activity. The
club soon hosted the Haymakers of Troy and the Actives of Clinton, and encouraging signs were found in both games. Following a
53-29 loss to the Iowans, the local paper wrote that "in batting" the
Peninsulars "can't be beat" and "only need practice to equal, if not
excel, any club in the country."[13] After the club lost 46-8 to the Haymakers the next week, the paper reported that the Peninsulars,
though "playing heretofore for mere amusement, were not to be
despised."[14] This phrasing suggests that ambitious clubs needed to
be successful to avoid a backlash in their hometowns. Undoubtedly,
this new reality discouraged the ambitions of many clubs.

As a result, competition did not generally extend beyond county
limits. Adrian and Tecumseh played on July 4 for a silver pitcher
that was supposed to be open to subsequent challenges, but after
Tecumseh won a close decision, it does not seem to have received
any challenges. County champions were also crowned in Oakland
County (the Hurons of Milford), Ottawa County (the Eagles of
Grand Haven), and Allegan County (the Otsego Club), but these
clubs also were content to rest on their laurels. The Regular Club of
Mt. Clemens won the championship of Macomb County, but the
only Detroit club it expressed interest in playing was a nine of
Advertiser and Tribune employees. Another telling indication of the
diminished status of baseball came when the Peninsulars of Ypsilanti cancelled a scheduled match with the Mutuals of Jackson
because a circus was coming to town and the players didn't want to
miss "seeing the elephant."[15]

Even with the Empires appearing vulnerable and so many clubs
claiming local championships, the state champions received only

one more challenge in 1871, from the Peninsulars of Ypsilanti. With no circus intervening, the game came off on September 8 in Detroit on the grounds of the Peninsular Cricket Club. The Empires won a close decision, 36-30, to finish the year as state champions.

One club that was showing the rudiments of ambition was the Nobby Club of Patterson's School, which changed its name to the Aetna Club out of a "desire to form a more prestigious organization." The club's initial claim to fame was its members' fashion-consciousness, their uniform being "the first of its kind shown in Detroit. It was of snow white cotton flannel, with a large AE in blue upon the breast of the shirt. The trimmings and stockings were all blue. The knickerbockers had not been worn by any club previous to this, and were considered quite an innovation."[16] Local papers wrote that the uniforms were "much admired" and "attracted considerable attention."[17] The Aetnas played six games in September and October, and their on-field performance showed promise. An 18-17 loss to the Unknowns was described as "perhaps the most exciting game played this season in Detroit."[18] The Aetnas got revenge on the Unknowns, by a 34-30 score, but apparently the club didn't consider itself ready to challenge the Empires.

About this time a group of boys including Joe Weiss, Billy Crofoot, Tommy Shaughnessy, Bob Sheeran, and Frank Brown split off from a club called the Hunkidoris and formed a new club. Known as the Red Hots, this club's home base was a vacant lot across from the Antisdel House. Like the Early Risers before them, the Red Hots, as Joe Weiss later recalled, had window troubles: "A photographer's car stood on the lot and Shaughnessy, who was a left handed pitcher, never failed to drive the ball through the window of this car, upon which the photographer would appear and attempt to 'take us' in a literal sense, but generally without success, as we were good base runners."[19]

In either 1871 or 1872, the Red Hots merged with another group of boys to form the Cass Club. Weiss remembered the Cass Club being formed one day on the grounds at the corner of Bagg and Second, while Louis Ives claimed that the club was formed at the home of his father, Albert Ives Sr. Both men's recollections were in accord about five of the original nine members of the Cass Club: Ives, Weiss, Charles Howard, Tommy Shaughnessy, and Billy Cro- foot.[20] Within a few years, the Cass Club and the Aetnas would forge Detroit's first great intracity rivalry.

But in 1871, as the season wore on, the doings of such clubs were overshadowed by growing hostility to the National Association. Michigan's initial interest in the new league was soon destroyed by stories about thrown games and drunken players. At the same time that baseball "arrived at the dignity of a profession, and a paying one, too," it appeared to many to have lost its integrity.[21] The Grand Rapids papers stopped reporting on the Fort Wayne club after an Eastern trip during which the Kekiongas "made the name of the club (hard as it is to speak) a by-word and reproach wherever they stopped by their wanton behavior."[22] A Hillsdale paper reprinted a lengthy article from an Eastern paper in which a ficti- tious gambler described techniques for fixing games and boasted that "when the nashunal game was first introduced, men used to play for the fun and exercise; but sense John Morrisey, Jim Fisk and our kind have taken the game up, they have to pay a member of a professional nine $1,000 for the season, his doctor's bill, and all he can make through his friends in side bets."[23]

By September, the once-supportive *Kalamazoo Telegraph* had changed its tune entirely and launched a vitriolic attack on profes- sional baseball:

> There may have been a time when for some reasons, "The National Game" was a national blessing, but, if so, that time has long since gone by, for now the most appropriate [name] . . . is "The National Swindle." . . . So long as Base-ball was confined to *amateurs;* so long as games were contests of genuine skill uninfluenced by the stakes of gamblers, without or within the Club; so long as it gave a healthy impetus to wholesome out-door sports, it was all very well. And even when played professionally as it was by the famous Red Stockings, during their first trip across the country, it was both pleasant to wit-

ness and, doubtless, left a good impression. . . . But now the game, as played professionally, has not only reached its highest stage of development, but has become both a swindle and a curse which ought no longer to receive countenance in any community. . . . If a town would raise up and send forth its own players, it might, perhaps, be entitled to some honor if they should be so fortunate as to win a closely contested game. But where the honor comes in, when a town imports a lot of drunken loafers from all corners of the country, to represent it on the contested field, we utterly fail to see.[24]

Needless to say, the *Telegraph* didn't cover baseball any more in the 1871 season.

With professional baseball now an institution, gambling was also increasingly being cited in litanies of the game's evils. Actual instances of gambling and related excesses were less common in Michigan, but not unheard of. A Cassopolis newspaper alleged that the Constellations of Dowagiac had deliberately fallen behind a Cassopolis club 22-12. Dowagiac backers then conned the Cassopolis supporters into betting on the game's outcome, at which point the Constellation Club started giving its best effort and won easily, 62-33.[25]

Even newspapers in remote regions were becoming hostile toward the game. A Cheboygan paper noted: "The boys have begun that break-neck, bloody-eye and stove-up game commonly known as Base-Ball. It generally costs a man two or three broken fingers and a sprained ankle to convince him there is no fun in it. Trading straight fingers for crooked ones, and little noses for big ones, with a little imaginary fun thrown in, is about the most fruitless enjoyment we can think of."[26]

New uses of the phrase "base ball fever" symbolized the changing attitude. These words had long been used to convey the boyish enthusiasm the game engendered, but now the negative connotations of the metaphor were being probed. A Grand Rapids journal described the "base ball mania" as "one of the necessities of the times, that makes its appearance with the approach of warm weather, and by some is considered one of the inconveniences and nerve-trying perplexities that have come to be a certain concomitant of the warm spell, not excepting flies, musketoes [sic] and dust."[27] The *Jackson Citizen* commented that "the base ball fever has broken out in Ann Arbor and Grand Rapids, but as yet no symptoms are observable here, for which let us give thanks."[28] Other newspapers went further, comparing "base ball fever" to the epidemics of potato bugs and cholera that tormented the state.[29]

Baseball was understandably in scarce supply at Michigan's county fairs that fall. Even the competitions that were arranged offered reminders of the declining interest in the game. In Saginaw, one of the two clubs that played "was only picked up to put in an appearance, so as to fill up the programme of the fair."[30] A silver cup was offered for the "championship of four counties" at a fair in Hubbardston, but only clubs from Palo, Matherton, and Pewamo entered. The Awkwards of Palo won and were challenged by a picked nine, many of whom had belonged to the Custer and Wolverine Clubs of Ionia "years ago, when the game was raging here." But after only four innings the game was abandoned so that some of the players could go on band duty.[31]

Nonetheless, baseball continued to make inroads in the Upper Peninsula in 1871. A tournament for a twenty-five-dollar purse took place in Negaunee on July 4, featuring two clubs from Marquette, one from Ishpeming, and one from the New York Mine. The tournament showed that profiteering was spreading even to outlying areas, as one spectator complained that the members of the host club did not participate because "they were too wholly occupied in selling lemonade and cigars to their visitors and was [sic] unable to do anything else than make money out of their invited guests."[32] Time permitted only two games on July 4, so the two winners met on July 15, when the First City Club of Marquette beat the Ishpeming Base Ball Club 50-26 to capture the purse. This game generated controversy when Ishpeming blamed the loss on partisan umpiring. The First City Club responded that its members had given the Ishpeming Club their own private conveyance to travel to the game and had walked themselves, but had received no thanks for the courtesy.

The spread of competitiveness to the Upper Peninsula continued when the First Nationals of Hancock made a tour of Marquette County in August. The First Nationals established themselves as the Upper Peninsula's best club by beating the First City Club of Marquette, the Negaunee and Ishpeming nines, the Independent Club of the New York Mine, and a picked nine from Marquette County. Most of these victories were by lopsided margins, including a 110-43 thrashing of Negaunee. The Ishpeming Club, however, lost only by a score of 29-23 and was encouraged enough to go into practice.

On September 25, the Ishpeming Club left home for a tour of its own. The beginning of the players' odyssey was inauspicious, as their boat was turned back by rough seas and they were stranded in Marquette for two days. Finally, they returned to Ishpeming and sailed by way of Portage. This trip was also fraught with hazards, but eventually they arrived in Houghton and beat that city's club 38-11 on the morning of September 29. Ishpeming then crossed the lake and played the champion First Nationals of Hancock the same afternoon. The Nationals led 20-19 after five innings, but Ishpeming rallied to win 52-29. Ishpeming continued on to Calumet for the next game, but a crowd of one thousand was disappointed when the two sides were unable to agree on an umpire and the game was finally called off.

The Ishpeming players returned home and, "having accomplished all they intended . . . now [hung] up their bats for the season and proclaim[ed] themselves the champion base ball players of the Upper Peninsula."[33] But such tidy endings were hard to come by in the newly contentious environment. The First Nationals challenged Ishpeming to a rematch, promising to provide a one-hundred-dollar purse and cover all expenses, but they were rebuffed. A newly formed club in Negaunee challenged Ishpeming, and when Ishpeming said it was done for the season, Negaunee declared itself champion of the county.[34] Obviously the Upper Peninsula was beginning to face the same problems that were plaguing the state's southern reaches.

In spite of the hostility, all of the National Association's clubs

The first professional baseball league, the National Association, was formed in 1871. That year's dramatic pennant race saw the first-place White Stockings of Chicago lose their ballpark, their uniforms, and most of their possessions in the Chicago fire. Playing out the season on the road in a melange of borrowed clothes, they were beaten out by the Athletics of Philadelphia. *Courtesy of Transcendental Graphics*

except Fort Wayne completed the league's first season. The pennant race had a most dramatic conclusion when the first-place White Stockings of Chicago had their ballpark and most of their possessions destroyed in the Chicago fire. The club played out its final three games on the road, wearing makeshift uniforms borrowed from other clubs. New acquisition Michael Brannock, for example, wore a Mutuals uniform with an Eckford belt. The demoralized White Stockings lost all three games and were nosed out for the pennant by the Athletics of Philadelphia.

NOTES

1. For details on the National Association, see William J. Ryczek, *Blackguards and Red Stockings*, the only history of this league. The National Association was denied major-league status by the Special Baseball Records Committee on the grounds of "erratic schedule and procedures."

2. *New York Clipper*, March 20, 1875; reprinted in Ryczek, *Blackguards and Red Stockings*, 203.

3. Fort Wayne won the game 2-0; this would remain the league's lowest-scoring game until 1875. James Carleton, the first baseman for Cleveland in this historic game, later settled in Detroit and formed a stockbroking partnership with Frederick M. Delano, former first baseman of the Brother Jonathans.

4. *Kalamazoo Daily Telegraph*, April 17, 1871: "Why can not the base ball fraternity of Kalamazoo induce two crack clubs to meet here, say during the Horse Fair? This feature would be particularly attractive, and would give at least variety, drawing many hundreds who otherwise would not come."

5. *Bay City Tri-Weekly Journal*, May 25, 1871.

6. Their names were Joseph L. Hull, T. Collins, M. Kinney, Dan O'Leary, Harry Spence, Robert Sheeran, C. Presley, C. Kelly, and Campbell, as best as can be reconstructed from the newspapers' habitual practice of referring to players only by their surnames.

7. *Saginaw Evening Express*, April 24, 1881

8. The Actives included Michael Brannock, who would later play in the major leagues and for the Cass Club of Detroit, and George Keerl, who would play briefly in the major leagues before settling in Menominee. The stature of the Empires was further diminished when the Actives beat the Mutuals of Jackson by the much narrower margin of 19-13 later in the month.

9. *Detroit Advertiser and Tribune*, August 8, 1871.

10. *Detroit Daily Post*, August 8, 1871.

11. *Detroit Advertiser and Tribune*, August 17, 1871.

12. Bellan had previously toured Michigan in 1868 with the Unions of Morrisania; he was also one of the first collegians to play professional baseball, having attended Fordham University.

13. *Ypsilanti Commercial*, August 26, 1871.

14. *Ypsilanti Commercial*, September 2, 1871.

15. *Jackson Daily Citizen*, August 1, 1871.

16. *Detroit Free Press*, February 24, 1889.

17. *Detroit Advertiser and Tribune*, September 23, 1871; *Detroit Daily Post*, September 25, 1871.

18. *Detroit Advertiser and Tribune*, September 23, 1871.

19. *Detroit Free Press*, January 13, 1889.

20. Weiss gave the others as Clarence Walker, Bob Sheeran, Len Barron, and Ed Aikman, while Ives remembered them as being Titchey Richardson, William Reid, Harm Vernor, and Billy Beck. Weiss's recollections are from the *Free Press* of January 13, 1889, while Ives's are from a letter to Clarence Burton, in the Burton Collection, Detroit Public Library.

21. *Adrian Times and Expositor*, October 7, 1871.

22. *Grand Rapids Daily Eagle*, July 22, 1871. The Kekiongas disbanded not long after this road trip.

23. *Hillsdale Standard*, August 1, 1871. The eccentricities of spelling are from the original.

24. *Kalamazoo Daily Telegraph*, September 14, 1871.

25. *Cassopolis Vigilant*, September 11, 1871.

26. *Manitawauba Chronicle* (Cheboygan), May 13, 1871.

27. *Grand Rapids Daily Eagle*, May 10, 1871.

28. *Jackson Daily Citizen*, May 9, 1871.

29. *Cedar Springs Wolverine Clipper*, June 17, 1874; *Grand Rapids Daily Eagle*, April 22, 1873.

30. *Saginaw Daily Courier*, September 28, 1871.

31. *Ionia Sentinel*, October 7, 1871.

32. *Marquette Mining Journal*, July 8, 1871 (signed "WITNESS").

33. *Marquette Mining Journal*, October 21, 1871.

34. *Marquette Mining Journal*, October 14, 1871.

21

"Playing in Our Own Shoes and Undershirts"

In the late 1850s, cricket and baseball had competed for the affections of Americans, but by the 1870s baseball was firmly established as the national pastime. However, as young men increasingly dominated baseball, cricket established a niche among those seeking a less physically demanding sport. Ford Hinchman, for instance, retired from the Detroit Base Ball Club at twenty-one but competed for another ten years at cricket, facing the All-England Club in 1879. Their older demographics meant that cricket clubs could secure comfortable grounds, while the much more popular game of baseball was relegated to makeshift diamonds on abandoned lots and public streets.

In early May 1872, the Peninsular Cricket Club of Detroit announced a new innovation in hopes of "populariz[ing] the game among Americans, many of whom are not accustomed to cricket."[1] On Tuesdays and Fridays their grounds would be reserved for cricket practice, but on Wednesdays and Saturdays they would be rented to baseball clubs. Rates would be two dollars, five dollars, or ten dollars, depending on the clubs' ability to pay and whether admission fees were charged. This new arrangement proved very successful, and it was a number of years before a Detroit baseball club felt the need to secure its own grounds for matches, although several had their own practice grounds. While a dramatic resurgence in cricket interest did not result, the exposure thus gained probably was a factor in cricket's continuing to thrive in Detroit into the 1880s.[2]

While baseball clubs in Detroit were happy just to have a place to play, much more ambitious plans were underway in Jackson. Local businessmen pledged five hundred dollars so the Mutuals

As can be seen from this undated photo of Detroit's St. George Cricket Club, by the 1870s older men were turning to cricket as baseball became a sport for young men. *Courtesy of the Burton Historical Library, Detroit Public Library*

could become a stock company, a format used by most successful National Association clubs to provide the capital to bankroll tours and make long-term plans. The Mutuals signed a ten-year lease for grounds with the Horse Breeders' Association at three hundred dollars a year, and work was begun on preparing these grounds for baseball.[3]

The Mutuals' first nine consisted of Fred Andrus, Hugh Ernst, Frank Wood, Ichabod Whiteman, James McGraw, Henry Lake, Robert Lake, Stephen A. Welling, and George Ismon. Andrus would become the first Michigan-born major leaguer, but in Jackson he made his living as a clerk in the freight office of the Michigan Central Rail Road, as a clerk at the Hubbard House, and as a printer for the *Citizen*, where he was known for being "as fast a type setter as he was a good ball player."[4]

Other clubs followed the Mutuals' example in adapting to baseball's new economics. The Unas of Kalamazoo made an apparently unsuccessful effort to form a stock organization and declined a challenge from the Clippers of South Bend because the Clippers lacked "enclosed grounds at which an entrance fee could be charged."[5] The Pastimes of Marshall formed a committee to call on local businessmen and ask them for small donations to the club in return for honorary membership, using the money raised to purchase uniforms and prepare their new grounds.

In this new environment, an amateur club like the state champion Empires of Detroit was accorded little respect. In mid-June, the Unas of Kalamazoo wrote to the Detroit newspapers challenging any club in Detroit to a best two-out-of-three series for the state championship, with the first match in Detroit, the second in Kalamazoo, and the third, if necessary, on neutral grounds. Harry Spence, the secretary of the Empires, responded by pointing out that the Empires were already state champions and explaining the rules long in effect governing challenges.[6] The Empires' credibility was further damaged when they lost 29-17 on July 4 to the Unknowns of Detroit, although their title was not on the line.

The state championship match between the Unas and Empires

finally came off on July 16. The Unas included such veterans as Johnny McCord, Tommy Dorgan, Will DeMyer, George Tremaine, and "Old Ez" White, and the Detroit papers held out little hope for the Empires. The *Post* even reported that the Unas were state champions and that there was "little betting since no one cared to bet on" the Empires.[7] But the Empires won convincingly, 36-14, and finally earned some respect. The *Advertiser and Tribune* wrote that the Empires "would 'make it lively' for any club in this state, and would not make a discreditable display against professionals."

The same paper complimented the Unas on their athleticism but noted that they were "evidently unacquainted as yet with those nice points of play upon which success in base ball now so greatly depends."[8] The reference was to a crucial moment in the second inning when one of the Empires deliberately dropped an easy pop fly with several runners on base and converted it into a triple play before the Unas realized what had transpired. This tactic had been used by the top clubs for years, and the Unas' unfamiliarity with it suggests how far Michigan baseball had fallen behind the rest of the country. The play unnerved the Unas, and by the time they recovered their poise the Empires had built a commanding lead.

The Detroit newspapers took this as a sign that heady play could enable one club to beat another with much more imposing physiques. When baseball fever was at its peak in the mid-1860s, its appeal had been aided by the perception that innate talent was less important than skills that could be developed by practice. The game suffered when its depiction as a test of character seemed less viable. So any indication that learned skills could overcome inborn ability—an obvious parallel to the American Dream—was welcome.

During the game itself, threatening clouds had limited the crowd to a few hundred. The *Advertiser and Tribune* regretted that "some of the spectators indulged in occasional merriment at the misfortunes of one of the Una players, whom they denominated 'Whiskers,' not knowing his real name, and that a few boys from the Eighth Ward yelled like Comanche Indians whenever any members of the Empires made a long strike or a brilliant play in the field. These things might better be omitted in the future."[9] Still, the Empires must have been pleased to have a few loyal supporters, even if they were overexuberant.

The Empires were beginning to gain some respect on the state level, the *Advertiser and Tribune* noting that they had "for a long time held the cup, and bid fair to retain it indefinitely."[10] But there were no illusions that the Empires were ready to compete with professional clubs. Chicago had dropped out of the National Association after the Chicago fire, so there were fewer clubs passing through the state. The Atlantics of Brooklyn considered a swing through Michigan, and the *Advertiser and Tribune* reported, "Detroit, Jackson and Kalamazoo, at least, can entertain them well, even if they are not able to make contests with them very exciting."[11] The Atlantics' visit fell through, but the Red Stockings of Boston did tour Michigan.

The Boston club featured five members of the Red Stockings of Cincinnati—George and Harry Wright, Charlie Gould, Andy Leonard, and Cal McVey—as well as legendary players A. G. Spalding and Ross Barnes. This all-star lineup was storming through the National Association with a twenty-two and two record, en route to the first of four straight championships. They met the Empires on August 21, and the game showed that Detroit fans would still turn out to see baseball's greatest stars. An hour before game time, spectators crowded the grounds on all sides and spilled out into trees and housetops. Even the usually dour *Free Press* commented that "the 'national game' has by no means died out in Detroit. . . . [I]t would take but little to incite in not alone the youthful, but the adult mind, as great enthusiasm for the game as ever existed."[12]

The papers emphasized the players' contrasting physiques. The *Advertiser and Tribune* commented that the "Empire nine is made up of vigorous and rather athletic young men, all of whom are just attaining mature life. The members of the Boston are athletes, brawny men, trained by long practice to immense muscular power and endurance."[13] The *Post* noted that the Empires looked "ludicrous by comparison" with their muscular counterparts.[14] The brawn of the Boston players was credited to hard work and progress; their muscle was built by "constant, incessant practice" during the off-season that enabled the players to resemble "machinery."[15]

While a physical advantage could be overcome against an inexperienced club like the Unas, the Red Stockings were superiors in all respects. In the third inning, the Empires had runners on first and second with no outs when Harry Spence lifted an easy pop fly to George Wright. The other Red Stockings began to yell "drop it," and the Empire base runners, alert to this strategy, began to run. Wright caught the ball, and Boston executed an easy triple play.[16] Boston won the game 35-2.

The day before, Boston had beaten the Peninsulars of Ypsilanti 40-3, so Ypsilanti indulged in the rather hollow boast that it had scored one more run than the Empires. The town was also pleased that Boston had scheduled to play its team because of a recommendation by the Haymakers of Troy. Unfortunately, rain and a fifty-cent admission charge kept attendance low, and it was the last time a major-league club played in Ypsilanti.

Although that was the extent of play against professional clubs in 1872, competition for the state championship continued. The Empires avenged their earlier loss to the Unknowns of Detroit, 34-17, and easily disposed of the Mutuals of Redford, 52-9. Their next challengers were the Peninsulars of Ypsilanti, a club that featured a star battery of pitcher Fred Emerick and future major-league catcher Frank Bliss.[17] But illness prevented Emerick from pitching and the Peninsulars were swept, 39-16 and 30-18.

The Empires next headed west to Kalamazoo for the second game of the series that had begun in July. The Unas had imported several professionals to help them avenge their earlier loss, including George Wilson of Chicago, whom they billed as the best shortstop in the West.[18] The Unas jumped to a 16-7 lead, but the game was rained out. The next day the Empires beat the Pastimes of Marshall 24-11, but on the following day in Jackson they were beaten 27-19 by the Mutuals.

The loss to the Mutuals did not deprive the Empires of the state title, but it was expected that the Jackson club would soon visit Detroit to complete the series. No such trip was forthcoming, however, as the Mutuals played no more games in the remainder of a rather mystifying season. Usually the amount of time employees devoted to baseball was a sore point with businessmen, but the Jackson business community had rallied to support the Mutuals only to find that the talented nucleus of players seemed disinclined to practice or play.

The Mutuals had earlier failed to appear for the scheduled game with the Empire Club, and in one of their two losses to the Unas of Kalamazoo they played listlessly. In a game against the Pastimes of Marshall, they jumped to a 19-3 lead but fell behind by the bottom of the fifth. The Mutuals then played "muff and monkey," trying to hide the ball and deliberately refusing to make the outs necessary to make the game official.[19] They also suffered an embarrassing loss to the Sooners of Greenville, a club whose hometown newspaper described them as boys from "among the pines . . . who make no pretensions."[20] The Mutuals' aversion to practice became notorious. The *Jackson Citizen* frequently chided them for indolence and at one point wrote that at their last practice "two of the nine and three or four bootblacks" had shown up.[21] So the unfinished series with the Empires seemed an appropriately apathetic ending to the Mutuals' season.

The Empires thus retained the state championship but they still received little respect. Some towns seemed unaware that a formal existed; the Unions of Berlin (now Marne), for instance, beat the Eagles of Grand Haven 38-17 and declared themselves state champions.

The waning interest in the state championship was symptomatic of a more general malaise; baseball, one newspaper observed, "appears to have lost its hold upon popular affection."[22] In Grand Rapids, where six clubs had flourished only two years earlier, a July 4 game was the only one played in 1872, and one of the nines called itself the Muffins because of its lack of practice. In the Upper Peninsula, the previous season's dispute over the championship of Houghton County led to the most involved competitive format yet devised in Michigan. Each entrant would play a home-and-home series with each other club, and the club winning the most games would receive a streamer.[23] However, not all the games were completed, although the First Nationals of Hancock were recognized as the county champions.

In October, the Mutual Club from the small town of Caro announced plans for a tour of the state. It had earned a strong reputation in its region by beating clubs from Watrousville, Hurd's Corner, Bay City, and East Saginaw and now scheduled matches with the state's top clubs. The tour attracted considerable interest, since, as one paper put it, "the Caro chaps do not come two hundred miles just for the fun of traveling."[24] But after losing to the Empires and easily beating the Dominoes of Pontiac, the Caro club failed to appear for its scheduled games in Jackson and Kalamazoo, "much to the disgust of the players of both cities."[25] Yet another enterprise that could have helped restore interest coming to nothing marked an appropriate end to the 1872 season.

In spite of the Empires' success in 1872, the 1873 season saw the game's popularity hit rock bottom in Detroit. When the Empires formed for the year on May 6, they announced that since they had held the championship cup since June 14, 1871, it would become their permanent possession unless they were defeated before June 14. For some time it looked as though the cup no longer held enough interest to elicit a challenge, but the Unknown Club of Detroit finally scheduled a match for June 13—one day before the deadline.

The game proved very low-scoring, with the Unknowns holding a 5-1 lead until the bottom of the ninth. Then the Empires mounted a stirring rally, scoring 3 runs and having two runners in scoring position before the Unknowns' second baseman, Fred Stearns, fielded a grounder and got it to first just in time to preserve a 5-4 victory. Unfortunately, wrangling overshadowed the exciting finish. The Empires protested the eligibility of several of the Unknowns—three of their players were former members of the Empires, while Fred Stearns was a member of both the Unknowns and the Aetnas.

Former Detroit Base Ball Club member Charles Vernor arbitrated the matter. He ruled that the three former Empires, having all left that club over a year before, were eligible to play for the Unknowns. But he deemed Stearns ineligible, rejecting the Unknowns' argument that one of his clubs was a junior club and the other a senior club. However, Vernor also found that the Empires were guilty of violating the rules of the championship cup for letting one of their own members officiate the game against the Unknowns. So he ruled that the two clubs should play again.

Vernor's decision didn't satisfy the *Advertiser and Tribune,* which pointed out that clubs that had violated the rules were specifically banned from competing for the cup. Why then, the newspaper asked, should two violators get to play for the cup again? It also pointed out that the Empires knew the rules and had deliberately violated them, whereas the Unknowns hadn't been furnished with a copy of the rules.[26]

Nonetheless, a rematch took place on July 5 that was won by the Empires 29-19. This time the Unknowns protested the eligibility of an Empire player, once again leaving the outcome up to Charles Vernor. Meanwhile, most observers were out of patience with all the bickering, and what little interest was still felt in the cup dissipated. The Detroit newspapers did not even bother to record Vernor's decision, and their growing antipathy to the game now turned to venom. When a young man named Hawkins was hit in the eye with a fly ball, threatening his sight, the *Post* fulminated, "If that young gentleman had been working a buck-saw up and down in somebody's back yard, instead of fooling around after 'fly balls,' he would to-day have been better off morally, physically and financially."[27]

The remainder of the season saw baseball interest in Detroit virtually die out. In August, the champion Red Stockings of Boston paid another visit to Detroit. With Chicago still recovering from the fire, the Red Stockings were the only professional club to pass through Michigan in 1873. The Empires realized that they were outclassed and attempted unsuccessfully to get Philadelphia to play Boston.[28] Still, even with the Empires forced to provide the opposition, the game attracted an overflow crowd.

Boston won easily, 37-4, the disarray of the Empires very evident. The Empires' pitcher M. Kinney was sick, so they had arranged for Charley Ward to pitch. Typically, Ward failed to appear, and a player named Crane had to make his pitching debut for the Empires against the country's best club. Crane's performance, sneered the *Post*, was as good "as can be expected from a player more closely resembling a base ball bat than any other in America. . . . [H]e lacks strength, experience, and accuracy."[29]

When Fred Stearns enrolled at the University of Michigan, he quickly discovered just how dead the sport was in Michigan. He later reminisced: "I remember in '73, when we started to revive interest in baseball, that we had no uniforms. So I stood in line at Van Amberg's Circus, with another boy, and collected ten cents apiece from those we could who were going in. I think we raised about $80, which bought us stockings, knickers and caps, but we had to play in our own shoes and undershirts."[30] Stearns and his teammates also had to overcome a shift in interest on campus to other activities. Wayne Hayman, who had played on the championship Ann Arbor Club in 1869 and 1870, was now captain of a campus football club and nearly managed to arrange what would have been the university's first intercollegiate football game, against Cornell in November of 1873.

Interest elsewhere was shifting to other sports as well. In Ypsilanti, "instead of ball-playing, sledge-throwing seems to be the order of the day."[31] In Buchanan, it was noted that several neighboring towns still had baseball clubs but that "this game seems to have given way entirely to croquet in our village as we have not a single base ball club organized at present."[32] A game called Chivalrie was introduced that seemed designed to appeal to society types who regretted that baseball had been taken up by the masses. As the pretentious spelling of the game's name suggests, Chivalrie was "an attempt to elevate croquet by loading it with a host of Norman-French names." The game's equipment cost two thousand dollars, prompting the observation that "if the snobs could only bind the patentees not to manufacture a set that should cost a cent less, the game would become highly popular." However, the game lost its appeal after the price of a set came within reach of the "common people."[33]

Individual sports were becoming much more lucrative than baseball. Henry Crandell won several postgame races as a pitcher for the Spear Club of Niles. He took up running seriously and earned one thousand dollars by winning a 150-yard footrace in twenty seconds, with some fifteen thousand dollars bet on the outcome of the race.[34] Crandell was later billed as "champion sprint runner of the world" after a successful tour in Europe.[35]

But competition from other sports wasn't always necessary to squelch baseball. A July 4 game between Greenville and Ionia ended after three innings when the Greenville players decided that they'd rather eat than expend "further effort to hit the balls of the Ionia pitcher."[36] The rivalry between the Wolverines of Benton Harbor and the Favorites of St. Joseph became "so intense that these games were discontinued in order to prevent a greater spread of ill-feeling."[37]

And businessmen continued to resent the game's tendency to distract workers. The Valley City Club of Niles announced that it had reorganized, "to the horror of all business men who have employes that are inclined to spend two hours a week in such a degrading way as our national game affords, 'when business is so urgent, you know.'" To allay such fears the club pledged to "play base ball for the good of the game, and not for an excuse to leave home . . . as has generally been the case heretofore."[38]

Despite the general decline in interest, a few hot spots developed in 1873. The most notable one was in Cass County, where a healthy rivalry emerged among a slew of clubs, including the Cassopolis Base Ball Club, the Vandalia Base Ball Club, the Mohawks of Jefferson, the Modocs and the Evening Stars of Cassopolis, the Jamestown Base Ball Club, the Constellations of Dowagiac, the Silver Stars of Vandalia, the Rising Suns of Oak Grove, the Prairie Boys of Penn, the Orientals of Edwardsburg, the Mocking Birds and the Lone Stars of Brownsville, the Last Chance Club of Calvin, the Ontwa Rangers of Ontwa, the Nottawas of Centreville, and the Hoboken Club of Redfield's Mill. A Newberg resident observed that his village was behind the times because it had no baseball club.[39]

A tournament was held in Cassopolis to capitalize on the flurry of interest. A prize fund of two hundred dollars was offered, and six clubs entered, with spectators paying twenty-five cents for admission. Two of the favorites, the Constellation Club of Dowagiac and the Lone Stars of Brownsville, met in the first round. After nine innings, the game was tied at 28-28. There was no scoring in the tenth, but the Lone Stars pushed across a single run in the eleventh to win 29-28. The Lone Stars then beat the Orientals of Edwardsburg 41-23 to claim the first prize. In addition to the standard prizes, the tournament organizers showed some ingenuity by giving awards to the Lone Stars for being the most gentlemanly club and to George Howe of the Valley Club of Niles for being the best umpire.

Unfortunately, there was a dispute over second prize. The Orientals of Edwardsburg assumed that, as the beaten finalist, they were entitled to the second-place money. Instead, the tournament organizers decided that the Orientals and Constellations would have to play for second prize. The Orientals refused to play the match, and eventually the game was forfeited to the Constellations. Thus, even in one of the state's few hot spots for baseball in 1873, matters ended with some dissatisfaction.

In spite of the generally bleak state of baseball in Michigan in 1873, there was one very bright spot in Jackson, where the Mutuals were emerging as the state's first great club since the Detroit Base Ball Club. The Mutuals had possessed much of the nucleus of a formidable club in the previous season but had lacked discipline and leadership. Both deficiencies were remedied when Will DeMyer, a "semi-professional" catcher who had played for the Unas of Kalamazoo in 1872, relocated to Jackson and became the captain and coach of the Mutuals.[40] He soon earned a reputation for "preserv[ing] perfect discipline" by "drilling the boys in their proper positions only."[41]

The Mutuals demonstrated their new seriousness by refurbishing the grounds they rented from the Horse Breeders' Association. The renovations included sodding the infield, packing the basepaths and the alley leading to the mound, and building a grandstand.[42] The club's hard work paid dividends when rain delayed one of its games. When the rain stopped, the outfield was naturally very wet, but the infield and basepaths showed the benefits of the "scientific principles" on which they had been constructed, proving very playable.[43] Later in the season, the Mutuals had the outfield plowed and rolled.[44]

The Mutuals' dedication also paid off on the field, as they showed themselves to be the state's best club. The Mutuals issued challenges to the Empires of Detroit and other strong clubs but found few takers. They did notch impressive wins against the Unas of Kalamazoo and the always strong club from the University of Michigan. Their toughest challenger was a club from Reading that included Clarence Terwilliger, who was rapidly emerging as the state's best pitcher.

Reading first faced the Mutuals on July 16. Reading clung to an 18-14 lead after six innings, with the onset of darkness leaving time for just one more rally. Jackson came through with 11 runs in its last at bat to pull out a 25-23 win. When the clubs met again in late August, Reading led 15-11 with two outs in Jackson's half of the ninth. But the "Mutes" rallied again, scoring six times before Reading could make the final out and then holding Reading to a single run for a dramatic 17-16 victory. The clubs played for a third time on September 10, and Reading took an 8-3 lead after five innings before Jackson staged yet another comeback to win 27-12.

The Mutuals also hosted the Red Stockings of Boston, who

were on their way to the second of four straight National Association championships. The Red Stockings were in the midst of a fourteen-game tour against nonleague clubs that saw them cumulatively outscore their opponents 524-48, including wins by such margins as 68-0, 64-0, and 66-1. Accordingly, Jackson was quite elated when it was only beaten 43-7, Robert Lake turning a handspring to celebrate after scoring Jackson's first run. However, an Adrian reporter felt that the visitors were "simply toying" with the Mutuals. He wrote that the Red Stockings would let the Mutuals get a few runners on base only to stymie them with a double play. On the basepaths, the Boston players "seemed to take delight in taking risks, starting to run, and then getting caught between bases. The Mutuals tried, time after time, to put them out, but, for six or seven times in succession, they failed to do it, the man making his base each time. Towards the last, however, they got caught twice in this manner."[45]

The game was a financial success, as spectators came from surrounding areas to witness the local heroes take on the champions. Some five hundred spectators paid fifty cents admission to watch the game. The Red Stockings were paid $150 for their appearance, leaving the Mutuals with a $100 profit to put toward further renovations of their grounds.

Baseball in Michigan was hardly in good shape when a 43-7 loss was cause for celebration, but at least there were glimmers of hope. Indeed, Boston's visit to Jackson directly led to a revival of interest in Grand Rapids. A businessman from that city attended the match, and Harry Wright assured him that the Red Stockings would visit Grand Rapids next season if a first-class nine were formed there. Wright even offered to send some top-notch ballplayers to Grand Rapids if they were assured employment.[46] More generally, the revival of the Mutuals was a sign that after three very slow years for baseball in the state the game might soon recapture its former glory.

NOTES

1. *Detroit Advertiser and Tribune*, May 4, 1872.
2. The Peninsular cricket grounds would again become the home of amateur baseball clubs in the 1880s. The *Detroit Free Press* reported on April 13, 1882, that the Amateur Base Ball Association had leased the grounds for three years.

3. *Jackson Daily Citizen*, May 10, 1872.

4. *Jackson News*, October 10, 1918.

5. *Kalamazoo Daily Gazette*, July 11, 1872.

6. *Detroit Advertiser and Tribune*, June 15, 1872.

7. *Detroit Daily Post*, July 17, 1872.

8. *Detroit Advertiser and Tribune*, July 17, 1872.

9. *Detroit Advertiser and Tribune*, July 17, 1872.

10. *Detroit Advertiser and Tribune*, August 7, 1872.

11. *Detroit Advertiser and Tribune*, July 25, 1872.

12. *Detroit Free Press*, August 22, 1872.

13. *Detroit Advertiser and Tribune*, August 22, 1872.

14. *Detroit Daily Post*, August 22, 1872.

15. *Detroit Free Press*, August 22, 1872.

16. That is how the play was described in contemporary accounts. An account in the *Saginaw Evening Express* on April 24, 1884, had Harry yelling, "Drop it," and George replying, "No, I won't." The batter and the base runners trusted George and did not run, so George dropped the ball and started the triple play.

17. Bliss played two games for the Milwaukee club of the National League in 1878 during his vacation from the University of Michigan Law School.

18. *Kalamazoo Daily Gazette*, August 1, 1872.

19. *Jackson Daily Citizen*, September 7, 1872; *Marshall Statesman*, September 11, 1872.

20. *Greenville Democrat*, September 7, 1872.

21. *Jackson Daily Citizen*, August 22, 1872.

22. *Big Rapids Magnet*, August 15, 1872.

23. *Portage Lake Mining Gazette* (Houghton), May 9, 1872.

24. *Kalamazoo Daily Telegraph*, October 15, 1872.

25. *Detroit Advertiser and Tribune*, October 24, 1872.

26. *Detroit Advertiser and Tribune*, June 26, 1873.

27. *Detroit Daily Post*, April 26, 1873.

28. *Detroit Daily Post*, August 5, 1873.

29. *Detroit Daily Post*, August 22, 1873.

30. *Michigan Alumnus* 29 (November 2, 1922).

31. *Ypsilanti Commercial*, July 19, 1873. "Sledges" are sledge-hammers.

32. *Berrien County Record* (Buchanan), April 24, 1873.

33. *Detroit Free Press*, August 4, 1873.

34. *Niles Republican*, August 21, 1873.

35. *Niles Democrat*, July 10, 1875. Another athlete in an individual sport whose income dwarfed that of any baseball player was wrestler James H. McLaughlin of Detroit, who wrestled for the world championship and a purse of five thousand dollars in May 1875.

36. *Ionia Sentinel*, July 11, 1873.

37. James Pender, *History of Benton Harbor and Tales of Village Days*, 74.

38. *Niles Democrat*, May 17, 1873.

39. *Cassopolis Vigilant*, September 4, 1873.

40. *Jackson News*, October 10, 1918. DeMyer was originally a New Yorker. When he died in Oakland, California, the *Jackson Citizen Patriot* of August 19, 1927, said his great-grandfather had been the first mayor of New York City. The first mayor of New York was Thomas Willett; I have not attempted to confirm their relationship.

41. *Jackson Daily Citizen*, May 15, 1878.

42. *Jackson Daily Citizen*, July 5, 1873.

43. *Jackson Daily Citizen*, July 17, 1873.

44. It is interesting to note that *infield* and *outfield* were originally Scottish farming terms; the infield was land near the farmhouse that was tilled and fertilized, while the outfield was land further from the farmhouse that was only cropped.

45. *Adrian Daily Press*, August 22, 1873.

46. *Grand Rapids Daily Morning Democrat*, August 22, 1873; *Grand Rapids Daily Times*, August 23, 1873. The businessman was George S. Cleveland, an assistant of Mr. Antisdel, a hotelier.

22

"The Resurrection of
This Noble American Game"

After three dismal years, Michigan baseball was in dire need of revival, and the 1874 season got off to a flying start. Leading the way was the Mutual Club of Jackson, eager to build on the success of the previous season. By mid-March the club had held meetings to elect officers; fill several subcommittees; and select the club's first nine, which consisted of Robert and Henry Lake, Will DeMyer, H. A. Lee, James McGraw, Fred Andrus, Lay Whiteman, William B. Montgomery, and Mark Benedict. The members of the nine had an average height of five feet eleven inches and an average weight of 156 pounds, which was large for the time and an important demonstration that Michigan baseball was finally becoming the preserve of men again.[1] The first nine then chose the members of the second nine and reelected DeMyer as captain.[2] Finally, the Mutuals voted down a proposal to change the game's basic dynamics to ten players and ten innings.[3] As the weather was still too cold for baseball, a dance was held to raise funds. Clearly, no one could accuse the Mutuals of not being organized!

There were encouraging signs that the renewal of interest would extend beyond Jackson. An early-season game in Niles between the Unknown Club and the local high school's nine was heralded as "the resurrection of this noble American game."[4] This revival was significantly aided by the fact that the press was again treating the game indulgently. A Houghton reporter wrote:

> To one who has been inclined to belittle the importance of base ball as a game of sport, the scene at the Hancock grounds last Saturday, when the Independents, of Ripley, and the First Nationals played, was surprising. The crowd present was large. It was composed of all classes, and included many strangers sojourning in the neighborhood. The ladies, too, were well represented, and apparently enjoyed the game. That many people are not only interested in base ball, but that they grow as enthusiastic over it as do the members of political parties during a hard-fought campaign over the respective issues in contest, was last week fully illustrated. Though the game was between two local clubs, the lines were well drawn, and each side was continually urged on and encouraged by the cheers and bravos of its friends. It can no longer be denied that base ball is in reality the national game in the United States. When, day after day, it can call together crowds of people throughout the land, it is useless to deny it the position it claims. That it does furnish innocent amusement and excitement to thousands is patent, and, so doing, much of its alleged abuse can be forgiven.[5]

Other newspapers showed a similar willingness to forgive the abuses and give the once-beloved game another look. Just as the last revival of the game had used the Red Stockings of Cincinnati as a model, this new one drew inspiration from Harry Wright's transplanted Red Stockings. A lengthy letter to a Cedar Springs newspaper observed:

> The present champions of the country are the Boston Red Stockings, and as such they form the ideal organization of the country—its members are honest men. They are never found in collusion with dishonest men to defraud such victims as may stake money on their games, by playing into the hands of opposing clubs, as some other

leading clubs do. This is a well known fact; and the fame of the Red Stockings is not more attributable to their professional skill than to their high-toned gentility. . . . A few years ago the Red Stockings of Cincinnati held the championship. The organization was strong in a professional way, but its members gradually gave way to habits of dissipation, some of them finally to downright drunkenness, and the club lost its existence altogether. Now we have in brief the career of two representative base ball clubs. The habits of each . . . [are] suggestive when taken in connection with the respective success of each.[6]

A New York paper opined that the Boston players were not individually as strong as those of other clubs but that they won because "there is nowhere in their ranks a man against whose character or honesty of purpose one breath of suspicion can be whispered. They are gentlemen . . . [who] have attained and continually maintain a higher degree of discipline than any other club."[7] Such glowing accounts of the Red Stockings' conduct persuaded many who were disillusioned with baseball to give the game another chance.

As the Red Stockings were being heralded as throwbacks to the age of chivalry, their play was paradoxically being linked to science and progress. Scientific progress had long been believed to emanate from renaissance men who mastered all branches of human understanding and used this knowledge to make breakthroughs. But this notion was gradually being replaced by the modern belief that specialists who devoted all their time and energies to a single field were better equipped to make new discoveries. The *Cassopolis Vigilant* attributed a club's success to "science and strict attention to their own business."[8]

The Red Stockings, en route to another championship under the astute leadership of Harry Wright, were perfect models for this new ideal. The postwar belief that practice could bring about infinite improvement had lost credibility, but now there was a new way to depict baseball as an ideological battle. Successful clubs were viewed as the sum of nine specialists who had mastered their own

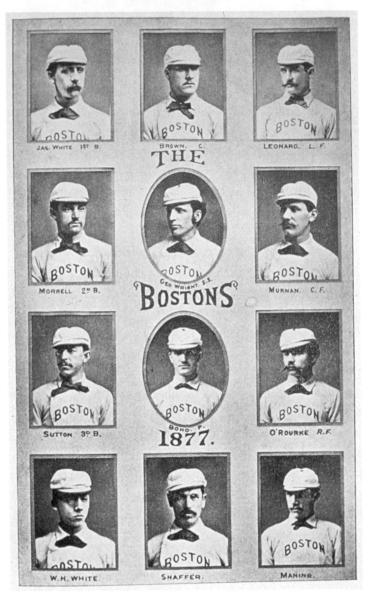

THE BOSTONS 1877.

JAS. WHITE 1ST B.   BROWN. C.   LEONARD. L.F.

MORRELL 2D B.   GEO WRIGHT. S.S.   MURNAN. C.F.

SUTTON 3D B.   BOND. P.   O'ROURKE R.F.

W.H. WHITE.   SHAFFER.   MANING.

Harry Wright's Red Stockings of Boston won four straight National Association pennants and made frequent stops in Michigan because Wright realized that games against amateurs were essential to a professional club's success. Wright's management of Red Stockings clubs in Cincinnati and Boston explains why these cities' major-league clubs still have "Red" as part of their nicknames. Jim "Deacon" White, one of the mainstays of the National Association champions, left for Chicago in 1876 and helped that club capture the first National League pennant. But Wright lured White back to Boston in 1877 and his league-leading hitting led this group to the pennant. *Courtesy of Transcendental Graphics* narrow realms. Thus, a game in Adrian was described as a triumph for the club on which "every man seemed to feel the responsibility of his particular position, and played accordingly . . . [and] every member of the club appeared to understand what his personal duty was," while the losing side trusted "too much to the mere matter of rushing in tallies."[9] The losers were advised to practice more often and to assign each player to "the position he is best capable of playing, and retain and play in that place in every game."[10] Another letter writer observed that, "There is something artistic, and there is something scientific, in a game of base ball . . . The silent play of science is to profit by position, to measure distance, and to poise the ball properly on its 'winged way.' "[11]

The game's return to respectability received another boost when Governor John J. Bagley donated a box of bats and balls to the State Reform School in Lansing. He sent this letter to the school superintendent along with the gift: "You know ball-time, top-time, marble-time and kite-time come as regularly for boys as seed-time and harvest do for the farmer. Thinking of this, I have sent you today by express a box of balls and ball-clubs for the boys, which you will give to them, with my desire that they will have lots of fun out of them and also that they will take good care of them and not lose either balls or clubs."[12] Bagley had been a neighbor of Henry Starkey when the Franklins were organized, but due to his corpulence, he apparently did not play the game as an adult. However, his letter suggests that he played as a child and that he believed that discipline and other important lessons could be learned from the game. He sent the reform school another dozen bats and balls in 1877, so he must have considered the experiment a success.[13]

While many of the men who had experienced baseball's postwar boom and its subsequent decline were willing to look at the game afresh, this did not necessarily mean that they were willing to participate again. The *Ionia Sentinel,* which had been instrumental in organizing Ionia's first club eight years earlier, now noted:

Baseball received much-needed credibility when Governor John J. Bagley donated a box of bats and balls to the State Reform School in Lansing, writing that "ball-time, top-time, marble-time and kite-time come as regularly for boys as seed-time and harvest do for the farmer." *Courtesy of the State of Michigan Archives*

The base ball fever is reviving once more, and we may soon look for the usual procession of limping, black-eyed, big-knuckled youths, whose devotion to the "noble game" is loyal to the death. As for us we have been thro' it—have traveled a hundred miles to play a match, and returned totally blind, with a base ball in one eye and a cinder in the other, and been accused of having "been on a bum," when under a training that allowed no stimulants and scarcely a full meal. We have had our fingers knocked out of joint by a "fly," and suddenly jerked back by a comrade; have stood on a base and had heel-spikes run thro' our foot; have been knocked down by a bat, and after all our personal sufferings, lost the game by shamefully partizan rulings of the umpire; and we have had enough of such fun; we are willing to retire on the glory won, and leave the bat and ball to be wielded by younger men, who have no families dependent upon them, to mourn their loss in case of their untimely death. It is an interesting game, and we love to look on and see some other man get a punch in the groin, or a "daisy cutter" on the nose, or a "hot one" in the stomach; we love to see 'em climb for first base, or chase a long fly, on a broiling hot day; but we don't hanker to do so any more ourselves. The memory of the time, when we used to beat the Grand Rapids boys at every match is enough for us, and we resign in favor of younger and more active muscle.[14]

The Ionia writer was not alone in handing down the once-beloved game to a younger generation. An article in the *Cedar Rapids Wolverine Clipper* described how, on a doctor's advice, an editor had joined a baseball club for exercise. Instead, after paying twenty-seven dollars for accessories and suffering a catalog of injuries that included a bunged eye, a broken finger, a bump on the head, a lame back, a sore jaw, a dislocated thumb, a sprained ankle, and a swollen leg, he decided his health could better be improved in other pursuits.[15]

Thus baseball was beginning its long tradition of being passed down from fathers to sons. That the revival of the game was essentially in the hands of a new generation of ballplayers meant that earlier mistakes would be repeated. The youthfulness of the players often alarmed older onlookers, such as one reporter who wrote that "the base ball malady rages with unabated rancor in these parts. Yesterday several children from Rockford escaped from the arms of their mothers and fled to this village where a like number abandoned their cradles and hied to the green for a game of base ball. The urchins were indignant at the old lady who mistook the occasion for a baby show."[16] But it also generated a new momentum for the sport, which soon manifested itself in the extension of competition beyond the rivalries between neighboring towns.

The now traditional Fourth of July games kicked off the tournament season and it soon became evident that the competition would be the most extensive in years. The Mutuals of Jackson successfully lobbied the organizers of the state fair in East Saginaw to recommence the tradition of a baseball tournament. A first prize of one hundred dollars and a gold medal was offered for senior clubs, with juniors competing for seventy dollars and a silver badge.

The Mutuals' effort to arrange a remunerative in-state tournament was one of many instances of the club's financially conscious outlook. The Mutuals declined to enter the Eaton Rapids tournament, openly stating that they were unable to afford two days' time and expense for the fifteen dollars offered as first prize. A new club in Grand Rapids received an invitation to play at the Mutuals' enclosed field, but the document reads suspiciously like a form letter, offering assurance that "you can make expenses, and most probably more, as their [sic] is considerable interest here."[17] Some might see this as cheapness or a mercenary spirit, but from the Mutuals' point of view, they were simply placing their club on a secure financial footing.

When the Red Stockings of Boston fulfilled their promise to play in Grand Rapids, there was still no club in that city strong enough to compete with the champions. The visit's organizers invited the Mutuals to provide the opposition and offered to pay all their expenses, but Jackson declined to play "on such unremunerative terms."[18] A Grand Rapids picked nine had to play the Red Stockings and were trounced 36-5 in spite of being allotted five outs per inning. The gentlemanly demeanor of the Red Stockings impressed everyone; the Boston players even loudly applauded when their opponents made a good play.[19] Over a thousand spectators attended, and after the Red Stockings were paid $150 and $200 in expenses, the game made a profit of $30.[20]

Boston also stopped in Jackson on the same trip, but the Mutuals objected to the five-outs handicap. Harry Wright explained that the Red Stockings played all amateur clubs on those terms because of the lopsided scores on the previous year's tour, and Will DeMyer finally conceded the point. But before the game could start, the Mutuals' first baseman, Hugh Ernst, loudly and dramatically announced that he would not play if any handicap were given. He was so insistent that the Red Stockings finally agreed to play the game on even terms. After four innings, Boston held a scant 3-0 lead, and although they finally broke the game open, the 19-4 final score was a very creditable showing for Jackson. Harry Wright pronounced the Mutuals the best amateur club that Boston had played.[21]

Encouraged by Wright's praise, the Mutuals wrote to such first-rate clubs as the White Stockings of Chicago, the Athletics of Philadelphia, the Mutuals of New York, and the Maple Leafs of Guelph to try to schedule games. There was even talk that the Jackson club might tour the East. But then the club received the bad news that the Horse Breeders' Association was evicting the Mutuals from the grounds that they had put so much money and labor into renovating.

The Mutuals joined forces with the local cricket club to search for a new home. They soon received permission from the Honorable J. C. Wood to enclose his grounds at the corner of Fourth and Franklin Streets. The club surrounded an area of 350 by 500 feet with an eight-foot fence, and within weeks the new grounds were being described as "all that can be desired" and as "if anything preferable" to the old grounds." A Grand Rapids reporter described the new locale as "nicely fenced, levelled and well calculated for base ball and cricket" and suggested that his hometown needed a similar ball field.[23] The new diamond became such an enduring home for baseball in Jackson that it was soon forgotten that baseball had ever been played anywhere else.[24]

One of the first visitors to the new grounds was the Mutuals' New York namesakes. While the New Yorkers won the game, the 21-6 score was very respectable. One of the New York players was John Hatfield, who was renowned for having made the longest recorded throw of a baseball—400 feet. Between the sixth and seventh innings, Hatfield wowed the locals with a 380-foot throw. The Mutuals of New York continued through Michigan, beating Eaton Rapids 20-3 and the Athletics of Grand Rapids 27-12, with Hatfield again showing off his throwing arm during the latter game.

While the earliest signs of renewed interest were outside of Detroit, the City of the Straits soon began to catch up. In an odd coincidence, as it had seventeen years earlier, the initial impetus came from a club of printers called the Franklins, which was formed on May 4. They immediately pronounced themselves "ready to dislocate fingers, sprain ankles and find fault with the umpire with any amateur club."[25] The Mutuals issued a challenge to the Franklins, and the *Jackson Citizen* scoffed at the claim that the players were actually printers: "the idea intended to be conveyed that they are amateurs of the simplest and weakest order . . . is too transparent not to be seen through. In all probability the nine will be the very best that can be raised in Detroit, whether printers or anything else."[26]

However, the Franklins turned out to be exactly as advertised, consisting of seven printers from the *Post,* one from the *Tribune,* and one from the *News.*[27] Worse, the players were small and clumsy and the only thing uniform about their motley garb was a white cap with a blue star.[28] The Mutuals won easily, 39-7, and the *Citizen* expressed chagrin at *not* having been duped! Clearly it would take a stronger club than this to restore luster to Detroit baseball.

Candidates soon began to emerge. The Cass Club beat the Unos of Detroit 20-16 on May 30. A new club called the Shamrocks was formed in early June that included three members of last year's Unknown Club and six new recruits, most of them from the Franklins. Another ambitious new club called the Mystics was organized in the city's west end. The Shamrocks beat the Mystics in Windsor on July 10 and then challenged the Aetnas to a best-of-three series for the championship of the city.

The two clubs met on July 25 at the Peninsular cricket grounds. The Aetnas were two-to-one favorites in pregame betting, but the Shamrocks won handily, 29-13. The attendance of five hundred spectators was described as "one of the largest seen on the grounds since the palmy days of base ball."[29] The public's willingness to support local rivalries represented an important breakthrough; with travel expenses dominating the game's economics, any revenue brought in without either club having to travel was a windfall.

This was not lost on the young men of Detroit, and a rush to form baseball clubs ensued in August. The National Base Ball Club, a first-rate nine formed in 1871 that had been inactive in 1873, reorganized. Other clubs soon followed suit. A meeting was held at the Russell House to attempt to "organize a base ball club which will scoop all creation."[30] The *Detroit Post* reported that the "idea would be to form a nine of amateurs with a professional pitcher and catcher."[31] (While the *Jackson Citizen* ridiculed the inconsistency of this concept, this was already a well-established compromise between competitiveness and full-blown professionalism.)[32] An unrelated meeting at the Biddle House sought to revive the Empire Base Ball Club.

On August 6, the Shamrocks beat the Aetnas for a second time, 47-18, to capture the city championship. However, the game again demonstrated that a renewal of enthusiasm for the national pastime was inevitably accompanied by undesirable developments. Both clubs had seen significant turnover in their lineups, with the Shamrocks having added three new players since their formation and the Aetnas employing three different players from the lineup they had used in their first match.

Although there is no way to know whether these particular players were paid for their services, once clubs became arbitrary units rather than groups of men who shared a common bond, mercenary behavior was inevitable. The child's game was now faced with basic economic principles—increasing revenue brought the expectation of compensation, and as demand for players increased, the amount expected also rose.

Such developments could be anticipated, but there was a novel component to baseball's economics. In business, a more successful enterprise could drive out its rivals and thereby reap greater profits. But baseball clubs were dependent on each other's competitiveness in order to have a marketable product. Too often there were vicious cycles: when one team got new players, other clubs had to improve to stay competitive, which in turn compelled the first club to get more players, until the stakes were too high for one or all to play. If the stakes were too high for a few clubs, the whole house of cards would inevitably collapse. A simple game was becoming increasingly complex.

And there was one additional factor. While baseball aficionados had shown that they would support a rivalry between clubs rather than between cities, this did not necessarily mean that they would support a rivalry between clubs whose players constantly changed and even switched allegiances. The importation of club members understandably diluted the loyalty of local supporters. Writer George Will's explanation of why modern fans are jarred by similar upheavals applies equally to baseball enthusiasts of the 1870s:

> The Seaver trade, and the restless mobility of "free agent" superstars, strains fan loyalty. Baseball is a business but such unsentimental capitalism is bad business. Baseball capitalism that respects only market forces is profoundly destructive because it dissolves the glue of sentiment that binds fans to teams. Besides, as Jacques Barzun says, baseball is Greek because it is based on "rivalries of city-states." Athens would not have traded Pericles for Sparta's whole infield.[33]

In most cases, locals did support successful teams of mercenaries, but they were quick to turn on such organizations if they didn't win. Clubs responded to the new atmosphere by cloaking their efforts in anonymity, with one game in Flint featuring the No Names of East Saginaw and the Unknowns of Fenton. The efforts to remain anonymous became unintentionally comical when the secretary of the No Names wrote to the local paper complaining that a loss attributed to that club had actually been played by a picked nine including five members of the No Names and that the game had been played "with the understanding that it would not be published."[34]

Another consequence of the transition of club members from being representatives of a town to simply belonging to an arbitrary unit was the continued erosion of the standard of hospitality. The Bark Peelers of South Haven, after having to pay their own expenses on trips to St. Joseph and Kalamazoo, nonetheless vowed to treat their guests "as visitors and not as intruders."[35] The *Benton Harbor Palladium* had to suggest to the Comets of St. Joseph that they at least assist visitors in finding accommodation, while the St. Joseph paper counseled the Comets to never "forget to be gentlemen."[36] The neighboring towns of Cedar Springs and Rockford had such a bitter dispute about allegations of inhospitable behavior to visiting clubs by the Rockford Club that the *Osceola Outline* wrote that "base ball is what is the matter between Rockford and Cedar Springs."[37]

When the Challengers of Mason played in Portland they were not offered a meal afterward and concluded that "evidence of civilization seems not to have reached as far north as Portland."[38] But another game played by the Challengers demonstrated the sometimes strange disparities in behavior. The game ended after five innings due to a dispute over the rules, but nonetheless the host Corn Huskers of Aurelius furnished the Challengers with dinner afterward.[39]

Nevertheless, these incipient problems remained beneath the surface for the most part. Over the next couple of years, the new rivalries would create more baseball excitement in the state of Michigan than at any time since the oft-cited "halcyon days of the old Detroit Base Ball Club."[40] On August 14, the Cass Club beat the Aetnas, 37-19. It is unlikely that any of the spectators realized that they were witnessing the beginning of one of the legendary rivalries of Michigan baseball.

NOTES

1. *Adrian Daily Times and Expositor,* May 26, 1874.
2. *Jackson Daily Citizen,* March 19, 1874.
3. New York journalist Henry Chadwick had spent the winter campaigning for his pet scheme of adding a tenth player—a right shortstop between the first and second basemen—and an extra inning for symmetry. Most of the country joined the Mutuals in rejecting the idea, but Chadwick was regarded as such an authority that many clubs mistakenly assumed the proposal was an official rule change. Ypsilanti played with ten players a side throughout 1874, and outlying areas sometimes used the tenth player for years afterward. A game in Grand Rapids featured "two short stops as is now the custom in the east" (*Grand Rapids Daily Morning Democrat,* May 28, 1874), as did quite a few other games in the ensuing years. Ten-player baseball ("piten") was also the norm in Cuba throughout the nineteenth century.
4. *Niles Republican,* May 7, 1874.
5. *Portage Lake Mining Gazette* (Houghton), June 18, 1874.
6. *Cedar Springs Wolverine Clipper,* September 9, 1874.
7. *New York Herald;* reprinted in Preston D. Orem, *Baseball (1845–1881) from the Newspaper Accounts,* 192.
8. *Cassopolis Vigilant,* August 28, 1873.
9. *Adrian Daily Times and Expositor,* April 27, 1874.

10. *Adrian Daily Press*, April 27, 1874.

11. *Adrian Daily Times and Expositor*, May 7, 1874, from a letter signed "By-Stander."

12. *Grand Rapids Daily Eagle*, April 13, 1874.

13. *Adrian Daily Times and Expositor*, June 28, 1877.

14. *Ionia Sentinel*, August 28, 1874.

15. *Cedar Springs Wolverine Clipper*, August 19, 1874. The *Adrian Daily Press*, May 21, 1874, reported that boys were again feeling a "strange fascination" for baseball but added that "our ardor has been cooled."

16. *Cedar Springs Wolverine Clipper*, July 1, 1874.

17. *Grand Rapids Daily Times*, May 13, 1874.

18. *Jackson Daily Citizen*, June 26, 1874.

19. *Grand Rapids Daily Morning Democrat*, July 4, 1874.

20. *Grand Rapids Daily Times*, July 4, 1874.

21. *Jackson Daily Citizen*, July 8, 1874. Just over a week later, the Red Stockings sailed for England with the Athletics of Philadelphia in an ambitious though unsuccessful attempt to popularize baseball in England.

22. *Jackson Daily Citizen*, August 6, 1874.

23. *Grand Rapids Daily Times*, September 15, 1874.

24. *Jackson News*, (October 10, 1918), termed the grounds "a modern elysium" and noted that "from the close of the [Civil] war until 1890 there was no spot in Jackson more actively associated with enjoyment, in the minds of the young and athletically inclined than 'corner Fourth and Franklin streets.' There were located the ball grounds, and there were few better natural ball fields in the country than those same grounds." The Jackson club was not alone in fixing up its grounds. For example, in Big Rapids, "the enterprising base ballists have erected a 'grand stand' on their ground for the accomodation [*sic*] of those who wish to witness their playing" (*Big Rapids Pioneer*, August 13, 1874).

25. *Detroit Daily Post*, May 5, 1874.

26. *Jackson Daily Citizen*, June 25, 1874.

27. The *Daily Citizen* eventually conceded that the players were printers, a fact that is confirmed by Detroit city directories. Patrick O'Grady was a *Tribune* printer, and James Murtagh was a *News* printer, while Bernard and Henry McAndrews, Albert Stewart, Converse Cook, Marcus Heaslip, and John Walker were *Post* printers. The ninth player, J. Dougherty, could not be located in the city directories under that occupation, but the *Daily Citizen* said he was also a printer for the *Post*.

28. *Jackson Daily Citizen*, June 27, 1874.

29. *Detroit Advertiser and Tribune*, July 26, 1874.

30. *Detroit Advertiser and Tribune*, August 4, 1874.

31. *Detroit Daily Post*, August 6, 1874.

32. *Jackson Daily Citizen*, August 6, 1874.

33. George F. Will, *Bunts*, 34.

34. *Saginaw Daily Courier*, July 4, 1874. On October 26, 1875, the *Fenton Independent* recorded a game between the Unknowns of Fenton and the No Names of Fenton. At least the players' names were given.

35. *South Haven Sentinel*, August 15, 1874.

36. *Benton Harbor Palladium*, July 31, 1874; *St. Joseph Traveler and Herald*, August 8, 1874.

37. Reprinted in the *Cedar Springs Wolverine Clipper,* September 16, 1874. Ironically, the whole dispute was based on a misunderstanding, according to the *Grand Rapids Daily Times,* August 30, 1874.

38. *Ingham County News* (Mason), July 30, 1874.

39. *Ingham County News* (Mason), August 13, 1874.

40. *Detroit Advertiser and Tribune,* October 9, 1874.

23

"MORE FOR INSTRUCTION THAN ANYTHING ELSE"

Several recent springs had seemed to promise a resurgence of Michigan baseball, only to lose momentum over the summer. However, the summer of 1874—for the first time since 1866—fulfilled the spring's promise and the geographic diversity of the renewed interest was particularly encouraging. From all over the state came reports of outbreaks of "base ball fever." Tiny Bowen Station had six clubs within a four-mile radius.[1] Big Rapids suddenly had several clubs, two of which, the Unions and the Anti-Crusaders, played a best-of-seven series for the city championship and a silver cup.[2]

The game also finally caught on in Iosco County, where two players from the 1869 state champion Ann Arbor Club had settled. Brothers Henry Nelson Loud and George Loud had grown up in Boston. As teenagers they moved in 1867 to Oscoda, where their father founded a lumber factory that would become the region's principal employer. After going to school in Ann Arbor, Henry Nelson at the university and George at Ann Arbor High School, both returned to the region and assumed important roles in its development as a leader in the lumber industry. Both also eventually gravitated to public service. George served as a congressman, while Henry became known as the "father of conservation and reforestation in Michigan" and also helped establish "Eastern Central Time," which was initially known as "Loud's time."[3]

The Louds nevertheless found time in their busy schedules to help bring baseball to the area in 1874. Three years earlier, the *Iosco County Gazette* had commented: "We are strongly in favor of organizing [a base ball club]. Who else?"[4] The question had fallen on deaf ears then, but by 1874 the region was prospering and attracting settlers, making the time right for an outbreak of "base ball fever."

Two East Tawas clubs, the Red Stockings and the Clumsies, played on Independence Day. After a closely contested game, the two clubs decided to consolidate as the North Star Base Ball Club and arranged a game with the Rough and Ready Club of Au Sable and Oscoda, which included the Loud brothers. The stage was set for a period of intense interest in the game characterized by an extraordinarily high level of hospitality, with players acting as representatives of their region—a notion that was becoming obsolete in southern Michigan.

On July 18, the North Star Club traveled to Au Sable on the tug *Wesley Hawkins,* accompanied by friends, including several women. The party was met at the dock by a throng that included the Rough and Ready Club and a band and were escorted to the Lee House for dinner. The visitors were given a tour of the town after their meal, and the game followed, with the North Stars winning 26-21. Then the clubs returned to the Lee House for more "mirth and song." Finally, the guests were escorted back to the dock by the band, and cheers were exchanged. After a pleasant ride, a large crowd loudly cheered the players and tug captain, welcoming the ballplayers home.[5] Obviously, this was an area where road clubs were still treated as "visitors and not as intruders." Six days later, in Tawas, the Rough and Readys evened the series in a match again characterized by good feeling on both sides.

Local businessman D. H. Hawes offered a rosewood bat trimmed with velvet and gold to the winner of the rubber game. It is not entirely clear when the deciding game was played, but the club from East Tawas won.[6] A photograph of the winners was preserved, as was the bat, which was described many years later as "beautifully polished; it is thirty-nine inches long, and weighs three pounds. It lies in a velvet-lined black walnut case, fashioned especially for it by an old-time cabinet maker. The hinges, handle and clasps of the box are beautiful antique hardware."[7]

The bat's beauty was surpassed by the symbolic value attached to it by the players who captured it; years later one of them would claim that they would not have traded the bat "for the Kohinoor diamond. We won it without masks, protectors, gloves of any kind or shin guards, and our bats were often parts of peavy or cant-hook stocks, but we always had a good supply of arnica and rags, and a ball that needed sewing up after every game."[8]

Eager to measure themselves against outside competition, the North Stars and Rough and Readys invited the Nationals of Bay

The winner of the rosewood bat was the North Star Base Ball Club of East Tawas and Tawas City. Playing on that club were (in no order) Harry L. Cameron, George Davey, James E. Dillon, Hi Sims, Jack Sims, Fred Levenseller, Fred Whittemore, Nels Brabon, Sam Lobdell, and Nelson Sims.

City for a visit. They again were magnificent hosts, the Nationals concluding that the "Tawas and Au Sable boys were vieing with each other to see who could use us best."[9] The Nationals' first stop was on September 1 in Au Sable, where business was generally suspended to watch the game. The visitors were chauffeured to the field in an omnibus and, after winning 20-17, were presented with a bouquet of flowers. After both clubs' members had replenished themselves from the refreshment tent, a special purse of fifty dollars was raised to entice the players to play again. This time the Rough and Readys won, 35-32, but the Nationals received another bouquet for their efforts, and a brass band performed for them upon their return to the hotel.

The next morning, the Nationals took a tug to East Tawas and were escorted to their hotel for breakfast and then shown about town. In the afternoon, the two clubs played, with Bay City winning 21-12. After the game, the Tawas players continued to "not let us look at our pocket books," paying for dinner and in the evening renting a hall where music and dancing were enjoyed. The Bay City players returned home raving about the hospitality they had received.[10]

Meanwhile, a similar scenario was unfolding in Delta County in the Upper Peninsula. The Fayette Base Ball Club and the Stars of Escanaba both celebrated the Fourth of July by playing intersquad games, and soon a match between the two clubs was arranged, more than sixty friends joining the Stars in traveling to Fayette on a tug. During the trip, several singers accompanied by an accordion player gave an impromptu concert. The visitors were met at the dock by the members of the Fayette Club, who accompanied them to the Fayette House for dinner and then on to the grounds.

During the game, the guests were treated to lemonade and afterward to ice cream and homemade root beer. Festivities after the Stars' 45-29 win included a tour of the furnace, an "admirable" supper, a boat ride, and a dance. When the tug whistle sounded, the hosts urged their guests to stay the night and see more sights in the morning. However, the Escanabans reluctantly elected to go home, singing such songs as "A Starry Night for a Rumble" and "John Brown's Body" on their return journey.

The Stars gratefully acknowledged that "never were visitors better treated," but they tried to return the favor the next weekend.[11] They treated the members of the Fayette Club to dinner and supper, escorted them around town in a four-horse shay, and held a baseball dance in the evening. In only one respect were they less generous hosts than the Fayette Club had been: they won the ball game.

The *Sand Lake Journal* commented similarly that their town's new club had "only been formed two weeks—consequently they had nothing to loose [*sic*] and all to gain. . . . They were only conquered in the kindness they received."[12] The high standards of courtesy and the "patience of hope," both disappearing in areas where baseball was long established, were thus reemerging naturally as the game entered new regions.[13] This is an important example of baseball's ability to "[pour] new life into its veins."

Back in Detroit, the Aetna Club responded to its recent losses by "reorganizing"—a euphemism for replacing its players with better ones. Reorganization had been unheard of in the old days of amateur baseball clubs, but it would soon become a staple of Michigan baseball. However, this year's reorganization was minor in comparison with the ones that would soon follow, as it only entailed promoting a few club members to the first nine and changing pitchers. Meanwhile, the two clubs that had beaten the Aetnas, the Cass Club and the Shamrocks, began a best-of-three series for city supremacy on September 3. The Cass Club got the first leg up with an exciting 19-11 victory. Before the second game of the series could be played, both the reorganized Aetnas and the Cass Club traveled to Greenville for a tournament.

The Greenville tournament had been announced only two and a half weeks before it opened on September 8. First prize in the first class was one hundred dollars and a set of flags and bases, second prize was fifty dollars and a gold-mounted bat, and third prize was twenty-five dollars and a black walnut bat. In the second class, first prize was fifty dollars, second prize was twenty-five dollars, and third prize was a gold-mounted bat. The generous miscellaneous premiums included a twenty-five-dollar silver ice pitcher to the best thrower, ten dollars to the best pitcher, ten dollars to the best catcher, a ten-dollar silver cup to the fastest base runner, ten dollars for the best uniform, and five dollars for the best score.

The bounty of renewed interest resulted in eighteen entrants and necessitated a makeshift format. The Cass Club ended up in the second class, where it won easily. Joe Weiss of the Cass Club later described one of its opponents as "a rural club composed of men with long flowing beards. I don't think one in that club weighed less than 200 pounds."[14] The Aetnas played in the first class and won fifty dollars by beating the St. Aldines of Cedar Springs, 23-21, and a club called the Sooners of Greenville (whose name signified that the players preferred lazing in the shade to running the bases).[15]

In spite of winning both their games, the Aetnas were not awarded first prize in the first class. That honor went to the Eaton Rapids Club, which beat the Challengers of Mason 7-2 and then defeated the Athletics of Grand Rapids 5-4 in a controversial game that was claimed to be the best ever played in the state. The Athletics contended, however, that they had actually won the game 6-5. They conceded that their sixth run had been disputed but claimed that both clubs' scorers had agreed that the score was 5-5 without counting that run. They were therefore shocked when umpire Lewis Cass Rumsey of Howell announced the final score as 5-4 and left the field. One Grand Rapids newspaper intimated that the ruling had gone against the Athletics because many of their players belonged to the Grand Rapids Guard, which had helped quell a riot in Greenville.[16] Another Grand Rapids paper sarcastically listed Rumsey as "A. B. Galoot" in the box score.[17]

Eaton Rapids' success was largely due to its fine battery of pitcher Clarence Terwilliger and catcher E. Wilder. Wilder employed a style that was new to many Michigan observers, coming up behind the hitter with runners on base.[18] This tactic revolutionized the position by greatly increasing the catcher's ability to throw out would-be base stealers and catch foul tips. It was also lethally dangerous, as unprotected catchers could be grievously injured by foul tips. Catchers soon began wearing equipment for protection—first rubbers for their teeth, then masks and chest protectors—but the position remained an extremely hazardous one.[19]

The history of this repositioning of the catcher is murky. Jim "Deacon" White is often credited with inventing the tactic in 1875.[20] However, Wilder's 1874 use of this position was not a first for Michigan—Frank Phelps was playing up close as early as 1866 (see chap. 9). Another Detroit Base Ball Club catcher, George Dawson, was also specifically credited with standing "close to the batter" in an 1868 game against the Niagara Club of Buffalo.[21]

But the innovation almost certainly predates even those two. According to early baseball historian George Moreland, "The first man to catch a ball up behind the bat was F. R. Boerum of the Athletic [sic] Club in 1859. Nat Hicks was credited by many as the first to do so, but such is not the case."[22] *Sporting News* founder Alfred H. Spink cites Bob Ferguson of the Atlantics of Brooklyn, Nat Hicks of the Mutuals of New York, and Fergy Malone of the Athletics of Philadelphia as members "of the old army who caught up close to the bat without glove or mask to protect them."[23] Indeed, Deacon White was not even the first member of his family to use this tactic. In 1870, his cousin Elmer White was described as having "played up close to the bat" to catch Deacon's pitching.[24]

It is difficult to determine how often these brave early catchers ventured up close and how close to the batter they came. Given the danger involved and the fact that many observers thought this was a new tactic in 1874, it seems likely that such positioning was rare and relatively cautious and that Deacon White did draw attention to the new stratagem. The notice Wilder received suggests that he deserves some credit for both courage and innovation.

The Aetnas returned home from the tournament far from empty-handed. They won a prize for the best uniform, and Charley Wood won a silver water pitcher with a throw of 309 feet against the wind. Among the competitors he defeated was Ed Thayer of Grand

Rapids, who had won a similar contest in Rockford. Other prizes went to Wilder for his innovative catching, to Thayer for his pitching, to M. Barber of Eaton Rapids for the swiftest baserunning, and to Terwilliger for having scored 5 of Eaton Rapids' 11 runs. Frederick Stearns of the Aetnas and Charles Howard of the Cass Club expressed themselves as being very pleased with the results of the tournament. The *Greenville Independent* observed that "all the boys seemed to go away full happier than when they arrived," though obviously it was overlooking the Grand Rapids contingent.[25]

Later in the season, Eaton Rapids and the Athletic Club of Grand Rapids had a rematch of the controversial game at the Greenville tournament. Eaton Rapids won 17-10 in Ionia in a match that was billed as being for the championship of the west side of the state. The $125 in gate receipts allowed the organizers to cover the $100 purse and pay their expenses, which no doubt encouraged Ionia to host very ambitious tournaments the next two summers.

The Mutuals, again acknowledged as Michigan's top club, had decided to skip the Greenville tournament to host a club from Staten Island on September 8. The Staten Island Club was made up of former major leaguers and Eastern collegians, and the game was billed as being for the amateur championship of the country.[26] The Mutuals won the game 16-8, although the result was at least partly attributable to the exhausting schedule the visitors had been playing.

The next major event on the baseball calendar was the state tournament in East Saginaw, which began on September 16. There were four entrants in the senior division until the last-minute arrival of the Rough and Ready Club of Au Sable caused controversy. The Mutuals, always conscious of the financial realities of the game, argued that a fifth club would add at least one extra day to their stay. The Rough and Readys contended that they had entered on time and felt outraged and betrayed when the Nationals of Bay City, whom they had hosted so graciously two weeks earlier, sided with the Mutuals.

Eventually Au Sable was disqualified. While this ruling simplified the tournament, it was certainly a low point for the game.

The Rough and Ready Club, which had brought to the game a level of decorum not seen in many years, was left on the sideline, bitterly reflecting that "the association set aside honorable dealing for the 'babes from Jackson and Bay City.' "[27] The Mutuals beat the Athletics of Grand Rapids 9-3 to advance to the championship game against the Ogemas of Flint, who had beaten the Nationals of Bay City. The Mutuals easily beat the Ogemas, 32-12.

The dissension carried over to the junior division, where the Forester Club of Charlotte beat the Dominos of Pontiac 14-5 to claim top honors. Most of the complaints came from the Junior Mutual Club of Jackson, which had been eliminated by the Dominos. The Junior Mutuals responded with some colorful allegations, claiming that most of the Dominos were "bearded like the pard," that one Domino was the father of "five little Dominos," and that the pitcher was a Methodist minister.[28] The Junior Mutuals then challenged the Foresters to play them in Jackson, and when the Foresters indicated that they would play only in Charlotte, George Mintie, secretary of the Junior Mutuals, insinuated that they too included overage players.[29]

The tournament afforded other reminders that the public and press quickly lost interest when games were not played in an appropriate spirit. The *Bay City Tribune* alleged that the Nationals had used three or four revolvers from the Saginaw Club and that their opponents, the Ogemas, had bribed those same players to throw the game. While the charges were heatedly denied, the hypocrisy of expecting loyalty from revolvers was apparent. The *Detroit Post* reported that the tournament was "of little interest to the general public, and [that] the games have drawn but few spectators, except infatuated small boys and friends of the players. There has been any amount of wrangling and disputing, and charges of fraud and swindling, and a feeling of general relief is experienced, now that the agony is finally over."[30] While the state fair as a whole was a big enough success for East Saginaw to host it again in 1875, there was no effort to reprise the baseball tournament.

Although the fractious behavior of the Jackson clubs did not bode well for a sustained revival, the game was continuing to expand at a greater rate than at any time since the postwar boom. In the Upper Peninsula, escalating competition was accompanied by many of the excesses of the Lower Peninsula along with some new ones. Several July 4 games were played in Ishpeming for cash prizes, but controversy arose when one of the clubs was not allowed to use substitutes for two players who were injured during practice. Another club, after being soundly beaten, sent the score to the *Marquette Mining Journal* but reversed the names.

Cash featured prominently in the Upper Peninsula's burgeoning competitiveness. The White Stockings of Republic challenged the Negaunee Club to play them for fifty dollars. The Mutuals of Ishpeming topped that by offering to play any club in the county for one hundred dollars. After Ishpeming beat Negaunee, the latter club talked about playing a rematch for a purse of two hundred dollars.

A tournament for three hundred dollars began in Houghton on August 11 with three clubs entered—the Independents of Ripley, the First Nationals of Hancock, and a picked nine from Keweenaw County. The double round-robin settled nothing, as the First Nationals beat Keweenaw twice, Keweenaw beat the Independents twice, and the Independents beat the First Nationals twice. So another round was played, and this time the Independents won twice to claim the three hundred dollars. Indicative of the increased level of competitiveness, the tournament featured accusations of imported players and thrown matches.[31] Now that they were champions of the copper region, the Independents were reported to be "casting a wistful eye toward the iron region for further conquests."[32]

The Independents got their wish when a tournament for all Upper Peninsula clubs began in Ishpeming on September 8. The organizers initially proposed a format in which all the clubs but the Mutuals of Ishpeming would play a round-robin, with the winner then facing Ishpeming for the championship. The format was justified on the grounds that the "Mutuals will necessarily be very busy in carrying out the arrangements" and should be excused from games "in consideration of the fact that they will be very busy in look-ing to the comfort of their visitors."[33] This reasoning understandably proved unpopular with other clubs, and eventually a more equitable format was devised. The tournament drew the best clubs in the region but also attracted clubs like the Stars of Escanaba, who entered "more for instruction than anything else, as the club is new and a game with good players would benefit our boys greatly."[34]

Six clubs entered the tournament, meaning that no fewer than fifteen games would have to be played. Bad weather made this impossible; several clubs were unable to play their final game, leav-ing the final standings a mess. Nonetheless, the Independents of Ripley were the undisputed champions and earned another $150. The Mutuals of Ishpeming took second and $50, while both Negaunee and the First Nationals of Hancock claimed third. The Stars of Escanaba, who had competed "more for instruction than anything else," voiced some mild complaints about the umpiring but thanked their hosts for having done "everything in their power to make the visiting clubs enjoy themselves."[35] In spite of a few problems, the tournament was a success, and, as one observer noted, "everybody and his wife seem[ed] to be in attendance."[36]

The enthusiasm for baseball in the Upper Peninsula was begin-ning to conflict with work. The *Sault Saint Marie Enterprise* gave this description of a practice of a baseball club composed of tugmen: "With three tugs at the bay, tied up to the dock, with one man left to blow the whistle if a wild tug comes in sight, the rest go out and prac-tice. At the first signal from the lookout, all hands run, helter-skelter, get up steam and run up as far as the mission, discover a steam barge coming with three vessels in tow, they hold a hurried consultation and agree to d——n the barge and then return to practice."[37]

Activity on college campuses was also on the rise in 1874, with two of the state's earliest intercollegiate games taking place. The Praktikois of Hillsdale College beat Albion College 31-10 on June 6. Two Detroit business schools squared off on September 19 when Goldsmith's Bryant and Stratton College faced Mayhew College.

Meanwhile, the flurry of competition in Detroit continued in September. The Clipper and Excelsior Clubs played a match that was billed as being for the championship of the Sixth Ward! The Cass Club beat the Shamrocks 33-21 in the second game of their series and, having beaten every other top club in Detroit, triumphantly claimed the city championship. However, the Aetnas were continuing to post impressive wins, and the Cass Club soon accepted a challenge from them.

On October 7, the Aetnas won the first game of the series, 26-16; on October 18, the Aetnas again emerged victorious, 15-9, wresting local bragging rights away from the Cass Club. This was the Aetna Club's eighth straight victory since its reorganization—an impressive turnaround that inspired a flurry of such moves in the ensuing seasons by clubs hoping for similar results. In their final game of the season, the Aetnas hosted Toledo on October 23, but the game ended in a 21-21 tie due to darkness.

Detroit baseball enthusiasts also had the chance to witness the return to the diamond of many stalwarts of the Detroit Base Ball Club in a pair of October games between the Detroit and Excelsior Boat Clubs. These were billed as muffin games, but with the two clubs' lineups featuring such familiar names as Charley and Milton Ward, Eugene Robinson, John Horn, Jack and Ford Hinchman, Butler Ives, Frank Folsom, and Jim Craig, they undoubtedly were fine exhibitions of ball-playing. These games also offered a painful reminder of the passage of time, and "at the close the veterans who had participated went down town and made liberal investments in liniments and ointments."[38]

County fairs were once again including baseball games as featured events. A tournament at the Berrien County Fair in Niles on September 29 and 30 featured one hundred dollars in premiums. The tournament showed glimpses of the "patience of hope," which had been in short supply in recent years. Although the field of six clubs led to some arbitrary pairings, no dissatisfaction was expressed by any of the clubs. And even though clubs from Indiana took the top two spots, the Michigan clubs "did not despair," taking comfort in the fact that one of the local clubs had "only organized the night previous to match [*sic*], and that, too after nine o'clock in the evening."[39]

The 1874 season ended with state bragging rights again belonging to the Mutuals of Jackson, who had completed their second consecutive season without a loss to a Michigan club. In thirteen matches, they had outscored their in-state opponents 299-86. While the only Detroit club they had played was the Franklins, they had handily defeated challengers from all over the state, including strong clubs from Eaton Rapids (twice) and Chelsea, the Unknowns of Hillsdale, the Ogemas of Flint, the Athletic Club of Adrian College (twice), and the Athletic Club of Grand Rapids (three times). These wins and the one over the club from Staten Island, combined with respectable showings against the Mutuals of New York and the Red Stockings of Boston, left no doubt that the Mutes were again the state's top club.

Near the end of the season, a benefit game between the Mutuals and the Junior Mutuals was played as a token of appreciation for the efforts of captain Will DeMyer. The Junior Mutuals were allowed five outs per inning, an advantage that almost perfectly balanced the two squads, as the senior club had to rally to win 27-25. DeMyer was also presented with an autograph album that featured the fist imprints of all the club members. Several newspapers reported that the Mutuals were considering becoming a professional club in 1875, but the *Jackson Citizen* denied this, describing the players as "all business young men, whose only object in perfecting themselves in the game is to enjoy the exercise, recreation and social meetings which the game fosters."[40] Nonetheless, the paper acknowledged that the club was considering touring and hosting a major tournament in 1875.

After the 1874 season, the state-fair organizers presented the Mutuals of Jackson with an elaborate championship medal, which was described as follows:

From an arc of orange gold upon which the word "Champion" is chased, is suspended a wreath of laurel, crossed by two foul flags, with an "M" in the centre, from this is suspended the medal proper, which is in the form of a star, on one side two bats are crossed over a belt, with an open score book at the centre, and in the points of the star are shoes, cap, base and home plate, all these in bold relief in lemon gold on a ground of rich orange. On the upper part of the star is a silver ball, while all the rest of the badge is gold. On the reverse side of the medal are the inscriptions, around the centre—"To Mutual Base Ball Club, Jackson, Mich." And in the points of the star—"First Senior Prize—State Fair Tournament—awarded by the Michigan State Agricultural Society." The medal is mounted on blue ribbon, is enclosed in a handsome morocco case, and is valued at $100.[41]

And while no one could dispute the Mutuals' right to the medal, there must have been some, especially in Iosco County, who found the medal's ostentation equally fitting.

NOTES

1. *Grand Rapids Daily Times*, September 12, 1874.
2. The Unions won the series, apparently in four straight games.
3. See the *Alpena News*, August 31, 1935, for a tribute to Henry Nelson Loud's eighty-fifth birthday. Also see his obituary in the *Alpena News* on August 26, 1938.
4. *Iosco County Gazette* (Tawas), August 10, 1871.
5. *Iosco County Gazette* (Tawas), July 23, 1874.
6. Edna M. Otis, *Sawdust Days: When the Tawas Area Was Young* (East Tawas, Mich.: n.p., 1973), 20–22; Edna M. Otis, *Their Yesterdays: Au Sable and Oscoda, 1848–1948* (n.p.). The latter book can be found at the Library of Michigan but contains no publication information or pagination.
7. Otis, *Sawdust Days*, 20.
8. Otis, *Sawdust Days*, 21–22; Otis, *Their Yesterdays*, n.p.. The deciding game may have evoked more competitiveness than the first two games. According to Otis, tradition has it that the Rough and Readys spiked their opponents' drinking water with gin.
9. From the *Bay City Tribune* (not extant); reprinted in the *Iosco County Gazette* (Tawas), September 17, 1874.
10. From the *Bay City Tribune* (not extant); reprinted in the *Iosco County Gazette* (Tawas), September 17, 1874.
11. *Escanaba Tribune*, August 15, 1874.
12. Reprinted in the *Cedar Springs Wolverine Clipper*, July 15, 1874.
13. *Escanaba Tribune*, August 22, 1874.
14. *Detroit Free Press*, January 13, 1889.
15. *Detroit Daily Post*, July 1, 1872. Another club with similar inclinations was the Lazy Nine

of Chester, who "come fully up to their illustrious name in playing" (*Charlotte Republi-can,* September 25, 1874).

16. *Grand Rapids Daily Morning Democrat,* September 12, 1874.

17. *Grand Rapids Daily Times,* September 11, 1874

18. *Greenville Democrat,* September 22, 1874.

19. Rubbers were in use by 1874, masks by 1877, and chest protectors by 1883. See the *Grand Rapids Morning Democrat,* September 4, 1883: "It was in the year 1877 that F. W. Thayer, then a student at Harvard college and captain of the university base ball club, was in want of a catcher. [Jim] Tyng was asked to take the position, but he said he did not care to, as he was afraid to fill a position that would afford a catcher no protection from the foul tips, hot balls and other risks that might threaten him. Before this the catcher's rubber had been the only safeguard adopted by the catchers, but this did not come into general use, and protected the teeth and mouth only. Thayer talked over the matter with Tyng, and the result was the conception of the base ball mask. An experimental one was made and satisfactorily tested in the college gymnasium. Thayer soon after visited the club room of the Boston nine, then at 39 Eliot street, and spoke to Harry and George Wright and others of the players present about the new invention. Most of them laughed at the idea of a man going around with a cage on his head. Harry, however, always ready and curious enough to look at anything new in base ball, asked Thayer to bring in the affair. The young man accordingly did so, and stood at one end of the room with it on, allowing the players to throw balls at it, which he easily butted off."

The first documented user of a chest protector was Charley Bennett of the Detroit Wolverines, as noted in the *Detroit Free Press,* May 1, 1883. As previously mentioned, gloves were in use in the early 1860s, and catcher's mitts began to evolve around 1875, according to the *New York Sun,* April 27, 1890. Those were the only protective devices used by nineteenth-century catchers; shin guards and the rest of the modern catcher's armor were not introduced until the twentieth century.

20. In the *Sporting News,* March 23, 1895, Al Pratt claimed that Deacon White was the first catcher to play up close. Pratt was wrong, but his expertise means that the tactic must have been uncommon before the 1870s. David Q. Voigt, *American Baseball,* 85, is one of many sources that credit this innovation to White.

21. *Detroit Advertiser and Tribune,* September 10, 1868.

22. George L. Moreland, *Balldom,* 274. Folkert Rappelye Boerum was the catcher for the Atlantics of Brooklyn from 1857 to 1861.

23. Alfred H. Spink, *The National Game,* 92. All three were catching in the late 1860s and/or early 1870s. The quotation cited refers specifically only to Hicks and Malone, but Ferguson is described as "one of the first to catch the ball up close to the bat" (Spink, *The National Game* 10).

24. *New York Daily Tribune,* August 19, 1870.

25. *Greenville Independent,* September 9, 1874.

26. The players included three major leaguers: Fraley Rogers, E. P. Beavan, and Fred Crane. Crane had nearly moved to Detroit seven years earlier.

27. *Iosco County Gazette* (Tawas), September 24, 1874.

28. *Jackson Daily Citizen,* September 18, 1874. The pitcher was Reverend Parker. The *Saginaw Daily Republican,* September 29, 1874, quoted the *Pontiac Gazette* as saying of Reverend Parker that "his pitching is characteristic of the arguments in his excellent sermons—they are sent home with telling effect."

29. *Jackson Daily Citizen*, October 6, 1874. Mintie died a month later of typhoid fever at age nineteen (*Jackson Daily Citizen*, November 9, 1874).

30. *Detroit Daily Post*, September 19, 1874.

31. *Northwestern Mining Journal* (Hancock), August 19, 1874; *Portage Lake Mining Gazette* (Houghton), August 13, 1874.

32. *Portage Lake Mining Gazette* (Houghton), August 20, 1874.

33. *Marquette Mining Journal*, August 22, 1874.

34. *Escanaba Tribune*, August 29, 1874.

35. *Escanaba Tribune*, September 19, 1874.

36. *Marquette Mining Journal*, September 12, 1874.

37. Reprinted in the *Ishpeming Iron Home*, September 19, 1874.

38. *Detroit Advertiser and Tribune*, October 9, 1874.

39. *Niles Republican*, October 1, 1874; *Niles Democrat*, October 3, 1874.

40. *Jackson Daily Citizen*, October 13, 1874.

41. *Jackson Daily Citizen*, March 4, 1875.

24

"A GAME WHICH HAS BECOME
PECULIARLY AMERICAN"

The revival of baseball in Detroit continued that winter, as the Aetnas began planning for the 1875 season shortly after the 1874 campaign ended. On November 27, 1874, the businessmen of Detroit offered their support for the Aetnas. Forty-five honorary club members, including Richard Fyfe, D. M. Ferry, David Peirce, Governor John J. Bagley, John Horn, and James Vernor, signed a pledge that affirmed in part their belief

> that exercise in the open air is promotion of physical strength and health and that such exercise cannot be safely neglected and should not be omitted either by the youthful or middle aged and recognizing in the game of Base-Ball, not only a means for this exercise, but a game which has become peculiarly American and in which therefore all Americans may well feel any interest and just pride, akin to the income and pride of all Englishmen in the Cricket game.[1]

More important than the sentiments were the ten dollars each man contributed to the Aetnas' coffers. The game itself was not entirely dormant during the winter, as the Aetna Club split into two nines to play baseball on ice on January 8, 1875.

The Mutuals of Jackson also organized early, and there was

understandable confidence in Jackson that the new season would yield more success. When the *Grand Rapids Times* suggested a state baseball club of players from Detroit, Grand Rapids, Ann Arbor, Kalamazoo, and Jackson, the *Jackson Citizen* replied brashly, "Leave Jackson out, if you please, and we can then whip all the rest."[2] The *Adrian Times* observed that the "Jackson Mutuals have begun this summer's work of practising and bragging."[3]

However, the assumption that the Mutuals would again dominate the Michigan baseball scene would prove to be ill founded. An important change that had been developing for several years would create vigorous competition and throw the race for state supremacy wide open for the first time in years.

Baseball had been a very high-scoring game in the early 1860s, with defenses powerless to prevent clubs from pounding the lively ball at will. As the decade progressed, both pitching techniques and fielding skill improved, which caused a reduction in scoring that was described as "scientific."

This very natural development was accelerated by less organic developments. Once low-scoring games were perceived as scientific by the newspapers and the public, clubs began using "dead balls" to earn praise. At an NABBP convention in New York on November 30, 1870, the amount of rubber allowed in the ball was reduced from two-and-a-half ounces to one ounce. Other changes reduced scoring even further, especially the liberalizing of pitching deliveries and the positioning of catchers closer to the plate.

The trend toward lower scores would turn baseball on its head. Early baseball gave so many advantages to the hitters that an out was an event. By the 1870s, that advantage had shifted to the pitchers and fielders, and it was runs that were at a premium. The *Detroit Post*, even while writing sentimentally about the glory days of the Detroit Base Ball Club, claimed that the new style of baseball was vastly superior:

> The "close and exciting" contests of those days, however, would rank but little higher than a first-class "muffin" game of the present time.

The player who captured a "fly" in the out-field received the plaudits of the spectators; a double play awoke thunders of applause, and a score of only twenty runs or less on a side was gazed at with admiring eyes. Now the player who misses a "fly" is liable to be laughed at, it takes a triple play to awake any particular enthusiasm, and if the runs in a majority of the innings are not denoted by a "o," lookers-on do not hesitate to declare that "the nines are playing loosely; are running up a big score."[4]

This dramatic change was also beginning to be used in the depiction of baseball as an indigenous American game. The *Kalamazoo Telegraph* gave an example of this reasoning: "This invigorating and manly pastime may now be justly termed the American game of ball, for though of English origin, it has been so modified and improved of late years in this country as almost to deprive it of any of its original features beyond the mere ground work of the game."[5]

The effect of the continuing trend toward less scoring was to breed an optimism in baseball clubs reminiscent of the faith during the postwar boom that clubs were capable of near infinite improvement. That initial faith had quickly evaporated when it met the harsh reality that no amount of perseverance could overcome superior athletic skills. It became accepted that success on the ball field necessitated assembling nine talented players, something that few small towns had any chance to accomplish.

However, the pitching of Clarence Terwilliger and the revolutionary catching technique of E. Wilder at the Greenville tournament had demonstrated that a new formula for building a strong club was possible. Even with an indifferent supporting cast, a small town like Eaton Rapids with a strong battery could realistically compete against a club drawing its players from a much greater population base. The philosophy that "good pitching stops good hitting" was starting to become one of baseball's articles of faith.

From around the state came more indications of renewed interest, as clubs were eager to develop the next great battery. Charlotte had "no less than a dozen different clubs."[6] It was reported that "the base ball fever which annually infests the whole country has reached Niles," and five different clubs were soon thriving.[7] Berrien Springs also soon boasted five clubs.[8] The *Fowlerville Review* reported, "Fowlerville glories in four base ball clubs."[9]

Perhaps the best example of the "patience of hope" returning to Michigan baseball was a club formed at the Michigan Agricultural College. William K. Prudden, a member of that club, later recalled: "In the spring of 1875 a baseball nine was organized, and called the 'Nine Spots.' After much solicitation and delay we managed to raise enough money to buy suits. I remember them well, white flannel trimmed with brown. We simply bought ten suits, one extra only. A baseball club in those days meant nine players with one substitute. The 'sub' was supposed to be able to play any position, and when not playing to carry water for the others." Naturally, this position proved difficult to fill: "I can't give you the name of the 'sub,' as he was generally a kicker on account of menial duties performed (or rather to be performed) and was 'fired' or 'resigned' once in two weeks."

Adding to the unglamorous portrait of being on a baseball team is Prudden's description of fitting practice in after the day's strenuous labor: "In those days three hours' work on farm and garden was required. Clearing land, digging ditches, and sundry light work for three hours, one until four, put us in prime condition for baseball practice from four to six, three times a week."[10] Obviously it took quite a love of the game to persevere under such circumstances![11]

While the perception that two players could turn around the weakest club did much to reinstill the "patience of hope," it paradoxically also led to increased impatience, as struggling clubs hurried to dump their pitcher and catcher in search of a quick fix.

The Mutuals of Jackson, who had dominated the state for two years with their battery of Robert Lake and Will DeMyer, became caught up in the pursuit of faster pitching and catchers who could handle such deliveries. They attempted to convert large, powerful third baseman Fred Andrus to pitching, but "Andrus and his speed

While William K. Prudden was a student at the Michigan Agricultural College (now Michigan State University), he was captain of a touring club called the Nine Spots. There were actually ten players on the Nine Spots, but "the 'sub' was supposed to be able to play any position, and when not playing to carry water for the others. . . . [H]e was generally a kicker on account of menial duties performed (or rather to be performed) and was 'fired' or 'resigned' once in two weeks." By the time this picture was taken at a reunion, Prudden had founded a company that would become the Motor Wheel Corporation.

were too much for the anatomy of DeMyer, and a new catcher named Joe Lawler was imported from Chicago."[12] Lawler, too, was soon deemed inadequate and shifted to another position. His replacement was another Chicagoan, Jack Carbine, from the recently disbanded Westerns of Keokuk, Iowa, of the National Association. Before long, yet another professional catcher, John Foley, was brought in. The *Jackson Citizen* complained in vain about the "folly of changing positions" and contended that the club should have stuck with DeMyer, who had been unceremoniously let go.[13]

As for the Athletics of Grand Rapids, at the end of the 1874 season they had vowed to import a battery from Chicago the next season to make themselves competitive.[14] But in the spring of 1875, faced with the reality that the "only way in which to start and keep up a first class club is on the stock company basis," they discovered that only half the club members wanted to proceed, with the remainder "contrary or lukewarm." Consequently, plans to organize for the upcoming season were put on hold.[15]

Meanwhile, in Detroit, hopes were high that the Aetnas would bring first-class baseball back to the city, ending a long drought during which "from time to time clubs have been formed, but from a lack of funds, friends and proper management, have been short lived, 'dying unwept, unhonored and unsung.'"[16] The always fashion-conscious Aetnas debuted new uniforms for their first game on May 29, sporting silver-gray caps, shirts, and knee breeches, with red facings, red stockings, and white canvas shoes.[17]

The Aetnas were outplayed by a University of Michigan club appareled in simple white uniforms and blue stockings. The collegians won 15-10 in front of five hundred spectators, eighty of whom were students who had traveled up from Ann Arbor for the game. The result, combined with the fact that the Mutuals of Jackson had already beaten the college team 7-5, signaled that the Aetnas still had a long way to go to reclaim state supremacy. Moreover, in the new environment of scientific play, dead balls, and liberalized pitching styles, the 15 runs allowed were considered very poor.

Much of the blame for the high score was placed on Aetna catcher Pete Morris, who had struggled to catch the fast, erratic pitching of Charley Wood. The Aetnas moved quickly to upgrade their catching by hiring Frank Bliss. Eager to avenge their loss before the university closed for the summer, the reinforced Aetnas traveled to Ann Arbor for a rematch on June 12. During their morning practice, Wood fell and dislocated his nonpitching shoulder. The shoulder was put back in place by a surgeon, and Wood pitched the Aetnas to a 7-6 victory with his "left arm hanging useless by his side."[18]

When the University of Michigan closed for the summer, it was a bountiful source of talent for clubs looking to recruit players. Fred Stearns and William Johnson rejoined the Aetnas, and, with Wood still nursing his shoulder injury, the Aetnas also added pitcher George Abbott for their first game with the Cass Club on June 17. The Aetnas won by a surprisingly easy 35-7 margin.

It was becoming evident that the Cass Club was struggling to adjust to the changing game. The Cass Club had been among the state's top clubs in 1874 and would regain that status in 1876. But in 1875, the club never hit on a winning formula, even though its directors included such prominent men as Butler Ives, James McMillan, and W. G. Thompson.[19] It lost successive matches to the Domino Club of Pontiac, the Foresters of Charlotte, and the Unknowns of Hillsdale and by the end of the season was playing as a junior club.

Thus the Aetna Club had to look outside of Detroit for competition. In late June, the Aetnas traveled to Canada to play in London and Guelph. After an exciting 16-15 win over the Tecumsehs of London, they were defeated 7-2 by the Maple Leaf Club of Guelph. The Tecumsehs then visited Detroit for an Independence Day match with the Aetnas, but the game was rained out in the fifth inning with the visitors ahead 4-3.[20]

Heavy rains ruined many other planned Independence Day games, but a few areas escaped. The Red Stockings of Sand Lake nosed out the host Actives of Howard City 16-15 to win a twenty-five-dollar purse. In Chesaning, a club from St. Charles beat its hosts to win a bat and ball. The Mutuals of Jackson beat the Athletic Club of Grand Rapids 19-11 in Jackson. The Foresters of Charlotte, last season's junior champions, began establishing their ability to compete with senior clubs. They won a holiday tournament in Charlotte by defeating the Unknowns of Hillsdale and the White Stripes of Carmel and followed with a brief tour.

The Mutuals of Jackson followed the Aetnas' example by looking to Canada for competition. The Tecumsehs of London journeyed to Jackson after the rainout in Detroit and were beaten 9-8 by the Mutuals. But the Mutuals were much less successful when they visited London and Guelph, losing 12-3 and 19-4.

Despite these two losses, the stage was set by the end of July for an excellent rivalry for the state championship. The Mutuals of Jackson remained the favorites, but their frequent roster changes and the changing game meant that they now had legitimate rivals, particularly the Aetnas. The two clubs met on July 23, and the Aetnas became the first Michigan club to beat the Mutuals in nearly three years, by a surprisingly easy 23-5 count.

The Mutuals pointed out that the game was just the first of a five-game series and that "honor won by three years hard labor cannot be transferred by a single game."[21] However, baseball enthusiasts around Michigan began to dub the Aetnas as "the Champions of the State."[22] Some even ridiculed the once-mighty Jackson club. The captain of a Grand Rapids club of small boys told a player who kept fumbling the ball, "We've had just about enough of this 'ere Mutual style of playing."[23] And when the Mutuals seemed disinclined to continue the series, it was taken by many as a tacit admission that the Aetnas were now state champions.

Interest in the state competition was bolstered by the growing number of clubs that were strong enough to provide stiff competition for the Mutuals and Aetnas, including the Unknowns of Hillsdale and the Foresters of Charlotte. All over the state, clubs were again swelling with ambition. The Wagon Makers of Buchanan, having lost only to a club from South Bend, Indiana, were reportedly "getting considerably conceited."[24] The members of the Shoo Fly Club of Stockbridge challenged several clubs, but only a picked nine was willing to play them. So they dreamed even larger, resolving that if nobody would play them after harvest they would travel east,

> expecting to return home crowned with laurels, and to have their names enrolled by the side of the cracked up clubs of our country, and to be known during the season of '76 as the Champions of America. And they expect to sit during the winter of '75–76 and relate to their wives and children the many curious sights of the East and South and to show on their persons broken noses, split fingers, misplaced cheek bones and jaws that are toothless, having to endure such perils to occupy the position they have reached.[25]

A more serious aspirant to the title emerged in August with the rebirth of the Unas of Kalamazoo. Reflecting the changing requirements for success, a Kalamazoo Base Ball Association was formed, its officers including Allen Potter as president and Johnny McCord as a director, and five hundred shares were issued. The selection of the Unas' nine also reflected the new emphasis on a speedy pitcher and a catcher who could hold him. Not only did the Unas secure

Clarence Terwilliger to pitch and "Chick" Myers to catch, but they hedged their bets in case of injury or poor performance by filling their outfield with three players—Will DeMyer, Clark Rowlson, and Tommy Dorgan—who had been star battery members for Michigan clubs in the recent past.

This strategy provided the Unas with backups at these critical positions and cannily prevented potential rivals from signing these players for their own batteries. However, baseball's unique economics meant that what was a good business practice in another industry could backfire on a baseball club. The Athletics of Grand Rapids had finally decided to upgrade their club by paying advance money to catcher John Foley, but Foley instead jumped to the Mutuals. With the Mutuals and the Unas both stockpiling pitchers and catchers, the Athletics again reversed course. Thus, a rivalry that could have enriched both the Mutuals and the Unas was squelched by those clubs' use of a traditional capitalistic practice.

The Foley incident also established the poorly kept secret that the top Michigan clubs were again employing professionals. Clubs' hometown papers still avoided alluding to this, but the *Pontiac Gazette* called the Aetnas and Mutuals "professional clubs."[26] Nonetheless, professionalism in Michigan was still on a very limited scale, and it is likely that only battery members were paid. The Aetnas' books show several five-dollar disbursements for "time lost" and "expenses" to Ed Thayer, Joe Lawler, and Frank Bliss in 1875.[27]

Even amateur clubs were following the Mutuals' lead in soliciting financial support from the community. The Athletics of Grand Rapids circulated a subscription paper to enable them to attend the Ionia tournament, though they cancelled after Foley's defection. After the Diamonds of Muir won their first game, a local wrote: "The news was sent to this village by telegraph, and a collection was taken up among the citizens and a keg of beer bought to greet their arrival home. Many subscribed for this who refused to subscribe money to purchase shirts for the club, and all who subscribed for the beer ought to feel ashamed of it as long as they live."[28] Obviously, the financial support of the community brought with it the expectation of on-the-field success as a return on the investment.

The stage was thus set for the 1875 tournament season to begin in earnest.

NOTES

1. *Aetna Base Ball Association Constitution and By-Laws.*
2. *Jackson Daily Citizen*, March 13, 1875.
3. Reprinted in both the *Homer Index* and the *Jackson Daily Citizen*, April 28, 1875.
4. *Detroit Daily Post*, May 27, 1875.
5. *Kalamazoo Daily Telegraph*, August 23, 1875.
6. *Grand Ledge Independent*, August 6, 1875.
7. *Niles Republican*, May 27, 1875. Also see the *Detroit Evening News*, April 29, 1875, which reported that one of these clubs was "a civil rights organization." Presumably that means that the club was either African American or racially mixed.
8. *Berrien Springs Journal*, quoted in the *Berrien County Record* (Buchanan), June 17, 1875.
9. *Fowlerville Review*, July 16, 1875.
10. *M.A.C. Record* 21, no. 29 (May 2, 1916).
11. William K. Prudden would found the Prudden Wheel Company in Lansing, which later changed its name to the Motor Wheel Corporation and became the world's largest manufacturer of automobile wheels.
12. *Jackson News*, October 10, 1918.
13. *Jackson Daily Citizen*, July 24, 1875.
14. *Grand Rapids Daily Times*, October 12, 1874.
15. *Grand Rapids Daily Morning Times*, April 16, 1875.
16. *Detroit Daily Post*, May 27, 1875.
17. *Detroit Daily Post*, May 31, 1875.
18. *Detroit Daily Post*, June 14, 1875.
19. Ives was a regular for the Detroit Base Ball Club and had become a prominent banker. McMillan was the business partner of John S. Newberry and later a U.S. senator. Thompson was another close friend of Newberry and, as mayor of Detroit, would help bring major-league baseball to Detroit in 1881.
20. With July 4 falling on a Sunday, celebrations were moved to either July 3 or July 5.
21. *Hillsdale Standard*, August 3, 1875, letter from an unidentified member of the Mutuals.
22. *Charlotte Republican*, August 6, 1875.
23. *Grand Rapids Daily Morning Democrat*, August 6, 1875.
24. *Berrien County Record*, June 10, 1875.
25. *Ingham County News* (Mason), July 29, 1875.
26. *Pontiac Weekly Gazette*, August 13, 1875.
27. *Aetna Base Ball Association Constitution and By-Laws.* Thayer, with the Athletics of Grand Rapids the previous season and now attending college in Ohio, briefly played for the Aetnas during his vacation.
28. *Ionia Sentinel*, August 6, 1875.

"EACH SIDE HAS ITS OWN STORY"

The first significant baseball tournament of the 1875 season took place in Vicksburg, Michigan, on August 6 and 7 and attracted six clubs. The problem of dealing with such an awkward number was simplified by an important side benefit of the trend toward lower-scoring games. Until recently games had often occupied four or five hours, but now they were being completed in less than three hours. This made it realistic to schedule more than two games per day, so three first-round games were played, with the Monitors of Kalamazoo, the Leek Diggers of Climax, and the Hungry Nine of Vicksburg emerging as winners. At that point, a vote was held to determine the next round's pairings, and the Kalamazoo club was awarded a bye into the championship game. The Hungry Nine of Vicksburg defeated the Leek Diggers but was beaten by the Monitors, who received a silver goblet for their efforts. The tournament also featured a concert and a dance.

Bay City, Wenona, Vassar, Lapeer, Romeo, and Orion were represented at an August 11 tournament in Orion for $50 in prizes, with the National Club of Bay City winning. A tournament of junior clubs in Charlotte featured the hometown White Stockings, the Alerts of Brookfield, the Unknowns of Jackson, and the Awkwards of Grand Ledge. The White Stockings beat the Unknowns to claim the title, but the third-place game was abandoned when one of the players, Howard Hubbard of Grand Ledge, broke his leg. At another tournament, in Pontiac, the host club won to claim $5 and a gold ball, while runners-up White Lake received silk flags and bases valued at $15.

These tournaments were small potatoes in comparison with a four-day tournament that began in Ionia on August 10. The top class offered a single prize of $200 and was open to all clubs. The second class, open to any club in the state of Michigan, featured prizes of $150, $75, and $25. The third class was restricted to clubs in Ionia County and offered payouts of $40, $25, and $15. An extra class for junior clubs was added belatedly, with $65 and $35 available to the top two finishers. Two fields were prepared, the primary one having been "leveled so that not a stone or knoll is left to interfere with the players."[1] Ten separate committees were set up to attend to every detail.

Although the tournament was not announced until July 21, the committees made up for lost time with hard work. Half-price fares were arranged on trains and steamers, and advertising was so extensive that a correspondent in Lyons complained, "Posters and bills announcing and giving the programme of the tournament are scattered about town in such profusion as to give one an idea that it is to be the grandest and most important event of the century, and that little villages were made for the sole purpose of proclaiming and making known to the public."[2] The bill posting, though annoying, did help ensure the tournament's success, as many residents of Lyons and other surrounding communities made plans to attend.

The format was carefully designed, giving an advantage to the homegrown clubs on whom the success of the tournament relied but also giving out-of-state clubs an opportunity to make their trip worthwhile. One out-of-state club did attend—the Livingstons of Geneseo, New York, a club consisting mostly of Cornell students who were spending their summer holidays "traveling and playing around the country from a pure love of the game."[3] The Livingstons' captain and sponsor, James W. Wadsworth, was the son of a Civil War general who had been killed in the Battle of the Wilderness, leaving his son a millionaire.[4] Wadsworth used his inheritance to pay "his nine for their time and [bear] all expenses."[5]

Four clubs signed up for the top division—the Livingstons, the Aetnas of Detroit, the Mutuals of Jackson, and the Unas of Kalamazoo. The Unas and Mutuals were scheduled to play in the first round, but the Unas withdrew at the last minute when several of their players were unable to make the trip. The Mutuals thought they should get a bye, but instead the pairings were redone: Jackson had to play the Livingstons, while the Aetnas received the bye.[6] Will DeMyer had returned to captain the Mutuals, and there was a corresponding improvement in their performance. The Livingstons beat the Mutuals 11-9 in a ten-inning thriller, after the Mutes had rallied with two in the bottom of the ninth to force extra innings.

The championship game thus pitted the Livingstons against the Aetnas of Detroit. The New Yorkers jumped out to an early 9-1 advantage and still held a 15-10 lead in the eighth inning. But the Aetnas staged a furious rally to pull out a dramatic 18-15 victory and capture the $200 prize. The collapse of the New Yorkers prompted rumors that the game had been sold to gamblers, though this seems very unlikely. Followers of the still-young game had a hard time accepting its uncertainty and were often too quick to conclude that any unanticipated result meant a fix.[7]

On the final day of the Ionia tournament, the Mutuals and Aetnas played in the state division for the $150 purse. The Mutuals prevailed 5-4 in a thrilling eleven-inning game, which many observers deemed the best game ever played in the state. The Mutuals scored the winning run when Mark Benedict, caught in a run-down between first and second base, was able to keep from being tagged until John Foley had scored the winning run from third base. The Aetnas won second prize in the state division. Since the Livingstons were not eligible in the state division, they were left out of the money altogether after having been within an inning of claiming the championship.

The top three prizes in the Ionia County class went to the Valley Club of Ionia, the Valley Club of Saranac, and the Star Club of Ionia.[8] (The Diamond Club of Muir beat the Stars of Ionia but was disqualified because its catcher, E. Wilder, had played for Eaton Rapids within the past sixty days.) The junior class was won by the Aetnas of Grand Rapids, who were on their way to a perfect 17-0 season.[9] However, the Cass Club of Detroit contended that the Grand Rapids club had used an ineligible pitcher, and the clubs elected to split the money rather than await the decision of the arbiter, the *New York Clipper*.

In spite of the disputes and a few rain showers, the tournament was a success, with gate receipts of over twelve hundred dollars. Expenses totaled one thousand dollars, leaving the stockholders with a 50 percent return on the four hundred dollars they had invested in the tournament.[10] The tournament was also character-ized by gentlemanly behavior on the part of both players and spec-tators, leaving the police hired to keep order with little to do. Plans were made for another tournament in Ionia in 1876, an event that would prove historic when James "Pud" Galvin pitched two no-hit-ters on a single day, including the first perfect game ever pitched at any level.

Before returning to New York, the Livingstons played three more games, beating the Mutuals 14-8 in Jackson on August 14 and the Athletics in Grand Rapids 27-5 on August 16, but losing again to the Aetnas 10-9 in Detroit on August 17. After the Livingstons left, interest shifted to the proposed visit to Michigan of the Red Stock-ings of Boston, who were on their way to their fourth straight National Association pennant and were compiling one of the most extraordinary records in baseball history. Managed by Harry Wright and led by the battery of A. G. Spalding and Deacon White, the Red Stockings would win their first twenty-six games, not lose a single home game all year, and finish with a seventy-one and eight record.

Scheduling difficulties forced the cancellation of a planned match between the Aetnas and Red Stockings, but the Boston team did play two games on its swing through Michigan. They beat the

Mutuals of Jackson 9-0, an eminently respectable result considering that in National Association games the Red Stockings averaged over 9 runs while allowing fewer than 4. Boston moved on to Kalamazoo and played the Unas at the National Park on August 24, a mere eighteen days after the club had reorganized. While a mismatch may have been anticipated, the clubs instead were tied at 2-2 after four innings before the Red Stockings broke the game open and won 14-6. Harry Wright called the Unas the strongest amateur nine Boston had met, "and better than some who style themselves professionals."[11] There was now a third major player in the competition for the state's best baseball club.

The Aetnas got their chance to face major-league competition when the White Stockings of Chicago came to town on September 2. The game was a classic, with the Aetnas losing by a 7-4 score to a club that featured the pitching of James Devlin.[12] The game also afforded the first taste of major-league competition to Aetnas' first baseman Frederick K. Stearns, who would later be president of the world champion Detroit Wolverines. The White Stockings also made stops in Jackson and Kalamazoo, where they had an easier time, beating the Mutuals 10-3 and the Unas 28-7.

With the Mutuals and Aetnas having played numerous games against common opponents but only two games head-to-head, they recommenced their series for state supremacy. The Mutuals won 13-10 on September 10 to even the five-game series (by mutual agreement, the game in Ionia did not count). The Aetnas' student contingent returned to the university after the defeat, however, and the club lost interest in completing the series. The Aetnas were not the same thereafter and were beaten by the Cass Club 7-5 and trounced 26-4 in a rematch with the White Stockings of Chicago.

The sudden decline of the Aetnas did not mean that the Mutuals would be state champions for the third straight season by default. In spite of their extremely late start, the Unas of Kalamazoo were emerging as serious contenders. They demoralized the formidable Forester Club of Charlotte by a 12-1 score on September 14. The Foresters scored their only run in the eighth inning on a wild throw and then the players declared that they had had enough and, "in a miff, more like school boys than ball players, they . . . packed up their clubs, and silently crept away."[13] On September 22, the Unas hosted the Tecumsehs of London, who had previously beaten both the Aetnas and the Mutuals. The Unas debuted new white and maroon uniforms that had been manufactured entirely in Kalamazoo. Fears that "the *pretty boys* could not play ball" in their new

The University of Michigan Base Ball Club of 1875. *Back row, left to right:* Ogden W. Ferdon, third base; Willis R. Roberts, shortstop, *Middle row, left to right:* George H. Winslow, catcher; George H. Abbott, pitcher; Edgar D. Root, center field; Charles S. Burch, first base; Oscar P. Shepardson, left field. *Front row, left to right:* Frederick K. Stearns, second base; William C. Johnson, right field. Several of these players spent their summer vacation helping the Aetnas of Detroit beat the state champion Mutuals of Jackson, and the Aetnas were not the same after the students returned to school in the fall. Stearns became president of the National League Detroit Wolverines, and his free spending helped them win the world championship in 1887. *Courtesy of the Bentley Historical Library, University of Michigan*

outfits were unfounded, the Unas prevailing 12-2 behind Clarence Terwilliger's stellar pitching.[14]

The renewed interest in baseball extended to clubs with no aspirations to state supremacy. Michigan was accustomed to brief periods of baseball excitement that were followed by long periods of apathy, and to seasons that began with great interest and soon fizzled, but this year seemed different. "The base ball fever doesn't appear to be subsiding," observed the *Coldwater Republican,* "but on the contrary seems to be on the increase."[15]

The Empire Club of Detroit, though no longer competing with the state's top clubs, held a festival at Bois Blanc Island that included a shooting match and a barge race. And after a scourge of potato bugs caused a disappointing harvest, two clubs of farmers in mid-Michigan showed they hadn't lost their sense of humor by playing a series of games as "The Grasshoppers of Elba" and "The Potatoe [*sic*] Bugs of Elsie." Afterward, the two clubs combined to play a third team billed as the "Squash Bugs of Ovid."

In Galesburg, a tournament was described as "palm days in the history of our village. A great array of gentlemen in the bloom and pride of life, employed those days in joyful pastime, in competing for premiums. . . . The vivacity of their motion made them experts in the game."[16] The Monitor Club of Kalamazoo won the tournament, followed by the Actives of Galesburg and the Monitors' second nine, while the Tiger and Star Clubs of Climax and the Hickory Club of Hickory Corners also competed. An exciting base-running contest saw three players timed in fifteen seconds. In a second heat, Ed Webster and Will Sergeant of the Monitors again tied with times of seventeen seconds. At that point Sergeant declared that he would much rather let his teammate have the five-dollar prize than run the bases yet again!

Baseball's renewed prominence in September at rural county fairs and other festive occasions offered further evidence that it was again being seen as great fun. In Coldwater, the Sailors of Quincy beat the Actives of Coldwater and the Stars of Union City to win a belt signifying Branch County supremacy. Port Hope won a baseball tournament at the Huron County Fair, with White Rock coming in second. In Grand Rapids, the Aetna Club beat the Yates Club to claim twenty-five dollars. The agricultural society of Port Austin offered premiums of twenty-five dollars and fifteen dollars to the best baseball clubs. Lake, Osceola, and Clare Counties held a combined fair in Hersey, where the Evart Base Ball Club defeated Hersey 27-13 to win a purse of twelve dollars. A combined fair in Romeo for the counties of Lapeer, Oakland, and St. Clair saw the Pontiacs emerge victorious, followed by the Gauntlets of Romeo, the Maple Leaf Club of Port Huron, and the C.O.D. Club of Romeo. Even the Scottish games in Orchard Lake offered fifty dollars to the best baseball club, prompting the *Jackson Citizen* to inquire good-naturedly, "When, in the name of all that is good, was base ball made a Scottish game?"[17]

Another sign that baseball's revival would have staying power was the comparative lack of squabbling, even though the reduced scores created many tight games. After losing to the Red Stockings of Sand Lake, the Aetnas of Morley wrote to the *Big Rapids Magnet* to commend their hosts for their excellent ball grounds, gentlemanly behavior, and thoughtful hospitality, which made their trip a "very pleasant affair."[18] Such sentiments, once taken for granted, were now a welcome change from the bickering of rival clubs that had filled so many newspaper columns in the preceding seasons.

There were, of course, some exceptions, such as the now obligatory gripes about ringers being slipped into juvenile games. The Eurekas of Pontiac, for instance, claimed that their members were all fifteen-year-olds while their opponents were "a bearded nine called the Plow Boys, from White Lake, Clarkston, Waterford, Davisburgh, Drayton Plains, White Lake settlement, etc."[19] From Dexter came the complaint that the "Little Boy club" of Pinckney looked "like men from 20 to 30, and some look like men from Unadilla and Howell."[20]

In the latter instance, as so often happened, one dispute quickly led to others. A Dexter newspaper claimed that the Pinckney players "hugged each other and acted like savages whenever a tally was made" and jeered the mistakes of the Dexter players.[21] A response from Pinckney accused the Dexter Club of poor manners for not meeting the members of the Pinckney team at the depot and for expecting them to pay all their own expenses. The reply from Dexter claimed that such niceties no longer applied: "We do not know what may be the practice among traveling base ball clubs, but if they always expect to be dead-head to supper and cigars, wherever they go, the sooner base ball ceases to be the national game, the better. And if the Dexters did not once 'stand treat,' they deserve honoring for it."[22]

Dexter was not alone in distancing itself from the chivalric rituals that had once characterized the game. One of baseball's longest-standing traditions was that of the loser presenting the winner with a new ball. After losing to the Wolverines of Bennington, the Energetic Club of Owosso instead presented its vanquishers with the ball used in the game, prompting the Wolverines to lament

> that the trophies they received were a ball with the cover ripped and torn in several places, (perfectly worthless) and an old umbrella all faded, and rips between each bow a foot long. But we will keep and cherish the aged umbrella for the good it did a century ago; and providence permitting, it will accompany us to the Centennial Fair as one of the umbrellas that Christopher Columbus was the owner of when he discovered this country.[23]

Another exception to the general goodwill resulted from an attempt to organize a grand baseball tournament in Negaunee. A prize fund of $250 was offered, and reduced fares were secured in hopes of attracting clubs from all over the Upper Peninsula and northern Wisconsin. Unfortunately, the tournament was announced only two weeks ahead of time, and the only entrants were four local clubs. The organizers put together two picked nines so that the round-robin format used in Ishpeming the previous year could be duplicated. However, Ishpeming withdrew after charging that Negaunee had hired a pitcher from Connecticut for the tournament and had rigged the schedule so that Ishpeming always had to play Negaunee when its players were tired. Negaunee won, but that news was overshadowed by the familiar cycle of charges and countercharges.

Unfortunately, the most anticipated series of the 1875 season provided another example of bickering. In late September, the Mutuals of Jackson accepted a challenge from the Unas of Kalamazoo to play a two-out-of-three series for the state championship. Jackson and Kalamazoo had a long history of heated baseball rivalries that went back to 1866, but this was the first time the state championship was on the line, so both clubs were on edge.

The Mutuals had finally abandoned their experiment with fast pitching and returned to their reliable battery of Robert Lake and Will DeMyer. Jackson easily won the first game, 20-9, on September 30 in Jackson. Kalamazoo evened the series the next day, again in Jackson, with a 27-12 win. The *Kalamazoo Telegraph* complained bitterly of the treatment the Unas had received in Jackson. The crowd, the paper alleged, "acted like a set of blackguards and the players seemed to be their not very distant relatives." The *Telegraph* also charged that pitcher Robert Lake kept intentionally hitting the Unas with pitches and that his teammates encouraged him to do so. The paper speculated that the Mutuals were hiring their players from prison and likened the crowd to a "mob" that "howled about the grounds like a set of savage Ashantees" and spent their time abusing the umpire and relieving "the monotony of the game by throwing stones at some of our players."[24]

The *Jackson Citizen* dismissed these comments as the product of a reporter's overactive imagination. And indeed the *Kalamazoo Gazette* was much more restrained than the *Telegraph*, criticizing the Jackson spectators for having "groaned, hooted and howled at our boys in a most indecent manner" but excusing the Mutuals from blame for the behavior of these "loafers."[25] Nonetheless, the controversy heightened the already considerable tension.

The first attempt to play the third and deciding game was made in Kalamazoo on October 8, but the game ended in a 9-9 tie, with darkness preventing extra innings. The presence of a neutral umpire, S. D. Bradley of Chicago, helped reduce the on-field bickering, but the *Kalamazoo Gazette* chastised the spectators for inappropriate remarks and added, "The Kalamazoos wish us to say that 'chin music' from spectators is not wanted in the future."[26] The Mutuals returned to Jackson after the tie, although the *Kalamazoo Telegraph* reported that the Mutuals had been offered one hundred dollars to stay. This time it was the *Gazette* that fanned the flames by attributing their departure to a lack of "sand."[27] The *Jackson Citizen* responded that the players would have jeopardized their employment by staying.

Nearly two weeks passed before another attempt to play the decisive game was made. Grand Rapids expressed interest in hosting the game, and perhaps a neutral site would have been best, but eventually the game came off in Jackson on October 21. No impartial umpire could be found, and Hiram F. Hatch of the Mutuals filled the position. Kalamazoo was clinging to a 7-4 lead with two out in the bottom of ninth.

There are widely divergent accounts of what happened next, but it seems that one player reached base on a close play, another reached by hit or walk, and then Sam Mettler hit a ground ball. After the throw to first, the Unas began celebrating, but Hatch (according to the Kalamazoo accounts) "amazed everyone by yelling 'Stand back. Safe on first!'"[28] The Unas heatedly argued that the game should be over, but to no avail. The next batter was awarded a base on balls, and this decision was protested even more vociferously. With the winning run for the Mutuals now on base, the Unas walked off the field. Hatch had no choice but to declare the Mutuals the winners by forfeit.

No one was satisfied with this result, and a third attempt was made to decide the state championship series on October 26. Even before the game the *Kalamazoo Telegraph* was alleging that the Mutuals had hired outside players, but the point proved moot when a mixture of rain and snow prevented the game from being played. There were no further attempts to complete the series.[29]

The question left on everyone's tongue was how so exciting a season could have ended in such an unsatisfactory manner. A Grand Rapids paper commented:

> A good deal of hard feeling appears to exist between the Kalamazoo and Jackson base ball clubs, and the partisans of each. Each side has its own story, which is one of discourtesy and blackguardism on the part of the other. This is all wrong. Both are excellent clubs. Both are supposed to be composed of gentlemen, and should act accordingly. The boy play which has been going on between the two for the past season has done much to belittle both in the opinions of outsiders. It should come to a pause.[30]

But such common sense was seldom followed by players in the thrall of baseball fever.

Nobody seems to have felt worse about the situation than umpire Hatch himself, and as umpires rarely if ever get the last word, it seems appropriate to close the account of this tumultuous season with his plaintive letter:

> DEAR SIR: In justice to myself, and to correct the misstatements which appeared in a correspondence in your paper, I desire to state to your readers some of the circumstances attending the game played here on the 21st inst. between the Kalamazoo club and the Mutuals. It was at the urgent solicitation of Mr. McCord [the Unas' captain] that I attempted to umpire the game, and only consented to do so with the assurance from him that the men should remain entirely quiet. I told him that mistakes would be made, but if his club would remain quiet I would do the very best I could. Yet the first strike that was called on one of the Kalamazoo men brought up at least half the club to protest against it, which action was continued throughout the game. I gave them a run on a dead ball. I put out Carbine of the Mutuals, and ordered two of the visitors safe on first, which were the only four decisions that I remember to have regarded as close up to the ninth inning. Then I determined to give the next close decision to the Mutuals,

which I did in giving Mettler safe at first, and I am sustained in that by nearly every one with whom I have conversed since the game. While Webster was at the bat I took more abuse than any man of ordinary spirit should submit to. I sent him to his base on three balls. He was the only one during the game. I believed then and do now, that I only performed my duty in so doing, yet I am not so positive of it as I am other decisions from the fact that I could not resist the impression that I was actually being threatened into giving strikes when I should not do so. Towards the close of the game I uniformly endeavored to give my decisions on strikes before judgment was called, for it was usually asked by at least one of their players in such a manner that no man of self respect would give it unless he was absolutely sure. One of the Kalamazoo players purposely preventing the Mutual catcher taking a foul bound, and then insisting on my ruling out one of the Mutual players for a great deal lighter offense of the kind; all had its effect upon me at this stage of the game. When I accepted the position, I determined to be *so fair,* that there would be no question, at least with the Kalamazoo men, but I believe now that it is impossible for a member of either club to umpire them and give satisfaction, for his decisions are watched with too much prejudice. I believe now that if a member of another club had made the same rulings as I made the Kalamazoo club would have acknowledged them fair.

The position of umpire is a hard one, particularly when there is so much talk to divert attention from the business. As an instance, I was undergoing a lecture when a suddenly pitched ball was struck at. I did not see it, and refused to give judgment until told. I do not write this to reflect upon the Kalamazoo club; perhaps other clubs would have done the same, but I did the best I could, and was very much in hopes to be able to bring in a better feeling between them. Dorgan claims that he was safe on third and Myers on first. I did not at the time regard them as close; yet I do not claim that I made no mistakes. I very much regret that any difficulty should have occurred, and I have promised myself never to be caught in such a place again.

Very Respectfully,

H. F. HATCH.[31]

NOTES

1. *Ionia Sentinel,* August 13, 1875.
2. *Ionia Sentinel,* July 23, 1875.
3. *Detroit Evening News,* August 18, 1875. The Livingstons took their name from their home county.
4. One article stated that Wadsworth was the nephew of General James Samuel Wadsworth, but Horace Andrew Wadsworth's *Two Hundred and Fifty Years of the Wadsworth Family in America* (Lawrence, Mass.: n.p., 1883) confirms that they were father and son. James W. Wadsworth later served in the House of Representatives. In a strange coincidence, George B. Catlin, the long-time *Detroit News* baseball writer and historian who compiled the list of the members of the Franklins used in chapter 2, played baseball for the Wadsworth-sponsored Livingstons in the late 1870s.
5. *Ionia Standard;* reprinted in the *Howard Record,* August 19, 1875.
6. The decision to redo the pairings was later condemned by the *New York Clipper,* the country's leading sporting journal (*Detroit Evening News,* September 14, 1875).
7. The *Jonesville Weekly Independent* of August 12, 1875, for example, alleged that catcher E. Wilder had accepted a ten-dollar bribe and sold out the Unknowns of Hillsdale in a game against the Foresters of Charlotte. The *Howard Record* went further, claiming that D. C. Höch, a Rockford physician who umpired a July 5 game between the Actives of Howard City and the Red Stockings of Sand Lake, had money on the game and therefore aided Sand Lake in winning. Melvin L. Adelman, *A Sporting Time,* 163–64, gives a more thorough account of the tendency to suspect a fix whenever an unexpected result occurs.
8. The captain of the Stars of Ionia, a club of boys aged fifteen to seventeen, was Walter Walker, later a one-game major leaguer. The tragic life of Walker, who later would become prosecuting attorney of Isabella County and president of the minor league that first brought Sunday baseball to Detroit, is recounted in Peter Morris, "One of Baseball's Odd Lives," *National Pastime* 15 (1995): 97–99.
9. The club's complete record appeared in the *Grand Rapids Daily Eagle* on November 1, 1875.
10. *Ionia Sentinel,* August 20, 1875.
11. *Kalamazoo Gazette,* August 27, 1875.
12. Devlin is today remembered only because while pitching for Louisville two years later he helped throw the National League pennant. Had he resisted temptation, he might today be considered one of the greatest pitchers of all time, as his outstanding pitching had put Louisville in a position to win the pennant.
13. *Kalamazoo Gazette,* September 11, 1875.
14. *Kalamazoo Daily Telegraph,* September 23, 1875.
15. *Coldwater Republican,* September 7, 1875.
16. *Kalamazoo Gazette,* September 3, 1875.
17. *Jackson Weekly Citizen,* September 7, 1875.
18. *Big Rapids Magnet,* July 22, 1875.
19. *Detroit Evening News,* June 7, 1875.
20. *Detroit Evening News,* July 19, 1875.
21. *Dexter Leader,* July 16, 1875.
22. *Dexter Leader,* July 30, 1875.
23. *Owosso Weekly Press,* July 28, 1875.

24. *Kalamazoo Daily Telegraph*, October 2, 1875.

25. *Kalamazoo Gazette*, October 8, 1875.

26. *Kalamazoo Gazette*, October 15, 1875. "Chin music" means talk, particularly back talk.

27. *Kalamazoo Gazette*, October 15, 1875.

28. *Kalamazoo Daily Telegraph*, October 22, 1875.

29. The Unas did play two more games, which established how much the college players had contributed to the Aetnas' success over the summer. On October 22 the University of Michigan, with Frederick Stearns and William Johnson, beat the Unas 5-2. In Detroit the next day the Unas routed the depleted Aetnas 11-1.

30. *Grand Rapids Daily Morning Democrat*, October 24, 1875.

31. *Kalamazoo Daily Telegraph*, October 17, 1875.

26

"THE PHENIX-LIKE PERFORMANCES OF THE PASTIME"

The National League was formed on February 2, 1876, and its continuous operation ever since leads many people today to regard that date as the beginning of baseball history. However, it should be clear by now that such a perception would not have been shared at the time. In reality, in the twenty years prior to 1876, baseball saw more dramatic changes than it has in any similar period since.

Michigan's earliest baseball clubs offered a harmless alternative to the evils of city living. Baseball provided exercise and fresh air and seemed to promise to uphold social stability. Its alignment with gentlemen's clubs and chivalric customs gave the impression that the game would always remain a source of wholesome amusement.

This in turn made it possible to present baseball as a test of character in which the traditional values of discipline, hard work, and subservience to authority were rewarded. As in the American Dream, success was the inevitable consequence of adherence to these precepts, and failure could be reversed with enough diligence. Athletic ability barely figured into the equation.

Unfortunately, such laudable ideals had a hard time surviving on the baseball diamond. Matches had a disquieting way of revealing that raw talent could have more to do with success than the best character traits, and gentlemanly behavior was often the first casualty of this revelation. Baseball had to adapt to these realities, in the process abandoning many of the alliances that had initially bolstered it.

The common code of shared beliefs governing play was replaced by a rulebook, and the mode of competition was refined accordingly. Clubs promoting social cohesion were replaced by teams devoted to winning baseball games. As matches became competitions instead of social rituals, a diversion was reinvented as a business. Many of the game's earliest supporters understandably felt betrayed. A veteran ballplayer voiced a common sentiment when he lamented in 1868 that "they don't play ball nowadays as they used

An 1892 game in Mt. Pleasant. *Courtesy of the Clarke Historical Library, Central Michigan University*

to. . . . [T]hey don't play with the same kinds of feeling or for the same objects they used to."[1]

The dawn of openly professional baseball in 1869 was a concept ahead of its time. The strong Eastern bias threatened to turn the game into a fad, while the creation of a few enormously talented clubs diminished everyone else's efforts. As historian Tom Melville suggests, baseball had "established a 'national' standard . . . but this standard had also been virtually imposed upon America's ball playing culture, it hadn't slowly evolved or developed 'up' from a broad network of geographically dispersed areas of interest. This path of development would make it possible for communities to quickly access the game's highest achievement level, but to do this they also had to abandon an equally strong, and deeply rooted, obligation that this achievement be an expression of place and locality."[2]

The National Association had been formed in 1871, but its five year existence was a struggle. A lack of leadership gave it little control over its players, so behavioral problems and links to gamblers were common. More seriously, the league allowed any club willing to pay the minimal entry fee to join. This inclusive structure led to parasite clubs that entered only to attract visits from a few big-name clubs and then dropped out. On the other end of the spectrum, a dominant club like the Red Stockings of Boston could destroy competitive balance.

By the end of the 1875 season, William Hulbert, president of the Chicago club, had had enough. He covertly signed Boston's "Big Four" of A. G. Spalding, Jim "Deacon" White, Ross Barnes, and Cal McVey to 1876 contracts and began planning a new league run on more businesslike principles. In a word, that meant exclusion.

Hulbert called a meeting to unveil his plan, and legend has it that he began by walking to the door, locking it, and pocketing the key.[3] Although likely apocryphal, this detail emphasizes that exclusion was the essence of the new league. As Melville observes, "No longer would clubs or communities, on the basis of their own qualification assessment, be entitled to championship competition. This prerogative was now exclusively in the hands of the 'charmed circle' of National League participants, derisively dubbed the 'Great I ams' by the Philadelphia *City Item*."[4]

As suggested earlier, however, barriers erected to keep things out sometimes end up keeping them in—men excluded from competitive baseball rediscovered their love of the game through muffin games, while spectators paid admission to enter enclosed ballparks and, in their shared fandom, rediscovered a sense of community. Similarly, the National League excluded most of the country yet made the game truly the national pastime.

This final paradox makes more sense than it would appear. The National Association was dominated by East Coast clubs, making the game's success in other areas irrelevant. But since the National League forged into markets like Louisville, Cincinnati, St. Louis, and Chicago, it depended on the involvement of the whole nation. As they crisscrossed the country, clubs could earn much-needed revenue by stopping and playing local nines. The National League and the first of its many rivals, the International Association, needed teams and supporters in all the regions between its far-flung clubs, and that feeling of being needed was the impetus for a renewed sense of belonging.

Success still came slowly for professional baseball. The dramatic fluctuations in interest continued, prompting a reporter to note in 1897: "But a few short years ago it was no uncommon occurrence to find intelligent persons asking, and in the most serious way, 'What is going to take the place of baseball, now that the sport is dying out?' The interrogations came mostly from parties who had not followed the national game from the early seventies and therefore were not familiar with the phenix-like performances of the pastime in nearly every quarter of the United States."[5] Through all the ebbs and flows, a broader base of interest was gradually built.

The founding of the National League in 1876 prompted three Michigan clubs—the Mutuals of Jackson and the Aetnas and the Cass Club of Detroit—to pursue professional baseball with additional resolve. The mixed success of this enterprise led to a couple of lean years, and another professional club in Detroit in 1879 was short-lived. But in 1881, the Detroit Wolverines entered the National League. The Wolverines struggled for several years, until Frederick K. Stearns took over as club president.

A dozen years earlier, Stearns had "stood in line at Van Amberg's Circus, with another boy, and collected ten cents apiece" to fund his baseball club, but now he was a pharmaceutical heir and flush with money. He purchased a second "Big Four," which again included the ageless Deacon White, and won the "World's Series" in 1887. The Wolverines dropped out of the National League a year later, but by then baseball had a foothold in Michigan.

By the start of the twentieth century, baseball had built the base of support necessary for a fever to become a permanent condition. Detroit, with the Detroit Tigers, reentered the major leagues in 1901 with the fledgling American League and has remained ever since. The game that Philadelphians were so amused to see men playing in the 1830s still endures as we enter the twenty-first century.

Baseball has come a very long way from matches played for ham and eggs and scores kept by making notches on sticks. But in some ways, we are not so far from baseball's beginnings. Baseball is still a game of routines that—in spite of domed stadiums and artificial turf—reflects the changing seasons. Today's players are more likely to take separate cabs to the ballpark than walk together and sing the team song, but the term *club* is still used to describe a team. In countless other ways, too, modern baseball still embodies its earliest days.

Early clubs relied on ballparks, team nicknames, and uniforms to create an identity, and modern fans feel a sense of nostalgia for these items that they often cannot explain. Jerry Seinfeld has observed that in the modern era of free agency, the fan is essentially rooting for clothes. And yet fans continue to root, even though the elevation of modern ballplayers to millionaires has added another barrier of exclusion that is deeply felt by many. But as long as fans believe that baseball belongs to them—and that it needs them—the game will continue to inspire "base ball fever."

Notes

1. Old Peto Brine [Pete O'Brien], "Ball Talk," *American Chronicle of Sports and Pastimes,* January 9, 1868.
2. Tom Melville, *Early Baseball and the Rise of the National League,* 35.
3. Albert G. Spalding, *America's National Game,* 210.
4. Melville, *Early Baseball and the Rise of the National League,* 81.
5. *Boston Globe,* March 28, 1897.

APPENDIX A

ABNER DOUBLEDAY

Abner Doubleday did not invent baseball, nor did he play a significant role in its development. However, the facts surrounding this erroneous attribution are so frequently misstated that it is worth reviewing them.

In 1905, A. G. Spalding assembled a panel of well-known baseball figures to determine the origins of baseball. The Mills Commission solicited information from the public, but its six members do not seem to have reviewed the submissions with much care. After two years, the commission announced its conclusion that Abner Doubleday invented baseball in Cooperstown, New York, in 1839. The basis for that finding was a single letter from an elderly man named Abner Graves.

The conclusion is absurd, as many historians have shown. However, in debunking the "Doubleday Myth," they have frequently misinterpreted Graves's letter. It is usually pointed out that Doubleday was at West Point at the time Graves claimed that he was inventing baseball. But the reasonable inference to draw from this fact is not that Graves was lying or deluded but that he was confused about which Abner Doubleday was involved.

For in fact there were two Abner Doubledays in Otsego County, and they were first cousins. The elder was born in 1819 and became a Civil War general. The younger one, Abner Demas Dou-

bleday,

bleday, was born in 1829 and also fought in the Civil War. Graves did say at one point that Doubleday became a general, but that is an understandable mistake. Abner Graves, born in 1834, described Abner Doubleday as a playmate "several years older" than himself and attending another school. He can only have meant the one born in 1829. Since the other Abner Doubleday was at West Point at the time, the obvious conclusion is that Graves was describing Abner D. Doubleday.

The younger cousin, Abner D. Doubleday, was born in Otsego County, New York, on March 9, 1829, and lived there until after the Civil War. He then moved to Kalamazoo, Michigan, where his two sons formed Doubleday Bros. and Company, one of the state's largest printers. (In 1999, it merged with another company and became Fidlar Doubleday.) Abner D. Doubleday died on November 20, 1903, only a few years before Abner Graves's letter was written. I could find no indication that he took any interest in baseball after moving to Kalamazoo.

Once again, it is important to stress that whatever Abner D. Doubleday did, he certainly did not invent baseball. In fact, Abner Graves's claims about what Doubleday did are actually quite modest (Spalding and Mills Commission chairman A. G. Mills embellished them considerably). In all likelihood, Abner D. Doubleday did help popularize an early version of baseball in Cooperstown around 1840, but that is the extent of his contribution to the game.

Appendix B

<hr>

CLUBS

The number of clubs in Michigan and the number of cities and counties represented, 1857–70

	Clubs	Cities	Counties
1857	1	1	1
1858	2	1	1
1859	10	6	4
1860	12	7	5
1861	9	6	6
1862	11	7	6
1863	8	7	5
1864	4	3	1
1865	16	13	11
1866	102	59	26
1867	240	117	36
1868	190	81	30
1869	113	52	27
1870	263	129	36

POPULATION DATA

	1854	1860	1864	1870
Michigan	n/a	751,110	803,745	1,184,059
African American residents	n/a	6,799	n/a	11,836
Detroit	40,373	45,387	52,970	79,603
Adrian	4,857	6,213	7,064	8,438
Kalamazoo	4,817	6,070	6,797	10,447
Grand Rapids	4,278	8,084	8,770	16,507
Ann Arbor	3,339	5,094	5,731	7,363
Jackson	3,326	4,799	5,544	11,447

Earlier state population:

1850	397,654
1840	212,267
1830	31,689
1820	8,896

Source: U.S. censuses

FIRST POST-1857 BASEBALL CLUBS BY COUNTY

Allegan	1867	Pine Browse Club of Wayland; Island Club of Plainwell; Renescule Club of Allegan
Alpena	1869	Alpena Base Ball Club
Barry	1867	Hastings Base Ball Club; Lone Star Club of Hastings; National Club of Middleville; Hickory Corners Base Ball Club; Fleet Club of Spaulding's Corners
Bay	1865	Chippewa Club of Portsmouth; Washington Club of Bay City
Berrien	1863	Monitor Club of Niles
Branch	1866	Coldwater Base Ball Club; Coldwater College Nine
Calhoun	1861	Pastime Club of Marshall; Red, White, and Blue Club of Marshall
Cass	1861	Dowagiac Base Ball Club
Clinton	1866	Maple Valley Club of Ovid; Star Club of St. Johns; Monitor Club of St. Johns
Delta	1870	Escanaba Base Ball Club
Eaton	1866	Olivet Base Ball Club
Genesee	1866	Wolverine Club of Flint; Ogema Club of Flint; Genesee Club of Flint
Gratiot	1867	Sheridan Club of Ithaca; St. Louis Base Ball Club
Hillsdale	1860	Reading Base Ball Club; Hillsdale Base Ball Club

Houghton	1868	Independent Club of Houghton
Ingham	1865	Capital Club of Lansing; Sheridan Club of Mason; Star Club of Agricultural College; Lansing Lower Town Base Ball Club
Ionia	1866	Ionia Base Ball Club; Wolverine Club of Ionia; Custer Club of Ionia; Defiance Club of Saranac; Lyons Base Ball Club; Otisco Club of Cooks Corner
Jackson	1860	Daybreak Club of Jackson
Kalamazoo	1859	Kalamazoo Base Ball Club; Galesburg Base Ball Club; Schoolcraft Base Ball Club
Kent	1859	Pioneer Club of Grand Rapids; Valley City Club of Grand Rapids
Lapeer	1866	Tiger Club of Lapeer; Star Club of Almont
Lenawee	1865	Anchora Club of Adrian
Livingston	1862	Hickory Club of Howell
Macomb	1866	Inland Club of Romeo; Union Club of Romeo
Marquette	1866	Marquette Base Ball Club
Mecosta	1870	Big Rapids Base Ball Club; Hungry Nine of Big Rapids; Active Club of Big Rapids
Monroe	1867	Union School Base Ball Club
Montcalm	1867	Greenville Base Ball Club; Eagle Club of Greenville; Star Club of Greenville
Muskegon	1867	Wolverine Club of Muskegon
Oakland	1867	Pontiac Base Ball Club; Oakland Club of Holly; Lightfoot Club of Holly; Continental Club of Pontiac; Agrestic Club of Farmington
Oceana	1867	Hart Base Ball Club; National Union Club of Pentwater
Ontonagon	1868	Ontonagon Base Ball Club
Ottawa	1867	Syskowits Club of Grand Haven; Star Club of Lamont
Saginaw	1866	East Saginaw Base Ball Club
Sanilac	1867	Telegraph Club of Lexington
Shiawassee	1865	Owosso Base Ball Club
St. Clair	1867	Welkin Club of Port Huron
St. Joseph	1865	Three Rivers Base Ball Club
Tuscola	1868	Cass River Club of Centreville (Caro); Vassar Base Ball Club; Athletic Club of Vassar; Star Club of Watrousville
Van Buren	1866	Lafayette Club of Paw Paw; Decatur Base Ball Club
Washtenaw	1859	Ypsilanti Base Ball Club
Wayne	1857	Franklin Club of Detroit

Note: Counties not listed did not have a baseball club until after 1870.

SELECT BIBLIOGRAPHY

MICHIGAN NEWSPAPERS, 1857–79

Adrian Expositor, Adrian Press, Adrian Times, Adrian Times and Expositor, Adrian Watchtower, Albion Recorder, Allegan Journal, Alpena Argus, Michigan Argus (Ann Arbor), *Ann Arbor Courier, Ann Arbor Journal, Ann Arbor Local News, Ann Arbor Local News and Advertiser, Ann Arbor Peninsular Courier, Ann Arbor Peninsular Courier and Family Visitant, Ann Arbor Register, Michigan State News* (Ann Arbor), *University Chronicle* (Ann Arbor), *Bangor Reflector, Battle Creek Journal, Michigan Tribune* (Battle Creek), *Bay City Chronicle and Tribune, Bay City Evening Observer, Bay City Journal, Bay City Morning Chronicle, Bay City Observer, Bay City Tribune, Belding Home News, Benton Harbor Palladium, Berrien Springs Era, Big Rapids Current, Big Rapids Independent, Big Rapids Magnet, Big Rapids Pioneer, Mecosta County Pioneer* (Big Rapids), *Big Rapids Pioneer-Magnet, Berrien County Record* (Buchanan), *Tuscola Advertiser* (Caro/Centreville), *Cassopolis Vigilant, Cedar Springs Clipper, Cedar Springs Wolverine Clipper, Charlevoix Sentinel, Charlotte Leader, Charlotte Republican, Eaton County Republican* (Charlotte), *Manitawauba Chronicle* (Cheboygan), *Cheboygan Free Press, Chelsea Herald, Chesaning Argus, Clare County Press* (Clare), *Coldwater Republican, Coldwater Sentinel, Constantine Weekly Mercury and St. Joseph County Advertiser, Detroit Advertiser, Detroit Advertiser and Tribune, Detroit Evening News, Detroit Free Press, Detroit Post, Detroit Post and Tribune, Detroit Tribune, Detroit Western Home Journal, Dexter Leader, Dowagiac Monitor, East Saginaw Courier, Eaton Rapids Saturday Journal, Edwardsburg Argus, Traverse Bay Progress* (Elk Rapids), *Escanaba Iron Port, Escanaba Tribune, Evart Review, Fenton Independent, Flint Sunday Democrat, Flint Wolverine Citizen, Fowlerville Review, Fremont Indicator, Fremont Times, Gladwin County Record* (Gladwin), *Grand Ledge Independent, Grand Rapids Democrat, Grand Rapids Eagle, Grand Rapids Enquirer, Grand Rapids Enquirer and Herald, Grand Rapids Leader, Grand Rapids Times, Grand Rapids Saturday Evening Post, Grand Rapids Weekly Democrat, Crawford Avalanche* (Grayling), *Greenville Democrat, Greenville Independent, Northwestern Mining Journal* (Hancock), *Alcona County Review* (Harrisville), *Oceana County Journal* (Hart), *Hart-*

ford Day Spring, Hastings Banner, Hillsdale Standard, Holland City News, Oakland County Advertiser (Holly), *Holly Register, Homer Index, Houghton Mining Gazette, Portage Lake Mining Gazette* (Houghton), *Howard Record* (Howard City), *Livingston Republican* (Howell), *Hudson Gazette, Hudson Post, Ionia Sentinel, Ishpeming Iron Home, American Citizen* (Jackson), *Jackson Citizen, Jackson Eagle, Jonesville Independent, Kalamazoo Gazette, Kalamazoo Telegraph, Kalkaska Leader, Lansing Journal, Lansing Republican, Lapeer Clarion, Lapeer Democrat, Leslie Local, Lowell Journal, Ludington Appeal, Mason County Record* (Ludington), *Manchester Enterprise, Manistee Advocate, Manistee Standard, Manistee Times, Lake Superior Journal* (Marquette), *Marquette Mining Journal, Lake Superior Mining Journal* (Marquette), *Marquette Plain Dealer, Marshall Chronicle, Marshall Democratic Expounder, Marshall Democratic Expounder and Calhoun County Patriot, Marshall Statesman, Ingham County News* (Mason), *Midland Times, Milford Times, Monroe Commercial, Monroe Monitor, Isabella County Enterprise* (Mt. Pleasant), *Muskegon Enterprise, Muskegon Journal, Muskegon Lakeside Register, Muskegon Lakeside Weekly, Muskegon News and Reporter, Muskegon Reporter, Nashville News, Negaunee Mining Review, Negaunee News, Newaygo Republican, Newaygo Tribune, Niles Democrat, Niles Enquirer, Niles Mirror, Niles Republican, Niles Times, Northville Record, Ontonagon Miner, Lake Superior Miner* (Ontonagon), *Orion Good News, Allegan County Record* (Otsego), *Otsego Union, Ovid Register, Owosso Press, Parma News, Parma Public Advertiser, Van Buren County Press* (Paw Paw), *Paw Paw True Northerner, Petoskey City Record, Emmet County Democrat* (Petoskey), *Wayne County Tidings* (Plymouth), *Pontiac Bill Poster, Pontiac Bill Poster and General Intelligencer, Pontiac Commercial, Pontiac Gazette, Huron County News* (Port Austin), *Port Huron Commercial, Port Huron Times, Portland Advertiser, Portland Observer, Reed City Weekly Clarion, Rochester Weekly Era, Presque Ile County Advance* (Rogers City), *Saginaw Courier, Saginaw Enterprise, Saginaw Morning Herald, Saginaw Republican, Saginaw Saginawian, Saginaw Spirit of the Times, St. Clair Republican, Clinton Independent* (St. Johns), *Clinton Republican* (St. Johns), *St. Joseph Herald, St. Joseph Herald-Traveler, St. Joseph Traveler, Saugatuck Commercial, Lake Shore Commercial* (Saugatuck), *Schoolcraft Dispatch and News, South Haven Sentinel, Iosco County Gazette* (Tawas), *Tecumseh Herald, Three Rivers News Reporter, Three Rivers Reporter, Three Rivers Tribune, Three Rivers Western Chronicle, Grand Traverse Herald* (Traverse City), *Utica Sentinel, Vicksburg Commercial, Whitehall Forum, Ypsilanti Commercial, Ypsilanti True Democrat*

BOOKS

Adelman, Melvin L. *A Sporting Time: New York City and the Rise of Modern Athletics, 1820–70.* Urbana: University of Illinois Press, 1986.

Aetna Base Ball Association Constitution and By-Laws. Unpublished log-book. Burton Collection, Detroit Public Library.

Alexander, Charles C. *Our Game: An American Baseball History.* New York: Henry Holt, 1991.

Bak, Richard. *A Place for Summer: A Narrative History of Tiger Stadium*. Detroit: Wayne State University Press, 1998.

———. *Turkey Stearnes and the Detroit Stars: The Negro Leagues in Detroit, 1919–1933*. Detroit: Wayne State University Press, 1994.

Barth, Gunther. *City People*. New York: Oxford University Press, 1980.

Benson, Michael. *Ballparks of North America*. Jefferson, N.C.: McFarland and Co., 1989.

Burk, Robert F. *Never Just a Game: Players, Owners, and American Baseball to 1920*. Chapel Hill: University of North Carolina Press, 1994.

Charlton, James, ed. *The Baseball Chronology*. New York: Macmillan, 1991.

Church, Seymour R. *Base Ball: The History, Statistics and Romance of the American National Game from Its Inception to the Present Time*. 1902. Reprint, Princeton: Pyne Press, 1974.

Coffin, Tristram Potter. *The Old Ball Game: Baseball in Folklore and Fiction*. New York: Herder and Herder, 1971.

Collins, Wilkie. *Man and Wife*. 1870. Reprint, London: Pocket Books, 1970.

Curran, William. *Strikeout: A Celebration of the Art of Pitching*. New York: Crown, 1995.

Dickson, Paul, ed. *The New Dickson Baseball Dictionary*. New York: Harcourt Brace and Company, 1999.

DiClerico, James M., and Barry J. Pavelec. *The Jersey Game: The History of Modern Baseball from Its Birth to the Big Leagues in the Garden State*. New Brunswick: Rutgers University Press, 1991.

Dunbar, Willis F., and George S. May. *Michigan: A History of the Wolverine State*. Grand Rapids, Mich.: William B. Eerdmans, 1995.

Fox, Stephen. *Big Leagues: Professional Baseball, Football, and Basketball in National Memory*. New York: William Morrow, 1994.

Freedman, William. *More Than a Pastime: An Oral History of Baseball Fans*. Jefferson, N.C.: McFarland and Co., 1998.

Gershman, Michael. *Diamonds: The Evolution of the Ballpark*. Boston: Houghton Mifflin, 1993.

Gilbert, Arlan K. *Historic Hillsdale College*. Hillsdale, Mich.: Hillsdale College Press, 1991.

Goldstein, Warren. *Playing for Keeps: A History of Early Baseball*. Ithaca: Cornell University Press, 1989.

Guschov, Stephen D. *The Red Stockings of Cincinnati: Base Ball's First All-Professional Team and Its Historic 1869 and 1870 Seasons*. Jefferson, N.C.: McFarland and Co., 1998.

Gutman, Dan. *Banana Bats and Ding-Dong Balls: A Century of Unique Baseball Inventions*. New York: Macmillan, 1995.

Guttmann, Allen. *From Ritual to Record*. New York: Columbia University Press, 1978.

Hardy, James D. *The New York Giants Base Ball Club, 1870 to 1900*. Jefferson, N.C.: McFarland and Co., 1996.

Henderson, Robert W. *Ball, Bat, and Bishop: The Origin of Ball Games*. 1947. Reprint, Urbana: University of Illinois Press, 2001.

Humber, William. *Diamonds of the North: A Concise History of Baseball in Canada*. Toronto: Oxford University Press, 1995.

Ivor-Campbell, Frederick, Robert L. Tiemann, and Mark Rucker, eds. *Baseball's First Stars*. Cleveland: Society for American Baseball Research, 1996.

James, Bill. *The Bill James Historical Baseball Abstract*. New York: Villard Books, 1986.

Kent Base Ball Club By-Laws and Constitution. Unpublished log book. Grand Rapids Public Library.

Larkin, Jack. *The Reshaping of Everyday Life, 1790–1840*. New York: Harper and Row, 1988.

Leifer, Eric M. *Making the Majors: The Transformation of Team Sports in America*. Cambridge: Harvard University Press, 1995.

Levine, Peter. *A. G. Spalding and the Rise of Baseball: The Promise of American Sport*. New York: Oxford University Press, 1985.

Light, Jonathan Fraser. *The Cultural Encyclopedia of Baseball*. Jefferson, N.C.: McFarland and Co., 1997.

Lowry, Philip J. *Green Cathedrals: The Ultimate Celebration of All 271 Major League and Negro League Ballparks Past and Present*. Reading, Mass.: Addison-Wesley, 1992.

Mack, Connie. *My Sixty-Six Years in the Big Leagues*. Philadelphia: John C. Winston, 1950.

McLuhan, H. Marshall. *The Gutenberg Galaxy*. Toronto: University of Toronto Press, 1962.

Melville, Tom. *Early Baseball and the Rise of the National League*. Jefferson, N.C.: McFarland and Co., 2001.

Moreland, George L. *Balldom*. 1914. Reprint, St. Louis: Horton Publishing, 1989.

Names, Larry D. *Bury My Heart at Wrigley Field*. Neshkoro, Wis.: Sportsbook Publishing, 1990.

Nemec, David. *The Beer and Whisky League*. New York: Lyons and Burford, 1994.

———. *The Great Encyclopedia of Nineteenth-Century Major League Baseball*. New York: Donald I. Fine Books, 1997.

———. *The Rules of Baseball*. New York: Lyons and Burford, 1994.

Okkonen, Marc. *Baseball in Muskegon*. Muskegon, Mich.: MICR Graphics, 1993.

———. *Minor League Baseball Towns of Michigan*. Grand Rapids, Mich.: Thunder Bay Press, 1997.

Orem, Preston D. *Baseball (1845–1881) from the Newspaper Accounts*. Altadena, Calif.: n.p., 1961.

Pender, James. *History of Benton Harbor and Tales of Village Days*. Chicago: Braun Printing, 1915.

Peverelly, Charles A. *The Book of American Pastimes*. New York, 1866.

Quigley, Martin. *The Crooked Pitch: The Curveball in American Baseball History*. Chapel Hill: Algonquin Books, 1988.

Rader, Benjamin G. *American Sports*. Englewood Cliffs: Prentice-Hall, 1983.

———. *Baseball: A History of America's Game*. Urbana: University of Illinois Press, 1992.

Rhodes, Greg, and John Erardi. *The First Boys of Summer*. Cincinnati: Road West, 1994.

Riess, Steven A. *City Games: The Evolution of American Urban Society and the Rise of Sports*. Urbana: University of Illinois Press, 1989.

———. *Touching Base: Professional Baseball and American Culture in the Progressive Era*. Westport, Conn.: Greenwood Press, 1980.

Ryczek, William J. *Blackguards and Red Stockings: A History of Baseball's National Association, 1871–1875*. Jefferson, N.C.: McFarland and Co., 1992.

———. *When Johnny Came Sliding Home: The Post–Civil War Baseball Boom, 1865–1870*. Jefferson, N.C.: McFarland and Co., 1998.

Seymour, Harold. *Baseball: The Early Years*. New York: Oxford University Press, 1960.

Smith, Robert. *Baseball*. New York: Simon and Schuster, 1947.

———. *Baseball in America*. New York: Holt, Rinehart and Winston, 1961.

Spalding, Albert G. *America's National Game*. 1910. Reprint, Lincoln: University of Nebraska Press, 1992.

Spink, Alfred H. *The National Game*. 1911. Reprint, Carbondale: Southern Illinois University Press, 2000.

Sullivan, Dean A., ed. *Extra Innings: A Documentary History of Baseball, 1825–1908*. Lincoln: University of Nebraska Press, 1995.

Sutherland, Daniel E. *The Expansion of Everyday Life, 1860–1876*. New York: Harper and Row, 1989.

Thorn, John, and Pete Palmer, eds. *Total Baseball*. 4th ed. New York: Viking, 1995.

Tiemann, Robert L., and Mark Rucker, eds. *Nineteenth Century Stars*. Kansas City: Society for American Baseball Research, 1989.

Voigt, David Q. *American Baseball: From the Gentleman's Sport to the Commissioner System*. 1966. Reprint, University Park: Pennsylvania State University Press, 1983.

Ward, John Montgomery. *Base-Ball: How to Become A Player, with the Origin, History and Explanation of the Game*. 1888. Reprint, Cleveland: Society for American Baseball Research, 1993.

White, Sol. *History of Colored Base Ball*. 1907. Reprint, ed. Jerry Malloy, *Sol White's History of Colored Base Ball, with Other Documents on the Early Black Game, 1886–1936*. Lincoln: University of Nebraska Press, 1995.

Will, George F. *Bunts*. New York: Touchstone, 1999.

Wright, Marshall D. *The National Association of Base Ball Players, 1857–1870*. Jefferson, N.C.: McFarland and Co., 2000.

Zang, David W. *Fleet Walker's Divided Heart: The Life of Baseball's First Black Major Leaguer*. Lincoln: University of Nebraska Press, 1995.

Zoss, Joel, and John Bowman. *Diamonds in the Rough: The Untold History of Baseball*. New York: Macmillan, 1989.

Articles of Particular Relevance

"Annual Meeting of the Detroit Club—Interesting Address by the President—Election of Officers." *Detroit Advertiser and Tribune*, April 7, 1868.

"Athletic Sports and Home Amusements." *Detroit Advertiser and Tribune*, August 16, 1869.

"Ball Tossers of Olden Days." *Kalamazoo Gazette*, February 11, 1906.

"Cass Club History." *Detroit Free Press*, January 13, 1889.

"Constitution of the Central Michigan Base Ball Association." *Lansing State Republican*, October 17, 1866.

"The Correspondence with the Excelsior Club of Chicago—The Championship Claims—Absurdity of the Chicago Pretensions and Excuses Exposed." *Detroit Advertiser and Tribune*, October 10, 1866.

"The First Ball Team." *Kalamazoo Telegraph*, December 10, 1901.

"First Baseball Club in Michigan." *Detroit Free Press*, April 19, 1897.

"The First Detroit Base Ball Club Formed in the Free Press Office Twenty-Seven Years Ago." *Detroit Free Press*, April 4, 1884.

Freedman, Stephen. "The Baseball Fad in Chicago, 1865–1870: An Exploration of the Role of Sport in the Nineteenth-Century City." *Journal of Sport History* 5, no. 2 (summer 1978): 42–64.

"Further from the Excelsiors of Chicago." *Detroit Advertiser and Tribune*, October 16, 1866.

Ford, Adam. "A Game of Long-Ago Which Closely Resembled Our Present National Game." In "A Critical Examination of a Source on Early Ontario Baseball: The Reminiscence of Adam E. Ford," by Nancy B. Bouchier and Robert Knight Barney. *Journal of Sport History* 15 (spring 1988): 75–90. First published in *Sporting Life*, May 5, 1886.

"The Game of Base Ball—Its Recent but Rapid Growth and Popularity—The Clubs of Detroit, Both Living and Dead—Matches of the Detroit Club." *Detroit Advertiser and Tribune*, May 2, 1867.

"How the Detroit Base Ball Team Just Missed a Championship in the Ancient Year of 1866." *Detroit News-Tribune*, March 15, 1903.

"Jackson Mutuals Helped Make Baseball History." *Jackson Citizen-Patriot*, July 24, 1927.

McGee, Melville. "The Early Days of Concord, Jackson County, Michigan." *Michigan Pioneer and Historical Collections*, v. 21 (1892): 418–31.

"Old-Time Base Ball." *Detroit Free Press*, December 26, 1884.

"Record of the Aetnas." *Detroit Free Press*, February 24, 1889.

"Rules Governing the Championship of Kent County." *Grand Rapids Daily Eagle*, May 26, 1868.

"St. Johns Monitors Were Baseball Champs Back in '66." *Clinton County Republican-News*, June 28, 1956.

Schaefer, Robert H. "The Lost Art of Fair-Foul Hitting." *National Pastime* 20 (2000): 3–9.

"Some Excelling Participants in Sports of Earlier Jackson." *Jackson News*, September 22, October 10, and October 13, 1918.

"Then and Now." *Detroit Free Press*, August 27, September 3, and September 16, 1881.

Thompson, George A., Jr. "New York Baseball, 1823." *National Pastime* 21 (2001): 6–8.

"When D. M. Ferry Played Ball." *Detroit Free Press*, June 14, 1903.

"When They Yelled 'Attaboy' at the 1859-ers." *Detroit Free Press*, March 25, 1928.

Special Collections

Ann Arbor Public Library; Bentley Library, Ann Arbor; Burton Collection, the Detroit Public Library; Grand Rapids Public Library; Jackson Public Library; Library of Michigan, Lansing; Western Michigan University Archives and Regional History Collections, Kalamazoo.

INDEX

Note: Page numbers in italics refer to illustrations. An index of Michigan cities follows this index.

Note: Baseball clubs of particular significance are included as subentries. Page numbers in italics refer to illustrations.